BLACKS & BLACKNESS IN CENTRAL A

BLACKS & BLACKNESS IN CENTRAL AMERICA

Between Race and Place

EDITED BY Lowell Gudmundson & Justin Wolfe

DUKE UNIVERSITY PRESS

DURHAM & LONDON

2010

© 2010 Duke University Press
All rights reserved
Printed in the United States of America
on acid-free paper ∞
Designed by Katy Clove
Typeset in Minion by Achorn International, Inc.
Library of Congress Cataloging-in-Publication
Data appear on the last printed page of this book.

CONTENTS

ACKNOWLEDGMENTS

This book emerged out of an international conference hosted at Tulane University. We invited scholars from Central America, the United States, and elsewhere to explore the history of people of African descent throughout the mainland Caribbean in an effort not just to insert Central America into the African diaspora, but to expose the deep connections between this region and the wider Caribbean. Our related goal was to challenge diaspora scholars everywhere to expand their analytical approaches to include areas whose own diasporan histories do not always fit so readily into traditional frameworks.

This effort would not have been possible without the generous support of the Stone Center for Latin American Studies at Tulane and the Dean of Faculty's Office at Mount Holyoke College. Support was also provided by Tulane University's Center for Scholars, the Department of History, the Department of Spanish and Portuguese, and the Latin American Library. Thomas Reese, director of the Stone Center for Latin American Studies, always understood the importance of this research and championed our cause. Thanks to him and the staff of the Stone Center, our contributors found a welcoming reception at Tulane and the conference reached a wide and engaged public. Denise Frazier, Amisha Sharma, Richard Conway, and Edith Wolfe at Tulane and Dawn Larder and Mary Heyer at Mount Holyoke all contributed to the smooth running of the conference. The research leading to the essays by Cáceres, Meléndez, and Gudmundson was funded by the National Endowment for the Humanities Collaborative Research Program (Grant #RZ-20704-01), whose support is gratefully acknowledged. Gudmundson translated from the Spanish original the essays by Cáceres and Meléndez for this volume. The map for our introductory essay was prepared by Donald Sluter of the Department of Geography at the University of Massachusetts.

The participants in the conference made for an exceptionally rich experience. In particular the commentaries by George Reid Andrews, Jane Landers, Paul Lovejoy, and Christopher Lutz helped us and our authors sharpen our arguments and our comparative perspective. We particularly thank our contributors, without whom neither the conference nor this collection would have been possible. Bringing together scholars working in disparate time periods and geographies challenged us all and has made our work better for the effort.

Throughout the editorial process Valerie Millholland has been helpful and enthusiastic, as well as patient at the right moments. So, too, were Miriam Angress and Neal McTighe as we headed toward final production, and Scott Smiley, whose index marvelously bridges our themes and ideas across the chapters. We thank the anonymous readers, whose critiques pressed for the collection to speak more widely across fields and regions. With their help we hope to offer novel perspectives to a broad social science and historical readership. At the same time we offer fresh paths and clues for those inhabitants of the region seeking to remember and reframe historical legacies and processes so assiduously forgotten by Central American nation-states and citizens alike.

INTRODUCTION

Lowell Gudmundson & Justin Wolfe

The remarkable flowering of scholarship on the history of Africans and their descendants in the Americas produced since the Second World War has been one of the most fruitful developments of historical and sociological knowledge worldwide. The great majority of that scholarship has focused on nations and areas where African-descent populations are both recognized as such today and comprise the majority population either regionally or nationally. The islands of the Caribbean, the United States, and Brazil have been the preferred setting for this extraordinary expansion of knowledge and remain so for scholars today.

On the margins, both geographically and conceptually, of that emerging Black Atlantic framework can be found the Hispanic mainland Caribbean nations from Mexico through Central America and Panama, to Colombia and Venezuela. Here one finds little recognition, in either popular or scholarly terms, of the region's dominant role in the earliest colonial slave trade or of the fact that people of African descent constituted the majority of nonindigenous populations long thereafter. Similarly, despite (or perhaps because of) the centrality of these people and imageries of blackness in the later development of national identities and historical consciousness, these same nation-states have often countenanced widespread practices of social, political, and regional exclusion of blacks. These histories should trouble our analyses of race and diaspora. This region is not an anomaly or a marginal case, but rather the setting of historical trajectories that necessarily challenge both empirical and theoretical scholarship. Research on the isthmus must be seen as more than additive—the inclusion of forgotten peoples and histories; it has been transformative. Histories of slavery, segregation, and racism in the mainland Hispanic Caribbean underpinned the emergence of new ideals of freedom, equality, democracy,

MAP 1 Central America and the Caribbean. Map by Donald Sluter.

and honor. Yet unlike in many other regions of the African diaspora, these histories were not simply whitewashed, but so often were displaced or denied. How do we account for such results?

Each of these nations has witnessed the postcolonial development of *mestizo* or mixed-race ideologies of national identity that have systematically downplayed African roots and participation in the process in favor of Spanish and Indian antecedents and contributions. Thus both their colonial history, so central to the peopling of the Americas with Africans, and the very contributions of mixed-race populations of African descent since then have been relegated to an episodic, peripheral rendering of one after another of the individual national histories. Indeed the very success of such an assimilationist blurring of ethnic categories in the more recent past has played a large part in a relative lack of scholarly interest in research on these cases, as well as profoundly misguided popular images of their historical past. Moreover that same nationalist success story has worked as a disincentive for any understanding of the story of African Americans in Middle America in a larger, regional framework or for scholarly discussions of these topics across those same national boundaries.

Following up on a number of conversations among researchers, we convened an international conference on the history of African Americans in Middle America at Tulane University (5–6 November 2004) with a view to developing this framework for the comparative discussion of historical experiences shared by and perhaps unique to the nations of the mainland Hispanic Caribbean. In two days of intensive discussions among colleagues across borders and disciplines we engaged each other in the common goal of revising notions of hybridity whose historical importance and precocity can hardly be overstated. One of our goals for the conference was to measure the progress of research on Afro–Central American issues by inviting the participation and critiques of scholars working in the relatively better developed cases of Mexico and Colombia.

If Mexico set the terms of this conversation with its early twentieth-century development of postrevolutionary imagery, it is no less true that each of the Central American nations pursued similarly complex processes of identity formation thereafter. However common the mestizo prototype that resulted, the conference's comparative conversations allowed us to better contextualize our individual and collective research, subjecting relatively isolated, nationally based research to commentary and criticism from foreign but similar fields and cases. Indeed overcoming the professional and geographic separation that has long characterized those working on Afro–Central America as a group, not to mention the separation from scholars working on Mexico and Colombia, was a major goal of the conference, its discussions, and the process of revising and editing these papers for publication. Thus the collection we have brought together represents a broad sampling of the pioneering work on the experiences of people of African descent and the changing meanings of blackness (and thus of necessity whiteness, Indianness, and mixedness) being undertaken by this generation's Central Americanists.

Collectively our focused reflections can make important contributions to the profound reimaginings being pursued in both the fields of African diaspora studies and Latin American history. To African diaspora studies we not only add historical depth, especially to the earliest engagements of Africans in the Americas, but address the vexing problem of how to conceptualize the relationship of the African diaspora to places where

African-descended populations do not self-identify as such or have been written out of national histories. To Latin American history we offer fruitful approaches to thinking about ethnicity and hybridity that do not fall into the twin traps of naïvely reaffirming the region's own "cosmic race" theorizings and elisions or of blindly replicating the alternately color-obsessed and color-blind thinking of overly fixed and essentialized categories of race and color.

Our understanding of *race* is clearly constructivist and nonessentialist. While attentive to African origins and the earliest of colonial times, the analyses are clearly less concerned with African continuities than with creole and American cultural innovation. While the majority of Central America's non-Indian population was no doubt of part-African descent, clearly that defined the lives of only some of the people and only at certain times. Blackness for Central Americans was and is a relational or dialectical rather than self-evident or inherent category. Ironically this is perhaps most visible in the fact that so much of formerly black or mulatto culture (defined pejoratively at the time by elites) is now considered mestizo or Pacific coastal, national, or majority culture in so many places. In noting this, however, we also reject the old assimilationist or *mestizaje* arguments that consign Africanness, slave status, and blackness itself to an unknowable, faceless past or prelude to the main event of national, mestizo-driven history. Race is constructed or imagined, of course, but also all too real, and not just in colonial or slavery times. Our evidence for this argument spans nearly four centuries and should finally lay to rest any idea that ours is a topic relevant only to the distant past. Better still, given the episodic and regionally diverse experiences of Africans and their descendants in Central America, the region offers a distinct set of opportunities to deepen our understanding of the role that cultural continuities and innovations have played in the formation of diasporan identities.

Central America also reveals the importance of place in conceptualizing blackness and diaspora. In one sense the racializing of space has long been recognized and finds detailed expression in many of our essays, especially those focused on the Atlantic coast of Nicaragua and Costa Rica. That imagery tended to emerge as part of a nineteenth-century nationalist ideology for (re)incorporating regions long semiautonomous or recently ceded to foreign enclave interests. It vigorously developed a "black as other" component, which only deepened national and other regional self-conceptions as "anything but black." The groundbreaking work of Peter Wade and Nancy Appelbaum on the Chocó and Antioquia regions in neighboring Colombia suggests the regional breadth of this discourse and should further invigorate our analyses of the links between regional and national identities.[1]

In parallel, but not always consonant, with this racialization of space is the way individual towns and communities have been inscribed with blackness in regional and national narratives, as well as how these communities have made claims on resources both locally and nationally based on such traditions and self-images. Just as Laura Lewis's local informants from the Costa Chica of Mexico embraced their *moreno* identity (at odds with surrounding Indians and outside whites or Spaniards) while vigorously rejecting any hint of foreign or African origin, Afro–Central Americans have often subscribed to a validating discourse of "rootedness" in (eternally) "being from here." Place trumps race very often in this second usage, because "belonging" in the national, mestizo-driven narrative requires it, lest one be confused with those truly other, black people of the Atlantic coast. At other times, however, African descent itself can be enabling if not ennobling, such as in several colonial sugar towns, particularly those of Dominican traditions such as San Gerónimo and Amatitlán in Guatemala. In either case, whether place trumps or reinforces race, blackness or African descent is quite distinctively equated with the hyper-rootedness and thus legitimacy imagined to most powerfully characterize indigenous communities.[2] Nowhere is this more openly expressed, however fancifully, than in the San Gerónimo community hymn recalling a foundational Indian and black fraternity of oppression:

The residents were Indians
and blacks their allies
turned into slaves
of a mistreated lineage
A race that's not pure
nor a shadow its figure
together in brotherhood
with the Indian and the African
Gone is that past
we're free and no longer slaves

we're children, brothers and sisters
of this beautiful Guatemala.[3]

Place proves fundamental to analyzing and understanding what Edmund Gordon has referred to as these "disparate diasporas."

Central America offers an important testing ground for theorizations of diasporan identities and cultures, as it is simultaneously geographically compact and structurally complex. While the countries of the region share institutional, legal, and religious frameworks inherited from the colonial period, not to mention an administrative unity within the structure of the kingdom of Guatemala, they encompass diverse geographies, economies, demographics, and international relations. Furthermore, in expanding upon understandings of the African diaspora that have been dominated by North Atlantic and Anglophone scholarship, we are also pushing to move beyond the tendency in Latin America to focus on Brazil and those islands of the Spanish Caribbean that Tannenbaum long ago described as "slave societies."[4]

PATHS NOT TAKEN

The history of research on African-descent populations in Central America has many parallels with work on Mexico, with scores of intriguing studies that failed to stir scholars from a decidedly Euro-Indian vision of the region's history. The classic works of Aguirre Beltrán on Mexico had some weaker echoes in Central America. Perhaps it would be more accurate to say that there were many studies that could have been, but were not, the points of departure for sustained interest in the topic. The first bust of the cycle, then, can be assigned to Central America. These early works included classic texts by Barón Castro for El Salvador and Castro y Tossi for Costa Rica, and even turn-of-the-century volumes such as those by Ayón for Nicaragua and the later president of Costa Rica González Víquez.[5]

A particularly instructive example from Costa Rica can be found in the classic work by Samuel Stone, *La dinastía de los conquistadores* (1975). Stone's claims for elite marital endogamy and continuity of rule from earliest colonial times to the (then) present have generated debate at times, but his use of a deracialized or racially homogenizing language both escaped notice and reflected an unfortunate turning away from the insights available in the work of preceding generations. Those authors had long pointed not to a vaguely mestizo colonial past but to a very decidedly mulatto one, appropriate to a nation whose patron saint is a black Virgin (La Negrita) housed in the parish church of colonial Cartago's black and mulatto neighborhood of Los Angeles. Indeed the early authors were often very explicit in their own writings about the nation's origins in the bacchanalia traditions shared by whites and blacks in La Negrita's festivities.[6]

In the 1970s, at the high point of Central America's faith in a social science driven by class, not race, Stone's model claimed not only an oligarchic framework for Costa Rica's most admirable democratic achievements, but a framework in which second-class, mixed-race descendants of the conquerors driving forward the democratic process were mestizos whose smuggler origins in the cacao trade on the Atlantic coast led them to break away from Cartago to found San José. And the rest is history, as it were. Those who have documented and critiqued Stone's tendency to confuse elite biological ancestry with marital endogamy and legitimate birth have also shown that very often these were *mulatto* and not *mestizo* descendants, a point reiterated with numerous examples in the essays by Lohse and Meléndez in this volume.[7]

Guatemala's historical literature offers another example of just how powerful were the later ideological conceptions and orthodoxies of class over race, and mestizo (emerging majoritarian), not mulatto (receding or colonial and minoritarian), frameworks, eliding even the most obvious of inconvenient facts. During the upheavals of the late colonial and early independence eras both elite and commoner critics of the coastal plains populations of southwestern Guatemala and El Salvador referred to them disparagingly as mulattos, with adjectives such as "barbarous," "fearsome," or "intruder" tacked on for effect. Among their most famous military leaders in the successful Carrera revolt of 1838, the Mejía brothers of Santa Rosa, Guatemala, proudly identified themselves and their followers as "brown folk" (*gente parda*) bitterly opposed to the snobbery and oppression of capital city politicians. Carrera himself was claimed to be mostly mulatto in ancestry by one well-meaning mid-twentieth-century biographer quite out of step with the pro-mestizo ideology of the time but in keeping with the by then dominant Guatemalan tradition of avoiding recent Indian ancestry at all costs. All of this in a nation whose capital city elite was mocked by its most famous ideologue and leader of the Liberal Revolution of 1871, the Spanish-born Miguel García Granados, as having an African heritage whose "ears showed."[8]

Mexico would soon suffer a similar disappointment when the pioneering work of scholars such as Colin Palmer in the 1970s was met by a generation of near silence in Mexico and even more so abroad. The second bust of the cycle was felt more acutely perhaps in Mexico in the 1980s. Scholars such as Patrick Carroll in the United States kept alive interest in the field, but it was not until the 1990s that a new wave of research led to an extraordinary flowering of work on Mexico's so-called Third Root, both at home and abroad. That work has run the gamut from archival-based colonial-period work, to widely read art history analyses, to contemporary oral history and anthropological accounts far too numerous to attempt anything like a representative listing.[9]

Central America's most systematic published interest in African-descent populations emerged roughly simultaneously with the work that Palmer best exemplified for Mexico. The most remarkable work within that tradition was no doubt Christopher Lutz's dissertation at the University of Wisconsin, published in Spanish in Guatemala in 1982 and much later in an expanded version in English in 1994. Similarly Afro- or mulatto-oriented research could be found in the late 1970s in work by Romero for Nicaragua and Gudmundson for Costa Rica.[10] There, once again, things came to an unexpectedly abrupt end as the civil war generation in the isthmus had other concerns and as the 1970s-inspired, heavily quantified, "social-demographic-economic" historical traditions foundered at home and abroad.

Even MacLeod's grand synthesis, *Spanish Central America* (1973), with its powerful focus on the Atlantic world vocation of the isthmus, based on slavery, cacao, and the contraband trade that fueled both, failed to generate any systematic challenge to the modern national obsession with Pacific-oriented Central America or its relegation of African-descent peoples to the Caribbean coast, otherness, and isolation.[11] Yet today the widely read novelist Francisco Pérez de Antón, born in Spain but long resident in Guatemala, can masterfully re-create a fictional account of the mulatto regiment of early eighteenth-century Antigua, where he affirms, "The mulattoes began to disappear from Santiago as their blood was mixed in the exceedingly complex sea of race mixture, until it vanished completely from the urban environment. Thus, it is only right to underline the fact that their social and cultural integration was carried out without tensions of any kind."[12] Ironically, amid this tensionless resolution even Antigua's very architectural legacy had been reinscribed as a Spanish or white cultural legacy rather than being traceable to its mulatto master builders of the Porres family. That the University of San Carlos itself and many other beneficent institutions owed their endowments to the sugar and African slave-driven wealth of the Dominican order in the region somehow continues to escape notice entirely in such a happy-ending version of the region's drama of mestizaje.[13]

Until recently scholarship on people of African descent in Central America has been caught in one of two analytical domains, worlds apart in time and place: the colonial past and the Caribbean coastal enclave. In earlier and some recent studies of colonial Central America race exists, but all too frequently as the nominal end of a project of colonial racialization. In these works these *negros, morenos, pardos, mulatos,* and even *bozales* are so lacking in social and cultural identity as to seem irrelevant to the more recent debates over African survival and creolization.[14] Studies of Central America's Caribbean coastal communities of African descent, by contrast, have been far more nuanced and alive to debates in African diaspora studies, but they have at the same time tended to reproduce Central American nationalist discourses that located blackness outside of national history and only marginally within national territory. Although some Central Americanists—notably Lokken, Lohse, and Cáceres in this collection—have begun to take Africa seriously in their analysis of the African diaspora, most remain more strongly tied to Latin Americanist historiography. While this has limited the conceptual scope of most scholarship on the African diaspora in Central America, it offers the advantage that as this scholarship develops it can take the more productive, dynamic, and integrative approach to the creolization debates heralded by such scholars as Tiffany Patterson and Robin Kelley, David Eltis, Philip Morgan, and David Richardson.[15]

Analysis of class and mestizaje has been the hallmark and limitation of Latin American social history, and this has made discussions between Anglophone and Latin American–based diaspora scholarship particularly difficult. Scholars working on the African diaspora in Central America, and most of Latin America for that matter, need to more thoughtfully and fully engage with the transnational—and perhaps more important, translocal—flow of people, ideas, and resources.[16] At the same time, Anglophone scholarship must contend with the ambiguous and variegated nature of black identities and experiences in Latin America. In an important agenda-setting essay on the study of the African diaspora Tiffany Patterson and Robin Kelley argue both for the continuing analysis of "the construction and reproduction of diasporic identities . . . the creation of a diasporan consciousness" and to enmesh this within the complex and crosscutting worlds of class, gender, colonialism and anticolonialism, social and revolutionary movements, and subaltern politics—all areas in which Latin Americanist literature is well developed.[17]

PATHS EXPLORED

The contributions to this volume offer a more complex alternative to the mythic version of the pacific, tensionless disappearance of Afro–Central Americans beginning in the colonial era itself. We have grouped our eleven essays in two broadly temporal categories: the colonial worlds of slavery and freedom, and postcolonial nation building by suppressing, remembering, and reinscribing color and race on both bodies and regions. However, while the five essays by Lokken, Lohse, Offen, Cáceres, and Komisaruk share a colonial temporal frame, they are equally inviting of thematic comparisons with later essays on the national period. The six essays by Wolfe, Gudmundson, Hooker, Putnam, Harpelle, and Meléndez pursue issues of blackness, whiteness, mixedness, representation, and nationality into the nineteenth and twentieth centuries, often with surprising findings in light of the overwhelming weight of the commonsensical understandings of black disappearance or confinement to the Atlantic coast in the isthmus. However, they too show repeatedly just how intimately related many of these processes are to the all too quickly forgotten history of colonial Central America. Thus cross-temporal comparisons are perhaps as important as the more traditional comparisons between the colonial and the national.

Central America's early and midcolonial realities were based on a very heavy reliance on both the wider Atlantic world trading system and the

African slave-descended populations brought to the isthmus by that trade. Wherever the tax man focused his eyes on a regional or international trade, there too one would find populations of African descent in some capacity. Where there were Spaniards (and as Offen's essay shows, Englishmen) there were those of African descent as well. Not only were they domestic servants, artisans, cattle ranch hands, and laborers in and independent producers of sugar, chocolate, liquor, and cloth dyes, but they were very often the blood relatives of those Spaniards as well. As Lutz long ago pointed out, those of African descent outnumbered Spaniards and Indian Spanish mestizos in the very colonial capital of Antigua until the mid-seventeenth century at least; Romero has shown the same was true in every major city of late colonial Nicaragua. Only when we accept later nationalist historiography's invitation to ignore the very different basis of colonial trade—its concentration on extremely high value to weight export and import flows, where long-distance trade involved no bulky commodities such as coffee or bananas typical of the nineteenth and twentieth centuries—can one fail to recognize the ubiquitous presence of African-descent peoples in the far corners of the isthmian imperial outpost.

And present they indeed were. The essays in part I, "Colonial Worlds of Slavery and Freedom," document the extraordinary diversity of those positionings, from low-wage to high-wage economies, from the most urban to the most rural and remote settings, from Atlantic fort and port cities and regions to highland and Pacific plain sugar works. Indeed these analyses suggest that we should assume that slaves and free people of color formed key economic and social sectors in every region of the Americas until research shows otherwise. The essays by Lohse and Lokken reveal just how central Afro–Central Americans were to the most dynamic sectors—sugar and liquor in Guatemala, cacao and cattle in Costa Rica—of the midcolonial economy. And contrary to the all-powerful claim underpinning the integrationist view—that the slave trade ended early—both show that these peoples were not only slaves often born in Africa, but that they were born in knowable places and came to Central America in the hands of slave traders whose names can also be identified.[18] The slaves too had names and national origins that demonstrably mattered in the new societies they helped to create, whether in Lokken's "Angolans in Amatitlán" rendering or even more forcefully with Cáceres's royal slaves in Omoa and their overtly African naming practices on the very eve of both abolition and independence.

Komisaruk provides a view of late colonial Guatemala that demonstrates how, through slave initiative, slavery itself withered away long before formal abolition. Her findings can be compared quite directly with Hunefeldt's classic work on early nineteenth-century Lima and its environs.[19] But then Lima was markedly Afro-American in the minds of nearly all subsequent analysts, while nothing could be less true of Antigua and Guatemala City in the late colonial and early independence periods, despite the British merchant traveler Henry Dunn's classic diatribe on the subject.[20] Where Dunn saw all non-Indians, including the ladinos and mestizos, as mulattos, later Central American authorities spared no effort to discount any such African heritage. Not surprisingly, traditional views of limited Afro–Central American populations have tended to sap efforts to historicize Afro–Central American agency. Sofonías Salvatierra was typical in this connection: "The mulatto and the black, with very few exceptions, had no greater hopes than those inspired in them by the generous ideas of *criollismo*; they formed no resistance [*fuerza*], because they were very few in numbers."[21] Rather than simply countering this denial of demography and agency, continuing research should engage the contentious and complicated social and political lives of slaves and free people of color, attentive to regional variation, without either assuming the meaning of race or denying its salience altogether.

That very slave agency and initiative highlighted by Komisaruk is also powerfully suggested by the fact that freed populations did so well in both her setting of very low wages (owing largely to the competition of forced Indian labor in agriculture, no doubt) and in the setting of extreme labor shortages and high wages of Lohse's midcolonial Costa Rica. Indeed one of the most remarkable findings of both authors is that slaves and their descendants came to control substantial monetary resources, sufficient to purchase both their freedom and a relatively favorable position for their descendants well before abolition. None exercised that agency in quite so colorful a fashion as that reported by Cáceres for Omoa, where women slaves led a boycott of meat purchases from their royal owners as a form of pressure for improved conditions. In all these colonial settings slaves' and freed people's agency emerges as an inescapable part of their escape from bondage and their rise to more favored social positions. This argument for slow, painstaking ascent is brought full circle by Wolfe and especially Meléndez in his use of Romero's prescient expression, "the slow ascent of the marginalized," a particularly haunting reminder of just how fully the African descent of elite figures in Costa Rica and Nicaragua could be elided and indeed suppressed in more recent times.

The essays by Offen, Lohse, and Cáceres show just how deeply tied to the Caribbean slave and commodity trading world Central America was during the colonial period. They powerfully remind us once again of just how purposeful was the postcolonial myth of the Atlantic coast as an alien region to be conquered or reclaimed by the triumphant Liberals at the end of the nineteenth century. Offen's meticulous reconstruction of the complex worlds of the Mosquitia under colonial rule shows in great detail how Atlantic trading networks involved many different partners—and enemies—rarely to be easily defined by imperial or racial and ethnic identities alone. Likewise for Cáceres Omoa's royal slaves are incomprehensible without an understanding of the more or less open slave provisioning by Spanish authorities with their English enemies in Jamaica directly or through their commercial partners in Cuba. Lohse's marauding predators of the Matina Valley cacao fields are, of course, the same self-determining Sambo-Mosquito traders of the northern half of Offen's Mosquitia, while their southern brethren, the Tawira Mosquitomen, more often sought a local alliance with the mulattos of Matina and their Spanish authorities in Cartago.

All three studies show that trade relations and political alliances were extraordinarily complex and subsequently subject to myth-making of the first order. They also show how fully ethnicized or racialized became the terminology employed, with specific economic activities and political allegiances effectively racialized to such an extent that subsequent historians have had great difficulty sorting out conflicting claims about who did what and why. The rise of twentieth-century eugenics, anthropology, and sociology of race have further complicated these issues as notions of "homogeneous" mestizo nationalisms of the Pacific and "authentic" (read: historically unique) black and Indian identities on the Atlantic coast have militated against seeing their deep imbrications. The works in this collection make it clear that researchers should bridge the shared histories of slavery, trade, migration, and nation-state formation that connect the

Pacific and Caribbean regions of the isthmus and link them to the Atlantic world, seeing this history not simply or always as adversarial, but also as mutually constituted.

For Offen various activities (lumbering, fishing, transport, subsistence cropping, etc.) were racialized early on in Mosquitia, but all involved trade with "the enemy" of the moment, usually Spanish authorities in Honduras, Nicaragua, or Costa Rica. For Cáceres the entire provisioning enterprise of the Omoa fortress was part and parcel of a Caribbean trade reliant on both Spanish networks based in Cuba and English networks in Jamaica. For Lohse the mulatto and black cacao producers of Costa Rica's Matina Valley were also investors in and traders with Nicaragua's cattle and cacao economies southwest of Granada, extending into today's Costa Rican province of Guanacaste. While the Machiavellian formula "The enemy of my enemy is my friend" may overstate things, it is no less true that blackness in Central America's Atlantic-oriented world, far from occupying a fixed identity or political position, fluctuated dramatically, however much it may have also been "assigned" to certain places and activities. The irony of this fact is great indeed for the subsequent reinvention, analyzed in particular in Hooker's essay of this collection, of Nicaragua's and by extension the entire isthmus's Atlantic coast as a uniquely black, fixed, nonnational space in more modern times.

Once nation-states began the process of reinscribing race and color on both bodies and regions, a novel complicating, external factor was to be added with the arrival after the 1870s of thousands of black West Indians as part of the railroad-building and banana-exporting initiatives. As never before, notions of blackness, whiteness, and mixedness, seemingly so secure in their brotherhood and invidious distinctiveness in relation to Indianness in Central America, were suddenly up for grabs once again in ways they had not been for decades, if not centuries. However, a close reading of Offen's essay will have already alerted us to some deep historical parallels. Just as had been the case with the Spanish throughout the isthmus, the English in Mosquitia had been forced by the circumstances of their multiple weaknesses to admit many of their mixed-race children as "local whites," many of whom would be rejected by white Belizeans after their removal there in the 1770s. Moreover both the Sambo (or mulatto) and the Tawira Mosquitomen had repeatedly asserted their own superiority over their English brethren in Jamaica, alternately affectionately and derisively referring to them as their "grandfather's children."

The essays by Putnam and Harpelle in particular explore the critical ways both blackness and whiteness were redefined by the simultaneous arrival of the banana industry's managerial (white, largely U.S. citizens) and laboring (black, mostly anglophone West Indians) immigrant populations. However, far more than white zones (fenced, whites-only residential quarters for the managers) and black belts (plantation work sites and port and dock center cities) were to emerge anew here. Entirely new conceptions of racialized class authority emerged in highly gendered domestic and private spheres in the white zones. Showing that white women with little or no prior experience as racial masters or authority figure employers struggled to adapt in their new dual roles, Harpelle pulls back what the domestic curtain of racialized privacy had long hidden. Even more significant were the ways the serially diasporic West Indian community invented a series of markedly progressive traditions uniting blackness and a multinational or supranational modernity. Putnam thus shows not only how remarkable and far reaching was the West Indian impact in redefining black and white in Central America, but how far beyond the isthmus—from Panama to Cuba to New York, London, and beyond— these simultaneously progressive and unsettling processes first visible in Central America were clearly visible and historically transformative.

Central Americans outside the banana zones were also reinventing ways of signifying and comprehending race. Perhaps nowhere was that more visible and meaningful than in Nicaragua. Unique in the region, Nicaragua's very existence as a nation-state was challenged not only by its own civil wars but by William Walker and the filibustering army he led in the 1850s. Along with Costa Rica, Honduras, and Panama, Nicaragua experienced the most systematic and heavy-handed influence from investor and interventionist North Americans, the purveyors of a uniquely strident and novel white supremacist doctrine throughout Central America. Thus the focus of the essays by Wolfe, Gudmundson, Hooker, and to a lesser extent Meléndez on the Nicaraguan case not only helps remedy that nation's extraordinary isolation in terms of scholarship on the nineteenth century and early twentieth; such a sustained national focus also engages a case long thought paradigmatic of successful assimilation through mestizaje and the disappearance or invisibility of any non–Atlantic coast blackness in that mixed-race prototype: the "myth of mestizaje" so successfully challenged by Gould and others in terms of its anti-Indian teleology but not yet in terms of its African elisions.[22]

The paradoxes facing the reader may prove challenging. The very same Hispanic or mestizo legislators and intellectuals discussed by Hooker as creators of Atlantic or black otherness over the past two centuries are shown by Wolfe to have been mulatto presidents themselves, prior to their reinscription as mestizo or even white figures of commemoration, and by Meléndez to have African forbearers in even the most irreproachable (and often either pro-mestizo or white supremacist traditions) elite family trees. Gudmundson shows not only how, and how much, color mattered in the late nineteenth century, but that it was in these very same mixed-race districts of decidedly mulatto hue that the most virulent of pro-mestizaje ideologies, and the Left-Liberal politics that fed them, flourished. The politics of race had clearly shifted from the early to the late nineteenth century, yet the history of this shift remains almost unknown. Whether due to difference in class, education, historical memory, or other factors, the mulattos of early nineteenth-century León in Wolfe's essay are decidedly not the same as those of the rural coffee-boom towns of Carazo and Granada in Gudmundson's essay. A blanket conceit of blancophilia as the means to understand these differences or Afro–Central American invisibility and disappearance is simply insufficient. The research presented here shows once again how the African heritage and race of postcolonial Central Americans must be accounted for with fine-grained readings of both place and position that acknowledge how much deeper our research must plumb. The national focus on Nicaragua of many of our later essays also helps to make clear to those who would follow our lead that, contrary to popular and widespread academic belief—and the best efforts of many a government official outlawing racial or ethnic designations after 1824—the paucity of archival materials available to study those of African descent in postcolonial Central America is not the problem. Rather their lack of study is symptomatic of the deeper problem of the powerfully hegemonic and homogenizing nationalist traditions of most historical work to this point. In that sense, and the Nicaraguan focus of this work notwithstanding, the essays by Hooker and Meléndez clearly remind us that the question is not of the inability of Nicaraguans and Costa Ricans to see any black in their union of red and white, any east coast in the west, or any Atlantic world in the Pacific plain or highlands. Central America as a whole suffers from and with the same myopia. Dealing with this deficiency rests not simply on working with the postcolonial sources, but in bridging the study of race in the colonial and postcolonial worlds.

PATHS FORWARD

The very ambitious agenda of research questions we engaged at the conference could never have been fully addressed, much less resolved, in a single gathering.[23] Substantial advances are visible in the contributions that follow, but many areas remain to be explored in depth. Perhaps most pressing remains research exploring how incorporating Central America more fully into the African diaspora implies a rethinking of the more established narratives of diaspora and race. Within the context of research on Central America it is clear that scholars must dig deeper into the politics of race and, as the critic might say, the antipolitics of race in the suppression of public recognition of categories of African descent. In addition historical and ethnographic analysis of the politics of representation surrounding ethnic or place-centered identities throughout Central America must explore both the processes of historical memory formation and transmission, be they official or contestatory, high- or low-brow, and the gendered formulations of these issues, whether interpersonal or regional, as well as the experience of them by gendered historical subjects.

One of the greatest ironies of Afro–Central American history and research into it is the fact that the greatest achievements of that population are shrouded in the deepest silence and prohibition of any ethnically specific recognition. Just as in Colombia and Mexico, where militia service and armed politics, usually but not always on the Liberal side during the nineteenth century's interminable conflicts, were at the heart of both a civic consciousness and a set of demands for political inclusion as communities, major successes along the way were framed within the same color-blind, supraethnic citizenship discourse that could be used to deny the relevance of that same ethnically and racially rooted agency.[24]

Research into this place- and race-specific mobilization process is just beginning and will no doubt prove critical in our evolving understanding of what black, mulatto, and *zambo* came to mean in modern Central

America. Black and mulatto Central Americans successfully defeated ethnically specific head taxation, the *laborío*, in colonial times, by highlighting (i.e., threatening to withhold) their key military service and made some of their greatest gains as citizens of national states through militia participation. Knowing this, it is only reasonable to assume, unless it can be otherwise demonstrated, that both these groups and their color were central actors and issues of isthmian politics from colonial times to the twentieth century.[25]

There does not appear to have been any equivalent in Central America of the Afro-Colombian "democratic societies," Leftist factions of the Liberal Party first dedicated to raising funds to liberate the enslaved and then to radical action in favor of freedmen's rights, discovered by Sanders in the Cauca Valley region. Still, that the mulatto Liberals in Wolfe's essay manifest the same concern with "absolute equality" that Sanders finds in Afro-Colombia's democratic societies suggests that scholars pursue, rather than ignore, such possibilities. In any event, everywhere one looks in Central America militia membership and service, more often than not in the partisan Liberal cause, marked the single most effective means of acquiring the vote and land distributed by the state, whether from public or previously Indian village lands. And just as in Mexico, this pattern is quite logically connected back to colonial times, when militias were disproportionately black and mulatto as well as key avenues for social mobility among those of African descent.[26]

Similarly it was precisely the Left or popular wing of the Liberal parties that most militantly demanded the suppression of distinctions among citizens based on background or condition. Thus the difficulties that subsequent historians have had in researching these populations' history were, in large part, the creation of that same group's successful agency. However, as we will see in several essays, this obstacle can be gotten around when one focuses in depth on individual families and social and political networks using non-census or secular official records, on towns and regions ("sugar towns" in particular) notorious for their Afro heritage, or when one discovers official mistakes or throwbacks, such as the Nicaraguan census material from 1883. Subsequent work will simply need to refuse to take no for an answer when devising archival strategies. Prior to this most recent outpouring of interest, for example, no one knew that militia records, sugar town court cases, or even official records long sworn to silence on the subject could offer the riches already discovered.

The task of developing textual materials and a deeper analytical understanding of Afro–Central American communities' historical memory is perhaps the least developed agenda item of our common enterprise. As part of the resurgence of ethnic politics under the aegis of Pan-Mayanism since the 1980s there has been a marked tendency to spatialize or territorialize ethnic identity and historically redemptive (not to mention contemporary political) claims. Within this framework, only the Garifuna in Guatemala, Honduras, and Belize, the Miskitu in Nicaragua and Honduras, the Creole in Nicaragua, and black West Indians in Costa Rica and Panama have tended to qualify as "historically black" in the minds of both popular political commentators and academics. In neighboring cases this has been equally notorious, but there at least the emerging work on the Costa Chica (the Pacific coast areas of Guerrero and Oaxaca) and the Gulf Coast states of Veracruz and Tabasco in Mexico and Colombia's Chocó Province and the Cauca River Valley in Antioquia has been able to make a regional research virtue of the intellectual vice of essentializing race by territory or contemporary self-identification. Wider historical analysis will push scholars to engage with Wade's recent call to explore both the lived and ideological forms of mixedness, to see race and nation in their lived complexity rather than simply in terms of exclusive authenticity.[27]

Many of the essays in this collection make reference to the complex ways historical memory emerges and is subsequently shaped. Perhaps the most detailed examination we have to date comes from the Dominican slave plantation of San Gerónimo, Baja Verapaz, Guatemala. To judge by this single, perhaps extreme case, historical memory studies would reward the researcher not only with a deeper understanding of both contemporary attitudes and events in the distant past, but also with clues as to how those very events actually unfolded, often misleadingly presented matter-of-factly in the official record. It is no criticism perhaps of this late-emerging work to say that it lags far, far behind both Mayan-identity studies locally and Mexico's Costa Chica research traditions. More important, we need to learn from those achievements, particularly from the sustained conversations between anthropologists and historians, between visual and material culture analysts and documentary historians.[28]

The feminization of subalterns and of entire subordinate regions is now readily recognized in most historical scholarship, just as is the re-masculinization or heroizing of subalterns by their supporters and leaders in modern political struggles over citizenship and its meanings. Classic studies by Gould, Hale, and Smith in particular have shown how deeply embedded such notions are for Indian and non-Indian categories in Central America.[29] How that dynamic played itself out involving ethnic and racial categories of African descent is, however, far from clear. Indeed to the extent that colonial sugar towns or districts were involved, female-headed households often controlled much of the wealth in the communities, owing to women's roles as domestic distillers and rumrunners, giving entirely new meanings to the traditional male-dominant rhetoric of rights and citizenship. Nevertheless traditional imageries of inferiority were, as we have seen, deeply encoded in terms denoting both blackness and disreputable femaleness and womanhood. Sorting out the many uses of gendered and racialized languages, for purposes of both exclusion and inclusion, as well as the way women and men experienced their resulting categorization will no doubt occupy Afro–Central American research for a long time to come.

That much remains to be done to fill in the historical record of blacks and blackness in Central America is all too obvious to those who convened the multidisciplinary working group at Tulane University in the fall of 2004. That the time had come for a more ambitious and comparative rendering of that history was also our firm belief. We trust that the following essays make good on that promise to contribute to documenting a long neglected historical record. Central Americans of all backgrounds, and those abroad who study their history, are invited to enjoy the essays that follow, filling in the black where only red and white could be seen before.

NOTES

1   Wade, *Blackness and Race Mixture*; Appelbaum, *Muddied Waters*.

2   Lewis, "Of Ships and Saints." Maria Elena Díaz's study *The Virgin, the King, and the Royal Slaves of El Cobre* offers a powerful example of precisely this place-focused and neo-indigenous cultural politics.

3   The full lyrics of the hymn are available on the Mount Holyoke College website, http://www.mtholyoke.edu/acad/latam/africania.html.

4   Tannenbaum, *Slave and Citizen*, 117. For important recent overviews of the broad thrust of scholarship on the African diaspora, see T. R. Patterson and Kelley, "Unfinished Migrations"; Manning, "Africa and the African Diaspora." See also the Latin Americanist engagements of Ben Vinson III, "Introduction: African (Black) Diaspora History," and Herman Bennett, "The Subject in the Plot."

5   Aguirre Beltrán, *La población negra de Mexico*; Barón Castro, *La población de El Salvador*; Castro y Tosi, "La población de la ciudad de Cartago"; Ayón, *Historia de Nicaragua*; González Víquez, *Apuntes estadísticos.*

6   Stone, *La dinastía de los conquistadores*, 244–57. The classic reference to the festivities of colonial Cartago's mulatto and white residents appears in Fernández Guardia's *Crónicas coloniales de Costa Rica* ("La Cofradía de Los Angeles," 156–63).

7   Stone's expression "segundones" did not even openly recognize the out-of-wedlock or illegitimate birth of those involved. Mauricio Meléndez has produced detailed genealogical evidence of the African and Indian backgrounds in many of these family lines, following the mulatto descendants of the conqueror Juan Vázquez de Coronado and the mestizo children born to the indigenous woman Catalina de Tuía. See Meléndez Obando, "Descendientes mulatos del conquistador Juan Vázquez de Coronado," and his forthcoming study *La dinastía de los conquistados.*

8   García Granados, *Memorias del general Miguel García Granados*, 7. For the genealogical claims about Carrera, see Cobos Batres, *Carrera*, 11. The self-description as *la gente parda* (brown folk) by the Mejía brothers was found by Ann Jefferson; see "The Rebellion of the Mita."

9   C. Palmer, *Slaves of the White God*; P. J. Carroll, *Blacks in Colonial Veracruz.* Some of the most influential recent works on Mexico are Bennett, *Africans in Colonial Mexico*; Chávez Carbajal, *El rostro colectivo*; de la Serna, *Pautas de convivencia étnica*; Herrera Casasús, *Piezas de indias*; Lewis, "Of Ships and Saints"; Martínez Montiel and Reyes G., *Encuentro nacional de Afromexicanistas*; Martínez Montiel, *Presencia Africana en México*; Naveda Chávez-Hita, *Esclavos negros*; Naveda Chávez-Hita, *Pardos, mulatos y libertos*; Restall, *Beyond Black and Red*; Vaughn and Vinson, *Afroméxico*, as well as Vaughn's website, Afromexico; M. E. Velásquez and Correa Duró, *Poblaciones y culturas de origen africano en México*; Vincent, *The Legacy of Vicente Guerrero*, and his website on black-Indian Mexico; Vinson, *Bearing Arms for His Majesty.* The works that analyze so-called *casta* painting in late colonial Mexico include Carrera, *Imagining Identity*; Katzew, *Casta Painting*; Velázquez Gutiérrez, *Juan Correa.*

Among the most influential book-length works on Colombia, in addition to those cited in note 1, see Arocha, *Ombligados de Ananse*; de Friedemann and Arocha, *De sol a sol*; Camacho and Restrepo, *De montes, ríos y ciudades*; Helg, *Liberty and Equality*; Lasso, *Myths of Harmony*; Mosquera, Pardo, and

Hoffman, *Afrodescendientes en las Américas*; Sanders, *Contentious Republicans*; Wade, *Music, Race, and Nation*. See also the Colombian journal *América Negra*.

10 Lutz, *Historia sociodemográfica*; Lutz, *Santiago de Guatemala*; Romero Vargas, *Las estructuras sociales de Nicaragua*, based on his French doctoral dissertation, written in the early 1970s; Gudmundson, *Estratificación socio-racial y económica*. Examples of this earlier generation's interest in the topic include Aguilar Bulgarelli, "La esclavitud en Costa Rica"; Barrantes Ferrero, *Un caso de la esclavitud en Costa Rica*; Houdaille, "Negros franceses en América Central a fines del siglo XVIII"; Fiehrer, "Hacia una definición de la esclavitud"; Fiehrer, "Slaves and Freedmen"; Gudmundson, "De 'negro' a 'blanco'"; Leiva Vivas, *Tráfico de esclavos negros en Honduras*; Martínez Durán and Contreras, "La abolición de la esclavitud en Centroamérica"; Meléndez Chaverri and Duncan, *El Negro en Costa Rica*; Riismandel and Levitt, "Un estudio cuantitativo de algunos aspectos de la esclavitud"; Olien, "Black and Part-Black Population in Colonial Costa Rica"; Rodríguez, *The Cádiz Experiment*; Tobar Cruz, "La esclavitud del negro en Guatemala."

11 M. J. MacLeod, *Spanish Central America*.

12 "Por lo demás, los mulatos fueron desapareciendo de Santiago a medida que su sangre se diluía en el complejísimo mar del mestizaje, hasta desvanecerse por complete del entorno urbano. En tal sentido, es justo subrayar que su integración social y cultural se llevó a cabo sin tensiones de ninguna clase." Pérez de Anton, *Los hijos del incienso y de la pólvora*, 541.

13 On the conflictive and complex family history of the Porres architects in colonial Guatemala, see Meléndez Obando, "Las raíces mulatas." See also his photo essay on the same topic on the Mount Holyoke College website. On the basis of much of the Dominican order's financial and political empire, the source of these institutional endowments in colonial times, in slavery and sugar, see Belaubre, "Poder y redes sociales en Centroamérica"; Gudmundson, "Firewater."

14 On these debates, see the classic elaboration of creolization by Mintz and Price, *The Birth of African American Culture*, and the more recent and varied Africanist approaches of Thornton, *Africa and Africans*; Gomez, *Exchanging Our Country Marks*; Lovejoy and Trotman, *Trans-Atlantic Dimensions of Ethnicity*.

15 T. R. Patterson and Kelley, "Unfinished Migrations," 15–19; Eltis, Morgan, and Richardson, "Agency and Diaspora."

16 See Seigel's excellent discussion in "Beyond Compare"; T. R. Patterson and Kelley, "Unfinished Migrations," 22–24.

17 T. R. Patterson and Kelley, "Unfinished Migrations," 14–15, 29–32.

18 On the identities of the slave traders in late colonial Central America, see Cáceres, "Migraciones forzadas y mercancías."

19 Hünefeldt, *Paying the Price of Freedom*.

20 Henry Dunn, English traveler in 1829, reprinted in Parker, *Travels in Central America*, 114, n. 105, citing page 90 of Dunn's original work as follows: "The Mulatto, or mixed race, form, in fact, the physical force of the nation. . . . The offspring of Negroes and Indians, of Whites and Indians, as well as the descendants of African Negroes, are included under the term Mulattoes, by which they are generally known; sometimes, however, they are called Mestizoes, or Ladinos."

21 Salvatierra, *Contribución a la Historia de Centroamérica*, 2:372.

22 Gould, *To Die in This Way*; Gould, Hale, and Smith, *Memorias del Mestizaje*; Gould and Henríquez Consalvi, *1932, Scars of Memory/Cicatriz de la memoria*; Euraque, *Conversaciones históricas*.

23 We proposed to participants a common research agenda or set of questions, which included the following: What were the defining experiences of Africans and African Americans in colonial and national times in the region or nation studied? How have African Americans and blackness been portrayed in regional and national literatures? How and when were African Americans of mixed race defined such that their African descent no longer counted? How have the struggles and contributions of African Americans, in particular those of mixed race, been built into mestizo, national, or otherwise homogenizing narratives? Do contemporary populations identify (culturally, politically, or in other ways) with an African heritage? What texts, images, or artifacts do those populations consider emblematic of their history and identity? How have you, as a researcher, dealt with what Peter Wade has termed the challenge of interacting with the populations whose history you study, and of thinking "reflexively" about race and ethnicity in contemporary Latin America?

24 Sanders, *Contentious Republicans*; Mallon, *Peasant and Nation*; Guardino, *Peasants, Politics*; Gould, *To Die in This Way*; Gudmundson, "Firewater."

25 Lokken, "Useful Enemies."

26 Sanders, *Contentious Republicans*, especially chap. 3, "A New Politics"; Gudmundson, "Firewater." Vinson, *Bearing Arms for His Majesty*, makes this colonial connection most directly. For Guatemala's early independent militia and mulattos, see Jefferson, "The Rebellion of the Mita." Another important source for understanding the colonial-national connections of mulatto militia service in Guatemala is Gómez, "*Al servicio de las armas.*"

27 Wade, "Rethinking *Mestizaje*."

28 Gudmundson, "Firewater." While Lewis's "Of Ships and Saints" is a model contemporary study of memory and ethnic identity inscribed in spatial and cultural terms, her research has also produced a colonial-era study of Inquisition materials: *Hall of Mirrors*. For a Guatemalan study with many parallels, see Few, *Women Who Lead Evil Lives*.

29 Gould, Hale, and Smith, *Memorias del Mestizaje*; C. A. Smith, "Race-Class-Gender Ideology."

I

COLONIAL WORLDS

OF SLAVERY & FREEDOM

ANGOLANS IN AMATITLÁN

Sugar, African Migrants, and
Gente Ladina *in Colonial Guatemala*
Paul Lokken

In early 1613 an official of the Audiencia of Guatemala inspected a "cargo" of ninety-seven men and boys and thirty-nine women and girls aboard the ship that had transported them from Angola to the decade-old Caribbean port of Santo Tomás de Castilla.[1] These 136 West Central Africans were among tens of thousands brought against their will to Spain's American empire in the early seventeenth century, when forced African migration to mainland areas of colonial Spanish America peaked.[2] The colonial heartlands of Peru and New Spain absorbed the majority of these unwilling immigrants, but mining and agriculture in northern South America and Central America also drew them in by the thousands.[3] The Angolans and others who ended up in the territory of the present-day republic of Guatemala played a more important role than is often realized in the early development of the nonindigenous sector of the population that is now defined as *ladino*. Their role was nowhere more crucial than in the region surrounding Lake Amatitlán, just south of present-day Guatemala City and home in the midcolonial era to several large sugar plantations employing hundreds of enslaved Africans and their American-born descendants.

These properties were investigated several times between 1670 and 1680 by royal officials charged with ferreting out abuses of indigenous laborers distributed to plantation owners by means of the labor draft known as the *repartimiento*. In conducting their investigations the officials recorded head counts of the enslaved workers of African descent who, long designated by legal and other considerations as the preferred labor force in sugar production and similarly arduous tasks, resided permanently on each plantation.[4] Several scholars have published these numbers, but the precise antecedents of the enslaved individuals they represent, and the ties of those individuals to the rest of seventeenth-century Guatemalan society, have remained largely unexplored.[5] This essay examines those antecedents, mostly West Central African, and demonstrates that the impact of forced African migration to the Amatitlán region extended well beyond the plantations themselves. Indeed by the late seventeenth century free people of part-African ancestry appear to have dominated demographically the rapidly expanding sector of the surrounding population whose members were classified neither as *indio tributario* (tribute-paying Indian) nor as *español* (Spaniard). In other words, around Lake Amatitlán many *gente ladina* (ladino people)—a classification just beginning to be used, although not consistently, in a sense akin to the modern one—were but a generation or two removed from Angola.

The location of Africans and their descendants at the center of the Amatitlán region's early demographic and social history has important implications for analyses of the interrelated histories in Guatemala of the term *ladino* and the people defined by it. On the one hand, the evidence presented here directly challenges the notion that modern ladinos are exclusively of mixed Spanish and indigenous descent, that *ladino* and *mestizo* are synonyms. This lazy "racial" claim continues to appear in authoritative and widely read sources, most strikingly right alongside a common and opposing scholarly definition of the term as a designation of a person or group as nonindigenous based on language or other aspects of cultural practice, not ancestry.[6] At the same time, neither the latter definition nor the "Indian-ladino dichotomy" it conjures up has been a timeless feature of the Guatemalan social landscape. If the initial outlines of both can be glimpsed in the history of the African experience in seventeenth-century Amatitlán, so can competing definitions of the term, as well as a more complex set of colonial social relations.[7]

The ultimate significance of this history for the Guatemalan national imaginary is left to the judgment of students of the postindependence era, some of whom have begun to attend closely to rather than ignore the fact that many nineteenth-century ladinos were better known as *mulatos*.[8] The focus here is on evidence of the impact of Africans on colonial Guatemalan society and of colonial Guatemalan society on Africans. Early seventeenth-century plantation records reveal the extent of the Amatitlán region's integration into the wider networks of the contemporary Atlantic slave trade precisely at a time of unprecedented West Central African migration to Spanish America. Matrimonial and other records produced later in the century hint at the demographic, social, and classificatory processes by which the descendants of African migrants began to acquire an emerging Guatemalan identity that would eventually carry few, if any, connotations of African origins.

SUGAR PLANTATIONS AND ANGOLANS

Writing in the 1640s of his experiences a decade earlier as a priest in the villages of San Juan Amatitlán and San Miguel Petapa, the Englishman and renegade Dominican friar Thomas Gage recalled a nearby sugar plantation thus: "[It] seemeth to be a little Town by it selfe for the many cottages and thatched houses of *Blackmore* slaves which belong unto it, who may be above a hundred, men, women, and children."[9] The property to which he referred was formally named Nuestra Señora de la Encarnación but more commonly called the Ingenio de Anís after its founder, Juan González Donis, who had begun producing sugar there during the late sixteenth century.[10] By the time it passed to González Donis's heirs in 1621 the property was the site of "a mighty sugar mill and cane fields where a great deal of sugar [was] made."[11] Gage actually underestimated the size of the ingenio's workforce a decade later, despite his reputation for exaggerating the riches of Central America as a goad to an English invasion. An inventory drawn up in 1630 indicates that 191 slaves of both sexes and all ages then resided on the plantation.[12]

Gage's stay in Guatemala between 1627 and 1637 coincided with the final years of the era during which forced African migration to the Spanish American mainland peaked. Nearly 270,000 Africans are estimated to have arrived there between 1595 and 1640, when Portuguese merchants held the Spanish slave-trading monopoly known as the *asiento* and otherwise enjoyed unprecedented access to Spain's American colonies as a result of a sixty-year union between the Spanish and Portuguese crowns (1580–1640).[13] The Portuguese were at the same time both implicated in and benefiting from a series of wars in Angola, where they had established themselves at Luanda in 1575.[14] As a consequence West Central Africa became the most important source of slaves for Spanish America in the late sixteenth century and early seventeenth. Most of these slaves passed through Veracruz and Cartagena, the two ports designated by the Spanish crown for the receipt of slave imports, but at least ten ships brought more than a thousand Africans directly to the coast of Central America between 1613 and 1628 alone. Most, if not all, of these ships proceeded from West Central Africa.[15]

Inventories from Guatemalan sugar plantations bear out at the local level the sense of a notable spike in African immigration in the early seventeenth century. The emergence of major operations like the Anís ingenio led to higher demand for imported African labor in and around the capital of the Audiencia, Santiago de Guatemala (now the town of Antigua), where the traffic in slaves had been relatively light for much of the sixteenth century.[16] Up until the 1590s most Africans arriving in Central America appear to have ended up in the silver mining areas of Honduras and Nicaragua, but as silver production began to decline an increasing number went instead to the sugar-producing region near Santiago, where royal decrees banning the use of the diminishing indigenous labor force in sugar work and similarly "onerous" activities threatened economic expansion.[17] Documentation of a recent influx of Africans into the region appears in the inventory of the Anís ingenio in 1630. Of 137 slaves identified as being at least eighteen years of age, as many as two-thirds were African-born. The key position of West Central Africa in the contemporary Atlantic slave trade is evident in the designation of no fewer than forty-eight of the plantation's residents as *angola* and another sixteen as either *anchico* or *congo*.[18] Meanwhile the plantation's skewed sex ratio reproduced an especially notorious characteristic of the transatlantic trade in humans. Some three-quarters of the enslaved immigrants were men, while the property's total enslaved population was 128 men and boys and just 63 women and girls.[19]

Similar demographic circumstances were to be found on other sugar plantations for which roughly contemporary information is available. When Gonzalo de Peralta died in 1625 the inventory of a *trapiche* he owned near Petapa named twenty-three slaves: fourteen men and boys and nine women and girls. Eleven of the sixteen adults listed were identified as migrants, all of them West Central African in origin. Four men and three women were defined as *angola,* and three men and one woman as *congo*.[20] More than a decade earlier the prominent Santiago merchant Francisco de Mesa employed twenty-eight slaves, including eighteen who

TABLE 1 African Immigrants on the Anís Ingenio, 1630

ASCRIBED ORIGIN	MEN	WOMEN
Angola	33	15
Anchico	9	2
Bran	4	2
Congo	3	2
Bañon	2	1
Other	10–18	0
Totals	61–69	22

Source: Archivo General de Centro América, Guatemala City, A1.20, leg. 536, fol. 296v–302.

were African-born, on a trapiche named Santa Cruz, located south of Santiago along the Guacalate River near the community of Escuintla. Ten West Central Africans represented the majority of the newcomers in this labor force, and there were also seven individuals identified by diverse Senegambian origins as well as one Pedro "Mazanbique." Remarkably just three of the twenty-eight slaves listed were female.[21]

Other large sugar operations in early seventeenth-century Guatemala probably shared the demographic conditions evident on these properties. Along with the Anís ingenio, the "three Farmes of Sugar" Thomas Gage saw in the Amatitlán area during the 1630s included the ingenio of Esteban de Zavaleta, formerly the Peralta operation and now employing some sixty slaves, and a nearby trapiche belonging to the Augustinian order, home to another twenty slaves. Gage also reported that a new trapiche was under construction in the area when he left, on property owned by one Juan Bautista between San Juan and San Cristóbal Amatitlán (today Palín).[22] North in the Verapaz meanwhile the Dominican order had been developing a large ingenio called San Gerónimo near Salamá since the late sixteenth century. The terms of an obligation placed on the property in 1633 reveal that more than a hundred slaves "of different nations" were then toiling on it. By the late colonial era it would be the largest sugar-producing enterprise by far in all of Central America, employing hundreds of slaves.[23]

Sugar was hardly the only regional employer of slave labor. The capital, with a total population estimated at more than thirty-three thousand by the 1650s, may have been home to more enslaved people of African origins in the early seventeenth century than all of the ingenios and tra-piches combined.[24] Others worked in small groups in rural household la-bor and on wheat farms, indigo plantations, and cattle ranches, mostly in territory east of Santiago and south along the Pacific coast but also, if more unexpectedly, in the vicinity of major Maya population centers like Quezaltenango in the western highlands.[25] But sugar production was the only local economic activity that regularly concentrated large numbers of Africans and their descendants in dense residential settings. As a result the impact of African immigration may have been especially profound in the plantation zone.[26]

Initially that impact was felt on the plantations themselves. As Gage's comments reveal, these seemed to be self-contained "villages," and they may well have been close-knit communities at a time of heightened im-migration, when large numbers of newly arrived Africans had yet to de-velop any social networks outside the narrow bounds of the properties on which they worked. The forging of new relationships on the proper-ties themselves was no doubt assisted by the mutual intelligibility of West Central African languages like Kimbundu and Kikongo, as well as the ex-perience many migrants already had replacing ties of real or fictive kin-ship that in many cases had been disrupted several times since their initial enslavement.[27] The inventories cited earlier reveal that immigrants indeed tended to be involved in family relationships internal to the workforce of the property on which they resided, at least where possible. But there was a major and obvious barrier to the formation of heterosexual family units, a rare area of mutual interest for most slaves and their owners: the demo-graphic imbalance between women and men. The impact of this barrier was felt in varying degrees on the Mesa, Peralta, and Anís properties.[28]

On the Mesa trapiche the one enslaved woman who was clearly identi-fied as an African immigrant, María Angola, was noted to be the wife of Pedro Mazanbique. A recount in 1620 of the property's labor force reveals that they had a child, Juana, not long after the first inventory was made. The second woman in the trapiche's slave population in 1612 was the "es-clava negra" Isabel, identified as the wife of Antón García, also labeled simply a "black slave." Isabel and Antón may or may not have been immi-grants, as they were among the few slaves on the property who were iden-tified neither by a specific African origin nor as *criollos* (American-born slaves). The only other woman listed, Agustina, was identified as both "mulata" and "criolla." She perhaps stood apart socially from the other slaves, since she was not linked in the inventory to any of the property's male residents. It may be significant in this regard that only two were classified, like her, as being of mixed ancestry.[29]

Clearly the Mesa trapiche provided few opportunities for the men of its enslaved labor force to form families with their female counterparts. As a consequence at least five of those men developed relationships with women who were neither enslaved nor, with one exception, African in origin. The wives of the two slaves listed in the inventory as skilled workers—Gregorio, the sugar master, and the cartwright Juan Grande—were identified as "Indian," in this area perhaps Pipil.[30] Two other enslaved men, including one immigrant, Antón Angola, also had native spouses. Another Angolan, Pablo, was alone in having found a free partner of African origins, Inés, identified as a free black woman.[31] Pablo and Inés made for a rare couple in rural Guatemala, where free women of exclusively African ancestry seem to have been even scarcer than female African immigrants.

The inventory of the Peralta trapiche offers a rather different picture from the one that emerges from the Mesa property's records, owing to a more balanced sex ratio among its enslaved workers. Fully nineteen of the twenty-three slaves named in the inventory were associated with one of six conjugal units said to exist among those workers, including two families with a total of seven children between them. One of these families involved Mateo Congo and Agustina Conga, both said to be about forty, and their four children, who ranged in age from three to roughly eighteen years. The other was composed of Margarita, Antón Angola, and three children of indeterminate age.[32]

The apparently successful establishment by these two couples of cohesive and relatively large family units must be balanced against the ever-present threat of involuntary family breakup. The seriousness of that threat is evident in the fact that Justino, the oldest of Mateo's and Agustina's four children, no longer lived with his family in 1625, but instead had been working in the capital for three years for a new owner, the bishop of Guatemala. Legal maneuvering upon the death of an owner could destabilize families as well. By the time the Peralta inventory was drawn up the deceased's widow had removed Margarita and her three children to Santiago, perhaps to ensure the protection of her dowry, while Antón remained behind on the trapiche. Margarita and Antón seem to have had difficulty exploiting the famed protections slave marriage enjoyed under Spanish slave law, even if other slaves were more successful in this respect. That same year, the decision of Pedro Angola and Lucía Negra to marry following the death of their owner, don Alonso Alvarez de Villamil, forced the executors of Alvarez's will to sell them together with their five children at a price far lower than their sales as individuals would have garnered.[33]

The Peralta inventory does appear to confirm that enslaved women, evidently always in the minority on early seventeenth-century Guatemalan sugar plantations, were highly likely to be involved in conjugal relationships with enslaved men who lived on the same property. The six conjugal units identified in the Peralta inventory involved all of the adult women listed. At least four of those women had come directly from Africa, while none possessed the mulata status that may have set the unattached criolla, Agustina, apart from the rest of the slaves on the Mesa trapiche. Ironically the benefits of these relationships accrued most obviously, if not necessarily most fully, to the slave owner, and not just in the realm of reproduction. Unbalanced sex ratios on plantations generally increased the likelihood of escape, and indeed two of the four unattached men on the Peralta trapiche had fled the property shortly before the inventory was made in 1625 and remained missing.[34]

Patterns of family formation similar to those existing among the Peralta slaves were evident among the residents of the much larger Anís plantation in 1630. At least thirty-three of the thirty-seven women said to be eighteen or older, along with three sixteen-year-old girls, were listed as spouses of men who were also slaves on the plantation. Of the remaining four adult women, two were identified as partners of men whose names do not appear elsewhere in the inventory, and two were said to be unattached (*soltera*). In all no fewer than 130 of the plantation's 191 slaves, including all fifty-four of those identified as being under eighteen, were linked by family ties to other slaves on the property. The precise number of conjugal relationships internal to the enslaved workforce itself is difficult to ascertain due to inconsistencies in the use of names in the inventory, but there were at least forty and as many as forty-seven. Roughly half of these couples had at least one child, and six had three or more children, although the exact nature of the family relationships inferred from the inventory is not clear since it never identifies more than one parent of any of the children listed. Nevertheless one assumes that, as in most societies, close biological ties were not a prerequisite to the formation of strong family relationships.[35]

This evidence of extensive family formation on the Anís ingenio suggests that the "little town by itself" that Gage described may well have exhibited some aspects of a cohesive and inward-oriented community. The stark imbalance between the sexes, however, left two-thirds of its adult men with limited options for establishing families with the enslaved women of the plantation, if they so wished. The Anís inventory gives no hint of the relationships that any of those sixty-four men may have sustained as a consequence with other, probably free women.[36] Such relationships surely existed, though, contributing directly to the steady growth in the surrounding region of a nonindigenous population composed largely of individuals identified as free mulattos by the late seventeenth century. That term, significantly, was applied in colonial Guatemala as often to people of African and native as of African and Spanish ancestry.[37]

SUGAR PLANTATIONS AND MULATTOS

By 1640 forced African migration to Guatemala had largely ceased due in part to Spain's loss of Portugal and a temporary halt to the asiento system. Despite intermittent smuggling and the eventual revival of the asiento, slave imports to Central America remained low for decades.[38] Slave-driven sugar production, however, lost none of its vitality, at least in the short term. Writing in the late seventeenth century, the chronicler Francisco Antonio de Fuentes y Guzmán indicated that local plantations largely satisfied domestic demand.[39] A *visita* of ingenios and trapiches conducted on behalf of the Audiencia by the *oidor* don Gerónimo Chacón Abarca y Piedra in 1679–80, the last and most extensive in the series of investigations of sugar plantations begun a decade earlier, reveals that the Amatitlán region was then home to four ingenios of sufficient productive capacity to employ more than a hundred slaves each. Five smaller operations in the immediate vicinity were reported to hold another 135 slaves between them, while dozens more labored on nine properties located elsewhere in the *corregimientos* (districts) of the Valley of Guatemala and

Escuintepeque (also Escuintla).[40] Unfortunately for historians the ingenio of San Gerónimo in the northern district of Verapaz was not also investigated. Its likely status as the largest operation of all in Guatemala in 1680 means the demographic and social effects of intensive sugar cultivation were not confined to the areas visted by royal inspectors.

A notable feature of sugar production later in the seventeenth century was the increasingly critical role that religious orders, particularly the Dominicans, played in it. By the 1660s the Dominican order controlled not only San Gerónimo but also two of the four largest plantations in operation near Lake Amatitlán: the Anís ingenio and a nearby property named Nuestra Señora del Rosario. They had also acquired a fourth, smaller ingenio in the corregimiento of Escuintepeque, known simply as Santo Domingo. In 1679 the Anís and Rosario properties were reported to hold 119 and 111 slaves, respectively, while thirty others worked on the smaller operation in Escuintepeque.[41]

Three other religious orders had joined the Dominicans by this time in exploiting the profits to be gained from the slave-driven production of sugar. The Jesuits, although the most commercially successful of the orders in many parts of Spanish America, played second fiddle to the Dominicans in the province of Guatemala, where they owned but a single ingenio near San Cristóbal Amatitlán (today Palín). That property, La Santíssima Trinidad, nonetheless rivaled the Dominican ingenios with respect to the size of its workforce, holding 108 slaves in 1679. The Mercedarians owned a somewhat smaller plantation east of the lake called San Ramón de la Vega, where eighty-four slaves lived and worked in 1679. Just to its north was San Nicolás, the Augustinian trapiche described a half-century earlier by Gage and still a relatively modest enterprise with an enslaved labor force numbering just twenty-eight persons.[42]

The only major local sugar-producing operation not run by a religious order as of 1679 was the ingenio owned earlier by Gonzalo de Peralta and then Esteban de Zavaleta. On Zavaleta's death in 1635 this estate, Nuestra Señora de Guadalupe, passed to his heirs, Juan and Domingo de Arrivillaga, who in 1638 reported the presence of more than eighty slaves. That number continued to grow over the following four decades, reaching 115 in 1675, by which time don Tomás de Arrivillaga Coronado had inherited the property, and 121 in 1679, when don Tomás's heirs controlled it. Fuentes y Guzmán, a jaundiced observer of the religious orders' economic expansion, averred with more than a touch of vicarious pride that the family-run Arrivillaga operation, located near his own, smaller one, was "the most outstanding" of all the ingenios in the surrounding area.[43]

Altogether the nine ingenios and trapiches surveyed by royal officials in the Amatitlán region were said to employ 594 slaves in 1679. The stark imbalance between the sexes that marks earlier plantation inventories had now moderated, with the Arrivillaga and Mercedarian properties actually holding female majorities. Nonetheless the 333 enslaved men and boys who were enumerated easily outnumbered the 261 enslaved women and girls. More than 250 free people, most identified as mulattos, also worked on these nine properties, whose owners were furthermore allotted a total of 440 native laborers by the repartimiento. The majority of these came from the nearby villages of San Juan Amatitlán, San Cristóbal Amatitlán, San Miguel Petapa, Santa Inés Petapa, and Santa Catarina Pinula. The workers sent out on a weekly basis from these communities, mostly Pogomam Maya, were supposed to be employed only in the wheat fields that plantation owners also maintained. As the investigations revealed, this regulation was regularly flouted.[44]

The indigenous population of these five villages totaled at least eight thousand at the time the visita was made, and may have been substantially higher, as the multiplier of three used in this case to derive the figure from the number of tributary heads of household is more commonly set

TABLE 2 Slaves by Gender on Amatitlán Sugar Plantations, 1679

INGENIO/TRAPICHE	MALE	FEMALE	Total
Arrivillaga	54	67	121
Anís (Dominican)	74	45	119
Rosario (Dominican)	71	40	111
Jesuit	59	49	108
Mercedarian	37	47	84
Augustinian	19	9	28
Arochiguí	10	4	14
Fuentes y Guzmán	7	0	7
Melgar	2	0	2
Total	333	261	594

Source: "Autos hechos sobre la visita de ingenios y trapiches en que trabajan indios, año de 1679," Archivo General de Indias (Seville), Guatemala, 27, R. 9, N. 29, block 5, images 148–76.

at four or even five.[45] The enslaved residents of local sugar plantations therefore composed far less than 10 percent of the total population in the region. Nevertheless they may have constituted as much as one-third of the local *non*tributary sector, which included Spaniards, mestizos, all people who were defined by African origins, whether free or enslaved, and *indios laboríos* (from the Taíno word *naboría*), native people who were not tied by tribute and labor obligations to a specific village.[46] While indios laboríos, like free people of African origins, did owe an alternative tribute, known as the *laborío*, they were clearly distinguished legally from the indios tributarios who formed the vast majority of the native population and in that sense were part of the nontributary sector. It has been estimated that during the late seventeenth century roughly six hundred people belonged to that sector in San Miguel Petapa and another four hundred in San Juan Amatitlán, the only two local communities with significant nontributary populations.[47] The sugar plantations, with some 850 resident workers, both free and enslaved, may have been the only other places in the region where large numbers of nontributaries were concentrated.

While the precise size of the area's nontributary minority remains largely a matter for speculation, records of *diligencias matrimoniales* (prenuptial investigations) involving local residents suggest that people of African origins, both enslaved and free, easily dominated. These records also hint at the processes by which plantation slaves moved their descendants into the surrounding free population.[48] Only a few of the records were found for the period before 1671, but one that may date from the early 1630s identifies María Casilda, a slave of the Anís ingenio, as the legitimate daughter of Diego and María, "black slaves" of the same property, and the future spouse of a certain Vicente Samayoa of unknown status. Another slave of the ingenio, Luis Antonio, said to be forty-four, testified on María's behalf during the prenuptial investigation. This record clearly illustrates the ability of slaves on Amatitlán plantations to formalize their marriages in accordance with official church policy, as well as the legal standing they enjoyed as witnesses in ecclesiastical investigations.[49]

Two other diligencias matrimoniales from the Amatitlán area before 1671 begin to reveal the impact of previous African immigration on the local free population. The investigation in 1638 of Vicente Solada and María Lorenza Catalán identifies them, and all three witnesses, as free mulattos of San Juan Amatitlán. Third cousins through mothers who were likely indigenous (Catalán's is identified as Josepha Mexicana), the prospective spouses may both have been linked through their fathers to the enslaved workforces on local plantations.[50] Direct evidence of the development of such connections emerges in a record of 1655 documenting the marriage to a free woman of Pedro de la Cruz, a "black man of the Angola nation." Pedro was the property of Francisco de Fuentes y Guzmán, the chronicler's father, and probably a laborer on the family's trapiche near Petapa. He may have met his intended spouse, a free mulata named Micaela de la Cruz, on the nearby Ingenio de Anís, her birthplace and home until the Jesuits took her on as an employee a few months before the record was filed. The witnesses in this case included the prospective bride's brother, a free mulatto named Nicolás Manuel, and three enslaved men: Domingo de Fuentes, "Angolan"; Diego de la Cruz, "black"; and Pascual de la Cruz, "mulatto." Domingo testified that he and Pedro had been brought together to the province by a Portuguese trader named Pedro Gomes in the early 1640s, evidently after the official cessation of slave imports. They had arrived thus at the very end of the major wave of Angolan migration to the region.[51]

More extensive evidence drawn from diligencias matrimoniales produced at ten-year intervals between 1671 and 1711 confirms that the impact of earlier African immigration on the population of the Amatitlán region was substantial.[52] Sixty-six percent of the prospective spouses, or *contrayentes*, appearing in these records are identified either as black or mulatto, and more than 20 percent of them as slaves. It is significant in light of the drastic slowdown in African arrivals to Guatemala after 1640 that only three of twenty-one prospective spouses who are identified as slaves in these records, and none of the eight slaves who are defined as black, appear after 1691. The data provide the sense of an enslaved population that was declining in numbers by the beginning of the eighteenth century and increasingly of mixed ancestry.

Meanwhile the free people of African descent who appear as contrayentes in these records are identified almost exclusively as mulatto, and they outnumber slaves two to one. The growth of this free rural population of plural ancestry probably owed extensively to earlier relationships, both marital and nonmarital, between enslaved men like the Angolan Pedro de la Cruz and free women of indigenous or mixed origins like Micaela de

	1671	1681	1691	1701	1711	*Total*
Enslaved black	2	2	4			8
Enslaved mulatto			10	2	1	13
Free black	1			1		2
Free mulatto*	13	5	16	2	4	40
Indigenous**	1	1	1		1	4
Indigenous laborío	1	2	1	1	2	7
Indigenous tributario			2			2
Mestizo			6		3	9
Spanish			1		3	4
Not defined			1	4	2	7
Total	18	10	42	10	16	96

* Includes two individuals defined simply as "mulatto" who are assumed to have been free in the absence of any reference to slave status.

** No additional designation.

Source: Archivo Histórico Arquidiocesano "Francisco de Paula García Peláez," Guatemala City, A4.16, Informaciones Matrimoniales.

la Cruz.[53] Any children born to Pedro and Micaela would have been free owing to the "law of the womb," by which a child inherited the mother's legal status. The implications of this law help explain why none of the eight enslaved women who appear in the diligencias matrimoniales examined here was marrying a free man, while five of thirteen enslaved men who turn up were marrying free women. The latter proportion is in fact extremely low in comparison with many other areas, as Russell Lohse's essay on Costa Rica in the present volume demonstrates.[54] If direct evidence of enslaved men's relationships with free women, marital or otherwise, is scarcer for the earlier seventeenth century, the inventory of the Mesa trapiche in 1612 suggests that they had long been important.

Planters' efforts to prevent the loss of "property" through such relationships probably intensified as the drought in new imports persisted. Marital investigations involving enslaved residents of the Arrivillaga and Jesuit ingenios lend some support to this notion. There are two records from 1671 involving the Arrivillaga ingenio, each listing an enslaved man and a free woman as the prospective spouses. Meanwhile all three records from 1691 involving residents of the property identify both partners as

TABLE 4 Intended Marriages of Prospective Spouses from Table 3

MAN	WOMAN	*Total*
Free mulatto	Free black/mulata	15
Other	Other	11
Enslaved black/mulatto	Enslaved black/mulata	8
Free mulatto	Other	6
Enslaved black/mulatto	Free black/mulata	3
Other	Free mulata	3
Enslaved black/mulatto	Other	2

Note: Other = indigenous, mestizo, Spanish, or undefined.
Source: Archivo Histórico Arquidiocesano "Francisco de Paula García Peláez," Guatemala City, A4.16, Informaciones Matrimoniales.

enslaved.[55] The fact that women had come to outnumber men on that plantation as of 1679 surely influenced its marriage patterns too, but the situation was not much different on the more male-dominated Jesuit ingenio. The sample contains four cases, none dated earlier than 1691, in which slaves from that estate are listed as contrayentes. All involve a marital union between two enslaved residents of the property.[56]

While these limited and evidently incomplete marriage data can provide no more than a rough approximation of overall demographic trends in the Amatitlán region, it is perhaps not stretching their usefulness too far to note that the proportion of all partners identified by African origins in Table 3 falls from nearly 90 percent of the total in 1671 to just over 30 percent in 1711. At the same time the mestizo, Spanish, and undefined categories, empty prior to 1691, hold 50 percent of all partners two decades later. There were of course individuals identified as Spaniards and mestizos living in the Amatitlán region long before 1691. They seem to have been concentrated most heavily in San Miguel Petapa, while the inhabitants of San Juan Amatitlán, closer to the Anís ingenio, were more likely to have African ancestors. Whatever the distribution, the striking shift in the data may reveal something else. The ranks of people defined as either Spanish or mestizo were probably being swelled throughout the region by free people of partial African ancestry, who were increasingly slipping the bounds of a classification, mulatto, that tied them to specific legal disabilities like the laborío tribute.[57]

The clearest conclusion to be drawn from these records is that the enslaved population of the Amatitlán region contained very few African immigrants by the end of the seventeenth century. A slave from the Arrivillaga ingenio, Domingo de España, is the lone individual clearly identified as African-born in diligencias matrimoniales after 1670, and he was transported from Cape Verde to Spain and then on to Guatemala around 1657.[58] While some African-born slaves do turn up in Santiago's parish registers during the last decades of the century, their impact in the main sugar-producing area of the region must have been minimal.[59] By 1700 most members of the local enslaved population, not to mention free people of African ancestry, must have been two or more generations removed from Angola and its neighboring territories, the natives of which had so thoroughly dominated the workforces of Guatemalan sugar plantations seventy years earlier.

SUGAR PLANTATIONS AND GENTE LADINA

If the impact of early seventeenth-century African immigration on local society in the Amatitlán region was profound, it was not unprecedented. Processes of biological and cultural *mestizaje* had been operating locally ever since the Spanish invasion of 1523–24, with an intensity that was probably unmatched elsewhere in Guatemala outside the capital and its immediate environs. What Christopher Lutz calls the "gradual decay" of local Pogomam Maya villages was well under way already by the mid-sixteenth century owing to the early influx of Spanish, African, and Mexican outsiders into the Amatitlán area as well as the crucial role its indigenous labor force and agricultural products played in the economy of nearby Santiago.[60] One might see evidence of that decay, or, if one prefers, transculturation, in Gage's description of Pogomam villagers "us[ing English] Morris dances, and Blackmore dances with Sonajas in their hands, which are a round set of small Morris dancing bells." More telling, though, is the same writer's recollection of witnessing bull-baiting contests in Petapa on the feast of San Miguel "with some *Spaniards* and *Blackmores* on Horse-backe, and other *Indians* on foot."[61]

The latter observation speaks volumes about the nature of social relationships in Guatemala's most important plantation zone. Simply put, many Africans coming into the Amatitlán region do not seem to have experienced the status of slave as total social degradation, what Orlando Patterson has famously called "social death."[62] Indeed, as in other parts of Spanish America, slaves of African origin often found themselves in the position of supervising indigenous workers on rural estates. Not surprisingly, given that these enslaved overseers were directly responsible for extracting the maximum amount of labor from their charges, repartimiento laborers complained frequently and bitterly about them. For example, of nine supervisory personnel imprisoned for abusing indigenous workers in the wake of the visita of ingenios and trapiches in 1679–80, eight were identified either as black or mulatto and seven as slaves.[63]

Spaniards' dependence on Africans and their descendants for assistance in controlling the indigenous population extended well beyond the realm of economic production. Gage, an honorary Spaniard while a priest in Guatemala, recalled the crucial aid he received from the "Blackmore" Miguel Dalva during a campaign to extirpate idolatrous practices on the part of a prominent native family in the village of Mixco. Dalva, who frequently served the English cleric as a sort of bodyguard, was charged in this instance with organizing a force of "those *Spaniards* that knew the businesse, and some more Blackmores his friends" to protect Gage from possible retaliation from the targets of the investigation. One imagines that the distinctions of color and origin these outsiders drew among themselves may have meant as little to the affected indigenous villagers in this case as they had in the earliest days of the Conquest.[64]

Those distinctions did of course mean something to Spaniards, who endeavored to maintain them strictly by imposing the laborío tribute and other legal and social disabilities on free people of African origins.[65] In the Amatitlán region, though, neither legal nor social exclusion seems to have been enforced very effectively, if for no other reason than that there were few Spaniards around to do so. The social license that many free people of color apparently believed they enjoyed as a consequence is illustrated in an incident in 1675 in San Juan Amatitlán, in which a Spanish *vecino* named Lázaro del Castillo accused a free black resident of the village, Joseph María, of having abused his hospitality and insulted his wife and family. The aggrieved Spaniard claimed his generous offer of lodging to a down-at-the-heels acquaintance had been repaid by thievery and, following the offender's ejection from the house, an assault "in word and deed" in the street outside. "It cannot be right," he complained, "for a black man to exhibit such insolence towards Spaniards." Joseph's sentence of two years' hard labor on the fortress at Granada, Nicaragua, commuted because of illness to permanent exile from the village, indicates that Castillo's concern about the threat posed to social order was shared in this instance by officials, who saw before them an offender who had failed to acquire a proper sense of social inferiority.[66]

Unfortunately for the defenders of that social order, the Amatitlán region appears to have operated as a refuge for many individuals like Joseph María. Its residents were frequently censured by leading residents of the capital for their "impure" origins and unwillingness to submit to proper social and religious control.[67] Fuentes y Guzmán intimated that the "great number of Spanish, mulatto, mestizo and black vecinos" in San Juan Amatitlán, vagrants all, might best be employed at the remote fortresses of the realm, and he vigorously opposed efforts by residents of both that village and San Miguel Petapa to remove their communities from Santiago's direct jurisdiction.[68] Among the more notorious area residents were people seeking to escape unwanted scrutiny of illicit sexual relationships, particularly those crossing boundaries of color and class. During the investigation in 1670 of a married Spaniard who fled the capital to live in San Juan Amatitlán with a mestiza who was not his wife, one witness declared that many such couples lived in town.[69] The most remarkable of these may have been don Pedro Henríquez de Castellanos, son of a prominent Santiago family, and an enslaved woman named Nicolasa Morán. These two pursued a scandalous love affair against stiff opposition before eventually securing permission to marry in 1682. The possibility that they too relocated to San Juan Amatitlán is suggested by the fact that their son, the free mulatto Juan Antonio de Castellanos, wed a free mulata named María de la Candelaria there in 1691.[70]

The unwillingness of the region's residents to observe proper social and moral standards occasionally attracted personal attention from officials eager to correct their unruly behavior. In 1684 Bishop Andrés de las Navas y Quevedo tracked down a number of individuals guilty of transgressing the bounds of sexual propriety in the course of a war on adultery in Petapa. Among those ensnared in the prelate's net were Lucía de la Cruz, a free black widow who had set up house with a Spanish bachelor named Nicolás de Alvarado, and, perhaps more striking, the free mulatto Juan de Miranda, who had abandoned his wife in the capital for a relationship with Juana Muñoz, identified as Spanish. The bishop sentenced eighteen sinners in all to exile from the village, excepting only women who agreed either to marry or take a nun's habit.[71]

The disapproval of Fuentes y Guzmán and the bishop aside, some of the Amatitlán region's "undesirables" may have enjoyed relatively high status locally, including a few free people of African origin. Family connections were especially likely to result in the sort of irksome social mobility that had long led the crown to complain, as in a letter in 1622 to the Audiencia, about "persons of little account such as mulattos and mestizos" requesting appointment to official posts "without making mention of the said conditions."[72] The very next year, in an action that underscored the inefficacy of such royal warnings, Antonio Meléndez de Valdés, resident of the Petapa area and the son of an enslaved woman named Juana de Aguilar, audaciously demanded the rights and privileges due the illegitimate children of prominent Spaniards. His father, Capitán Gonzalo Meléndez de Valdés, a native of Asturias and the former governor of Soconusco, would no doubt have supported the petition vigorously had he still been alive. He had freed Antonio at birth, mandated his treatment as an *hidalgo* (minor noble) "although he is a mulatto," demanded of a bailiff attempting to seize his son as security for an unpaid debt, "What, you want to seize my son who is freer than I am?" and left him land near Jalpatagua, southeast of Lake Amatitlán in the district of Guazacapán.[73]

No doubt the lives of most free children of slaves exhibited less evidence of such striking social mobility, given that most did not have wealthy or prominent fathers. The lot of Felipa de Jesús was surely more typical. Daughter of a Jesuit-owned slave, Diego de Godoy, and a free mulata named Polonia de la Cruz, she was herself working for the Jesuits on their ingenio when she wed a fellow employee, a free mulatto named Alonso Cristóbal, in 1671.[74] Nevertheless such opportunities for the accumulation of wealth and status as existed in a poor and radically unequal colonial society like Guatemala's were not entirely closed to free people of African origins, even in a major sugar-producing zone where slavery was important. Given the dependence of that society primarily on the labor of the indigenous tributary majority, not enslaved Africans, it was Indians above all who needed to be kept in their place.

The social mobility available as a consequence to people of African descent, modest as it may have been, appears to have worked in the direction of undermining a strong sense among free mulattos of a corporate identity tied to African origins.[75] By the late seventeenth century the free population of African descent in the Amatitlán region was in many ways already integrated into a larger and more amorphous group that stood apart from the indigenous tributary majority. Within that group distinctions based on ancestry were not necessarily paramount. On the one hand, the diligencias matrimoniales examined earlier suggest the operation of a strong tendency toward endogamy among people who were defined on the basis of African origins, as some five-sixths wed other individuals who were similarly identified. But that endogamy may have owed largely to their clear demographic preponderance in the local nontributary population, for the sample also shows both mestizos and indios laboríos marrying mulattos about half the time. Little wonder, then, that individuals assigned to these three categories were being lumped together locally under the classification *gente ladina* as early as 1655.[76]

There remained nonetheless at least two significant legal bases for distinguishing among mestizos, indios laboríos, and free blacks and mulattos in the late seventeenth century. The first was the laborío tribute, imposed at differing rates on indios laboríos and free people of African descent, and not at all on mestizos. The second flowed from the development after the 1640s of a largely segregated militia in which free blacks and mulattos usually served in their own units, a powerful counterweight to the dissipation of a corporate identity based on African ancestry. Mestizos meanwhile tended to enroll in Spanish companies, while indios laboríos appear in general to have been entirely excluded from militia, like the rest of the indigenous population.[77]

These legal distinctions, if increasingly arbitrary and difficult to sustain with each passing generation, were far from giving way entirely to a broader category such as ladino, at least in its modern sense. For one thing, the most common usage of the term in the late seventeenth century remained its application to members of the indigenous population who spoke Spanish, captured in the phrase "indio ladino en lengua castellana," which appears countless times in contemporary sources.[78] A more narrow association with *indio laborío* was also cropping up, although indigenous people said to be both ladino and tributary continue to appear in later records.[79] Reporting in 1675 on the foundation in San Juan Amatitlán of a *cofradía* (religious confraternity) dedicated to the recently canonized Santa Rosa of Lima, the prior of the local Dominican monastery informed the bishop of Guatemala that the saint's image was the object of veneration on the part of "all the Spaniards, pardos [people of part-African ancestry] and ladinos" of the community. The association is more explicit in a roughly contemporary complaint to the bishop from the indigenous officers of a cofradía in the valley of Almolonga, near Santiago. The plaintiffs referred first to the "naboríos, Spaniards, blacks and mulattos" whom they accused of usurping their resources, and later to "the said ladinos, Spaniards, blacks, and mulattos."[80]

At the same time, though, the dissociation of *ladino* from any sense of being *Indian* was also emerging. In one definition along these lines, Fuentes y Guzmán wrote that the word was used to refer to "Spaniards, mestizos, mulattos, and blacks in Indian villages," although the traditional implication of linguistic dexterity was not entirely lost, as he immediately added, somewhat paradoxically, that the Indians were those who "only [spoke] their mother tongue."[81] A Franciscan report from 1689 offers a more unambiguously ancestry-focused meaning for the term in a count of the "ladino persons (that is, Spaniards, mestizos and mulattos)" in communities under the order's jurisdiction.[82] By the end of the seventeenth century, then, the word was beginning to be used, if only occasionally, as shorthand for emphasizing what was arguably the most carefully constructed social division in colonial Guatemala: the one between the tributary Indian majority and everyone else.

In the sugar zone surrounding Lake Amatitlán *everyone else* was a category constituted in large part by the free descendants of African immigrants. Those of mixed African and native ancestry were in a sense doubly ladino, descended in many cases both from indios ladinos and from *negros ladinos*, the term long applied to African-born slaves who had learned Spanish or otherwise acquired the ability to manipulate Iberian cultural practices with a substantial degree of sophistication.[83] This process of adaptation to Iberian ways was captured succinctly in places like Guatemala in the designation of African immigrants who had embarked on it as being "between bozal [newly arrived African] and ladino."[84] But the vast majority of slaves in the Amatitlán region's population were no longer experiencing this process in the late seventeenth century. American-born, they instead grew up ladino.

If the term was at the same time beginning to be transformed into one with a quasi-ethnic meaning, that transformation was in its initial stages.[85] Parish priests continued to distinguish assiduously between mulattos and mestizos in the Amatitlán region, where the African roots of the children and grandchildren of Angolan migrants had hardly begun to recede into the more remote corners of memory. Slavery itself persisted for more than a century, if for the most part on a reduced scale.[86] Signs of future trends were evident in the slow decline of local sugar plantations, lamented around 1720 by the Dominican historian Francisco Ximénez, and the increasing tendency toward exogamy revealed in diligencias matrimoniales.[87] Such signs, however, were unlikely to have been obvious to the area's contemporary residents. They were probably far more conscious of the relatively recent past than of the unknowable future. In that past sugar production had been expanding, and numerous Angolans and other African strangers had arrived to alter substantially the character of local society. Evidence that their society had never been shaped exclusively by relations between Spaniards and native peoples was all around them.

NOTES

Versions of this essay were presented as papers at LASA 2003 in Dallas and the conference in 2004 from which this volume emerged. Research was funded in part by a Tinker Foundation Field Research Grant and a Beveridge grant from the American Historical Association. I am grateful for scholarly assistance and commentary to Franz Binder, Robinson Herrera, Jane Landers, Chris Lutz, Murdo MacLeod, Doug Tompson, and Stephen Webre, as well as the editors and anonymous reviewers.

1   Visita de la Nuestra Señora de Nazarén, 12 February 1613, Archivo General de Centro América, Guatemala City (hereafter AGCA), A3.5, leg. 67, exp. 1291, fols. 15v–17v. The Audiencia of Guatemala extended from what is now the Mexican state of Chiapas through present-day Costa Rica and was governed by a high court of the same name. The port of Santo Tomás de Castilla allowed direct access from the Caribbean to the territory of the modern republic of Guatemala via Amatique Bay.

2   Eltis, "The Volume and Structure of the Transatlantic Slave Trade," 24, 33, 44.

3   Bennett, *Africans in Colonial Mexico*, 22–25; Tardieu, "Origins of the Slaves in the Lima Region," 43–54; Lane, *Quito 1599*, 53–82; Ferry, "Encomienda, African Slavery," 621–23; Lutz, *Santiago de Guatemala*, 83–86. For seventeenth-century Central America, see also Cáceres, *Negros, mulatos*; Lohse, "Africans and Their Descendants."

4   Reports of these investigations dating from 1670, 1675, and 1679–80 are contained in "La Audiencia de Guatemala informa a v.m. con testimonios sobre los obrajes y ingenios que hay en esta jurisdición" (1681), Archivo General de Indias, Seville (hereafter AGI), Guatemala, 27, R. 9, N. 29 (digitized format). This document is available online through Portal de Archivos Españoles (PARES). On the repartimiento, see M. J. MacLeod, *Spanish Central America*, 206–9.

5   Hernández Aparicio, "Problemas socioeconómicos"; Pinto Soria, *El valle central de Guatemala*; Luján Muñoz, *Agricultura, mercado, y sociedad.*

6   See the Central American definitions of *ladino* in *Diccionario de la lengua española*, 22nd ed. (Madrid: Real Academia Española, 2001), and the discussion of "ethnic groups" by Ralph Lee Woodward Jr., the noted historian of modern Central America, in "Guatemala," *Microsoft Encarta Online Encyclopedia 2006* (Redmond, Wash.: Microsoft, 1997–2006), accessed 29 January 2007. Efforts to illuminate the contradiction between racialized and cultural constructions of ladino identity include R. N. Adams, *Encuesta sobre la cultura de los ladinos*, 19–20; C. A. Smith, "Introduction," 4; Casaús Arzú, *La metamorfosis del racismo*, 59–61.

7   A similar dynamic is evident in recent work on other regions and groups in colonial Guatemala. See Rodas Núñez, *De españoles a ladinos*; Matthew, "Mexicanos and the Meanings of Ladino," accessed 25 January 2007.

8   Gudmundson, "Firewater," 274–75; Jefferson, "La Gente Parda"; Little-Siebold, "'Where Have All the Spaniards Gone,'" 107–33, especially 119–20. By contrast, a widely cited older analysis of the term *ladino* is striking for its dismissal of the historical relevance of the word *mulato*, based on the alleged "numerical scarcity of blacks in the Kingdom of Guatemala, together with their limited racial mixing and the slave status of many of them." See Taracena Arriola, "El vocablo 'Ladino,'" 98.

9   Gage, *The English-American*, 134, italics in original.

10 Falla, *Extractos*, 1:21. For one reference to the founder as Juan González "de anis" see his redemption of a *censo al quitar*, a credit instrument similar to a mortgage, on 25 February 1609, AGCA, A1.20, leg. 1483, fols. 224–25v. An *ingenio*, like a *trapiche*, was a sugar mill, although the terms were often applied in Guatemala to the surrounding rural estate as well. By standard definition, if not always so in practice, a trapiche was an animal-powered mill while an ingenio, larger and more technologically sophisticated, was powered by water. Compare Rodríguez Morel, "The Sugar Economy of Española," 97–99; de la Fuente, "Sugar and Slavery," 134–38.

11 Vásquez de Espinosa, *Compendio y descripción*, 206; Falla, *Extractos de escrituras públicas*, 2:285–86.

12 "Negros de la hacienda," AGCA, A1.20, leg. 536, fols. 296v–302 (1630).

13 Eltis, "Volume and Structure," 24, 33, 44; Vila Vilar, *Hispanoamérica y el comercio de esclavos*, 197–211.

14 Miller, *Kings and Kinsmen*, 176–203, 210–21; Thornton, "The African Experience," 421–34.

15 See Lutz, *Santiago*, 85; the records of ship arrivals and slave sales in AGCA, A3.5, leg. 67, exp. 1291 (1613); A1.20, leg. 4553, exp. 38611 (1614); A1.20, leg. 812, fols. 65–66 (1614); A1.20, leg. 755, fols. 155–56, 179–87v, 191–95v, 203–6 (1617); A1.20, leg. 812, fols. 286–286v (1619); A1.20, leg. 810, fols. 298–99, 307–8v (1620); A1.20, leg. 756, fols. 1–1v, 19v–22, 207–9v, 237–38v (1621); A1.20, leg. 756, fols. 209v–12 (1622); A1.56, leg. 5356, exp. 45251 (1622); A1.20, leg. 813, fols. 6–6v, 28–29v (1624); A1.20, leg. 757, fols. 151v–152v, 163–64 (1625); A1.20, leg. 812, fols. 436–37v (1625); A1.20, leg. 757, fols. 240–44 (1626). See also Vila Vilar, *Hispanoamérica*, 151–52, table 2.

16 Herrera, *Natives, Europeans, and Africans*, 112–19, especially table 2 on 113.

17 See Reales Cédulas of 24 November 1601, AGCA, A1.23, leg. 4576, exp. 39529, fols. 45v–50; 24 November 1602, A1.23, leg. 1514, fols. 33–34; 26 May 1609, A1.23, leg. 1514, fol. 67. See also "Recopilación de las Reales Cédulas que gobiernan en el Supremo Tribunal de la Real Audiencia de Guatemala," *Boletín del Archivo General de la Nación*, 2nd series, 1, no. 1 (1967), 23, 37, 85, 108. On slavery and sixteenth-century mining, see M. J. MacLeod, *Spanish Central America*, 60–61, 148–51; Chamberlain, *The Conquest and Colonization of Honduras*, 117, 220–24, 238; Melida Velásquez, "El comercio de esclavos," 206–8.

18 I have been helped in tracking down other, more obscure terms in the inventory by the maps and other commentary in Thornton, *Africa and Africans*, x–xxxvi; Thornton, "Cannibals, Witches, and Slave Traders," 276; Sweet, *Recreating Africa*, 17–21.

19 "Negros de la hacienda," AGCA, A1.20, leg. 536, fols. 296v–302 (1630). For an argument that, overall, the sex ratio imbalance in the slave trade has been exaggerated, see Eltis and Engerman, "Was the Slave Trade Dominated by Men?," 237–57.

20 "Inventario de los bienes de Gonzalo de Peralta," 29 September 1625, AGCA, A1.43, leg. 5925, exp. 51614, fols. 4–5.

21 "Escritura de venta y censo," 28 April 1612, AGCA, A1.15, leg. 4103, exp. 32523, fols. 4–5. The ascribed origins of the immigrants: Angola (6), Congo (4), Mandinga (2), Bañon (2), Biafara (1), Balanta (1), Berbesi (1), Mozambique (1).

22 Gage, *The English-American*, 134, 179; Falla, *Extractos de escrituras públicas*, 3:354.

23 "Censo impuesto sobre el ingenio de San Gerónimo y otros bienes del orden dominico," 22 March 1633, AGCA, A1.20, leg. 1124, fols. 2v–3; Gage, *The English-American*, 137; Ciudad Suárez, *Los dominicos*, 264; Belaubre, "Poder y redes sociales," 52–53; Gudmundson, "Los afroguatemaltecos a fines de la Colonia," 257, table 1.

24 Lutz, *Santiago*, chap. 4, 242.

25 Lokken, "From Black to Ladino," 45–48.

26 For a striking late colonial exception, see Rina Cáceres's examination in this volume of the intensive use of enslaved African labor in the construction of the fortress of Omoa, on the Caribbean coast of present-day Honduras.

27 Sweet, *Recreating Africa*, 33–34; Sandoval, *De Instauranda Aethiopum Salute*, 89; Thornton, "Central Africa," 95–96.

28 For evidence of negotiations over the specifics of family life on eighteenth-century South Carolina rice plantations, see Berlin, *Many Thousands Gone*, 163.

29 "Escritura de venta y censo," 28 April 1612, AGCA, A1.15, leg. 4103, exp. 32523, fols. 4–5; "Inventario," 3 January 1620, AGCA, A1.15, leg. 4103, exp. 32523, fols. 31v–33.

30 Fowler, *The Cultural Evolution of Ancient Nahua Civilizations*, 51–56.

31 "Escritura de venta y censo," 28 April 1612, AGCA, A1.15, leg. 4103, exp. 32523, fols. 4–5.

32 "Inventario de los bienes de Gonzalo de Peralta," 29 September 1625, AGCA, A1.43, leg. 5925, exp. 51614, fols. 4–5.

33 "Inventario de los bienes de Gonzalo de Peralta," 29 September 1625, AGCA, A1.43, leg. 5925, exp. 51614, fols. 4–5; Mortual of Alonso Alvarez de Villamil, AGCA A1.43, leg. 4877, exp. 41807 (1625). The debate over the practical effects of Iberian Catholic slave legislation, centered on the much criticized "Tannenbaum thesis" of Iberian exceptionalism, has yet to end. For a recent challenge to those who reject the thesis outright, see Landers, *Black Society*, 1–2. For the original, see Tannenbaum, *Slave and Citizen*. For an extended analysis of Spanish slave law as codified in the medieval Siete Partidas and applied in the late colonial Guatemalan context, see Komisaruk's essay in the present volume.

34 "Inventario de los bienes de Gonzalo de Peralta," 29 September 1625, AGCA, A1.43, leg. 5925, exp. 51614, f. 5; Lokken, "A Maroon Moment," 52; Schwartz, *Slaves, Peasants, and Rebels*, 105.

35 "Negros de la hacienda," AGCA, A1.20, leg. 536, fols. 296v–302 (1630).

36 Three of sixty-four men had children but no spouse listed, having perhaps lost them to death or sale.

37 The term *zambo* almost never appears in seventeenth-century Guatemalan documents.

38 Crown to Audiencia of Guatemala, 19 May 1670, AGCA, A1.23, leg. 2199,

exp. 15755, f. 50; Lutz, *Santiago*, 86; M. J. MacLeod, *Spanish Central America*, 298; Bowser, "Africans in Spanish American Colonial Society," 362; Elliott, *The Count-Duke of Olivares*, 457–599. On smuggling, see the case of the ship *Santa María de los Remedios y San Lorenzo* in AGCA, A1.24, leg. 1559, exp. 10203, fols. 35–37v, 93–95v (1641–42); Crown to Audiencia of Guatemala, 1 December 1662, A1.23, leg. 1519, exp. 10074, fols. 90–90v; Alonso Moratalla Tebar to Crown, 10 February 1644, AGI, Guatemala, 16, R. 5, N. 30.

39 Fuentes y Guzmán, *Recordación florida*, 1:224.

40 "Autos hechos sobre la visita de ingenios y trapiches en que trabajan indios, año de 1679," in "La Audiencia de Guatemala informa a V.M. con testimonios sobre los obrajes y ingenios que hay en esta jurisdición" (1681), AGI, Guatemala, 27, R. 9, N. 29, block 5, images 1, 117–253.

41 "Autos hechos sobre la visita de ingenios y trapiches," AGI, Guatemala, 27, R. 9, N. 29, block 5, images 148–49, 169–70, 192–93; Ximénez, *Historia*, vol. 3, book 5, pp. 100, 104.

42 "Autos hechos sobre la visita de ingenios y trapiches," AGI, Guatemala, 27, R. 9, N. 29, block 5, images 150–51, 170–73; Konrad, *A Jesuit Hacienda*; Cushner, *Lords of the Land*.

43 Censo, Domingo and Juan de Arrivillaga, 24 May 1648, AGCA, A1.20, leg. 846, fols. 170–72; Censos, Domingo de Arrivillaga, 8 August and 14 October 1639, AGCA, A1.20, leg. 760, fols. 55–57v, 289–91v; "Autos hechos sobre la visita de ingenios y trapiches," AGI, Guatemala, 27, R. 9, N. 29, block 5, images 174–76; "Autos hechos sobre la visita de los ingenios y trapiches de hacer azucar de este balle de Guatemala el juez el señor doctor don Jacinto Roldán de la Cueba oidor y alcalde del crimen de la Real Audiencia que reside en la ciudad de Santiago, año de 1675," in "La Audiencia de Guatemala informa a V.M. con testimonios sobre los obrajes y ingenios que hay en esta jurisdición" (1681), AGI, Guatemala, 27, R. 9, N. 29, block 5, image 114; Falla, *Extractos*, 1:363; Fuentes y Guzmán, *Recordación florida*, 1:224; M. J. MacLeod, *Spanish Central America*, 304.

44 "Autos hechos sobre la visita de ingenios y trapiches," AGI, Guatemala, 27, R. 9, N. 29, block 5, images 117–76.

45 Luján, *Agricultura*, 26; M. J. MacLeod, *Spanish Central America*, 131; Rodas Núñez, *De españoles a ladinos*, 24.

46 On the history of naborías and laboríos, see Lutz, *Santiago*, 96–99, 253–54; Sherman, *Forced Native Labor*, 102–11, 218–20.

47 Luján, *Agricultura*, 30; Mörner, "La política de segregación y el mestizaje," 147.

48 The records are held in Guatemala City's Archivo Histórico Arquidiocesano, "Francisco de Paula García Peláez" (hereafter AHA), A4.16, Informaciones Matrimoniales. Prenuptial investigations were aimed at confirming

the free will of prospective spouses, preventing bigamy, and blocking unions between close relatives without a proper dispensation. The records held in the AHA primarily reflect the marriage patterns of the nontributary sector because indios tributarios turn up in investigations sent for approval to the bishop in Santiago only in cases of marriage outside the home parish or the tributary population. On church dictates regarding these investigations, see Remesal, *Historia general*, 2:346; Contreras Gallardo, *Manual*, 64–72; Socolow, *The Women of Colonial Latin America*, 11. A helpful guide to the records cited here, although it omits the racial designations employed, is Mazariegos Anleu, *Indice General*, vol. 1, book 1.

49 Diligencia matrimonial, María Casilda and Vicente Samayoa, 1630?, AHA, A4.16, T5 1.21 (1618–69, caja 192), unnumbered expediente. For an extended analysis through the lens of matrimonial records of the encounter between enslaved Africans and the Catholic Church in seventeenth-century Mexico, see Bennett, *Africans in Colonial Mexico*, chap. 4.

50 Diligencia matrimonial of Vicente Solada and María Lorenza Catalán, 4 November 1638, AHA, A4.16, T5, 1.21 (caja 192), unnumbered expediente. Josepha was probably from nearby Santa Inés Petapa, where descendants of Pedro de Alvarado's Mexican allies were said to have settled.

51 Diligencia matrimonial of Pedro de la Cruz and Micaela de la Cruz, 5 July 1655, AHA, A4.16, T5, 1.21 (caja 192), unnumbered expediente. As likely shipmates during the Middle Passage, Pedro and Domingo had probably forged the sort of fictive kinship conveyed, at least in Brazil, in the Kimbundu-derived term *malungo*. See Sweet, *Recreating Africa*, 33–34.

52 The data set includes forty-eight records either produced in or involving residents of San Miguel Petapa (17), San Juan Amatitlán (8), the Arrivillaga ingenio (6), the Jesuit ingenio (6), the Anís ingenio (4), the Rosario ingenio (3), the Augustinian trapiche (3), and Santa Inés Petapa (1). The specific records are AHA, A4.16, T4 1.12 (1670–71, caja 157), exps. 94, 102, 125, 146, 190, 191, 195; T4 1.11 (1671, caja 197), exps. 216, 293; T4 105 (1680–81, caja 2), exps. 244, 252, 271, 309, 361; T5 106 (1691, caja 200), exps. 16, 22, 23, 24, 32, 33, 61, 80, 81, 82, 95, 97, 100, 102, 104, 108, 115, 147; T5 107 (1691, caja 205), exps. 255, 295, 313; T6 105 (1701, caja 77), exps. 2368, 2392, 2413, 2417, 2421; T7 104 (1711, caja 110), exps. 3937, 3940, 3988, 4015, 4059, 4070, and one unnumbered expediente; T7 103 (1711, caja 124), exp. 4106.

53 The capital's high rates of illegitimacy were undoubtedly mirrored in rural areas. See Lutz, *Santiago*, appendix 3.

54 See also ibid., 88–89, 94; Lokken, "Marriage as Slave Emancipation," 190.

55 Diligencias matrimoniales, Domingo de España and Juana Mathias, 6 October 1671, AHA, A4.16, T4 1.12, exp. 190; Juan de los Santos and María Nicolasa, 6 October 1671, AHA, A4.16, T4 1.12, exp. 191; Ambrosio de Arrivillaga and Lucía de Ochoa, 18 June 1691, AHA, A4.16, T5 106, exp. 80; Pasqual de Ochoa

and Francisca de Ochoa, 18 June 1691, AHA, A4.16, T5 106, exp. 81; Juan de Arrivillaga and Simona de Ochoa, 18 June 1691, AHA, A4.16, T5 106, exp. 82.

56 Diligencias matrimoniales, Gabriel Matheo and Melchora de la Cruz, 14 May 1691, AHA, A4.16, T5 106, exp. 61; Santiago de la Cruz and Simona de la Cruz, 2 August 1691, AHA, A4.16, T5 106, exp. 100; Alejandro Bentura and Eugenia López, 23 April 1691, AHA, A4.16, T5 106, exp. 115; Manuel Delgado and Luisa Gonzales, 8 November 1701, exp. 2417.

57 One thought-provoking study of the widely noted instability of classification by color and ancestry in colonial Spanish America is Cope, *The Limits of Racial Domination*, especially chaps. 3–4. A classic and still useful analysis of the absurdities inherent in all systems of racial classification is Harris, *Patterns of Race*, especially chap. 5.

58 Diligencia matrimonial, Domingo de España and Juana Mathias, 6 October 1671, AHA, A4.16, T4 1.12, exp. 190.

59 Lutz, *Santiago*, 86.

60 Ibid., 53, 270 n. 27. See also Gage, *The English-American*, 133–34; Luján, *Agricultura*, chaps. 4–7; Pinto, *El valle central*, 17–42; Ghidinelli, "Reconstrucción histórica," 22–35.

61 Gage, *The English-American*, 134, 155, italics in original. On the concept of transculturation, see Ortíz, *Cuban Counterpoint*, 97–103.

62 O. Patterson, *Slavery and Social Death*, especially chap. 2. For recent scholarship arguing that the fact of enslavement was only one among many facets of an enslaved individual's identity, see Bennett, *Africans in Colonial Mexico*; Soulodre-La France, "Socially Not So Dead!"

63 "Autos hechos sobre la visita de ingenios y trapiches," AGI, Guatemala, 27, R. 9, N. 29, block 5, images 237–53. See also Hernández Aparicio, "Problemas," 608; Landers, *Black Society*, 19–20; Martínez Peláez, *La patria del criollo*, 276–77; Lutz and Restall, "Wolves and Sheep?," 196–204; Gutiérrez Brockington, *The Leverage of Labor*, 140.

64 Gage, *The English-American*, 171–78, quotation on 174, italics in original. See also Restall, *Seven Myths*, 52–63.

65 See, for example, Libro VII, título quinto, ley primera, "Que los Negros, y Negras, Mulatos, y Mulatas libres paguen tributo al Rey" (1574), and Libro VII, título quinto, ley tercera, "Que los Mulatos, y negros libres vivan con amos conocidos, para que se puedan cobrar sus tributos" (1577), in *Recopilación de leyes de los Reynos de las Indias*, 4 vols. (Madrid: Ediciones Cultura Hispánica, 1973), 2:285–285v; Mörner, *La corona española*, especially 94–99.

66 "Lázaro del Castillo español vecino de San Juan Amatitlán se querella criminalmente de un negro libre llamado Joseph María," 12 January 1675, AGCA, A1.15, leg. 5905, exp. 50087.

67 Few, *Women Who Live Evil Lives*, 120–28; Ruz, "Sebastiana de la Cruz," 55–66.

68 Fuentes y Guzmán, *Recordación florida*, 1:197, 254.

69 AGCA, A2.2, leg. 137, exp. 2472 (1670).

70 Diligencias matrimoniales, don Pedro Henríquez de Castellanos and Nicolasa Morán, 30 November 1680, AHA, A4.16, T4 105, exp. 232; Juan Antonio de Castellanos and María de la Candelaria, 5 December 1691; AHA, T5 106, exp. 147; Falla, *Extractos*, 2:195.

71 Ruz, *Memoria eclesial guatemalteca*, 1:355.

72 Crown to Audiencia of Guatemala, 16 August 1622, AGCA, A1.23, leg. 4578, exp. 39531, fols. 26v–27.

73 Petition of Antonio Meléndez de Valdés, 11 February 1623, AGCA, A1.29.2, leg. 2327, exp. 17286. For Gonzalo Meléndez de Valdés's will of 28 August 1614, see fols. 15–20. None of the ten slaves mentioned in it were favored like Antonio, least of all his mother, long since sold by her former sexual partner. For another contemporary example of the demographic impact of the sexual exploitation of enslaved women by their owners, see Gage, *The English-American*, 132.

74 Diligencia matrimonial, Alonso Cristóbal and Felipa de Jesús, 9 January 1671, AHA, A4.16, T4 1.12, exp. 94.

75 Bennett, "A Research Note," 207–13.

76 Testimony of Joseph de Melgar, 9 March 1655, in "La Iglesia del Pueblo de San Juan de Amatitlán de Guatemala," in Crown to don Martín Carlos de Mencos, 1663, AGI, Guatemala 72.

77 Lutz, *Santiago*, appendix 7; Webre, "Las compañías de milicia," especially 516–18, 525–29; Lokken, "Undoing Racial Hierarchy," 25–36; Vinson, *Bearing Arms for His Majesty*, especially 226.

78 For a concise review of the term's Iberian origins and later use in the Americas, see Adorno, "The Indigenous Ethnographer," 378–81.

79 See diligencia matrimonial of Gregorio Lobo, "indio ladino natural y tributario del Pueblo de San Cristóbal Amatitlán," and Teresa de la Peña, "india laboría," 12 August 1701, AHA, A4.16, T6 105, exp. 2390; Matthew, "Mexicanos and the Meanings of Ladino." Compare the claim that *indio ladino* was exclusively applied to "Hispanicized Indians who no longer paid tribute . . . as opposed to indio tributario" in Van Oss, *Catholic Colonialism*, 69–71.

80 Fray Francisco de la Trinidad to the Bishop of Guatemala, 31 July 1675, AHA, A4.14, T2 109, exp. 9; Officers of the Cofradía of the Rosary of Almolonga to the Bishop of Guatemala, 8 July 1664, AHA, A4.14, T2 108, exp. 21.

81 Fuentes y Guzmán, *Recordación florida*, 2:242.

82 "Descripción de los conventos de la Santa Provincia del Nombre de Jesús de Guatemala, hecha el año de 1689," transcription by J. Joaquín Pardo, in Vázquez, *Crónica*, 4:64.

83 The sense of hispanization beyond simple language acquisition, applied to native peoples, Africans, and other non-Spaniards, was often viewed negatively by Spanish commentators. See Adorno, "The Indigenous Ethnographer," 380–81.

84 See petition of Pedro de Armengol, 15 April 1638, AGCA, A1.15, leg. 4111, exp. 32578, fol. 17v; Falla, *Extractos*, 2:237–38, 245, 277, 374, 450; Láscaris, *Historia*, 194.

85 Compare Rodas Núñez, *De españoles a ladinos*, 169–70.

86 Palomo de Lewin, "Perfil de la población africana," 195–209; Komisaruk, this volume.

87 Ximénez, *Historia*, vol. 2, book 4, p. 196, vol. 3, book 5, p. 104.

CACAO AND SLAVERY IN

MATINA, COSTA RICA, 1650–1750

Russell Lohse

In the mid-seventeenth century Spanish colonists in Costa Rica began to establish cacao haciendas in the humid Atlantic lowlands, an area that by and large they declined to settle themselves.[1] After several frustrated attempts to work the haciendas in the Matina Valley with indigenous workers, by 1700 *hacendados* had turned to African slaves to supply the necessary labor. The relative absence of Spaniards in the region allowed male slaves in Matina an exceptional autonomy, especially striking when compared to the brutal control exercised over slaves in many other parts of the Americas. Like slaves in some plantation societies, enslaved men in the Atlantic zone organized the use of their own time, managing all stages in the cultivation, processing, and sometimes sale of cacao, the colony's most important export. Unlike work in the cane fields of the Caribbean and Brazil or the rice swamps of South Carolina, however, cacao cultivation did not impose the murderous labor demands that often accompanied a measure of autonomy. An unusual circumstance—the adoption of cacao as legal currency in the colony—further enhanced the independence of enslaved African men in Matina. With as ready access as anyone in Costa Rica to the cacao money, slaves purchased coveted imports from the British and Miskito contrabandists who frequented the coast. In some ways their quasi-free lifestyle compared favorably to that of free peasants.

Other conditions, however, especially the vulnerability of the region to foreign attacks, complicated the potential advantages of life in Matina. Frequent raids on the cacao haciendas confronted slave men with the risk of being kidnapped or killed. Such dangers, in addition, led Spanish masters to keep slave women in the Central Valley. This spatial separation of enslaved women from enslaved men reinforced the tendency of slave men to marry

MAP 1 Colonial Costa Rica. Map by Donald Sluter.

free women. By negotiating arrangements with their masters or growing the valuable crop on their own account, several enslaved men succeeded in purchasing their freedom with cacao. Conditions in Matina promoted the social advancement of African men and their assimilation into the broader creole culture, but they also prevented the formation of slave families, communities, and ultimately the reproduction of a distinct slave culture.

ANTECEDENTS

Cacao had been cultivated by indigenous peoples throughout Costa Rica before the Conquest. The Indians of Mesoamerican origin in Nicoya used cacao as money and consumed it at rituals, as Gonzalo Fernández de Oviedo observed in 1528.[2] In 1563 the conquistador Juan Vázquez de Coronado noted the cultivation of cacao by the Indians of Quepos in the South Pacific as well as the Votos of the northern plains.[3] Later ethnographic data suggest that like the Indians of Nicoya, the Talamanca of the southeast also imparted important symbolic meanings to cacao.[4] In 1610 Fray Agustín de Cevallos wrote that in Talamanca "cacao abounds, and [is] of the best in the kingdom in quantity and quality."[5]

As in northern Central America and Venezuela the first Spanish planters in the Atlantic region almost certainly took advantage of existing cacao groves, and certainly forced Indian laborers, to establish their haciendas.[6] In 1605 Spanish expeditionaries founded a settlement at Santiago de Talamanca on the Tarire River and divided the Indians for "deposit" (a euphemism for the illegal *encomienda de servicio*) among the conquerors.[7] By 1610 Felipe Monge had established a cacao hacienda at Doyabe near the Tarire. As one of the conquerors of Talamanca, Monge had been granted the Indians of the pueblo of Xicagua in deposit and probably simply appropriated an existing planting. Other colonists also owned fields (*milpas*) of cacao by then, also worked by the Indians in their deposit.[8] They brutally abused these Indian workers, whipping them, severing their ears, and inflicting additional gratuitous humiliations such as forced haircuts. Such mistreatment contributed to a general Indian uprising, which expelled the colonists from Talamanca in 1610.[9] Yet the Spaniards of Costa Rica never lost hope of regaining control of the area, and plans to establish cacao haciendas figured importantly in their projects. Diego del Cubillo included the "large quantity of . . . cacao" in the region as one of the reasons to reconquer Talamanca in 1617, as did don Francisco Núñez de Temiño in 1649.[10]

BEGINNINGS OF THE MATINA CACAO CYCLE

With the decline of the Central Valley's indigenous populations and the export trade with Panama, Costa Rican elites began searching for a new economic enterprise. Cacao seemed the perfect crop to develop for export. By the 1620s the established cacao-producing areas of Central America, such as Guatemala, El Salvador, and Soconusco, had entered a period of long-term decline exacerbated by rising competition from the Caribbean islands, Venezuela, and Ecuador.[11] At midcentury a series of disastrous setbacks, including a cacao blight, an earthquake destroying Caracas financial facilities, and a decline in trade with Mexico, combined to slash the price of Venezuelan cacao from thirty pesos per *fanega* (about 54.5 liters, or 14.4 gallons) in 1647 to just five pesos per *fanega* in 1654.[12] By that time Europeans were beginning to develop a taste for chocolate, promising an enormous market greater than the established market in Mexico. Markets for cacao were expanding, and other producers seemed unable to supply them. With ports on the Atlantic, a suitable climate, existing wild cacao groves, and a large if unconquered Indian population, Costa Rica's Atlantic region seemed ideal for cacao cultivation.

In the mid-seventeenth century colonial governors began actively promoting the conquest of Talamanca and cacao cultivation. The twin projects offered foreseeable solutions to Costa Rica's major economic problems: Cacao production would provide the colony with a valuable export crop, while the conquest of Talamanca would secure a new source of labor. Upon arriving in Costa Rica in 1650 Governor don Juan Fernández de Salinas y Cerda immediately endorsed plans to reconquer Talamanca. Hoping to revive exports to Portobello and Cartagena, he ordered the rehabilitation of the Atlantic port of Suerre in 1651.[13] Like several of his successors, Salinas personally invested in the new crop, acquiring a cacao hacienda in Matina.[14] Subsequent governors followed Salinas in looking to the Atlantic and cacao. While exploring the Atlantic coast in 1659, Governor Andrés Arias Maldonado wrote that the area near what is now Puerto Limón boasted "the best cacao groves that [he had] ever seen." Like his predecessor, Arias Maldonado established a small cacao hacienda of his own.[15] His son, the interim governor Rodrigo Arias Maldonado, renewed the conquest of Talamanca in 1662, partly in response to the growing labor needs of Matina cacao haciendas.[16]

Cacao production expanded rapidly, at least at first. By 1660 Costa Rican planters were producing quantities of cacao sufficient to export to Nicaragua.[17] In 1676 Governor don Juan Francisco Sáenz enthused that cacao already provided the "main income" of the province.[18] An inventory of haciendas in 1678 listed 103,250 trees in Matina and 26,230 more in the adjacent Reventazón Valley; nine other *rozas*, or groves of newly planted trees that did not yet produce fruit, were also listed.[19] Don Miguel Gómez de Lara estimated in 1681 that there were more than 150,000 trees planted in the Atlantic zone.[20] In 1682 Cartago hacienda owners compiled

TABLE 1 Contemporary Estimates of Costa Rican Cacao Production

DATE	SOURCE OF ESTIMATE	NUMBER OF TREES IN PRODUCTION	NUMBER OF YOUNG TREES
1675	Audiencia of Guatemala	200,000	No info
1678	Inventory	129,480	No info
1681	Governor of Costa Rica	150,000	No info
1682	Cacao hacendados	28,700	66,100
1683	Governor of Costa Rica	110,000	40,000
1691	Inventory	117,400	No info
1691	Cacao hacendados	120,000–140,000	No info

Sources: León Fernández, ed., Colección de documentos para la historia de Costa Rica, vols. 6–10 (Barcelona: Imprenta Viuda de Luis Tasso, 1881–1907), 8:349, 376–77, 398, 399–405, 428; Archivos Nacionales de Costa Rica, c. 83, fols. 3–7, 10v; c. 85, fols. [1v]–5.

their own count for tax purposes. As a tax was to be levied on each tree, their estimate seems extraordinarily low, with 28,700 "old" trees already producing, and 66,100 "new" trees in the Matina, Reventazón, and Barbilla Valleys.[21] Governor don Juan Francisco Sáenz Vázquez, himself a large cacao planter, was probably closer to the mark when he estimated in 1683 that of more than 150,000 trees in Costa Rica, 40,000 were already bearing fruit.[22] In 1691 Governor don Miguel Gómez de Lara undertook a census of Cartago residents, their occupations and property, again for purposes of tax assessment. Sixty-two persons claimed to own a total of 117,400 trees.[23] The same year a group of Cartago hacienda owners presented information on the cacao industry in Matina. Their estimates on the number of trees in cultivation ranged from 120,000 to 140,000.[24]

Available information on cacao exports in the 1680s and 1690s is certainly incomplete, as it fails to record the contraband trade that was probably equal to if not greater than legal commerce. Nicaragua provided Costa Rica's most important market for the legal export of cacao, but prohibitive transportation costs encouraged illegal exports from the Matina coast. Compiling data from the official records of the Real Hacienda, Philip S. MacLeod has traced the uneven growth of the cacao industry in the seventeenth century.[25] Again, the illegal trade might easily have doubled the scale of exports.

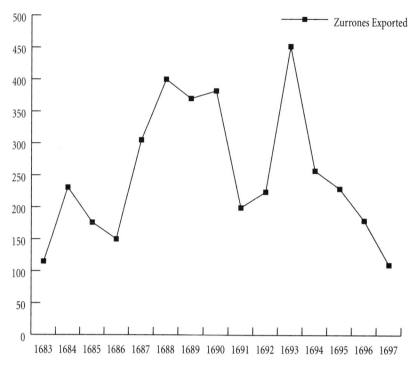

FIGURE 1 Recorded cacao exports in *zurrones*, 1683–97. *Source*: Based on Philip S. MacLeod, "On the Edge of Empire: Costa Rica in the Colonial Era (1561–1800)," Ph.D. dissertation, Tulane University, 1999, table 6.

FORCED INDIAN LABOR

The nearby Urinama Indians of Talamanca provided the first major source of labor for the Matina haciendas. In the 1650s Governor don Juan Fernández de Salinas y Cerda first "reduced" the Urinamas.[26] The effects of Salinas's efforts must have been limited, however, because the interim governor don Rodrigo Arias Maldonado set out again to conquer the Urinamas in 1662, accompanied by Franciscan missionaries. Arias Maldonado attracted Indians to the settlements mainly by promising gifts such as axes and machetes, which he advised the king were "the means to accomplish such ends."[27] The Urinamas readily accepted gifts such as tools and clothing, which continued as a cornerstone of both missionary and hacendado efforts to attract the Indians.[28] Many Indians showed interest in Christianity and the new technologies but opposed permanent settlement in the missions and, above all, work on the haciendas.

The Urinamas soon resisted the missions through both flight and rebellion. Just a few months after beginning his initially successful reduction, Governor Rodrigo Arias Maldonado was besieged by unconverted Indians, who expelled him from Talamanca in June 1662.[29] The Franciscans renewed their efforts to build missions in the 1670s, but in 1678 the Urinamas revolted again. Don Antonio Salmón Pacheco, a recent immigrant from Spain and the owner of a hacienda of four thousand cacao trees, led an expedition from Cartago to punish the rebels, which, in the words of historian Philip MacLeod, "provided the justification for Indian slavery" and allowed the reestablishment of the missions.[30]

The Franciscans came to see the greatest threat to the success of the missions not in Indian rebellions, however, but in the demands of the cacao planters of Matina. The hacendados abused the missions as bottomless reservoirs of Indian labor. They enlisted the governors of Costa Rica and their lieutenants to remove the Urinamas from the missions, often by force. In 1675 Visitor General don Antonio de Noboa Salgado prohibited Spaniards, mulattos, and mestizos from entering the Urinama pueblos except for "good ends" and with the permission of the governor.[31] No doubt because the governor himself participated in them, the drafts continued. As long as work on the plantations did not interrupt evangelization, the friars saw little objection to providing the hacendados with Indian workers. But as cacao production expanded, the needs of the haciendas clashed increasingly with the goals of the missionaries and placed ever greater demands on the Indians themselves. In the 1680s Urinama men not only cared for the Matina haciendas and harvested the cacao, but supplied the labor for a growing infrastructure needed to serve the expanding industry. Urinamas maintained the road from Cartago to Matina, built shelters along it to accommodate travelers, and hauled cacao between the haciendas and the capital.[32] In late 1689 the Franciscan missionaries asked Governor don Miguel Gómez de Lara to send the Urinama men in Matina back to the missions "so that they could receive the sacraments." Not only did the governor refuse to return the men already in Matina, but he asked the missionaries to send forty more Urinamas to the haciendas, provoking the friars to ask sarcastically "if they were his lieutenants."[33]

As the Franciscans charged, Indians were often removed from the Ta-lamanca missions by force.[34] Other Urinama men, promised "food to eat and machetes and arrows," probably preferred work on the cacao haciendas to the strenuous labor of building houses and churches.[35] In this competition for Indian bodies and souls hacendados held an advantage. Fray Melchor López and Fray Antonio Margil complained in 1690 that the Indians, "because they know we cannot whip them," abandon the missions whenever some "trivial fear or hunger tempts them."[36] Fray Pablo de Rebullida and Fray Francisco de San José agreed a few years later, writing, "With love [alone] everything necessary cannot be done with them."[37] Cacao planters, however, held no such reservations about using violence to bring Indians to the haciendas and keep them there.

In February 1690 Fray Diego Macotela, the Franciscan provincial of Ni-caragua and Costa Rica, petitioned the Audiencia of Guatemala for an order to stop the removal of the Urinamas to the haciendas of Matina. He held the governor of Costa Rica and his lieutenants primarily responsible for removing the Indians "for the cacaotales of Matina." The Indians had been so terrorized by the "slavery that they experience[d]" that when they heard the voice of the lieutenant governor they fled the missions, undoing all the Franciscans' hard work.[38] The Audiencia promptly acceded to the provincial's request, ordering in April 1690 that the governor and his lieutenants leave the Indians in the mission and not remove them "to Matina nor elsewhere, not for the reason of the benefit of the cacaotales, nor for any other." Violators would be subject to a fine of one thousand pesos as well as criminal prosecution and the loss of all their property.[39]

When word of the order arrived in Costa Rica the Matina hacendados wasted no time before protesting it. In January 1691 Manuel de Farinas presented a petition to the Audiencia in Guatemala City on behalf of the hacienda owner and onetime conqueror of the Urinamas, don Antonio Salmón Pacheco. Without the service of the Indians, Farinas warned, the Matina haciendas would be "extinguished and annihilated." Far from det-rimental to the Urinamas, work on the haciendas would benefit them by eventually providing them with money to pay tribute to the crown.[40] On the advice of the crown attorney, the Audiencia attempted to broker a compromise. Upholding the *reales cédulas* that prohibited personal ser-vice and *repartimiento*, the Audiencia ordered that Indians who wished voluntarily to serve the haciendas should not be barred from working there, as long as they continued to attend mass and receive the other sacraments. In this way neither the interests of the Church nor those of the hacendados or the crown would be sacrificed.[41] A second decree in May 1691, however, prohibited any "Spaniard, mestizo, black, or mulatto" from entering the missions without the express permission of the friars.[42] Just five months later one hacendado after another declared that the prohibition had already caused the total ruin of the Matina cacao industry. Since the order many haciendas had been reclaimed by the jungle, leaving their owners "without means to sustain their families." If the prohibition were not repealed the hacendados might quit Costa Rica altogether, abandoning Matina to the pirate enemy, which would jeopardize the entire province.[43]

Despite their threats the hacendados did not vacate Costa Rica, but began to search for another labor force. They continued to employ the Urinamas illegally, at least occasionally, but in the long term hacendados recognized that they needed another source of workers for their cacao haciendas.[44] Indians were simply less and less able to supply the necessary labor. A wave of epidemics in the late 1680s and 1690s afflicted the already weakened indigenous peoples of the Central Valley.[45] Although their effects were not as well documented, these diseases affected Talamanca as well. Fray Pablo de Rebullida wrote in 1698 and 1699 that some Talamanca feared the missionaries because they believed that the friars brought plagues.[46] This not unjustified perception contributed to a renewed Talamanca resistance to evangelization. Mass flight constituted the most common form of resistance, further reducing the number of Indians available for work in Matina.

THE SEARCH FOR A NEW LABOR FORCE

Once the Audiencia prohibited the coercion of the Urinama Indians, cacao planters considered and experimented with a number of labor sources for the haciendas. Between the 1650s and the 1690s Urinamas had provided the main labor source for the haciendas, but never the only one. From the beginning slaves, free people of color, mestizos, Indians of other origins, and even Spaniards also worked on the cacao haciendas. For example, Esteban Yapiro, an Indian from the Central Valley pueblo of Teotique, was working at a Matina hacienda when buccaneers sacked the valley in 1666. Yapiro escaped, but the pirates captured eight other Indians.[47] Magdalena de Sibaja, a free mulata who owned her own house near the Cartago neighborhood of El Tejar, died in the Reventazón Valley in 1670 while on the way to Matina "in the service of" Juan de Meza.[48]

The cacao planters of the Atlantic region did not switch to a slave labor force overnight; the transition from de facto Indian to de jure African slavery occurred over a period of decades. Although some cacao planters continued to use other workers, many came to prefer slaves for several reasons. Living conditions in the Matina and Barbilla Valleys were unpleasant and insecure. Throughout the colonial period and long after, the region suffered from a shortage of labor. Some of the same reasons that made Matina ideal for cacao cultivation, such as its heavy rainfall and high humidity, caused Spanish colonists to shun the area. In 1741 Governor don Juan Gemmir y Lleonart flatly declared the Matina Valley "uninhabitable" due to its "sickly, humid, and hot" climate.[49] "It is extremely hot and humid, and the rains very continuous," Bishop Pedro Agustín Morel de Santa Cruz agreed ten years later. "From these causes arise illnesses and fevers, so malignant that those who enter that country either die within a few short days, or if they escape with their lives, they lose their color entirely and contract a kind of paleness in their faces, which never leaves them."[50] The bishop's description probably referred to symptoms of malaria (*Plasmodium falciparum* or *Plasmodium vivax*) or yellow fever, to both of which people of African descent demonstrate greater resistance than whites or Indians do.[51] Morel claimed, "Only blacks enjoy good health in that intemperate climate."[52] Of course Africans were not immune to disease, notwithstanding the mistaken beliefs of whites such as the bishop. Luis, an enslaved African probably born on the Slave Coast, died of an "epidemic" in the Matina Valley in 1710, which must have affected others as well.[53]

In addition to the climate and disease environment wild animals also presented danger. Snakes posed a constant threat, especially in the shady undergrowth beneath the plantain and cacao trees. Manuel Aná was bitten on the leg in 1719; the following year a snakebite caused one of Francisco Mina's toes to swell.[54] Until the twentieth century crocodiles were common in the rivers along the Atlantic coast as far south as Cahuita.[55] "Lions and tigers" (pumas and jaguars) in the area were reputedly "so bold that they [threw] themselves at the houses of the residents" and occasionally attacked humans. Pedro, an African slave of Captain Juan Sancho de Castañeda, was killed by a big cat while working on his master's hacienda sometime before 1719, as was another African man on the road from Matina in 1702.[56]

As frightening as wild animals could be, the greatest threat by far came from humans, specifically from the foreign attackers who frequented Matina's shores. The British buccaneers Edward Mansfield and Henry Morgan landed on the Atlantic coast in 1666 with a multiethnic force of several hundred, sacking the haciendas and kidnapping resident workers. In 1687 the notorious mulatto pirate Lorencillo ravaged Matina for three months, killing several Spaniards.[57] Soon thereafter, in the 1690s, the Miskito Zambos of Honduras and Nicaragua, newly allied with the British, began to attack Matina. The Miskitos preferred to sack the valley at the time of the cacao harvest, when they could make off with thousands of pounds of cacao as well as prisoners.[58] In March 1705 they attacked Matina at harvest time and kidnapped six slaves as well as some Spaniards.[59] When a force of five hundred Miskito Zambos entered the Matina Valley in a surprise attack in April 1724 they took twelve slaves and twenty-one freemen (nineteen of them mulattos) prisoner.[60] After forcing the men to carry up to a thousand *zurrones* (107 tons, or 97 metric tons) of cacao to their boats, the Miskitos sailed away with them to their territory to the north.[61] Factors such as the climate, the disease environment, the danger posed by wild animals, and especially the threat of attack and imprisonment by the Miskitos and others led free workers to successfully demand high wages for work in Matina.

From the planter's perspective the cost of hiring free people to work the cacao haciendas was prohibitive. In 1703 the cacao planter Captain Blas González Coronel claimed that during the cacao harvests the workers (*gente de servicio*) in Matina, "because there [were] no Indians, [were] composed of Spaniards, blacks, mulattos, [and] mestizos" and earned two pesos per day, paid either in cacao or in clothing and other goods.[62] González Coronel might have exaggerated; Captain Francisco Pérez del Cote cited the lower figure of one to one and a half pesos daily.[63] These wages were twice to four times as high as the half-peso per day that one master sought as compensation for his slave's work the same year.[64] Wages remained high throughout the first half of the eighteenth century, although they were always paid in cacao or clothing, never in silver. Captain don José de Mier Cevallos noted that wage workers in Matina earned "a salary as high as twelve to fourteen pesos per month" in 1719.[65] By contrast, soldiers were paid just four pesos per month during an emergency the following year.[66] In 1724, after attacks by the Miskitos, prominent citizens of Cartago complained, "No person can be found to go down to the cultivation of the cacao haciendas, except at double salary, because of their fear of being taken prisoner."[67] "Double salary" presumably meant about twenty-five pesos, enough in those years to buy as many as five mules, a gold chain, a house in Matina, or more than a hundred acres of land (forty hectares) just north of San José.[68] In the 1720s and 1730s the usual wage for free workers in Matina was twelve to twelve and a half pesos per month, in addition to food and lodging.[69] In 1736 Cartago's *procurador síndico* Captain Juan José de Cuende complained that hiring workers for the cacao haciendas was "extremely costly": "They are not content with earning a regular wage as in other places, but [want] exorbitance and serve [only] with reluctance."[70]

Perhaps as important as high labor costs, land in the Atlantic regions was abundant and, for all intents and purposes, free to those who worked it. Although masters listed Matina cacao trees in testaments and inventories from the late 1650s, they never included the land itself because they never bothered to secure legal title to it as they did in the Central and Pacific Valleys. Nevertheless they bought, sold, mortgaged, and bequeathed their haciendas in all respects as if they owned the land on which they were established.[71] For much of the colonial period the lands of the Atlantic region officially remained the property of the crown (*tierras realengas*), and no law prevented an enterprising freeman from starting his own plantings on a piece of unclaimed land.

Using their influence with (or, just as frequently, as) colonial officials, hacendados strove to maintain exclusive control over the land and labor of the Matina Valley. Indeed apart from defense, control of workers constituted one of the only functions of an official presence in the region. Captain Luis Gutiérrez, a former lieutenant governor of Matina, said in 1719 that the duties of his former position consisted "only [of] that which [was] related to the defense of the port, and the orders given, and the obedience of the subjects who serve[d] in that Valley, who [were] the servants of the haciendas."[72] Officials repeatedly issued edicts designed to prevent a free peasantry from establishing itself in Matina by ensuring that all people resident there were bound to a master. In 1704 Governor don Diego de Herrera Campuzano issued an order barring "idle and vagabond people" from the Matina Valley. He instructed his lieutenant, the hacendado don Antonio de la Vega Cabral, to ensure that people in Matina "work for a wage [*jornal*] in the haciendas of the vecinos, who will pay them for their labor according to custom." Those who refused to enter into contracts with the hacendados were to be expelled from the valley.[73] Lieutenant Governor of Matina don Bernardo Marín issued a similar order in 1716, demanding that all the "resident hacendados, sharecroppers [*arrendatarios*], and black overseers" notify him of "the people each one ha[d] under contract." Anyone not bound by such a contract was to leave Matina within three days.[74] Three years later the procurador general of Cartago, don Pedro de Moya, another cacao planter, petitioned the governor to expel any person in Matina found "independent of administration of hacienda or contract, or any others of those who [went] to the said Valley without a contract with the owners of the haciendas."[75] In 1737 Governor don Francisco Carrandi y Menán issued a similar order, expelling "those who [did] not want to subject themselves to a labor contract with those hacendados" in the Matina Valley.[76]

At an average price of approximately 315 pesos in the century between 1650 and 1750, male slaves between the ages of sixteen and twenty-five constituted an expensive solution to the labor shortage.[77] Once the cacao was planted, however, the labor requirements on the haciendas were relatively light, so there was no special need to purchase men of prime working age. The strongest men could be used in clearing the thickly forested lands, "opening the mountain," in the evocative phrase of a freeman who worked in the cacaotales of the Barbilla Valley, and planting, while those less robust could keep the plants watered, shaded, and free of weeds.[78] Boys and older men could and did perform the work. For example, a black man named José was sold in 1706 at the estimated age of fifty-five with a hacienda of 1,300 trees in the Barbilla Valley.[79] The black creole slave Juan Román labored on his master's haciendas until he was nearly sixty.[80] As the Costa Rican historian Rina Cáceres has suggested, some elite Cartago families were able to survive the seventeenth-century depression by allocating enslaved workers to the cacao industry.[81] Cartago families who already owned slaves could send them to work in Matina without investing capital. As cacao exports increased, Costa Rican planters used a portion

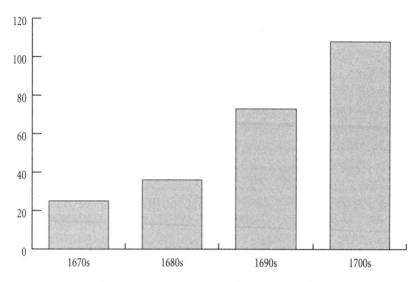

FIGURE 2 Slave sales by decade, 1670s–1690s. *Sources:* Archivos Nacionales de Costa Rica, P.C. 818 (1664, 1668–71) through P.C. 850, 853 (1697, 1699, 1700, 1701); Indice de los protocolos de Cartago, vols. 1–3.

of their profits to invest in more slave purchases. The late seventeenth century and early eighteenth saw a mini-boom in Costa Rica's small-scale slave trade and a re-Africanization of the colony's slave population. Registered slave sales in the 1680s rose 44 percent over the previous decade, 51 percent in the 1690s, and a further 48 percent in the 1700s.[82]

In an essay published in 1982 the Costa Rican historian Carlos Rosés Alvarado contended that the small-scale slave trade to Costa Rica was insufficient to provide a solution, even a temporary one, to the chronic labor shortage that plagued cacao production.[83] More recently Philip S. MacLeod drew attention to the variety of labor regimes employed on Atlantic cacao haciendas, including wage labor and sharecropping (*arrendamiento*), and suggested that slavery was of minor importance.[84] Both Rosés Alvarado and MacLeod seemed to argue from an assumption that cacao production required a large labor force. This was not the case. The hacendados recruited Urinamas on the order of thirty to sixty men at a time in the 1670s and 1680s.[85] When the agent of Antonio Salmón Pacheco presented a petition to the Audiencia of Guatemala in 1691, he requested that twelve Urinama men be allocated to "the service and cultivation" of Salmón Pacheco's haciendas.[86] Apparently he asked for more workers than he needed: in that year Salmón Pacheco owned haciendas with a total of four thousand trees, and according to a Venezuelan text dated 1721 it was "well known" that one slave could care for a thousand trees. According to the census of 1691, no planter in Costa Rica owned more than ten thousand trees in production, and the average cacao planter owned 1,894 trees.[87] Even owners of just one or two slaves, like many Costa Rican masters, could profitably cultivate cacao with slave labor, and many did.

The generally low costs of starting a cacao hacienda allowed Cartago elites to diversify their economic enterprises at a time when their traditional activities had foundered. In fact if not in law, land in Matina was free, but it was also worthless without men to work it. Although for most of the year the work was light, cacao trees required constant care. Most free workers found such work unattractive, and after the decree of the Audiencia in 1690 Indians could not be forced to do it. Slaves constituted by far the most expensive of the cacao hacienda's productive forces, but soon were considered part of a hacienda's essential "equipment." Accordingly enslaved men were sometimes sold as a package with the haciendas. In March 1718 doña María Josefa de la Vega Cabral inherited a cacao hacienda and two slaves from her late father. A few months later her husband don Juan José de Cuende sold a hacienda with Francisco and Sebastián, the two slaves who were "tied to said hacienda," along with the "musket, tools, . . . and other implements necessary to the work on the said hacienda."[88] In 1727 Diego de Angulo, born in West Central Africa, was auctioned with the Matina hacienda he had worked for decades.[89]

Once slaves were purchased, their maintenance costs in Matina were close to nil. Slave men met virtually all of their needs themselves. They built their own houses, roofing them with palm thatch. Plantains, "which serve in place of bread," formed the most important part of their diet.[90] Fruits such as oranges, avocadoes, and *zapotes* added variety and nutrients.[91] Rice provided another staple. In 1733 the free cacao worker Miguel Solano remarked that the creole slave Juan Román made his own "rice fields and other plantings" in the Barbilla Valley, "as other black slaves customarily" did in Matina.[92] Antonio Cabo Verde might have brought Old World knowledge of the crop to Costa Rica. His *casta* surname indicates an origin in Upper Guinea, where rice provided the dietary staple, or in the Cape Verde Islands themselves, where it was also cultivated. In other colonies, notably South Carolina, slave buyers prized West Africans like Antonio for their expertise in rice culture.[93] Wherever he learned to grow it, Antonio farmed rice successfully enough to sell a surplus to free people in the area. He also raised chickens and pigs. Cattle raised in the Barbilla Valley provided the area with beef.[94] No doubt slave men also hunted—in 1721 don Diego de Barros y Carbajal complained, "My negro is asking for his musket," which was being repaired—and fished the nearby rivers.[95] Every year the sea turtles that came to lay their eggs on the beaches provided another important source of meat.[96]

LIFE AND WORK ON THE CACAO HACIENDAS

On the cacao haciendas of the Matina, Barbilla, and Reventazón Valleys slave men lived remarkably independent lives. More comfortable in the temperate Central Valley, most hacendados came to Matina only once or twice a year to supervise the harvest, usually staying for two to three weeks.[97] The rest of the time slave men lived and worked largely on their own. The detailed inventories of the haciendas of doña Agueda Pérez de Muro provide a glimpse at the rustic conditions on a large cacao complex in the early eighteenth century. In 1722, when Pérez de Muro married for the second time, she owned four cacao haciendas in the Matina Valley, totaling 8,650 producing trees.[98] In the adjacent Barbilla Valley she owned another hacienda of 1,150 trees, also already bearing fruit.[99] The combined value of the trees was assessed at 16,406 pesos in cacao, or 11,718 pesos 6 reales in silver, a sizable fortune by Costa Rican standards. In addition she owned another 600 trees, planted four or five years before, which had not yet borne fruit and were valued at 425 pesos in cacao or 300 pesos in silver.[100] Five slaves administered the Matina haciendas. Two of them, José Congo and Nicolás Casasola, were described as "overseers" (mandadores). Another slave, Lorenzo, attended the hacienda in Barbilla.[101]

At the Matina hacienda the five men lived in three houses, "like those used in that Valley." The men surely built these themselves of wood and palm thatch. Each house was furnished with a grinding stone (piedra de moler) and a large iron pot used for cooking. For hunting and self-defense the men shared two "French muskets."[102] To cut wood, keep the cacao groves free of weeds, split cacao pods at harvest time, and no doubt occasionally to protect themselves against snakes and other animals, they used four axes and eleven iron machetes. To pick cacao at the harvest there were three *almaradas* (a tool consisting of a pole about one meter long, with a thin, sharp knife or hook attached to one end). A *canoa* listed in the inventory was probably not a boat but a large trough used for fermenting cacao. For drying cacao there were nineteen uncured cow skins and thirty-five more ready for use. In addition to the buildings used for housing, the hacienda had three terraces (*galeras*) used to "break cacao" and later to dry it in the sun. The men shared three needles to sew the leather bags in which cacao was transported and sold. A single pine box kept by the overseers was probably used to store valuables, although it had no lock.[103]

Because no colonial Costa Rican documents have yet been located that describe in narrative form the cultivation and processing of cacao, it is necessary to draw upon contemporary accounts from other American colonies to reconstruct the techniques used.[104] Cacao was first planted as seedlings, which were transplanted at six to ten months.[105] About eight feet (2.4 meters) was allowed between cacao trees. Next to each a plantain tree was planted to provide shade and shelter for the delicate plants.[106] Maintenance was relatively simple and required few workers, mainly to weed and periodically replant. Mature plants were harvested twice a year, around the time of the festival of Saint John the Baptist (24 June) and at Christmas.[107] The pods were lowered from the trees with almaradas (also called *cuchillones*). On the ground the workers opened the pods with axes, machetes, or knives, then extracted the seeds and placed them in tubs (*bateas*) for fermentation. Later the seeds were spread onto leather skins and dried in the sun, a step considered essential for the flavor of the cacao.[108] After drying the cacao was sewn into leather bags (*zurrones*), each one purportedly holding twenty thousand grains and valued at twenty-five pesos.[109] Some of the cacao was then sent to Cartago, from where it was exported to Nicaragua, the only legal outlet for much of the colonial period. Many haciendas, however, had their own wharves (*embarcaderos*), and contraband trade was extensive.[110]

Masters relied on black overseers (*mandadores*) to administer their Matina haciendas. Occasionally planters hired Spanish overseers to supervise their slaves but far more commonly chose a driver from among the slaves themselves. Despite a decree in 1708 requiring planters to employ a Spanish overseer on their haciendas, very few complied.[111] Most often drivers were Africans, as were the men they supervised. For example, Gregorio

Caamaño, of Slave Coast origin, and José Congo both served at different times as mandadores of doña Agueda Pérez de Muro's haciendas. Manuel, a Yoruba (aná), and Antonio de la Riva, a mina from the Gold Coast or Upper Slave Coast, were both overseers at don Juan de Ibarra y Calvo's cacaotales. Masters trusted these men with the equipment of the haciendas and, importantly, with calculating the number of trees on the properties. When Ibarra died in 1737 his executors trusted Antonio de la Riva with the care of his late master's cacao haciendas, simply formalizing an already current arrangement.[112] Taking an overseer's word for the number of trees on a hacienda amounted to relying on his assessment of the property's net worth. An undercount of the trees could allow slaves to appropriate and market the surplus for their own profit, and enslaved overseers were sometimes implicated in contraband trade.[113]

The point of having an overseer at all was to maximize cacao production, which could be done only through command of the other enslaved men on the haciendas. It is clear that more than mere administrators, drivers exercised authority over other slaves; for example, in 1718 the slave Antonio Cabo Verde purchased a mule only after gaining the approval of his enslaved overseer, Diego García, a slave of the same ethnic designation.[114] Unfortunately no sources have been found to clarify how drivers extracted surplus labor from the men they supervised, nor to identify potential sources of conflict between drivers and other slaves. Overseers probably enjoyed the authority to command as extensions of their master's power. Enslaved overseers reported to their masters on affairs of the haciendas, in at least one case by letter (probably dictated to a literate acquaintance).[115] If an overseer did not discipline a recalcitrant slave on the spot the master could be expected to do so later. Inventories of cacao haciendas, however, do not list the chains or shackles that sometimes appeared in masters' homes.[116] Overseers simply could not have ruled by force alone and must have negotiated and compromised with the enslaved men under their command.

The choice of Spaniards not to live in the Atlantic zone had important implications not only for the cacao industry, but for the defense of the province. As elsewhere in Caribbean Central America free mulatto militias made up the bulk of military forces in Matina.[117] But exceptionally in Matina slaves were regularly mobilized for service. When don Manuel Antonio de Arlegui reviewed the militiamen of Matina in January 1719 twenty-one slaves stood among them. Eight carried guns—their "own arms," the roster specified—and thirteen held lances. Slaves were better armed than their free counterparts in all respects: of the 120 free men mustered in Matina, thirty had firearms, sixty-one carried lances, and two wielded machetes. More than one-fifth of the men (twenty-six) reported for review with no arms of any kind.[118]

For enslaved men a sense of honor, independence, and even equality with white men sometimes developed from a knowledge of their importance in cacao production. After building their own homes and managing the cacao haciendas in every way, some slaves understandably felt a sense of proprietorship and regarded the semiannual visits of the hacendados as unwelcome intrusions. In 1696 the Spanish captain Juan de Bonilla went to Matina for the June harvest on an errand from doña Josefa de Santiago y Aguilar, who wished to ensure that no one collected cacao from her properties until her son arrived to supervise. Upon arrival Bonilla found Francisco de Flores collecting cacao from doña Josefa's groves. When Bonilla asked him on whose authority he was picking the fruit, Flores replied that he had been sent by Gregorio Sanabria, a mulatto slave of doña Ambrosia de Echavarría Navarro. Sanabria had sent Flores to collect a debt of two zurrones (436 lbs. or 198 kg) owed to him by Benito Mejía, doña Josefa's slave.[119]

Infuriated by the slave's initiative, the next day Captain Bonilla went with three servants to Echavarría Navarro's hacienda and called out to Gregorio, "Come here, mulatto, where will your shamelessness end? On whose authority did you go to pick cacao?" Gregorio replied, "On [my] authority alone." When Bonilla called him a scoundrel (*desvergonzado*), Gregorio rejoined that the shameless one was Bonilla, "for coming to his [Gregorio's] house like that."[120] Bonilla then raised the stakes by calling Gregorio a dog, at which Gregorio warned him to "watch how he talked" and observed that "there were many kinds of dogs; there were Spanish dogs, too."[121] Enraged, Bonilla took a machete from his belt and was about to start at Gregorio when, according to his account, he "contained [himself]" and, "as a Spaniard and a man of honor," told Gregorio, "Come now, man, let's leave it [alone]." Unsatisfied with the Spaniard's offer of a truce, Gregorio angrily threw down a cup of chocolate and wished aloud that he and Bonilla were alone.[122] Although brought up in slavery and, beyond any doubt, aware of the Spanish American assumption of white superiority, Gregorio gave no indication that he accepted that premise. On the contrary, he openly disdained the implication that he owed whites any special deference and considered Spaniards to be unwelcome interlopers in Matina. He resented their pretensions to superiority—"there were Spanish dogs, too"—their intrusion on "his" house, and their interference with his collection of cacao at the harvest.

African slaves also worked in the transport of the crop, both to Cartago and to the coast, where it was sold illegally to the British, the Miskito Zambos, and perhaps the Dutch.[123] In 1722 Francisco Plaza, a mina (from the Gold Coast or Upper Slave Coast) slave of doña Luisa Calvo, brought a train of mules from Cartago to Matina to transport cacao.[124] He may or may not have been the same *negro mina* who had driven mule trains between Matina and Cartago twenty years before.[125] Benito, a slave of don José de Prado, purchased a mule worth sixteen pesos on credit from Francisco de Cabrera; Antonio Cabo Verde bought one around 1718, no doubt to haul zurrones.[126] (Far more often, however, muleteers were free mulattos, mestizos, and Indians.)[127] Masters might even entrust their slaves with illegal operations. On several occasions in the early eighteenth century the African slaves Gregorio Caamaño and Juan Damián took a total of thirty-one zurrones (3.3 tons or 3 metric tons) of cacao to the Atlantic coast by mule. There they traded it with smugglers for yards of cloth, hats, and finished articles of clothing, among other items, all of which they remitted to their mistress in Cartago.[128]

The participation of African slaves in contraband trade presented one of Costa Rica's governors with a theoretical and legal conundrum. Ultimately don Diego de la Haya Fernández failed to resolve it and issued contradictory rulings. In theory slaves were merely extensions of their master's will, but when they participated in illegal trade, officials tried to hold them responsible for their own actions. In 1719 Governor de la Haya charged Juan Damián with illegal trade, "which he should not have carried out, even if it were by order" of his mistress, doña Agueda Pérez de Muro.[129] Don José de Castellanos, named by the governor to defend Juan Damián, argued that the slave was not responsible for his actions on two grounds: "He is an African-born black [*negro bozal*] who does not understand [the law], nor does he have his own will, because he is a slave." Doña Agueda therefore was legally responsible for the illegal sale, as well as neglecting to correct her slave's bad behavior. Furthermore, argued the advocate, Juan Damián could not be guilty of contraband trade "because he ha[d] no property of his own." Juan Damián and his companion Gregorio Caamaño would not have carried out the prohibited acts were it not for the will of their mistress. If the governor rejected the premise that Juan Damián had no will of his own to act illegally, Castellanos claimed ignorance of the law as the slave's excuse. Governor de la Haya found Juan Damián guilty, and Castellanos appealed the case to the Audiencia in Guatemala City.[130] In another case two years later, however, de la Haya accepted the defense that an African-born slave could not understand the legal import of his actions. Antonio García, a mina slave of Captain Manuel García de Argueta, confessed to having traded tobacco to the Miskito Zambos in return for some iron.[131] The governor absolved Antonio, stating that the African was "incapable by nature of understanding whether it is or is not a crime to trade with the said Mosquitos."[132] But as de la Haya surely knew, Africans as well as American-born slaves proved more than capable of exploiting all the opportunities open to them in Matina.

CACAO AND FREEDOM

A circumstance particular to Costa Rica gave male slaves rare bargaining power and further enhanced their independence. By the early eighteenth century cacao served as legal tender in the colony.[133] Each *zurrón*, a leather bag weighing about 214 lbs. (97 kg), was valued at twenty-five pesos in cacao. Cacao pesos were officially worth two-thirds of silver pesos, thus the value of a zurrón ostensibly equaled slightly more than sixteen pesos five reales in silver. Buyers, sellers, and appraisers, however, frequently negotiated their own values and might accept cacao pesos at just half the value of silver ones.[134] In any case, enslaved men had as easy access to cacao, and therefore money, as anyone in Costa Rica.

Because land in Matina was fully available, many slave men took the opportunity to plant and cultivate their own cacao groves. Some masters allowed this activity, provided the slaves cultivated their plantings only "on feast days and without missing other days in the service of their masters."[135] Other slaves appropriated some of the cacao they grew themselves without bothering to secure anyone else's permission. Cacao enabled slaves to purchase needed items from merchants or smugglers. While some Cartago vendors profited from selling merchandise to slaves, planters inveighed against the practice, presumably reasoning that slaves paid for the items with stolen cacao. Despite prohibitions the sales continued.[136] That masters spent little on clothing for their slaves can be inferred from the petition of one hacendado, who sought to prohibit the passage of merchants to Matina because they sold clothing to the slaves.[137] But slaves and others in the colony had other sources of merchandise connecting them to the broader Atlantic world. Like "everyone in Matina," slaves traded cacao with smugglers for goods ultimately from England, especially cloth, sometimes for their masters and sometimes on their own account.[138] On several occasions in the early eighteenth century Gregorio Caamaño took a total of thirty-one zurrones (3.3 tons or 3 metric tons) of cacao to the Atlantic coast by mule. There he traded it with foreign smugglers for yards of cloth, hats, and finished articles of clothing, among other items, all of which they remitted to their mistress in Cartago.[139] Antonio García, a mina slave of Captain Manuel García de Argueta, confessed to having traded with the Miskito Zambos in return for iron.[140] Some slaves accumulated enough cacao to lend money to free people. In 1717, for example, Isidro de Acosta acknowledged that he owed twenty-five pesos in cacao to Nicolás Barrantes, a mulatto slave of Captain don Nicolás de Guevara.[141]

All of the advantages related to residence in Matina were closed to slave women. Largely because of the threat of military attack, Cartago masters rarely, if ever, sent their female slaves to Matina. As a result Matina slave men saw slave women only on occasional visits to the capital. Even then masters tended to confine female slaves to their homes as domestic servants, subjecting them to heightened vigilance and constraining their opportunities to pursue outside relationships. Slave women rarely married in the Catholic Church. Of 322 children born to slave mothers who were baptized in Cartago between 1599 and 1750, 297 (92 percent) were born out of wedlock.[142] The inherent disadvantages of marriage to an enslaved wife—foremost among them the birth of one's children in slavery—made slave women unattractive marriage partners.

While Costa Rican slave owners sharply limited the kinds of family life available to female slaves, enslaved men faced fewer restrictions. Although they legally married relatively infrequently, they did so ten times as often as enslaved women. In Costa Rica no effective obstacles prevented marriage between slaves and free persons. Slave men celebrated legal marriages only rarely, but when they did they almost always chose to marry free women. This tendency proved strong in many areas of Spanish America, but the marriage patterns of enslaved men in Costa Rica exhibited several striking characteristics, perhaps unique in the continent. Enslaved black men were far more likely to marry than male mulatto slaves, and among black men Africans married more frequently than creoles.

Slave men elsewhere in Central America also preferred free wives. Paul Lokken and Christopher Lutz have documented that in colonial Guatemala an overwhelming majority of enslaved men married free women.[143] In Costa Rica enslaved men's strong preference for exogamy proved even more pronounced. Of seventy-two marriages of slave men recorded in Cartago parish registers between 1670 and 1750, a full sixty-six (92 percent) were to free women.[144] With marriage to free women a viable option, slave men almost never married slave women.

Just as strikingly, enslaved black men in Costa Rica were more than twice as likely than male mulatto slaves to marry, in contrast to many other societies. In Mexico and Guatemala, for example, mulatto slaves enjoyed substantially greater success in pursuing free wives than did enslaved black men in the century between 1650 and 1750. In Mexico City mulattos married free women up to twice as often as blacks did; in Guatemala about 24 percent more often.[145] In Costa Rica the reverse was true. Priests recorded the race of seventy-two of the seventy-five slave bridegrooms in Cartago parish registers between 1670 and 1750. Fifty-two (74 percent) were black men, while only nineteen (26 percent) were mulattos. The Costa Rican data challenge assumptions that free women found mulattos more attractive marriage partners than blacks, which should have been the case if blacks occupied the lowest rung on the ladder of the racial hierarchy. Even more surprising, of those enslaved men whose place of birth can be determined, more than one-third more Africans married in the Church than male black creoles (twenty-three Africans compared to fifteen creoles).[146] Although not too much should be made of these low figures, Costa Rica differed in this respect from plantation societies, where creoles generally enjoyed favored treatment over Africans in most aspects of life, including their access to marriage.

Who married enslaved African men? For nine of the twenty-three free women (39 percent) who married enslaved African men, no information about their race was recorded. They were certainly free women, however, because as far as is known functionaries never omitted the fact that a bride was enslaved, and surely the overwhelming majority, if not all of them, were *castas* and possibly Indians, not Spanish women. Of the remaining fifteen women, five were mulatas, five were Indians, and five were mestizas.[147] Only one enslaved African woman married an enslaved African man: Agustina, a Yoruba (aná), married Antonio García, a mina, in 1733. Both were slaves of the same master and had arrived on the same slave ship twenty-three years before.[148]

Race and ethnicity mattered on Costa Rica's marriage market, but for slave men other factors proved more important. I suggest that the differences in intermarriage ratios between enslaved African, creole, and mulatto men can be attributed largely to the unique position of African men in Costa Rica's cacao economy. Poor and often illegitimate, free women who married slaves generally counted on few resources of their own. Diego García, a *cabo verde* born in West Africa who eventually earned his freedom, married twice while still a slave. When he composed his will in 1743 he stated plainly, "The said two women brought nothing at all to my possession."[149] For free women with few other marriage options, enslaved men living in Matina must have seemed viable marriage partners. They held several advantages over other slave men and even some of the free poor. Although they and all their property technically belonged to their masters, for all intents and purposes African men in Matina lived in their own homes and grew provisions on their own land, just as poor farmers or ranchers did. They exercised much greater independence than slaves or free servants who lived closer to their masters. With cacao money, slave men furnished their modest homes with goods such as iron pots and coveted European cloth, which they bought from the smugglers who frequented the coast. Most important, cacao could provide the means to freedom itself, and ultimately a path to financial and social advancement. Free wives must have seen a promise in their husbands that mitigated the men's slave status.

Although myriad individual circumstances surely influenced the decision to marry, marriage to free women could form part of a long-term strategy by slave men to acquire freedom itself. Sometimes the link was direct. In 1742 the mulatto slave Ramón Poveda proposed marriage to a free mulata, María Nicolasa Geralda. Her father, a captain in the mulatto militia, lent his daughter's suitor two hundred pesos toward the purchase of his freedom.[150] Even with the help of free family members it often took decades to amass the cacao necessary to buy freedom. Soon after his marriage to the free Manuela Gutiérrez in 1721 the cabo verde Diego García leased a cacao hacienda for fifty pesos per year in cacao from one of her relatives, Juan González. García was so successful that he was not only able to meet his obligation to González, but with a surplus of "many zurrones of cacao" lent money to Francisco Morales, the Spanish captain of the Matina Valley.[151] In 1738 he contracted with his master, Sergeant Major José Felipe Bermúdez, for his freedom in return for the care of a cacao grove and was freed some time before his death in 1744.[152] Diego Angulo, born in West Central Africa around 1690, married the free mulata Felipa Chavarría in 1709. The couple eventually had four children, born in freedom.[153] Over a period of years and with the help of his son Juan Manuel, working "on feast days and without missing other days in the service of their masters," Angulo succeeded in amassing 375 pesos' worth of cacao and purchasing his freedom in 1730.[154] As a free man he continued to grow cacao, now on his own account. At the time of his death in 1745 he owned a sizable hacienda in the Barbilla Valley with a small house, 1,265 trees in production, and five mules to transport the crop, as well as another home in Cartago's free colored neighborhood, the Puebla de los Pardos, and two nearby lots. He owed his freedom and advancement largely to the help of his free family.[155]

African men such as Diego García, Diego Angulo, and others all earned the money to buy their freedom by growing cacao. In the valleys of Barbilla and Matina they lived and worked with little supervision from their masters, managing cacao production at every step. More attractive mates than slave men who lived closer to their masters, enslaved men in Matina secured freedom for their children by marrying free women. Growing their own provisions and cacao groves they were able to provide for the subsistence of their families, and because cacao was legal currency, to acquire needed goods, and sometimes even freedom itself.

After winning their freedom several former slaves remained in the Atlantic region and continued to grow cacao on their own account, earning a comfortable living. Many more chose to live in Cartago or, increasingly, as independent small farmers in the valleys to its west. From the mideighteenth century the free population of African descent continued to rise as the enslaved population dropped sharply. Mixed marriages favored the further integration of people of African descent into the broader creole culture. Within a few decades the descendants of Costa Rica's slaves disappeared as an identifiable group, becoming part of the majority mestizo population. Ironically the cacao haciendas offered enslaved men opportunities for freedom and social mobility only because they were located in an unhealthy and dangerous place that Spaniards deemed fit only for blacks.

NOTES

1   In keeping with contemporary local usage, I use "Spaniard" and "Spanish" to refer to people of European ancestry, regardless of place of birth.
2   Pérez Valle, *Nicaragua en los cronistas de Indias*, 67, 68, 436. See also Ibarra Rojas, *Las sociedades cacicales de Costa Rica*, 84; Newson, *Indian Survival*, 52–53.
3   Fernández Guardia, *Cartas de relación de Juan Vázquez de Coronado*, 25, 18.
4   Bozzoli de Wille, "Continuidad del simbolismo del cacao," 229–40.
5   Fernández, *Colección de documentos*, 5:157.
6   P. S. MacLeod, "On the Edge of Empire," 206–7; M. J. MacLeod, *Spanish Central America*, chaps. 4–5; Ferry, "Encomienda, African Slavery," 611.
7   Fernández, *Colección de documentos*, 5:116–30.
8   Ibid., 2:124, 125, 130, 151, 5:126–27, 128; P. S. MacLeod, "On the Edge of Empire," 204.
9   Fernández, *Colección de documentos*, 2:129, 131, 139, 151.
10 Ibid., 5:220, 332.
11 M. J. MacLeod, *Spanish Central America*, 242, 244.
12 Ferry, "Encomienda, African Slavery," 625–27.
13 Testimonio de cómo el puerto de Suerre está navegable mediante lo hecho por el Gobernador don Juan Fernández Salinas y Cerda, Cartago, 30 June 1651, Archivo General de Centro América, Guatemala City (hereafter AGCA), A1 (6), exp. 1177, leg. 83; Fernández, *Colección de documentos*, 5:334, 337–38; P. S. MacLeod, "On the Edge of Empire," 211.
14 Auto de la Real Audiencia, Guatemala, 17 October 1669, Archivo de la Curia Metropolitana de San José, Costa Rica (hereafter ACMSJ), Sección Cofradías, Serie Cartago, libro 5, fols. [34–37]; Thiel, *Datos cronológicos*, 44.
15 Gobernador Andrés Arias Maldonado al Secretario del Consejo de Indias, Cartago, 8 July 1659, Archivo General de Indias, Seville (hereafter AGI), Audiencia de Guatemala (hereafter A.G.) 39, ramo 42, no. 193; Gobernador Andrés Arias Maldonado al Secretario del Consejo de Indias, Cartago, 8 July 1659, AGI, A.G. 39, ramo 42, no. 193; P. S. MacLeod, "On the Edge of Em-

pire," 213. For the identification of the site as Puerto Limón, see Fernández Guardia, *Reseña histórica*, 73.

16   "Fragmentos del juicio de residencia del gobernador don Rodrigo Arias Maldonado.—Año de 1665," *Revista de los Archivos Nacionales* (Costa Rica) 1, nos. 11–12 (1937), 649–50; P. S. MacLeod, "On the Edge of Empire," 214–17; Fernández Guardia, *Reseña histórica*, 74–81.

17   P. S. MacLeod, "On the Edge of Empire," 213.

18   Fernández, *Colección de documentos*, 5:361.

19   Ibid., 8:376–77.

20   Ibid., 8:398.

21   Ibid., 8:399–405.

22   Ibid., 8:428; P. S. MacLeod, "On the Edge of Empire," 229.

23   Padrón y memoria de todos los vecinos y moradores de Cartago, Cartago, 27 March 1691, Archivo Nacional de Costa Rica, San José (hereafter ANCR), Sección Colonial Cartago (hereafter C.) 83, fols. 3–7, 10v.

24   Declaración del Teniente Tomás Macedo Ponce de León, Cartago, October 1691, ANCR, C. 85, fol. [1v]; Declaración del Capitán don Juan Rodríguez Plaza, Cartago, 19 October 1691, ANCR, C. 85, fol. [3v]; Declaración del Capitán don José de Guzmán, Cartago, 19 October 1691, ANCR, C. 85, fol. [5].

25   P. S. MacLeod, "Auge y estancamiento de la producción de cacao," 83–107; P. S. MacLeod, "On the Edge of Empire," chap. 5.

26   Declaración del Teniente Tomás Macedo Ponce de León, Cartago, October 1691, ANCR, C. 85. fol. [1v]; Declaración del Ayudante Francisco Barquero, Cartago, 20 October 1691, ANCR, C. 85. fol. [9]; Fernández, *Colección de documentos*, 8:276, 277.

27   Gobernador interin don Rodrigo Arias Maldonado al rey, 1663, ANCR, Sección Complementario Colonial (hereafter C.C.) 5175, fols. 1–1v, quoting 1v; "Fragmentos del juicio de residencia del gobernador don Rodrigo Arias Maldonado.—Año de 1665," *Revista de los Archivos Nacionales* (Costa Rica) 1, nos. 11–12 (1937), 649–50.

28   Fernández, *Colección de documentos*, 5:379, 407.

29   Ibid., 8:281–83.

30   P. S. MacLeod, "On the Edge of Empire," 231 (quoted); Fernández, *Colección de documentos*, 5:353, 8:376.

31   "Real cédula que aprueba las ordenanzas dictadas en favor de los indios por el Dr. don Benito de Noboa Salgado, oidor de la Audiencia de Guatemala y visitador de la provincia de Costa Rica.—Año de 1676," *Revista de los Archivos Nacionales* (Costa Rica) 1, nos. 3–4 (1937), 147, 148 (quoted).

32   Poder otorgado por los dueños de las haciendas de cacao del valle y costa de Matina, Barbilla, y Reventazón al Capitán Jerónimo Valerino, Cartago, 22 May 1691, ANCR, Protocolos Coloniales de Cartago (hereafter P.C.) 841, fol. 59.

33 Carta de Fray Sebastián de las Alas al Provincial Fray Diego Macotela, San Bartolomé de Ycarurú, 10 December 1689, AGI, A.G. 297, pieza 1, fols. 13v–14, quoting fol. 14. Many of the documents relating to Franciscan missions in Talamanca are printed in Fernández, *Colección de documentos*; I refer to the originals.

34 Carta de Fray Sebastián de las Alas al Provincial Fray Diego Macotela, San Bartolomé de Ycarurú, 10 December 1689, AGI, A.G. 297, pieza 1, fol. 14v.

35 Carta de Fray Sebastián de las Alas al Provincial Fray Diego Macotela, Ujarrás, 18 January 1690, AGI, A.G. 297, pieza 1, fols. 16 (quoted), 16v.

36 Carta de los Muy Reverendos Padres Fray Melchor López y Fray Antonio Margil al Guardián Fray Sebastián de las Alas, Cururú, 25 October 1690, AGI, A.G. 297, pieza 1, fols. 35v, 36.

37 "Carta de Fray Pablo de Rebullida and Fray Francisco de San José.—Año de 1699," in Fernández, *Colección de documentos*, 5:385.

38 Carta de Fray Diego Macotela a la Audiencia de Guatemala, León, Nicaragua, 20 February 1690, AGI, A.G. 297, pieza 1, fol. 9v.

39 Auto del Presidente de la Audiencia de Guatemala don Jacinto de Barrios Leal, Guatemala, 4 April 1690, AGI, A.G. 297, pieza 1, fols. 12v–13v, quoting fol. 13.

40 Petición de Manuel de Farías en nombre del Capitán de Caballos Corazas don Antonio Pacheco, vecino de Cartago, a la Real Audiencia, presentada en Guatemala, 16 January 1691, AGI, A.G. 297, pieza 1, fols. 18v–20, quoting fol. 19.

41 Respuesta del Sr. Fiscal Dr. don Pedro de Barreda, Guatemala, 3 March 1691, AGI, A.G. 297, pieza 1, fols. 20v–21v; Despacho de la Real Audiencia, Guatemala, 9 March 1691, AGI, A.G. 297, pieza 1, fols. 21v–22.

42 Respuesta del fiscal, 12 May 1691, AGI, A.G. 297, pieza 1, fol. 28; Despacho de la Real Audiencia, Guatemala, 22 May 1691, AGI, A.G. 297, pieza 1, fol. 30.

43 Declaración del Teniente Tomás Macedo Ponce de León, Cartago, October 1691, ANCR, c. 85, fols. [2] (quoted), [2v].

44 Fernández, *Colección de documentos*, 5:371, 436.

45 M. J. MacLeod, *Spanish Central America*, 98 (quoted); Ibarra Rojas, *Las manchas del jaguar*, 74.

46 Fernández, *Colección de documentos*, 5:379, 386.

47 "Fragmentos del testimonio de los autos hechos con motivo de la invasión de la provincia de Costa Rica por los piratas Mansfelt y Henry Morgan en 1666," *Revista de los Archivos Nacionales* (Costa Rica) 1, nos. 1–2 (1936), 7, 14, 15–16.

48 Auto del Capitán y Sargento Mayor Alonso de Bonilla, Alcalde Ordinario Más Antiguo de Cartago, 13 March 1670, Sección Mortuales Coloniales de Cartago (hereafter M.C.C.) 921, fol. 1; Declaración de Salvador de Avila, Cartago, 9 May 1670, ANCR, M.C.C. 921, fol. 4.

49 Relación geográfica de Costa Rica por el Gobernador don Juan Gemmir y Lleonart, Cartago, 21 May 1741, AGCA, A1.17, exp. 5016, leg. 210, fols. 252v–253.

50 Visita apostólica de los pueblos de Nicaragua y Costa Rica hecha por el Ilustrísimo Sr. don Pedro Morel de Santa Cruz, 8 September 1752, University of Texas, Benson Latin American Collection, Joaquín García Icazbalceta Collection, vol. 20, no. 7, fol. 57v.

51 Kiple, *The Caribbean Slave*, 14–21. For possible malaria in colonial Costa Rica, see Von Bülow, "Apuntes," 137, 471. David P. Adams provides an interesting thesis in "Malaria, Labor, and Population Distribution in Costa Rica." Unfortunately his essay contains numerous substantial errors on Costa Rican history.

52 Visita apostólica de los pueblos de Nicaragua y Costa Rica hecha por el Ilustrísimo Sr. don Pedro Morel de Santa Cruz, 8 September 1752, University of Texas, Benson Latin American Collection, Joaquín García Icazbalceta Collection, vol. 20, no. 7, fol. 58.

53 Petición del Capitán Felipe de Meza, presentada en Cartago, 18 October 1720, ANCR, C. 275, fol. 9; Auto de sentencia, Cartago, 22 November 1720, ANCR, C. 275, fol. 15.

54 Reconocimiento y avalúo de tres negros, Cartago, 7 November 1719, ANCR, Sección Colonial Guatemala (hereafter G) 187, fol. 14; Tasación de Francisco Mina, Cartago, 7 June 1720, ANCR, C. 258, fol. 13v.

55 Ibarra Rojas, *Sociedades cacicales*, 89; P. Palmer, "*What Happen*," 54.

56 Petición del Capitán don Bernardo Marín, Cartago, 17 August 1719, AGI, Escribanía 353B, fol. 634v (quoted); Razón de dos esclavos dada por el Capitán Juan Sancho de Castañeda, Cartago, 13 November 1719, ANCR, C. 231, fol. 61; Fe de muerte de un negrito bozal, Cartago, 5 April 1702, ANCR, C. 112, fol. 8v; Declaración del Capitán Vicente Andrés Polo, Cartago, 11 October 1703, AGI, A.G. 359, pieza 3, fol. 14v.

57 "Fragmentos del testimonio de los autos hechos con motivo de la invasión de la provincia de Costa Rica por los piratas Mansfelt y Henry Morgan en 1666," *Revista de los Archivos Nacionales* (Costa Rica) 1, nos. 1–2 (1936), 5–33; Declaración del Capitán Lucas Cervantes, Cartago, 22 October 1691, ANCR, C. 85, fol. [14v].

58 Romero Vargas, *Las sociedades*, 80.

59 Declaración del Capitán don José Pérez de Muro, Cartago, 12 November 1705, AGI, Escribanía 351B, pieza 1, fol. 165v.

60 Declaración de Diego Sánchez, pardo libre, Cartago, 8 May 1724, ANCR, C. 303, fols. 68v–69v; Memoria de los prisioneros libres y esclavos, Matina, 1 May 1724, ANCR, C. 303, fols. 66–66v.

61 Declaración de Diego Sánchez, pardo libre, Cartago, 8 May 1724, ANCR, C. 303, fols. 68v–69.

62 Declaración del Capitán Blas González Coronel, Cartago, 15 October 1703, AGI, A.G. 359, pieza 3, fol. 17v.

63 Declaración del Capitán Francisco Pérez del Cote, Cartago, 17 October 1703, AGI, A.G. 359, pieza 3, fol. 28.

64 Petición de Nicolás Granajo en nombre del Capitán don Antonio Mora Díaz de Silva, presentada en Guatemala, 26 November 1703, AGCA, A1.24 (6), exp. 10217, leg. 1573, fol. [498].

65 Petición del Capitán don José de Mier Cevallos, presentada en Cartago, 11 July 1720, ANCR, C. 266, fol. 31v.

66 Auto del Gobernador don Diego de la Haya Fernández, Pacaca, 20 February 1720, AGCA, A2 (6), exp. 3, leg. 1, fol. 25.

67 Junta de Guerra, Cartago, 10 February 1724, AGI, A.G. 455, fol. 534.

68 Mortual del Sargento Mayor José de la Haya y Bolívar, Esparza, 26 October 1723, ANCR, M.C.C. 838, fol. 38v (five mules); Capital de bienes de doña Agueda Pérez del Muro, Cartago, 16 April 1722, ANCR, P.C. 895, fol. 48v (gold chain); Mortual del Sargento Mayor Juan Francisco de Ibarra y Calvo, Cartago, 14 May 1737, ANCR, M.C.C. 850, fol. 26 (house in Matina); Venta de tierra, Barva, 18 June 1723, ANCR, Protocolos Coloniales de San José 412, fols. 21v–23v (caballería of land in Tibás).

69 "Informe de don Diego sobre su gobierno," in Chacón de Umaña, Don Diego de la Haya Fernández, 229; Petición de doña Gertrudis de Hinojosa, presentada en Cartago, 31 October 1735, ANCR, C.C. 4303. fol. [4]; Viaje del gobernador Carrandi Menán al valle de Matina. Año 1738 (San José: Imprenta Nacional, 1850), 15.

70 Petición del Capitán Juan José de Cuende, Procurador Síndico de Cartago, presentada en Cartago, 14 March 1736, ANCR, Municipal 772, fol. 94v.

71 P. S. MacLeod, "On the Edge of Empire," 206, 208; Aguilar Bulgarelli and Alfaro, La esclavitud negra, 177; Fonseca, Costa Rica colonial, 228–30.

72 Petición de descargos del Capitán Luis Gutiérrez, Cartago, 20 August 1719, AGI, Escribanía 353B, fol. 628.

73 Auto del gobernador, Cartago, 1 July 1704, ANCR, C. 127, fols. 1–1v.

74 Auto de buen gobierno, Matina, 8 August 1716, ANCR, C. 205, fols. 1–1v.

75 Petición del Capitán don Pedro de Moya, presentada en Cartago, 21 April 1719, ANCR, C. 269, fol. 2.

76 Bando de buen gobierno, Cartago, 26 March 1737, ANCR, C. 389, fols. 5v–6.

77 Gudmundson, "Mecanismos de movilidad social para la población de procedencia africana en Costa Rica colonial," in Estratificación, 23.

78 Declaración de Miguel Solano, Cartago, 27 August 1733, ANCR, C.C. 4292, fol. 20 (quoted); Ferry, "Encomienda, African Slavery," 631.

79 Venta de esclavo, Cartago, 25 October 1706, ANCR, P.C. 862, fols. 73v–75v.

80 Petición del negro esclavo Juan Román al Teniente de Gobernador don José Mier de Cevallos, presentada en Cartago, 27 July 1733, ANCR, C.C. 4292, fol. 1v.

81   Cáceres, *Negros, mulatos*, 40.

82   Number of sales in the 1670s, 25; in the 1680s, 36; in the 1690s, 73; in the 1700s, 108. Calculations based on ANCR, P.C. 815 (1654–55, 1664–67) through P.C. 853 (1697, 1699, 1700, 1701); *Indice de los protocolos de Cartago*, 6 vols. (San José: Tipografía Nacional, 1909–30), vols. 1–3.

83   Rosés Alvarado, "El ciclo del cacao," 235.

84   "Few cacaoteros used slaves on their haciendas, given their expense and scarcity in this peripheral society." P. S. MacLeod, "On the Edge of Empire," 255.

85   "Real cédula que aprueba las ordenanzas dictadas en favor de los indios por el Dr. don Benito de Noboa Salgado, oidor de la Audiencia de Guatemala y visitador de la provincia de Costa Rica.—Año de 1676," *Revista de los Archivos Nacionales* (Costa Rica) 1, nos. 3–4 (1937), 147, 148; Carta de Fray Sebastián de las Alas al Provincial Fray Diego Macotela, San Bartolomé de Ycarurú, 10 December 1689, AGI, A.G. 297, pieza 1, fols. 13v–14.

86   Petición de Manuel de Farinas, apoderado de don Antonio Salmón Pachecho, presentada en Guatemala, 16 January 1691, AGI, A.G. 297, pieza 1, fol. 19v.

87   Padrón y memoria de todos los vecinos y moradores de Cartago, Cartago, 27 March 1691, ANCR, C. 83, fols. 4v, 3–7; Piñero, "Accounting Practices," 41 (quoted).

88   Venta de esclavos, Cartago, 21 June 1718, ANCR, P.C. 885, fols. 109–113v, quoting fol. 110v.

89   Petición de Diego de Angulo, negro esclavo, presentado en Cartago, 12 September 1729, ANCR, C.C. 4259, fol. [2].

90   Auto del Gobernador don Diego de la Haya Fernández, Esparza, 28 April 1720, AGCA, A2 (6), exp. 3, leg. 1, fol. 39v.

91   Carta de libertad, Cartago, 2 March 1733, ANCR, P.C. 910, fol. 8.

92   Declaración de Miguel Solano, Cartago, 27 August 1733, ANCR, C.C. 4292, fols. 20 (quoted), 21v. See also Declaración de Juan de Salazar, Cartago, 7 May 1715, ANCR, C.C. 4036, fol. 4v.

93   Hawthorne, "Nourishing a Stateless Society," 1–24; Duncan, *The Atlantic Islands*, 167, 168; Carney, "Landscapes of Technology Transfer," 5–35; Carney, *Black Rice*; Wood, *Black Majority*, 58–62; Littlefield, *Rice and Slaves*; Joyner, *Down by the Riverside*, 13–14.

94   Petición del Sarg. Cristóbal de Chavarría, presentada en Cartago, 1 August 1719, ANCR, C.C. 4075, fol. 10v; Memoria de los gastos presentada por el Alférez Juan Bautista Retana, presentada en Cartago, 28 June 1710, ANCR, C. 187, fol. 205.

95   Don Diego de Barros y Carbajal al Ayudante Matías Masís, Cartago, 16 July 1721, ANCR, M.C.C. 941, fol. 16.

96   For a reference to turtling during the colonial period, see Declaración del Capitán Juan Cayetano Jiménez, Cartago, 18 March 1717, ANCR, C. 211, fol. 13v.

97 Declaración del Capitán de Caballos don Antonio de la Vega Cabral, Cartago, 28 June 1703, AGI, A.G. 359, pieza 1, fol. 10v.

98 Inventario de las haciendas de cacao de doña Agueda Pérez de Muro, Matina, 20 April 1722, ANCR, P.C. 895. fols. 94, 94v.

99 Inventario de las haciendas de cacao de doña Agueda Pérez de Muro, Barbilla, 22 April 1722, ANCR, P.C. 895, fol. 95v.

100 Avalúo de las haciendas de cacao de doña Agueda Pérez de Muro, Cartago, 12 May 1722, ANCR, P.C. 895, fol. 100v; Razón dada por el negro Nicolás, esclavo de doña Agueda Pérez de Muro, Cartago, 4 May 1722, ANCR, P.C. 895, fol. 99.

101 Inventario de las haciendas de cacao de doña Agueda Pérez de Muro, Matina, 23 April 1723, ANCR, P.C. 895, fols. 95v–96; Petición del Capitán don Francisco Garrido, presentada en Cartago, 2 May 1722, ANCR, P.C. 895, fol. 97v.

102 Razón dada por el negro Nicolás, esclavo de doña Agueda Pérez de Muro, Cartago, 4 May 1722, ANCR, P.C. 895, fols. 99, 99v.

103 Razón dada por el negro Nicolás, esclavo de doña Agueda Pérez de Muro, Cartago, 4 May 1722, ANCR, P.C. 895, fols. 99, 99v.

104 Rosés Alvarado, "El ciclo del cacao," 260–61; Aguilar Bulgarelli and Alfaro, *La esclavitud negra*, 176–77.

105 For a reference to replanting, see Declaración de José Guerrero, pardo libre, Cartago, 4 September 1733, ANCR, C.C. 4292, fol. 29.

106 Thus cacao groves were referred to as "plantained" (*plataneadas*). See Arrendamiento de cacaotal, Cartago, 15 June 1715, ANCR, P.C. 877, fol. 103; 9 May 1731, ANCR, P.C. 905, fol. 1; 31 October 1730, ANCR, P.C. 905, fol. 17v.

107 Declaración del Capitán Rafael Fajardo, Cartago, 10 October 1703, AGI, A.G. 359, pieza 3, fol. 9; Testimonio de arrendamiento de cacaotal, Cartago, 17 April 1724, ANCR, M.C.C. 700, fol. 12; Carta de libertad, Cartago, 3 October 1733, ANCR, P.C. 910, fol. 72.

108 See Prisión y embargo de bienes del Capitán Felipe de Meza, Matina, 15 May 1721, ANCR, C. 211, fol. 135; Testamento del Teniente don Pedro Jiménez de Mondragón, Cartago, 30 July 1732, ANCR, P.C. 908, fol. 38v; Inventario de los bienes del Sarg. Mr. don Juan Francisco de Ibarra, Matina, 23 March 1737, ANCR, M.C.C. 850, fol. 18; Inventario de los bienes de Agustín de la Riva, mulato libre, Matina, 4 March 1740, ANCR, M.C.C. 1165, fol. 4v; Inventario de los bienes de Francisco Guerrero, Matina, 30 December 1743, ANCR, M.C.C. 795, fol. 6v.

109 Carta de libertad, Barva, 19 November 1693, ANCR, P.C. 844, fol. 2.

110 Declaración de Juan Núñez, Cartago, 2 May 1724, ANCR, C. 304, fol. 3v.

111 Auto de buen gobierno, Cartago, 14 July 1708, ANCR, C. 166, fol. 5. For references to Spanish *mandadores*, see Declaración del Alférez Jacinto de Rivera, Cartago, 31 May 1720, ANCR, C. 237, fol. 14v; Declaración de Pedro Mina,

negro esclavo del Sargento Mayor don Juan Francisco de Ibarra y Calvo, Cartago, 6 June 1720, ANCR, C. 237, fol. 14v.

112 Declaración de José Congo, mandador de haciendas, Matina, 23 April 1722, ANCR, P.C. 895, fol. 95v; *Indice de los protocolos de Cartago*, 2:231–232; Declaración de Gregorio Caamaño, negro esclavo y mandador de haciendas, 14 August 1717, ANCR, C.C. 4111, fol. 6; Declaración de Antonio de la Riva, negro de casta mina y mandador de haciendas, 22 March 1737, ANCR, M.C.C. 850, fol. 17; Sargento Mayor don Juan Francisco de Ibarra y Calvo hace inventario de los bienes que aportó a su matrimonio con doña Catalina González del Camino, Cartago, 21 June 1718, ANCR, P.C. 886, fol. 12v.

113 Declaración de Juan Damián, negro esclavo y ladino de doña Agueda Pérez de Muro, Cartago, 14 August 1717, ANCR, C.C. 4111, fol. 3v; Confesión de Antonio Mina, negro esclavo del Capitán Manuel García de Argueta, Cartago, 2 December 1721, ANCR, C.C. 5805, fol. 2.

114 Petición de Juan Masís, presentada en Cartago, 14 August 1719, ANCR, C.C. 4075, fol. 18v; Venta de esclavo, Cartago, 27 March 1722, ANCR, P.C. 895, fols. 32v–35.

115 Carta del negro esclavo José de Moya a su amo el Capitán don Pedro de Moya, Matina, 16 August 1720, ANCR, C. 237, fols. 25–25v.

116 Mortual del Sarg. Mr. don Juan Francisco de Ibarra y Calvo, Cartago, 15 March 1737, ANCR, M.C.C. 850, fol. 11v.

117 Montoya, "Milicias negras y mulatas," 93–104; Lokken, "Undoing Racial Hierarchy," 25–36; Lokken, "Useful Enemies,"; Cáceres, *Negros, mulatos*, 98–105.

118 Revista general de las milicias, Matina, 23 January 1719, ANCR, C.C. 3797, fols. 24v–27v.

119 Querella por el Capitán Juan de Bonilla, presentada en Cartago, 17 July 1686, ANCR, C.C. 6403, fol. 1.

120 Querella del Capitán Juan de Bonilla, presentada en Cartago, 17 July 1696, ANCR, C.C. 6403, fols. 1, 1v; Declaración de Manuel de Mora, Cartago, 30 August 1696, ANCR, C.C. 6403, fol. 6.

121 Declaración de Francisco de Flores, Cartago, 30 August 1696, ANCR, C.C. 6403, fol. 5v.

122 Querella del Capitán Juan de Bonilla, presentada en Cartago, 17 July 1696, ANCR, C.C. 6403, fol. 1v (quoted); Declaración de Manuel de Mora, Cartago, 30 August 1696, ANCR, C.C. 6403, fol. 6.

123 Troy S. Floyd claimed that the Dutch of St. Eustasius and Curaçao were "eager to buy cacao" from Matina, but provided no sources for his assertion (*The Anglo-Spanish Struggle for Mosquitia*, 59).

124 Auto del Gobernador don Diego de la Haya Fernández, Cartago, 2 November 1722, ANCR, C. 283, fol. 9v; Declaración de Nicolás, negro de casta mina, Cartago, 25 April 1723, ANCR, C. 283, fol. 11.

125 Declaración del Ayudante Lázaro de Robles, mulato, Cartago, 6 October 1703, AGI, A.G. 359, pieza 1, fol. 43.

126 Testamento del Capitán Francisco de Cabrera, 5 February 1696, ANCR, P.C. 848, fol. 5v; Petición de Juan Masís, presentada en Cartago, 14 August 1719, ANCR, C.C. 4075, fol. 18v.

127 See Cuaderno de registro de las recuas procedentes de Matina que llegan a Cartago, ANCR, C. 285 (1724).

128 Declaración de Juan Damián, negro esclavo, Cartago, 14 August 1717, ANCR, C.C. 4111, fols. 3–5; Declaración de Gregorio Caamaño, negro esclavo, Cartago, 14 August 1717, ANCR, C.C. 4111, fols. 5–8; Confesión de Juan Damián, esclavo que fue de doña Agueda Pérez de Muro, Cartago, 11 May 1719, ANCR, G. 181, fol. 2v.

129 Auto de culpa y cargo contra Juan Damián, esclavo que fue de doña Agueda Pérez de Muro, Cartago, 7 May 1719, ANCR, G. 181, fol. 1.

130 Descargos dados por el Capitán José Fernández de Castellanos en nombre del esclavo Juan Damián, presentada en Cartago 8 June 1719, ANCR, G. 181, fols. 5–6, quoting fol. 5; Petición del defensor presentada en Cartago 12 July 1719, ANCR, G. 191, fol. 9.

131 Confesión de Antonio García, esclavo del Capitán Manuel de García Argueta, Cartago, 2 December 1721, ANCR, C.C. 5805, fol. 2v.

132 Auto de sentencia, Cartago, 21 June 1721, ANCR, C.C. 5805, fol. 7.

133 "Se dispone que el cacao corra en la provincia de Costa Rica para la compra de víveres por no haber en ella moneda de plata. Año de 1709," *Revista de los Archivos Nacionales* (Costa Rica) 1, nos. 9–10 (1937), 600–603.

134 Carta de libertad, Barva, 19 November 1693, ANCR, P.C. 844, fol. 2; Venta de esclavo, Cartago, 7 May 1726, ANCR, P.C. 899, fol. 45v.

135 Declaración de Antonio Masís, negro libre, Cartago, 26 August 1733, ANCR, C.C. 4292, fol. 16.

136 Auto del Gobernador don Diego de la Haya Fernández, Cartago, 8 January 1720, ANCR, C.C. 160, fols. 1–1v.

137 Petición del Sargento Mayor don Antonio de Utrera, vecino y Procurador General de Cartago, presentada en Cartago, 25 April 1727, ANCR, C. 323, fols. 1–1v.

138 Confesión de Juan Damián, esclavo que fue de doña Agueda Pérez de Muro, Cartago, 11 May 1719, ANCR, G. 181, fols. 2v, 3 (quoted); Declaración de Pablo José de Alvarado, indio ladino, 18 October 1703, AGI, A.G. 359, pieza 1, fols. 65v, 67v.

139 Declaración de Juan Damián, negro esclavo, Cartago, 14 August 1717, ANCR, C.C. 4111, fols. 3–5; Declaración de Gregorio Caamaño, negro esclavo, Cartago, 14 August 1717, ANCR, C.C. 4111, fols. 5–8; Confesión de Juan Damián, esclavo que fue de doña Agueda Pérez de Muro, Cartago, 11 May 1719, ANCR, G. 181, fol. 2v.

140 Confesión de Antonio García, esclavo del Capitán Manuel de García Argueta, Cartago, 2 December 1721, ANCR, C.C. 5805, fol. 2v.

141 Testamento de Isidro de Acosta, Cartago, 26 June (July?) 1717, ANCR, P.C. 882, fol. 82v.

142 ACMSJ, Libros de Bautizos de Cartago, nos. 1–6 (1594–1738), Family History Library, Salt Lake City, Utah (hereafter FHL), VAULT INTL film 1219701, items 1–5, VAULT INTL film 1219702, item 1.

143 Lutz, *Santiago de Guatemala*, 177–78; Lokken, "Marriage as Slave Emancipation," 175–200.

144 ACMSJ, Libros de Matrimonios de Cartago, nos. 1–6, FHL, VAULT INTL film 1219727, items 6–10.

145 Love, "Marriage Patterns," 87–89; Cope, *Limits of Racial Domination*, 81–82, table 4.10; Lutz, *Santiago de Guatemala*, 88–89, 177–78.

146 ACMSJ, Libros de Matrimonios de Cartago nos. 1–6, FHL, VAULT INTL film 1219727, items 6–10.

147 ACMSJ, Libros de Matrimonios de Cartago nos. 1–6, FHL, VAULT INTL film 1219727, items 6–10.

148 Partida de matrimonio, Cartago, 3 May 1733, ACMSJ, Libros de Matrimonios de no. 3, FHL, VAULT INTL film 1219727, item 8.

149 Testamento de Diego García, negro libre, 30 December 1743, ANCR, P.C. 931, fol. 10.

150 Declaración del Capitán José Nicolás de Haya, mulato libre, Cartago, 22 April 1744, ANCR, C.C. 6219, fols. 2–2v; Testamento del Capitán José Nicolás de la Haya, Cartago, 2 May 1747, ANCR, M.C.C. 841, fol. 2v.

151 Declaración de Tomás Rivera, mulato libre, 24 November 1724, ANCR, C.C. 4148, fol. 4v.

152 Testamento del Sarg. Mr. José Felipe Bermúdez, Cartago, 17 March 1738, ANCR, P.C. 919, fol. 32; Fe de muerte de Diego García, negro libre, Cartago, 5 January 1744, ANCR, P.C. 931, fol. 6.

153 Auto, Puebla de los Angeles, 8 February 1746, ANCR, M.C.C. 462, fol. 4v.

154 Declaración de Antonio Masís, negro libre, Cartago, 26 August 1733, ANCR, C.C. 4292, fol. 16; Carta del Teniente don Antonio de Angulo, Cartago, 9 September 1729, ANCR, C.C. 4259. fol. [1]; Diligencia de haber entregado los 325 pesos de cacao y recibo de ellos, Cartago, 29 September 1729, ANCR, C.C. 4259, fols. [9v–10]; Carta de libertad, Cartago, 20 February 1730, ANCR, P.C. 903, fols. 1v–4.

155 Inventario de los bienes de Diego Angulo, negro libre, Valle de Barbilla, 10 November 1745, ANCR, M.C.C. 462, fols. 1–2; Memoria de los bienes de Diego Angulo, presentada en Cartago, 7 February 1746, ANCR, M.C.C. 462, fol. 3v.

RACE AND PLACE IN

COLONIAL MOSQUITIA, 1600–1787

Karl H. Offen

In the early seventeenth century English settlers in the West Indies fashioned notions of race to explain difference, justify slavery, and advance white privilege. Older European categories that classified people as Christian or heathen gave way to associations of culture and physical features, "heritable difference that was hierarchically meaningful." This change was tied to the rise of plantation agriculture. As the profitability of the plantation system increased during the mid-seventeenth century, African slaves replaced indentured laborers. Miscegenation rates were high, as was the proclivity to create categories of caste such as white, negro, Indian, mulatto, mustee, etc. These categories provided the foundation upon which an ideology of race was produced in the British West Indies. While British ideas of race emerged from a shared Anglo-experience, their elaboration differed from place to place.[1]

At the intersection of British and Spanish colonial empires in eastern Central America and the western Caribbean, the Mosquitia provides a unique place to examine the relationship between ideas of race and their social and discursive manifestations among different peoples. Though the region never developed a viable plantation economy based on chattel slavery, by the second half of the eighteenth century some six hundred free settlers, half of whom were of mixed race, and their twenty-two hundred African and Amerindian slaves procured natural resources, raised cattle, traded with adjacent Spaniards, and grew crops at select points between Black River and Punta Gorda in what is today Honduras and Nicaragua, respectively. Although slaves of African descent predominated, the British also held indigenous and mixed-race slaves. Given the polyglot nature of Mosquitia society, race was initially a less important concept than class and legal status. With the creation of a British superintendency for the Mosquito Shore in 1748, however, ideas of race and their material and social manifestations became more important in the organization of people's daily lives. British settlement in Mosquitia came to an abrupt, if temporary, end in 1787, after the Convention of London upheld the Spanish interpretation of the Treaty of Versailles of 1783.[2]

Early notions of race in Mosquitia were complicated by the existence of the Mosquito Kingdom, an incipient African Amerindian polity that overlapped in space but was independent from the British superintendency. Consisting of four semi-autonomous districts, the kingdom was divided such that by the second half of the eighteenth century the two northern districts became the dominion of the mixed-race and so-called Sambo Mosquito, while the two southern districts fell under the jurisdiction of the native or Tawira Mosquito. Though the British sought to effect a chain of command with a lone Mosquito king at the top, a Mosquito ethnic and political geography necessitated that they bestow multiple titled commissions to other Mosquito leaders.[3] While new racial categories and ideologies helped divide the Mosquito people, both the Sambo and Tawira often referred to themselves as "a nation of Mosquitomen." The tenacity of Mosquito assertions of independence indicate that new notions of territorial nationhood became the foundation of a shared Mosquito identity during the eighteenth century. Though the Mosquito people were of African Amerindian or Amerindian descent, their independence and regional power distinguished them from other Indians or Afro-Amerindians. British reliance on the Mosquito for protection from the Spaniards and their own slaves further complicated the social and discursive manifestations of racial difference and served to weaken the enactment of racial ideologies and legal systems that emerged elsewhere in the British West Indies.

Emerging notions of race and racial difference also reflect geographic differences within the Mosquitia itself. The north, or Honduran, coast was distinct from the south, or windward, coast of what is today Nicaragua. These differences shaped and reflected economic opportunities, diverse slave populations, and dissimilar political proclivities among the Sambo and Tawira Mosquito. As such, this essay shares many findings with those of Rina Cáceres and Russell Lohse in this volume, particularly the way that generalized racial classifications and elite ideologies fail to explain how ideas of race were manifest in specific places. This essay also provides an extended Anglo and internally nuanced preamble to the Hispanocentric and externally imposed racialization of the Mosquitia that is the subject of Juliet Hooker's chapter.

The Mosquitia and related terms, such as *costa de mosquitos* and Mosquito Shore, came to replace earlier colonial terms such as Taguzgalpa through the spatial practices of the Mosquito people.[4] Constituted in this way, the Mosquitia became a large, albeit continually negotiated, triangular territory whose sides ran east from Cape Cameron to Cape Gracias a Dios and then south to Punta Gorda. Its figurative hypotenuse was a porous space inhabited by *indios caribes* and *jicaques*, or non-Christian Indians, whom the Spaniards, British, and Mosquito sought to influence (Offen Map 1). This frontier space included the Rama south of Bluefields, the Pech south and southeast of Trujillo, the Ulwa west and north of Bluefields, and the Mayangna peoples denoted by groups such as the Twahka and Panamahka, who lived throughout what is today northeastern Nicaragua and Honduras.[5] The Mosquitia is constituted by long meandering rivers, tropical rain forests, pine savannas, lagoons, tidal estuaries, and coastal mangrove and palm forests. Offshore a shallow marine shelf extends seaward for several miles, especially near Cape Gracias, and contains numerous shoals and keys. This important biophysical geography has significantly influenced regional history by constraining and enabling specific types of economic activities that have, in turn, affected social elaborations of racial difference.

Despite several descriptions of eastern Central America in the early seventeenth century, the ethnic label "Mosquito" does not appear in writing until William Dampier wrote about his visit in 1679 to the "Country of the Moskitos." Dampier stated that the Moskito were "but a small Nation or Family, and not 100 Men of them in Number, inhabiting on the Main on the North-side, near Cape Gratia Dios." Given Dampier's population estimate, he was referring only to the emerging group of Afro-Amerindians who spoke the Mosquito language.[6] In contrast, place names synonymous with the term Mosquito appear more than a century earlier. Spanish maps from 1536, 1562, and 1587 and two Dutch maps from 1595 and 1613 show

MAP 1 Colonial Mosquitia. Map by Donald Sluter.

a "R: de moschitos," a "Rio Mosquitos," a "R: de moscomitos," a "R. de Mesquitos," and a "rio de mosquitos," respectively.[7] English mariners of the 1630s through the 1660s referred to "ye Musquitos, which are Certaine little Islands, 14 leagues from ye Cape," while simultaneously referring to the "Indians of the Cape."[8] Convention posits naming from toponym to ethnic group, and this became cemented in regional historiography after a Spaniard wrote, "[The] Zambos have their origin from some Negros that shipwrecked many years ago at a [group] of Islands called Mosquitos that are immediately off the north coast. They mixed with the heathen Indians that rescued them."[9] While this discussion is academic, it is important to establish that Mosquito-speaking Amerindians inhabited the Cape Gracias region and had contact with Europeans before some of them incorporated African peoples.

We do not know when people of African ancestry first arrived in Mosquitia, but we know the Mosquito had met African-descended peoples by the end of the sixteenth century and had assimilated some by the mid-seventeenth century. In 1689 the Frenchman de Lussan noted, "[Cape Gracias] has been inhabited for a long time by mulattoes and negroes, both men and women . . . ever since a Spanish ship, out-bound for Guinea with a load of padres, was lost by coming too close in shore to land." In 1699 an English-man known only as M. W. wrote, "The Mosqueto-men, about 60 years past, murder'd above 50 Spaniards, amongst whom were several friars who liv'd amongst them, some near *Cape Grace a Dios.*" He described the Mosquito as having "a dark yellow or brown complexion, having long black hair, excepting the Mullattoes, whose black hair curls; and their bodies are nearer to the colour of negroes, from whose mixture with the Indians they first sprung, occassion'd 50 years since by a Guiney mer-chant ship which was driven to leeward." That a Guinea ship with Span-iards aboard sank near Cape Gracias in the mid-seventeenth century is confirmed by a Spanish report that the "zambos" originated in 1650 with the capsizing of a ship belonging to the Portuguese Lorenzo Gramalxo, "según su tradición."[10]

Africans also reached the Mosquitia in 1641, the same year the Span-iards took nearby Providence Island from the English. After privateers discovered Providence (Catalina) and Henrietta (San Andrés) Islands, English Puritans formed a colony on Providence Island in 1629. The colony is noteworthy because settlers quickly enslaved Africans at a rate unparalleled in any English colony at the time. The Mosquito were well connected with island society and thus by the early seventeenth century were exposed to African slavery, plantation agriculture, white indentured servitude, racial hierarchies, British decorum, and privateering. Most of the African slaves at Providence came from Dutch privateers, while at least one Dutchman was paid by the Providence Company "for buying Negroes at ye Cape."[11] English plans to settle the Mosquitia were cut short after a Spanish fleet removed settlers from Providence in 1641. The Span-ish captured 350 Englishmen and 381 African slaves, fewer than they ex-pected, while some investor reports claimed that 600 slaves had been lost.

Some slaves likely escaped to the Mosquitia, northwest of Cape Gracias, where they mixed with some Mosquito.[12]

When Esquemelin visited the Mosquitia in 1671, he noted, "[The Indians of Cape Gracias] have among them some few negroes, who serve them in the quality of slaves. These happened to arrive there, swimming, after shipwreck made upon that coast." He added, "[The] negroes that are upon this island live here in all respects according to the customs of their own country."[13] We can assume, however, that if some Africans were held captive among the Mosquito in the seventeenth century, their offspring were not. The rise of mixed African Amerindian Mosquito near the Río Kruta inspired some native Mosquito to move west and south. Of his experiences in 1711, the marooned Englishman Nathaniel Uring wrote, "Some of [the native Mosquito people] have separated from the main Body . . . and gave this Reason for it":

> They said, that some People who were not of the ancient Inhabitants, but new Upstarts, were got into the Government, and behaved themselves with so much Pride and Insolence that they could not bear it, and therefore had separated from the main Body. They related the Matter thus: A Ship with Negroes by Accident was cast away on the Coast, and those who escaped drowning mixed among the Native Muscheto People, who intermarried with them, and begot a Race of Mulattoes, which were the People that Society could not brook should bear any kind of Command amongst them.

Likewise de Lussan implied that the "original inhabitants of Moustique" moved south "ten or twelve leagues to windward of Cape Gracias a Dios" to Sandy Bay for similar reasons. He also noted that the primary residents of the immediate Cape Gracias area were "mulattoes." In short, differences developed between two Mosquito groups, and the catalyst was the rise of Afro-Amerindian leadership.[14]

A distinctive Mosquito settlement geography underscores contemporaneous associations of race and place. By 1700 some seven hundred predominantly Sambo Mosquito lived between the Río Kruta and Brus Lagoon along the north coast of Honduras. By the 1720s the north coast region was ruled by a Captain Hobby, a mulatto, "his Mother being a Negroe." Sambo Mosquito men also headed the Mosquito communities of the lower Río Wangki (Coco) by 1700 and Sandy Bay by 1730.[15] In contrast, no Sambo Mosquito communities existed south of Cape Gracias a Dios before 1712. Indeed M. W. describes numerous Mosquito "Indian" families at Sandy Bay and on the savannas to the south, while Uring considered Sandy Bay "the greatest body of Muscheto Indians."[16] This demography changes quickly after a small pox epidemic in 1727, because Sandy Bay is henceforth deemed the home of the now majority mulatto Mosquito and the first mulatto Mosquito king, Peter. This important epidemic was widespread, killing the last Tawira Mosquito king, Jeremy, and the Tawira governor, John Hannibal. The succession of Peter, a mulatto, to the position of king in 1729 created what he called "social unrest" among his people. As a result many Tawira Mosquito moved south from Sandy Bay and Dakura to the Río Grande and Pearl Lagoon for the first time.[17]

This distinct Mosquito geography foretells an evolution in naming conventions. M. W. often distinguished between Mosquito "mulattoes" and "Indians" in 1699, but he was the first to also use the label "Mosquetomen" to refer to both groups.[18] It is not until the 1740s that the term Sambo replaces mulatto in English-language texts:

> The Mosquito Shore extends from Cape Gracias a Dios to Great River 42 leagues southward, 12 of which viz. from the Cape to Sandy Bay, are inhabited by the Samboes, the other 30 by the native Indians; the said Shore extends likewise from the Cape to Black River 54 leagues, all which belongs to the Samboes, except [an] honors Guard (as they are called) of Indians at Brewers Lagoon and another at Black River. . . . The Samboes are about 500 fighting men, the native [Mosquito] Indians in all about 350. At the back of them both are several other small nations, some in commerce with the Mosquitomen, some with the Spaniards, others divided between them, both sides contending for their alliances. The Samboes are a race sprung from two ship loads of Negroes cast away about 90 years ago at the Cape and intermarry'd with the Indians, their friendship to the English is of about 70 years standing; their fidelity to us is reckoned to exceed that of the Natives, as is their dexterity when rous'd.[19]

This important narrative by Robert Hodgson, whose father was the first British superintendent of the Mosquito Shore, establishes four general characteristics of British writings throughout the second half of the eighteenth century. First, there are two groups of Mosquito people, the Sambos and the natives (Tawira). Second, the two groups inhabited distinct regions, the natives between Rio Grande and Sandy Bay, and the Sambos from Sandy Bay to Black River. Third, the descriptor "Mosquitomen" could be used when a distinction was not necessary. And fourth, Sambo fidelity to the British "[was] reckoned to exceed that of the Natives."

The geographically divided nature of Mosquito leadership required British officials to recognize other leaders by the 1720s. As Hodgson put it:

> Though [the Mosquito] are to all intents and purposes one people, yet they are not so properly a single state, as three united, each of which is nearly independent of the others. . . . [The southernmost group] inhabit from the southern extremity till about Bragmans, and are mostly the original Indians; their head man they call *governor*. The next extend to about Little Black River [Rio Kruta], and are mostly Samboes; their chief is called *king*. The last is to the westward, and consists of Indians and Samboes mixed; their head man is called *general*.[20]

Superintendent Richard Jones (1759–62) put it this way: "The Ancient Mosquito Indians of pure unmixed Blood possess the Coast and Country aback from the Bluefields to Sandy Bay; from thence as far as Plantain River, Sandy Bay included, is possessed by a race of Sambos." A fourth precinct centered around the Rio Grande, at what is today Sandy Bay Sirpi; headed by a Tawira admiral, it achieved equal stature with the other districts after the 1740s. A small cluster of Sambo villages in southern Pearl Lagoon remained the only Sambo presence south of Sandy Bay during the eighteenth century.[21]

Embryonic ideas of racial difference underscored ongoing Sambo-Tawira tensions. In 1740, during the Anglo-Spanish War of Jenkins Ear, Captain Robert Hodgson (the elder) came to the Mosquitia to seek Mosquito support. After a lengthy ceremony "under the British Standard" Hodgson got the Sambo and Tawira leaders, King Edward and Governor John Briton, to sign a declaration acknowledging themselves subjects of Great Britain: the declaration was signed "English, Mosquito Men, and all the Mosquito Nation both Samboes and Indians."[22] Hodgson then led some 230 Sambo and Tawira Mosquito on a military expedition against several Spanish strongholds stretching from Nicaragua to Panama. After a successful attack at the Matina Valley, Hodgson wrote that the Tawira "Governour released all the Indians & Mustee Prisoners," but that this upset the Sambos:

> The Sambos Insisting that their Colour was as good as the Indians, the Mulatos, Sambos, and Negroes were released too, & some of each Colour played upon their Guitars while their Masters [Spaniards] were obliged to make & fill their own Seroons; the Mosquito Men standing over them & telling the Indians that little Breeches [Spaniards] had made them (to whom ye Country belonged) work many a hard days work; but now they were come to give them a play day.[23]

This passage *suggests* that Mosquito ideas of "Colour" divided the Mosquito among themselves as well as others. But such developments cannot be understood outside of a social context in which most "Negroes" were enslaved and most "Indians" were not.

Power and the balance of power between the Sambo and the Tawira also played a role in constituting racialized distinctions among them. In a conversation with the Tawira Mosquito governor Timothy Britain, Superintendent Hodgson (the younger) reported, "[Britain] opened to me his Mind which was full of Jealousy at the King's Power." Governor Britain referred to the Sambo Mosquito king "and all the Sandy Bay People [as] Negroes & Strangers," but added that "his People . . . were the native Indian Breed & true old Friends & Allies of the English." Hodgson added parenthetically, "In this he was nearly right & I can add that this Breed is still rather more powerful than the other."[24]

Contemporaneous racial discourse surely influenced Mosquito thought. The Reverend Thomas Warren, who likely spoke for many elite whites, wrote in 1772, "[The Sambos] derive their origin from a Guinea Ship . . . [and] certain it is, that their hair, complexion, features . . . clearly prove an African ancestry, from whom they have also inherited some of the worst characteristics of the worst African mind: for they are generally false, designing, treacherous, knavish, impudent, and revengeful." In contrast, Warren wrote, "The Pure Indians are so called because they are free from any mixture of negro blood, and their general conduct gives a very favourable Idea of Indian nature, they are seldom guilty of positive evil, and often rise to positive good, when positive good does not require much exertion of mind." Warren's racial discourse is important for at least two reasons. First, he was Superintendent Hodgson's personal secretary for upward of four years and traveled the coast on numerous occasions. Second, the memorial from which this passage was taken was used almost verbatim by Edward Long, the well-read Jamaican historian who published one of the few contemporaneous works on the Mosquitia.[25] What the Mosquito thought of such discourse can be inferred principally from their actions, particularly their assertion of independence, their manipulation of British reliance on them, and their choosing to refer to themselves as Mosquito-men. In short, Sambo and Tawira Mosquito power struggles shaped and reflected the racialized context in which they developed.

MOSQUITO EXCEPTIONALISM

Before major European powers ended their official support for priva-teering in the late seventeenth and early eighteenth centuries, privateers attacked key trade routes and ports throughout the Caribbean. These activities were sustained by a network of safe havens of which the Mos-quitia figured prominently. Through these early encounters the Mosquito earned the respect of northern Europeans and became their allies. It was also through these interactions that the Mosquito began to see themselves as a different sort of Indian or mulatto. So while the Mosquito people both shaped and reflected the emerging ideas of racial difference that de-veloped in Mosquitia, their behaviors, status, and power helped subvert many racialized conventions forming around them.

Following the demise of the Puritan colony on Providence Island, Mosquito-English relations centered around fishing, sailing, piloting, pi-racy, and eventually the Indian slave trade. Pirates described the Mos-quito as "without dispute the most dexterous in fishing." For use of these talents the English gave the Mosquito "a great deal of Respect, both when they [were] aboard their Ships, and also ashore, either in Jamaica, or else-where, which they often [came] with the Seamen." Indeed Mosquito skills were "esteemed and coveted by all Privateers . . . it [was] very rare to find [British] Privateers destitute of one or more of them." Following the official demise of privateering in the late seventeenth century the Mosquito accompanied Jamaican sloops, where they got "good Wages too, and [were] treated in the friendliest manner by the Commanders, being always their companions, and called Brother."[26] Many of these ventures included the Amerindian slave trade. Merchants acquired Indians captured by the Mosquito and sold them to British planters for up to thirty pounds. Mosquito slaving increased significantly during the Wars of Spanish Succession (1700–1712) and became a genuine threat to Spanish settlements along the Mosquitia frontier. Following the war Mosquito slaving concentrated on Indians outside Spanish dominion and also reflected a distinctive Sambo-Tawira territorial jurisdiction.[27]

The Mosquito gradually retained more and more Indian, black, and mulatto captives, a development that reinforced their power and demographic growth. In 1699 M. W. noted that only members of the royal family possessed "a few" Indian slaves. In 1757 Hodgson believed that Indian captivity among the Mosquito was "rare." But he added that if the Mosquito king did not have "a few slaves of other Indians, he would be obliged to do all his own work."[28] Still, this position changed in the second half of the eighteenth century, and most Mosquito villages had some Indian, black, or mixed-race captives. After Indian slaves could no longer be legally sold in 1776 Superintendent Lawrie noted, "[There] still remains a number of Indian slaves amongst the Mosquitomen who were in their possession previous to the late regulations." Lawrie sought three thousand pounds to free all remaining Mosquitia slaves, suggesting that approximately 150 to 200 Amerindians were in bondage at this time, including those held by the British themselves.[29]

Anglo-Mosquito relations became more systematic in the early eighteenth century. In 1720 King Jeremy and Governor Hannibal, both Tawira Mosquito, signed an agreement with Governor Lawes to "scour the [Jamaican] woods for runaway negroes." Lawes sent Captain Togwood to bring King Jeremy to Jamaica along with fifty of his men "in the handsomest manner" to carry out this endeavor. Upon arrival at Sandy Bay, Togwood presented Jeremy and his people with rum, flour, and sugar and presented the new king with his commission in a solemn and well-choreographed ceremony. This is the first time a Mosquito king received his commission in the Mosquitia. It is also the first time the Mosquito were used as regular troops in the service of the British Empire.[30] Though the Jamaican maroons were never reduced, at least one hundred Mosquito went to Jamaica again in 1725, and a group of two hundred returned for the same purpose in 1738. These trips to Jamaica represent the most sustained Mosquito contact with British plantation society at that time. Presumably some Mosquito did not like what they saw, because after the success of their first outing the Jamaicans invited the Mosquito to settle there, "assigning them lands and let[ting] them enjoy rights of Englishmen." The Mosquito declined, however, saying they did not "want to leave their own country."[31]

Sustained economic and cultural contact with the English, coupled with participation in the slave trade, elevated Mosquito stature in their own eyes. As early as 1699, according to M. W., the Mosquito, "in regard that they have had some small commerce with the English, esteem[ed] themselves to be a very notable sort of people, affecting much to be call'd Mosqueto-men, and distinguishing their neighbours by the names wild Indians." Elevated distinctions were also held by the British. In the last sentence of his monograph Hodgson noted, "[The Mosquito] are so much superior to the neighboring Indians, that *their* calling *them* wild, is no great impropriety in the comparison." Meanwhile the self-ascriptor Mosquitomen suggests that the Mosquito began to see themselves as part of the larger international community of nations equivalent to Englishmen, Frenchmen, Welshmen, and Dutchmen. A sustained rhetoric of freedom and territorial independence backed up by flags, uniforms, and scepters supported a budding notion of nationhood while confounding incipient racial categories and hierarchies in Mosquitia.[32]

Despite using a plethora of racialized and denigrating rhetoric to describe the Mosquito, many Spaniards recognized Mosquito exceptionalism. During one Mosquito-Spanish overture in the late 1760s the Guatemalan captain-general Pedro de Salazar warned that Mosquito autonomy and independence must be respected:

It is now very clear that to think of obligating [the Mosquito] to pay taxes, or to even raise this question with them, will completely jeopardize our friendship. . . . The laws [dealing with Indians] speak of other classes of Indians, those that have not established treaties with the nations of Europe, those that do not possess arms, and those who do not possess such skills as these [Mosquito] have in their ability to defend themselves and to eschew the domination of Spain.[33]

Salazar's distinction between the Mosquito and "other classes of Indians" suggests that demonstrable power could transcend the way legal and cultural notions of race were operationalized in colonial Central America.

Following the British evacuation of Mosquitia in 1787 the long-time Irish resident Colville Cairns advised the Spanish to allow the Mosquito to retain their independence and privileges: "To bother them with this particular issue would create horrendous consequences." To emphasize his point, he added, "The Mosquito will not tolerate any type of rigorous punishment or scolding by a European."[34] The governor of Nicaragua, Don Juan de Ayssa, concurred. In organizing his efforts to exert Spanish authority in 1790 de Ayssa judged it convenient that the Mosquitia should remain divided into Sambo and Tawira domains. He also believed that the leaders of each faction "should have a salary assigned to them along with some uniforms": "He who is accustomed to live with a salary should not be forced to live without one."[35] If anything Mosquito privilege and power only grew under nominal Spanish dominion, a point made repeatedly in a study by Douglas Thompson.[36]

Although Mosquito power declined in the nineteenth century, their self-esteem withstood the deepening effects of racialized colonialism. One observer believed, "[The Mosquito have] an ever-increasing notion of their own importance, which is probably the foundation of the legend current to-day among the Mosquito men, that they once held Jamaica in subjection and sent annually to levy tribute from the people of that island." He added, "A common Mosquito designation of [black] Jamaicans is, 'My Grandfather's Children,' an appellation which is frequently thrown in the faces of the Jamaicans [Creoles] who now hold the reins of Mosquito government."[37] Moravian missionaries often mentioned that the Mosquito called themselves "real men": "Indeed they believe they are superior to all other races. A Miskito Indian . . . is proud of the fact that he has always been a free man."[38] Such notions might have seemed quaint to Anglo-Americans in the nineteenth and twentieth centuries, but in the eighteenth century a compelling Mosquito enactment of these beliefs was the norm and respected.

The Mosquitia was among the most diverse British colonies in the West Indies. While British settlements, often comprising only a few houses, existed at Punta Gorda, Bluefields, Corn Island, Saint Andrews, Pearl Lagoon, Brangmans, Sandy Bay, and Cape Gracias in what is today Nicaragua, British wealth, population, and influence concentrated along a short coastal stretch from Brewer's (Brus) Lagoon to the Cape (Cameron) River, anchored by the Black River settlement, in what is today Honduras (Offen Map 2). Some 70 percent of all British freemen lived around Black River in 1757, and this number had climbed to 80 percent by 1786. Likewise 70 to 80 percent of British-owned slaves also resided around Black River, which was divided internally by race and class. Approximately half of all British freemen were of mixed race, both mulattos (predominantly of African European ancestry) and mustees (predominantly of Indian European ancestry). Despite a large free population, wealth concentrated in the hands of a few white men, half of whom were of Scottish, Irish, and Manx heritage. Although shifting migration and investment patterns were linked to the Anglo-Spanish disputes of 1739–48, 1759–63, and 1779–83, and the conditions of peace between them, relative demographic distributions and proportions stayed roughly the same throughout the superintendency. Precarious settlements less than a hundred miles from Spanish towns left propertied white men beholden to poorer free classes, black and Indian slaves, and the Mosquito for their protection. This condition played an important role in how emerging ideas of race were put into practice, assimilated, and leveraged by mixed-race, subjugated, and Mosquito peoples.

At least a few Englishmen resided continuously in Mosquitia after the Spanish captured Providence Island in 1641. Still, pirate testimonies do not mention permanent European domiciles until 1689, when de Lussan wrote that Englishmen tried to make themselves "masters of the country," for they already had "a number of habitations." As late as 1700 no Europeans resided on the north coast, while only three Englishmen lived on the south coast. By 1724 some thirty Britons resided in the Mosquitia, including in eight huts on the Mosquito Cays, where three to four ships arrived each month.[39] When Spanish forces attacked the logwood cutters at the Belize River in 1730 William Pitt and other Baymen fled to Black

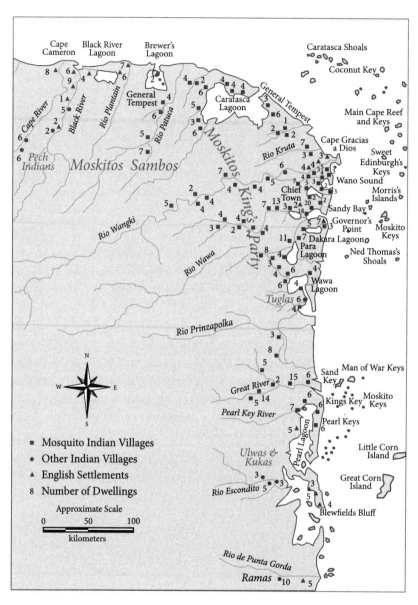

MAP 2 Miskitu and English settlements, colonial Mosquitia, 1770s. Note that "English settlements" include free black and slave residences. Map by Donald Sluter based on the author's redrawing of three maps in Thomas Jefferys, *The West-India Atlas; or, a Compendious Description of the West Indies* . . . (London: R. Sayer and J. Bennett, 1775).

River on the northeastern coast of Honduras. Although most returned to Belize, Pitt remained at Black River, where he reigned as the "master of trade" until his death in 1771.[40]

In 1748 Jamaican officials authorized a superintendency for the Mosquito Shore and approved Robert Hodgson as the first superintendent. Hodgson was instructed to "cultivate such an Union and Friendship with the Indians in those parts, as may induce them to prefer his Majesty's Alliance & Protection to that of any other Power."[41] Jamaican Governor Trelawny sought to restrict slavery in Mosquitia. He believed, "Slavery should not be allowed in the same manners it is in our other colonies." He reasoned, "As the same affect may be supposed to always flow from the same cause, there will be a few rich men with large tracts of land with a great number of slaves, the rest servants and some very few white artisans." Adding to his prophecy, Trelawny said, "If white men cannot work [in Mosquitia], they have no business here. If the settlement cannot be carried on without slaves, it had better not be carried on at all, and the government should not be put to any expense about it." These views notwithstanding, slavery became the foundation of British Mosquitia.[42]

The creation of the superintendency in general, and the formation of the Black River settlement in particular, marks the beginning of a largely mixed-race society whose principal language was English. On the whole, white settlers were young and miscegenation rates were high. Of the forty-two known white men in 1753, twenty-five were between twenty-two and thirty-five years old, and 72 percent were forty or under. White women were few, and they rarely lived outside of Black River. At least some white women were Spanish, as Pitt married a shipwrecked Spanish woman, and "the majority" of women at Brus Lagoon in 1746 were allegedly "Españolas" taken by "los Zambos" from Spanish dominions. Few white women combined with high percentages of African and Amerindian slaves helped to create a large population of mixed-race people, both free and enslaved.[43]

The percentage of peoples of African and mixed descent grew quickly. By 1751 twenty-nine white and fifty-five black men were capable of bearing arms at Black River, while eleven whites and twenty-seven blacks could do so at Cape Gracias, in addition to forty more blacks not well acquainted with arms. Thus less than five years after formal recognition of the British settlement black men outnumbered white men by more than three to one.

By 1757 free settlers held eight hundred slaves, approximately 20 percent of whom were Indians. Among the Indian slaves a large majority were held south of Cape Gracias. Thus three-quarters of all slaves were held around Black River, and they were primarily black.[44]

Hodgson's population figures from 1757 also show that among the three hundred free men and women half were "Mulattoes" and "Mestizoes," 80 percent of whom resided around Black River. The data show sixteen white women, all of whom lived west of Cape Gracias, and fifty-four free, mixed women, thirty-six of whom lived around Black River. Hodgson identified only five white children, compared to eighty-one children of free people of mixed race.[45] During the tenure of Superintendent Richard Jones (1759–62) "the Mosquito Shore was inhabited by 203 white people (the detachment of 30 soldiers included) with 189 free musteas and mulattos, about 3,000 Mosquito Indians and 914 Negroe slaves." In 1764, the year after the Treaty of Paris allowed British settlers to remain at Black River without fortifications, Superintendent Joseph Otway (1762–67) listed forty-five white families around Black River and twenty-two more for the remainder of the Mosquitia. He also identified 970 slaves, twenty-one "Mestize" families for the Black River area, and nine for the remainder of the Mosquitia. Otway defined mestizes as "free People and Christians": "They differ but little in complexion from White People, they are useful to the Community, most of them are Possessed of Property and they are, in general, good Handicrafts." Otway's mestizes were likely Christian in name only, because when the Moravian catechist Frederick Post arrived at Black River in 1765 he found two hundred to three hundred "Mustee people . . . almost a nation," who were uninstructed in the Christian religion. So-called mustees were bilingual and bicultural; Lawrie opined in 1774, "The Mustees or mixed breed betwixt the Indians & white generally speak the [Mosquito] language in greater perfection than the Moskittos themselves."[46]

On his visit to Black River in 1764 the Spanish engineer Luis Diaz Navarro drew a map that spatialized these figures. His drawing shows that the majority of "black slaves" and "los vecinos," or white Englishmen and slave owners, lived at the principal settlement surrounded by the earthen fortifications he was there to remove. Away from the main settlement lived "varios mestizos," described as "hijos de la tierra" (native born), as well as smaller settlements of other mixed groups whom Navarro labels fishermen and turtlemen. From this map we learn that slave-owning white men lived together while smaller, mixed-race settlements spread out from Brus Lagoon to Cape Cameron, five to ten miles east and west of Black River proper.[47] This map, along with others from the period, confirm that British communities in Mosquitia were internally organized around race and place.[48]

As the peace with Spain held, many British Loyalists from North America relocated to Mosquitia, increasing the free and enslaved populations.[49] Following clarification of the Treaty of Versailles with the Convention of London in 1786, 537 free people and their 1,677 slaves evacuated Mosquitia for Belize in early 1787. We know that a large percentage of the arriving free population in Belize were of mixed race by the way white Belizeans described them. Immediately after relocation white Belizeans believed that their property and color should allow them to discriminate against the "very different" classes originating from the Mosquitia. As the Mosquito Shore folks began to protest their second-class status, violence erupted. One commentator reported, "A few white people of the very lowest class, a number of Mustees, Mulattoes, and free Negroes are running about the streets and assembling under Arms to the infinite terror of the more respectable [white people]." Despite the violence Belizeans refused to accommodate the demands of "a set of men of Colour calling themselves the People of the Mosquito Shore." In addition to color the Belizeans dwelled on class. Records show that among the 537 Mosquitia freemen relocating to Belize, half held no slaves, while only forty owned 1,200, or three-fourths of the total. These records suggest that free people called white, mustee, or mulatto in Mosquitia were seen quite differently by whites elsewhere.[50]

PROTECTING SLAVERY AT BLACK RIVER

The Mosquitia was a precarious place for British slave owners. On the one hand, a large slave population ensured that settlers relied on the Mosquito for protection. Yet Mosquito fidelity had to be frequently cajoled with costly presents, and even then loyalty was never assured. On the other hand, the proximity of Spanish settlements and forts (particularly near Black River) meant that British settlers lived under the constant threat of a Spanish attack, particularly from Omoa. This forced them to rely on their slaves and the Mosquito for protection. Meanwhile the Spaniards sought to lure the Mosquito and slaves to their side, promising the former special privileges and the latter their freedom. In this context the Mosquito leveraged their importance to receive large and frequent gifts from the British, including weapons, shot, and powder. At the same time black, Indian, and mixed-race peoples manipulated the confines of their status to gain a measure of independence.

From the beginning of the Black River settlement William Pitt worried that the Spaniards would soon come and "take the place." In seeking more troops from Jamaica he argued that the few soldiers sent up to that point "proved of good effect, in regard to the Spaniards, as also to the Moskito men, and negroes." In 1751 Hodgson noted, "The Mosquitomen are growing cool and frightened at seeing us give way to the Spaniards. And not withstanding their promises while I am distributing presents among them, keep close upon every alarm." In 1768 Richard Jones reported that the Tawira of the south coast had entered into discussions with the Spanish governor at Costa Rica. This worried the Sambo Mosquito of General Tempest's district, creating what Jones described as "the late expected insurrection," in which Tempest threatened to kill the Tawira governor Colville Briton. Jones was worried about this because without a united Mosquito "the neighbouring Spanish settlements . . . would otherwise soon over run and expel the English."[51] In 1770 inhabitants of Cape Gracias wrote the governor of Jamaica concerning "the late dissatisfaction" among the Mosquito Indians. They thanked the governor for sending an agent to provide presents for the Mosquito, but feared, "As soon as that Gentleman and the Man of War leaves the Coast we shall again labour under the same disagreeable Circumstances." They begged him to send "a few soldiers which will keep the Musquito Men in Awe."[52]

Besides the Spaniards and the Mosquito, the British feared their own slaves. Many Black River slaves came from Jamaica, where they had been removed for unruly behavior. This unique situation, according to Superintendent Lawrie, meant that Mosquitia slaves had to be well treated. Like their counterparts at Belize, black slaves routinely owned guns, a long-standing Mosquitia tradition. Still, slaves rebelled and sought their freedom. The first recorded "negro rebellion" occurred around 1745 at Black River, but it was quickly put down.[53] Around the same time "the negroes belonging to the inhabitants of [Black River] . . . ran away in a

[boat] and settled in the neighbourhood, till they were reduced by the [Mosquito], the white men being utterly unable to do it themselves."[54] In 1776 some fourteen black slaves that were property of the crown escaped from Black River with weapons and tools and sought to form a settlement in the mountains. Settlers sought Mosquito help, and some 250 came to their assistance—"more than they really wanted," as Barbara Potthast put it—and destroyed the rebels' homes.[55]

Other slaves succeeded in their plans. At least one British settlement near Black River had to be abandoned "through the danger the Settlers were in from a great number of runaway Slaves who then infested this part of the Country."[56] In 1766 Otway reported the desertion of fifteen slaves "to the Spaniards [at Omoa] by whom they are received and protected." The Spaniards baptized runaway slaves, "by which means they [fell] under the protection of the Ecclesiastical Authority. . . . [Thus] the Spanish Commandants allege[d] that it [was] not in their power of military or civil officer or magistrate to release them." Otway added that a spread of this knowledge to other slaves would effectively end the settlement: "Without the labour of slaves, matters of commerce could neither be carried on nor improved in these parts. . . . Persons settled here usually estimate their worth in proportion to the number of their slaves."[57]

Above all, however, settlers feared that slaves would join the Mosquito. Just before the death of William Pitt in 1770 leading settlers wrote concerning "the turbulent disposition of [Pitt's] Negroes," "[They] are very numerous, and many . . . have declared they would serve no man after, and at the Event of his Death, it's more than probable that a prospect of Liberty may Induce many of our Slaves to Join with the Disaffected, some of the Negros having already made proposals to the [Mosquito] Indian Chiefs of joining them (this was discovered the other day by Capt. Morgan an Indian Chief [who told] Capt. Garrison an Englishman)." They hoped a company of soldiers could be sent because they "would awe the most turbulent [Negroes]" and Mosquito men.[58] But black slaves and the Mosquito continued to collude with one another. As Hodgson put it in 1771, "Some Mosquitoes, together with some of our own Negroes, lately made an attempt to kill eight Spaniards who were returning home [from here]."[59]

In the context of the larger Anglo-Spanish military conflict that engulfed Mosquitia, Spanish forces from Trujillo temporarily took Black

River in early 1780. The Spaniards assumed that the settlers would not be able to rely upon their slaves for protection. Instead they found that the slaves put up more resistance than the whites, most of whom fled. After the Spaniards destroyed the fields they quickly retreated for fear of Mosquito reprisals. With the settlers gone the slaves reoccupied and took charge of the town. When the British returned with troops from Belize the slaves demanded that the most inhumane slaveholders not be allowed to return. Though this was denied, the British negotiator did promise that the leaders of the slave uprising and their families would be granted their freedom. In addition those who were most courageous in defending the town were rewarded with a salary.[60] By 1784 a "Battalion of Free people of Colour" at Black River was formed that included thirty-seven male and nine female slaves.[61] But arming slaves only created new fears among the whites.

When news of the impending evacuation arrived officially in 1786 settlers feared a slave uprising instigated by the Mosquito. One settler wrote, "[The Mosquito are] enraged at being left to the mercy of the Spaniards [and] will not allow us peaceably to depart." The settlers tried to highlight their unique predicament, appealing to the fact that their slaves had a great "attachment to this Country" and that their freedoms had been very "different from the treatment in the West Indies in general": "[They] have all the reason to think without a sufficient force to awe them, a great part may be induced to join the Mosquito Men, and thus add (with their advice as it is well known they have an amazing influence over them) strength to those people, and endeavor to effect our Ruin."[62]

Settler fears were well founded. According to Lawrie, "[Sambo General Lee] has of late frequently declared . . . his determination to blow out the brains of the first white man who should attempt to desert him and his people and leave them to the mercy of the Spaniards." Lawrie added that Lee had promised to assemble Mosquito leaders to discuss the matter: "As those Chiefs will in all probability be numerously attended [by other Mosquito, one] can see how dangerous it will be for us." Lawrie believed that the Mosquito "disdain" for the Spaniards was so great that the settlers would likely be "cut in pieces" by them. Thus Lawrie was relieved to hear that General Lee would go to Jamaica to make his concerns known there, because "in this manner [he would] become a hostage for the good behaviour of his people in his absence." Just to be safe, however, he begged the Jamaican governor to send troops: "At least one hundred men will be wanted for Black River, an equal number at Cape Gracias a Dios and fifty men at Bluefields."[63] Even a decade later the Sambo Mosquito remained furious with the British for giving " 'away to their enemies their own country which God Almighty gave them,' as they emphatically expressed it."[64]

As the settlers were preparing to evacuate the Mosquito Shore in 1787 the council of settlers at Black River was preoccupied with a family of rebellious slaves known as "Flower's Negroes," who had "fled to the woods" and were "in a state of actual rebellion, after having assisted in Robbing some of the Inhabitants of Black River." After lengthy and panicked deliberation the council decided, "The very dangerous tendency of a Family so numerous and so generally connected to other Families, flying into the woods and in open defiance of all law and order at this very critical juncture, attempting to form an independent establishment in the heart of the settlement, [warranted extreme negotiation]." To avoid "a general desertion and open Rebellion of the Slaves . . . and taking into their serious consideration the state of Freedom in which this Family [had] lived for upwards of thirty years past and knowing of no legal claims to it," the council hoped to put "an immediate stop . . . to the defection and revolt already begun," by declaring Flower's Negroes "to be Free to all interest and purposes with their Issue and Increase forever."[65] The ability to rebel, run away, collude with the Mosquito, and offer necessary protection ensured that slaves at Black River enjoyed greater independence than those elsewhere in the British West Indies.

RACE, PLACE, ECONOMY: NORTH COAST

The Mosquitia was constituted by two separate British economies, a larger one at Black River anchored by the labor of primarily black slaves and a smaller one along the windward coast reliant on both Amerindian and black slaves. These distinct economic geographies influenced associations of race with slavery. In general enslaved Indian men fished, crewed boats, and hunted along the windward coast; black male slaves cut timber, laded ships, transported goods, and worked plantations wherever they resided, but especially along the north coast; free mixed-race people secured their own living through turtling, extracting resources, retailing, and trading with the Spaniards. We know that enslaved women washed clothes, cooked food, raised crops, and cared for children, but we know little about the activities of free women. For their part Mosquito men turtled, slaved, managed cattle, oversaw contraband trade, and moved goods across coastal bars, but the Tawira and Sambo participated in these activities to different degrees and in different places. As Superintendent Lawrie put it, "[Mosquito women] do all the Drudgery. Cut Firewood, clear, plant & clean the Plantation, Spin, weave Cotton Cloath. . . . In short they are perfect slaves."[66]

Most Mosquitia economic activity occurred in and around Black River. Throughout the superintendency mahogany cutting accounted for about one-third of annual exports and averaged about thirty thousand pounds. From about 1750 until the evacuation in 1787 mahogany exports averaged about 700,000 board feet; after the Anglo-Spanish Treaty in 1763 allowed settlers to remain at Black River, exports increased despite the fact that the value of mahogany declined. Mahogany cutting and shipping were seasonal and carried out by "gangs," mostly of black slaves in groups of eight to twenty, who went far up north coast rivers. Women likely accompanied these crews, making it relatively easy for whole families to escape to the Spaniards. The work cutting, sectioning, and trucking logs to river banks with oxen was labor-intensive and took place from February through May. With the start of the rainy season in late May logs were floated down to Black River, where they were squared or cut into planks and boards.[67]

Since Black River had no deep sea, port ships had to be loaded and unloaded while anchored offshore because large or full vessels could not cross the coastal bar. Ferrying goods, including timber, across the bar had to be done before the arrival of northers in late October because no ship could "lay a day on this Coast [after that time] until the middle or latter end of April."[68] Wealthy settlers who owned fifty or more slaves operated two or three gangs simultaneously. Poorer and mixed-race free settlers also participated in the mahogany economy but likely labored alongside their crews. Data from a single year of mahogany exports suggest that many cutters were small-time operators.[69]

Illicit trade with the Spaniards accounted for another third of all economic activity. This is partly evident from import and export statistics from 1772 in Great Britain that compared the Mosquito Shore with Belize. Although four times more goods were imported from Belize, three times more goods were exported to the Mosquito Shore.[70] Many of these "very considerable" imports of dry goods (cloth, grains, manufactured goods) were transported to the Spaniards from Black River by blacks and mulattos, both free and enslaved, who returned with sarsaparilla, cattle, mules, cacao, cotton, indigo, cochineal, tallow, tobacco, silver, and hides. Poorer settlers and slaves also gathered sarsaparilla, a forest vine used to treat syphilis, and turtle shell, which circulated widely as currency in eighteenth-century Mosquitia. Indeed these two resources accounted for about a third of Black River export values.[71]

The cattle business was another Mosquitia activity. While cattle, horses, and mules originated from the Spaniards, they quickly became semiferal on the northern savannas. Meanwhile black slaves managed "Penns of Black Cattle and provision grounds" along Black River.[72] Free men of color lived as ranchers on the savanna. In 1779, for example, Jopher Corey agreed to manage 150 horned cattle along the Río Patuca with the help of "one Indian or negroe man Slave."[73] Meanwhile the Sambo Mosquito of the north coast managed semiferal cattle and horses specifically for British markets at Belize and Jamaica. General Tempest's people were singled out for raising stocks of black cattle that "would not disgrace Leaden Hall market." With the evacuation British settlers took 270 cows and thirty-one mules and horses with them, but many more must have remained.[74]

There is no evidence that sugar or its by-products were ever shipped from Mosquitia. Cane juice was apparently distilled and consumed locally. Based on the names of rum retailers and increased efforts to regulate consumption, we can assume that liquor dealers and consumers were too poor to deal with or consume imported spirits.[75] Accounts of agricultural potential at Black River also suggest that sugar cane was not widely cultivated. As early as 1748 Richard Jones found that the land around the lagoons was "capable" of producing sugar cane "and other valuable Commodities," but that this was not happening.[76] Almost twenty years later Superintendent Otway noted that trade was "chiefly in mahogany, sarsaparilla, tortoise shell, and mules," but that indigo, cotton, sugar cane, coffee, cacao, rice, and ginger "could be" profitably produced.[77] As late as 1773 settlers still dealt principally in mahogany, sarsaparilla, turtle shell, and cattle.[78]

As on the south coast, sugar cane cultivation started only after 1770 and probably not before 1775, and then only on a limited scale. In 1779 a 1,200-acre "plantation or Sugar Work . . . up Black River" sold with all its

"Houses, buildings, etc. and Utensils and Materials used in the Manufacturing of Sugar and Rum," including seventeen "Negroe Men, Women, & Indian Slaves," twenty-one mules, and thirty-one horned cattle.[79] By 1785 Black River had three "Sugar Estates" and two mills.[80] Despite an increasing orientation toward sugar and other cash crops immediately before the evacuation, plantation agriculture was not a significant dimension of Mosquitia economic geography or slave experiences. Thus the brutal plantation system that had formed the foundation of social and economic life in the British West Indies since the mid-seventeenth century was essentially absent in Mosquitia.

RACE, PLACE, ECONOMY: SOUTH COAST

Indian labor and the Indian slave trade were central to the economy of the southern Mosquitia. As Superintendent Otway put it, "The Trade [on the south coast] mainly consists in taking the neighbouring Indians and selling them for Slaves."[81] Although the Indian slave trade in the British West Indies was outlawed in 1741 and Mosquitia Indian slaves were allegedly freed in 1777, Indian slavery and slave raids continued throughout the eighteenth century, and many Amerindians remained enslaved until the general emancipation in 1841. Slave raiding was in general seasonal and tied to the procurement of hawksbill turtle shell south of Bluefields. According to Hodgson, "Getting tortoise-shell is [the Mosquito's] grand employment, [yet] the valuable hawksbill turtle frequents the southern coast [only] from about Monkey Point as far as Chagres, [Panama]." This geography inspired Tawira leaders, twice before 1725 and again during the 1760s and 1770s, to make overtures to the Costa Rican governor to ensure their access to prime hawksbill turtling areas.[82] When diplomacy failed, Tawira turtling and slave raids remained seasonal and inextricably linked.

Hodgson tells us, "From fifteen to twenty peruaguas, (large canoes) with about twelve men in each, are employed in [the turtling] business from April to August. If they have formed a [slaving] expedition, they chose this time to execute it, and therefore set out and keep together till it is over; otherwise they straggle from the first, and spread all the way from Blewfields to Boca Del Drago."[83] On average the Mosquito returned with fifteen to twenty Indian slaves each turtling season. By the late 1770s traders paid "the common price" of twenty turtle backs "for a full grown Indian and for one half grown fifteen backs," or about twenty pounds Jamaican currency, and resold them for thirty to thirty-five pounds.[84] Twappi's Irish resident Colville Cairns wrote at the end of the turtle season in 1777 that only five Indian slaves "came [that] year," implying that he not only expected Indian slaves each season, but that he expected more than five. Cairns was the leading dealer in Amerindians; by 1776 he possessed sixty-eight Indian slaves, most of whom came from Costa Rica and Panama.[85]

The Amerindian slave trade was deemed unfavorable by some settlers and eventually by the Sambo Mosquito leadership. Superintendent Otway wrote that Indian slaving on the south coast was "detrimental to the general interest of the settlement." Instead of improving trade with the British, the neighboring Indians were "driven to seek protection from the Spaniards." In 1775 Mosquito King George sent a delegation to London to denounce Indian slavery in Mosquitia. While in London the king's brother Duke Isaac, his son George II, and two Ulwa Indians named "Richard, admiral" and "John, captain," laid "before his Majesty's ministers some representations and complaints [regarding] the conduct of the [Indian slave] trade." These efforts helped produce a British law nullifying the sale of Indian slaves in the Mosquitia after October 1776, but this legislation was unevenly enforced.[86]

Improving commerce and civilization in the eighteenth century inspired plantation agriculture, and the lack of both on the south coast was a constant lament of superintendents. Hodgson wrote that south coast settlers "entirely neglect[ed] cultivation, except for necessary provisionings." When Otway toured the south coast in 1765 he found that settlers had not yet complied with orders to establish plantations: "I should have found Land cultivated . . . [but] instead of the improvements . . . I found large Tracts of Land . . . laying waste and unimproved." According to Otway, residents understood that it was "their duty" to increase commerce: "But their situation was at present from a defenseless state, too precarious for them to think of investing their property in purchasing of [Negroe] slaves to cultivate land as they might be daily exposed to ruin if the Spaniards should ever succeed in effecting a commerce with the [Tawira] Mosquito Indians."[87] A summary of depositions from former Amerindian captives recorded in 1824 included the statement, "Almost the whole of the labor of the Southern part of the Mosquito Shore was performed by the Indian Slaves." This fact is also confirmed by period statistics. Of the ninety-four Indian slaves listed in 1757, eighty-eight were held south of Cape Gracias.[88] As we have seen, Cairns held sixty-eight Indian slaves at Twappi, the home of the Tawira Mosquito governor, but we know that he also owned a few "Negro and Sambo Slaves" because he bequeathed them to his two children, Anna and William, "begotten by the Body of Rachel Gill, a Fine Mustee Woman."[89] (The use of Sambo here and below implies the enslaved offspring of black-Indian unions and not the Sambo Mosquito.) The reliance on or preference for Indian slaves on the south coast reflects a relative insecurity, ease of acquisition, lower cost, and absence of plantation agriculture.

The general characteristics of slavery on the south coast are revealed in the unique records of the Bluefields estate of an Isle of Man trader, Henry Corrin. Corrin lived at Bluefields Bluff from 1752 until his death in 1769 (see Offen Map 2). He bequeathed his estate to the future child of his partner, Mary Brown, "a Mustee," if her child was a boy and survived his birth. This child was either not a boy or did not survive or Mary and her child were cheated out of their inheritance because the estate passed to Corrin's Isle of Man nephew, George Cummins, who died of alcohol poisoning soon after he arrived. The estate was then cared for by a series of overseers who relied on violence and coercion in an attempt to hold things together. Corrin had traded in mahogany, turtle shell, cacao, and Spanish silver, and he was the foremost contraband trader with the Nicaraguan provinces of Matagalpa and Chontales. He moved goods up the Río Escondido with the help of the Ulwa Indian leader Captain Garrison, whom the Spanish called Capitán Yarrince or Yarrinsen. Corrin had serious disputes with the Tawira of Pearl Lagoon, who repeatedly threatened "his commerce" Indians, but he maintained good relations with the Sambo settlements at the southern end of Pearl Lagoon.[90]

The inventory of Corrin's estate in 1771 shows that he owned seventy-five slaves: thirty-seven negroes (sixteen men, seven boys, fourteen women and girls) and thirty-two Indians (twenty men and boys, six women and girls, and six "Sambo" children). The overwhelming majority of Corrin's black men were listed as "sawyers," or timber men. A few were carpenters, smiths, or agriculturalists; in contrast, male Indian slaves were listed as fishermen, sailors, caulkers, turtlers, and hunters. Indian boys worked in the household or assisted the men, listed as "goes in craft" or "with the hunter." Women were cooks and washerwomen and raised children. In 1773 Corrin's Indian slaves were valued at 366 pounds, while his negro slaves were valued at 1,689 pounds. Together they accounted for 92 percent of his estate's total worth. These figures suggest that Indian slaves were tied to provisioning and other domestic duties, while most male slaves of African descent were valued more and linked to commercial enterprises.[91] The records reveal a sharp correlation between emerging ideas of race and labor, and they also reveal the birth of a new African Amerindian population, ancestors of the Creoles who emerged at Bluefields and Pearl Lagoon in the late eighteenth century.[92]

From a second inventory of Corrin's estate taken in 1772 we learn that twelve "Free Indians [were] staying about the estate." Five of these so-called free Indians were women living with enslaved black men and their children, and most were likely Kukra Indians.[93] Despite mixed backgrounds and origins, these slaves united to defend an accustomed lifestyle. After Superintendent Lawrie removed some of the Bluefields children to Black River to ensure compliance among those who remained, in 1774 he purchased several black and Indian men and women for 436 pounds Jamaican currency.[94] The separation of families did not sit well with those who remained behind. In September 1775 Colville Cairns reported, "[The] Negroes and Indians belonging to [Corrin's] Estate have possessed themselves of all the Great and small guns, powder and Shot of that Place and mounted the former on the Bluff and drove away all the White Men and bid defiance to the Whites and Moskito Men being resolved to keep their Ground and Defend themselves, and in short are now in open rebellion."[95] To make matters worse for settlers, the Tawira Mosquito refused repeated requests to intervene.

Corrin's slaves did not remain at the Bluff for long. Instead they sought protection from the Spaniards of Chontales up the Río Escondido. In November 1775 fifteen canoes arrived near Acoyapa with sixty-five "Negros mixed with Indians from Bocatoro [Panama] and Cuera [Costa Rica]." Among the thirteen negro men, five negro women, twenty-five "carive" Indians, and twenty-two "negrittas y sambittos" below age sixteen was Lorenzo García, a sixty-year-old "negro Christian" from Santiago de Veragua who served as the group's translator. Many of the people arriving were sick, and twenty-eight of them died within six months. The fate of the survivors is not known, but it was suggested that the blacks be removed to León and Granada. Meanwhile John McHarg, the Scot in charge of Corrin's estate, wrote don Antonio de Vargas, the comandante of Chontales, asking him to return the slaves that had been guided by "the Woolwas of Garrison's Tribe." He hoped that "the long good trust that . . . subsisted between [Corrin] and the Gentlemen in the Savanna," including Vargas, would ensure his cooperation.[96] These records suggest that black and Indian slaves would seek out Spanish settlements if their accustomed way of life changed for the worse.

As on the north coast, sugar production reached the south coast only after 1770. In 1776 the Londoner Dr. Charles Irving attempted to establish a sugar plantation on the Río Grande with black slaves hand-picked in Jamaica by the free Igbo Gustavus Vassa, or Equiano Olaudah. This project, along with an unrelated cacao plantation headed up by a Frenchman, introduced several dozen new black slaves to the south coast. This occurrence paralleled similar sugar developments at Cape Gracias a Dios. Some time after Vassa's enslaved "countrymen" arrived at the Río Grande, at least fifteen of them fled to the Spaniards, supporting the claim that security on the south coast limited greater settler investment. Meanwhile Irving's land grant in the governor's district had been acquired from King George.[97] This unprecedented Sambo usurpation of Tawira territorial authority pushed the Tawira to renew talks with the Spaniards at Cartago, León, Portobelo, and Cartagena. These contacts with the Spaniards initiated a decisive period of Sambo-Tawira conflict. In 1790, following the British evacuation, the Sambo and Tawira fought a "civil war" that led to Sambo subordination of the Tawira.[98]

CONCLUSION

Ideas of race and social manifestations of racial difference developed differently in colonial Mosquitia than in other British colonies in the West Indies, including mainland colonies such as Guyana and Belize. The reasons for this exceptionalism include the precarious location of British settlements in relation to Spanish forts and settlements, the relative lack of plantation agriculture, the labor requirements of far-flung extractive enterprises, the preponderance of mixed-race peoples, and the domineering presence of the Mosquito people. I have argued that the activities and relative power of the Mosquito problematized the relationship between emerging ideologies of race and an everyday hierarchical meaning of racial difference in Mosquitia. The Mosquito were Afro-Amerindian or Amerindian, but they had a different status from other Indians and free mulattos. They also lived royally, governed themselves, and interacted with the British and the Spanish as equals. By imagining themselves to be "a very notable sort of people, affecting much to be call'd Mosqueto-men," the Mosquito lived as a distinct social group within emerging racial categories in colonial Mosquitia. The fact that the Mosquito could exert "amazing influence over" black and Indian slaves, but were simultaneously essential to the slave system in Mosquitia, weakened the connection between ancestry, racial discourse, and slavery that was so emblematic of other British colonies in the West Indies.

NOTES

1   Chaplin, "Race," 168. See also Dunn, *Sugar and Slaves.*
2   For the British return to Mosquitia in the 1830s and the development of more Victorian ideas of racial difference, see Hooker's essay in this volume; Naylor, *Penny Ante Imperialism*; Offen, "The Geographical Imagination."
3   Olien, "The Miskito Kings"; Offen, "The Sambo and Tawira Miskitu." In this essay I use the most common English and Spanish historical term, *Mosquito*, to describe the people and kingdom instead of the neologisms *Miskito* or *Miskitu*. The term *tawira* means "much hair" in the Mosquito language, and though it had limited colonial use it was the title of Charles Napier Bell's book *Tangweera*, published in 1899. Bell, who spent his youth in Mosquitia during the 1840s and 1850s, wrote that the Mosquito Indians "call themselves Tangweeras (Straight-hair), to distinguish them from the half-breed Sambos, who speak the same language" (4).
4   Offen, "Creating Mosquitia."
5   Attempts to map these groups have been numerous but varied; see Conzemius, *Ethnographical Survey*; Helms, *Asang*; Davidson, "Etnografía histórica"; Davidson and Cruz, "Delimitación de la región habitada"; von Houwald, *Mayangna*; Offen, "The Miskitu Kingdom," 28–34.
6   Dampier, *A New Voyage*, 7, 15, 27, 28; Offen, "Sambo and Tawira Miskitu," 334. My point about Dampier's first use is hyperbolic. He published his book in 1697, but we have to assume that the Mosquito ethnic label was in use when he first visited the region in 1679. The ethnic term does not, however, appear earlier.
7   Alonso de Santa Cruz, "[Carta del Seno Mejicano]," 1536, *Mapas Españoles de*

América, Siglos XV–XVII, ed. Academia Real de Historia (Madrid: Academia Real de Historia, 1951), 45; Diego Gutiérrez, "Americae Sive Qvartae Orbis Partis Nova Et Exactissima Descriptio" (Antwerp, 1562); Juan Martínez, "[Carta del Seno Mejicano y del Océano Atlántico Septentrional]," 1587, *Mapas Españoles*, 163; Arnoldo Florencio Langren, "Delineatio Omnium Orarum Totius. Aus Tralis Partis Americae" ([Amsterdam], 1595); Joannes Oliva, "[Chart of North and Central America and West Indies]" (Marseilles, 1613), British Library, Eg. 819, Map 3 (fol. 4); William Blaeu, "West Indies" (Antwerp, 1635). See also Romero Vargas, *Las sociedades del Atlántico*, 124–26; Offen, "Creating Mosquitia," 259–62.

8   Harlow, "The Voyages of Captain William Jackson," 25; Nathaniel Butler, "A Diary, from February 10th 1639 of My Personal Employments," British Library, Sloane 758, 2 June 1639; Pargellis and Lapham, "Daniell Ellffryth's Guide to the Caribbean," 312, 313.

9   "Carta a la Audiencia de Guatemala sobre los establicimientos de los ingleses en la costa, 1704," in *Colección de documentos referentes a la historia colonial de Nicaragua* (Managua, 1921), 5.

10   De Lussan, *Raveneau de Lussan*, 285; M. W., "The Mosqueto Indian and his Golden River. A familiar Description of the Mosqueto Kingdom in America, with a Relation of the Strange Customs, Religion, Wars, &c. of those heathenish People," *A Collection of Voyages and Travels, Some Now First Printed from Oriental Manuscripts, Others Now First Published in English . . .*, ed. Awnsham Churchill (London: J. Walthoe, 1732), 289, 293; D. Pedro de Rivera, "Noticias Sobre los Mosquitos y medios de Exterminarlos, Guatemala, 25 Nov. 1742," in *Costa Rica y Costa de Mosquitos*, ed. Manuel M. de Peralta (hereafter cited as CRCM) (Paris, 1898), 121; "Informe de D. Fray Benito Garret y Arloví, Obispo de Nicaragua, sobre los mosquitos y el modo de reducirlos, Granada, 30 November 1711," in CRCM, 57–58; Potthast-Jutkeit, "Indians, Blacks," 54–55; Helms, "Miskito Slaving," 179; Romero Vargas, *Las sociedades del Atlántico*, 123–26.

11   Minutes of a Court for Providence Island, 31 January 1638, National Archives, Great Britain, Public Record Office (hereafter PRO), Colonial Office (hereafter CO) 124/2, 313.

12   Newton, *The Colonising Activities*, 150, 258, 303; Kupperman, *Providence Island*, 33, 84–88, 104–9, 116, 169–72, 199, 338; Potthast-Jutkeit, "Indians, Blacks," 54–55; Offen, "Miskitu Kingdom," 116–24, 174–75; Offen, "Sambo and Tawira Miskitu," 329–41.

13   Esquemelin, *The Buccaneers of America*, 234, 238.

14   Uring, *The Voyages and Travels*, 154–55; de Lussan, *Raveneau de Lussan*, 287; Offen, "Sambo and Tawira Mosquito," 329–41.

15   Uring, *Voyages and Travels*, 155; Romero Vargas and Solorzano, "Declaración de Carlos Casarola," 88; Hodgson to Lordships, 4 April 1744, PRO, CO

323/11, 67–68; D. Ambrosio Thomás Santella M., "Guatemala, 3 Oct. 1716, Sobre el cumplimiento de la Real Cédula de 30 Abril de 1714, acerca del exterminio de los mosquitos," in CRCM, 75–86; M. W., "Mosqueto Indian," 288–91; Offen, "Miskitu Kingdom," 141–91.

16   M. W., "Mosqueto Indian," 287–90; Uring, *Voyages and Travels*, 156; Romero Vargas and Solorzano, "Declaración de Carlos Casarola," 88; Offen, "Miskitu Kingdom," 184.

17   Peter to Governor Hunter, Sandy Bay, 3 October 1729, PRO, CO 137/18, 68–69; "Meeting 3 June 1730," *Journal of the Commissioners for Trade and Plantations*, 14 vols. (hereafter cited as JCTP) (London: His Majesty's Stationary Office, 1920–38), 6:120. See also Olien, "The Miskito Kings," 206; Romero Vargas, *Sociedades del Atlántico*, 163–67; Olien, "General, Governor, and Admiral," 283, 287; Offen, "Creating Mosquitia," 266–67.

18   M. W., "Mosqueto Indian," 286. Meanwhile expressions such as *indios y zambos mosquitos* and *zambos y indios* begin to characterize Spanish-language sources after 1700. "D. Carlos Marenco informa al general D. Manuel López Pintado sobre los indios y zambos Mosquitos, San Felipe de Portobelo, 16 Feb. 1731," in Fernández, *Colección de documentos para la historia de Costa Rica*, (hereafter cited as CDHCR) 9:187–205; "Granada se halla de ser invadida por los ingleses y sus aliados los zambos é indios mosquitos, Granada, 12 May 1757," CDHCR, 9:524–27.

19   Robert Hodgson to Lords of the Committee of Council, Black River, 1 April 1744, PRO, CO 323/11, 67–68.

20   Robert Hodgson Jr., *Some Account of the Mosquito Territory, contained in a memoir written in 1757* (Edinburgh, 1822), 46–47.

21   [R. Jones?], "Report on the Mosquito Shore," *The Kemble Papers*, vol. 2, *Expedition to Nicaragua, 1780–1* (New York: New York Historical Society, 1884), 419; "Letter of the Inhabitants of the Mosquito Shore to the late Earl of Chatham, 1766," *The Defence of Robert Hodgson* (London, 1779), appendix V, 4–5; Porta Costas, "Relación del reconocimiento geométrico y político," 57; Romero Vargas, *Sociedades del Atlántico*, 163; Ayón, *Historia de Nicaragua*, 3:169–70.

22   Declaration of Edward, King of the Mosquito Indians, Senock Dawkra, 16 March 1740, PRO, CO 123/1, 52.

23   "Robert Hodgson to Trelawny, Chiriqui Lagoon, 21 June 1740," *The States of Central America, Their Geography, Topography, Climate . . . Etc*, ed. Ephraim G. Squier (New York: Harper and Brothers, 1858), appendix D, 746; Hodgson to Trelawny, St. Jago de la Vega, 28 November 1740, PRO, CO 137/57, 39.

24   Diary of a Tour made by Robert Hodgson along the Mosquito Shore, 9 April 1772, PRO, CO 137/67, 105.

25   Memorial of Rev. Warren, 1773, British Library, Add. Ms. 12413, 4; Long, "Mosquito Shore," 1:316 (for Warren's passage).

26 Butler, "A Diary"; de Lussan, *Raveneau de Lussan*, 286; Dampier, *New Voyage*, 15–17, 67; Uring, *Voyages and Travels*, 161; Burney, *History of the Buccaneers of America*, 91–95, 105, 164.

27. M. W. "Mosqueto Indian," 287, 292; Romero Vargas and Solorzano, "Declaración de Carlos Casarola," 88–89; "Declaración de Micaela Gómez, mulata libre, 2 Jan. 1717," in CRCM, 89; Uring, *Voyages and Travels*, 156–57; Juan Geronimo Duardo, "Carta a la Presidente de la Real Audiencia de Goathemala," Guatemala, 26 July 1704, in CDHCR, 6–7; "Carta a la Audiencia de Guatemala sobre los establecimientos de los ingleses en la costa, etc. 1704," in CDHCR, 3–5; Floyd, *The Anglo-Spanish Struggle*, 64–67; Romero Vargas, *Sociedades del Atlántico*, 157–59; Conzemius, *Ethnographical Survey*, 84–87.

28 M. W., "Mosqueto Indian," 288, 290; Hodgson, *Account of the Mosquito Territory*, 48.

29 Lawrie to Germain, Black River, 28 May 1777, PRO, CO 137/72, 147; see also Lawrie to Governor of Jamaica, Black River, 3 April 1778, PRO, CO 137/73, 185.

30 Articles of Agreement between Gov. Lawes and King Jeremy, St. Jago de la Vega, 25 June 1720, PRO, CO 137/13, 268–69; Speech of Nicholas Lawes, Jamaica, 28 June 1720, PRO, CO 137/13, 263; Speech of Nicholas Lawes, Jamaica, 4 October 1720, PRO, CO 137/13, 285–86; Lawes to Board of Trade, Jamaica, 13 November 1720, PRO, CO 137/13, 280–82; "Gov. Lawes to Council of Trade and Plantations, 24 Aug. 1721," *Calendar of State Papers, Colonial Series, America and West Indies*, ed. Cecil Headlam, 39 vols. (London: His Majesty's Stationary Office, 1920–33), 27:126, 128; [Joseph Smith Speer], "Notes on That Part of the Map and Chart of the Continent, in the West Indies, Called the Bay of Honduras and the Mosquito Shore" [ca. 1765], PRO, Records of the Admiralty (hereafter cited as ADM) 7/837.

31 Roberts, *Jamaica*, 62–64; C. Robinson, *The Fighting Maroons*, 40; Uring, *Voyages and Travels*, 160; "Meeting June 3, 1731," JCTP, 6:206.

32 M. W., "Mosqueto Indian," 285–86; Hodgson, *Account of the Mosquito Territory*, 55; Offen, "Creating Mosquitia," 254–82.

33 "Pedro de Salazar, Guatemala, 11 Nov. 1769," *Boletín del Archivo General del Gobierno* (Guatemala) 5, no. 4 (1940), 343.

34 "Plano de Colville Cairns para mejor establecimiento del Gobierno Español en La Costa de Mosquitos, London, 24 Oct. 1786," and "El Marqués del Campo a Condé de Floridablanca, London, 24 Oct. 1786," both in *Costa Rica y Colombia de Mosquitos*, ed. Manuel M. de Peralta (San José, 1889), 254, 249.

35 Passage cited in Ayón, *Historia de Nicaragua*, 3:202.

36 Tompson, "Frontiers of Identity," especially chap. 4.

37 DeKalb, "Nicaragua," 239.

38 Schubert, "Some Experiences," 94.

39 De Lussan, *Raveneau de Lussan*, 288; M. W. "Mosqueto Indians," 288; "Relación de una cautividad," CRCM, 87–92; "Declaración del mulato Miguel Gutiérrez," Masaya, 10 October 1710, Archivo General de Indias, Seville (hereafter AGI) Guatemala, 300, 396; "Declaración de Gregorio López," Cartago, 25 April 1724, AGI Guatemala, 455; Offen, "Sambo and Tawira Miskitu," 344–45.

40 "Sobre el Fallecimiento del coronel Dn. Roberto Hogzon, é inventario de sus bienes, 1791," Archivo General de Centro América, Guatemala City (hereafter cited as AGCA) A2.1, leg. 9, exp.158; Dawson, "William Pitt's Settlement"; Dawson, "The Evacuation"; Offen, "British Logwood Extraction."

41 Duke of Bedford to Gov. Trelawny, Whitehall, 5 October 1749, PRO, CO 137/48, 186–87.

42 Gov. Trelawny to Duke of Bedford, 14 April 1750, PRO, CO 137/57, 532–34.

43 M. W., "Mosquito Indian," 288, 290; Uring, *Voyages and Travels*, 125; Trelawny to Duke of Bedford, Jamaica, 14 April 1750, PRO, CO 137/57, 533; Sorsby, "British Superintendency," 51–52; Romero Vargas, *Sociedades del Atlántico*, 102; Lawrie to Trelawny, Black River, 9 April 1751, PRO, CO 137/25; Pedro Gaxaycoechea, "Relación de las Poblaciones que Tienen los Yngleses en la Costa de Honduras," 1746, British Library, Add. Ms. 17566, 171.

44 Lawrie to Gov. Trelawny, Black River, 9 April 1751, PRO, CO 137/25; "Relato de una expedición a la costa norte hecho por Juan de Lara y Ortega, Comayagua, 18 Sept. 1759," *Boletín del Archivo General del Gobierno* (Guatemala) 5, no. 2 (1940), 138; Hodgson, *Account of the Mosquito Territory*, 15.

45 Hodgson, *Account of the Mosquito Territory*, 15, 16; "The First Account of the State of That Part of America Called the Mosquito Shore. In the Year 1757," PRO, CO 123/1, 55–80.

46 R. Jones to Gov. Elletson, Jamaica, 3 August 1768, PRO, CO 137/35, 27; Joseph Otway, "Inhabitants of the Mosquito Shore," Mosquito Shore, 21 April 1764, PRO, CO 137/33, 168; Klingberg, "The Efforts of the S.P.G. to Christianize the Mosquito Indians, 1742–1785," 314, 316; James Lawrie to Rev. William Robertson, Black River, 10 November 1774, National Library of Scotland, Edinburgh (hereafter NLS), Robertson-MacDonald Papers, Ms. 3942, 175.

47 Diez Navarro, "Costa, y poblaciones que ay en rio tinto," 1:81–82, 2: núm. 32. See also Davidson, *Atlas de mapas*.

48 Offen, "Creating Mosquitia," especially 278–80.

49 W. Brown, "Mosquito Shore," 43–64; S. J. Robinson, "Southern Loyalists." See also Dawson, "William Pitt's Settlement," 688, 693; Richard Owen, "Sketch of the Eastern Coast of Central America," 1839, Royal Geographical Society, Central America JMS 5/9, 11; A List of Settlers on the Mosquito Shore, 16 October 1786, PRO, CO 137/86, 164.

50 A List of Settlers on the Mosquito Shore, 16 October 1786, PRO, CO 137/86, 164; Bolland, *The Formation of a Colonial Society*, 34–35, 41; Romero Vargas, *Sociedades del Atlántico*, 100–102.

51 William Pitt to Gov. Trelawny, Mosketo Shore, 17 July 1749, PRO, CO 137/57, 530–31; Robert Hodgson to Duke of Bedford, Jamaica, 21 April 1751, PRO, CO 137/57, 550; Jones to Elletson, Jamaica, 3 August 1768, PRO, CO 137/35, 24; "Meeting Aug. 3, 1768," JCTP, 13:139.

52 Petition of the Inhabitants living at Cape Gracias a Dios, Cape Gracias, 28 February 1770, PRO, CO 137/65, 206.

53 [Richard Jones], "Part of the Moschetto Shore from Cape River to Brewers Lagoon, with the number of inhabitants residing on that part of the Shore and Fortifications at Black River," 28 May 1751, Map, Kingston, PRO, CO 700/British Honduras 4.

54 Trelawny to Duke, 14 April 1750, PRO, CO 137/57, 533.

55 "Copy of a Spanish Report on the Mosquito Indians," NLS, Liston Papers, Ms. 5531, 29–30; Potthast, *Die Mosquito-Küste*, 237–38.

56 "Report on the Mosquito Shore," 430.

57 Otway to Commissioners, Black River, 20 January 1766, PRO, CO 137/34, 11; "Meeting July 8, 1766," JCTP, 12:304.

58 Black River residents to Mr. Jones, Black River, 12 March 1770, PRO, CO 137/65, 208–9. Hodgson was happy to report, "The Strong Apprehension entertained by all the inhabitants here of an Insurrection of the Slaves at Mr. Pitts Death has proved abortive." Robert Hodgson to William Trelawny, Black River, 12 June 1771, PRO, CO 137/67, 46.

59 Robert Hodgson to Hillsborough, Black River, 1 November 1771, PRO CO 137/67, 41.

60 Potthast, *Die Mosquito-Küste*, 238–9; Report of Major Robert Hoare, 16 June 1780, PRO, CO 137/78, 305.

61 His Majesty's Battalion of Free People of Colour, Black River, 22 June 1784, Belize Archives, 3-Mos. Sho., 83.

62 Black River Settler's Committee to James Lawrie, Black River, Mosquito Shore, 14 October 1786, PRO, CO 137/86, 162.

63 Lawrie to Governor of Jamaica, Black River, 14 October 1786, PRO, CO 137/86, 156–60.

64 Robert Sproat to Col. Thomas Barrows, New Egypt, 5 April 1803, PRO, CO 123/15, 61.

65 This is an unusual but not infrequent event if one reads between the lines of prosaic records at Black River after 1774. Minutes of Council, 22 January 1787, Belize Archives, 1-Mos. Sho., 103–4.

66 Lawrie to William Robertson, Black River, 10 November 1774, NLS, Robertson-MacDonald Papers, Ms. 3942, 174.

67 Richard Jones to Gov. Elletson, Jamaica, 3 August 1768, PRO, CO 137/35, 27; Hodgson, Account of the Mosquito Territory, 19; Authorizing Mahogany Gangs, Kingston, 29 April 1783, Belize Archives, 3-Mos. Sho., 39–40; Offen, "British Logwood Extraction," 126–29; Offen, "The Geographical Imagina-

tion," 68–73; W. Brown, "Mosquito Shore," 49–50; Long, "Mosquito Shore," 1:318; "Report on the Mosquito Shore," 428.

68   Settler's Committee to James Lawrie, Black River, Mosquito Shore, 14 October 1786, PRO, CO 137/86, 161.

69   Export duties on mahogany shipped in 1785, Belize Archives, 1-Mos. Sho., 80.

70   Sir Charles Whitworth, *State of the trade of Great Britain in its imports and exports . . .* , 2 vols. (London, 1776), 2:89–90.

71   Joseph Otway to Commissioners of Trade and Plantations, Black River, 25 April 1764, PRO, CO 137/33, 168; "A List of Vessels Entering and Leaving Black River in 1770," Black River, October 1770, PRO CO 137/66, 129–130; Offen, "British Logwood Extraction," 126–29.

72   "Report on the Mosquito Shore," 428.

73   Agreement to manage Cattle herd on Patook Savanna, 21 April 1779, Belize Archives, Mos. Sho. bk. 4, 95–96.

74   Dawson, "William Pitt's Settlement," 704; Colville Cairns to James Lawrie, Tebuppy, 10 May 1777, PRO, CO 137/73, 197–202; José del Río, "Disertación del viaje hecho de órden del Rey, Trujillo, 23 Aug. 1793," in *Límites de Costa-Rica y Colombia*, 147–48; Romero Vargas, *Sociedades del Atlántico*, 100–101; Ayón, *Historia de Nicaragua*, 3:195; Porta Costas, "Relación del Reconocimiento," 56–57; "Record of Capt. Hodgson's Voyages and Expeditions refuting his Accusers," *Defence of Robert Hodgson*, appendix V, 83–85; Offen, "Ecología cultural mískita," 55–56.

75   Act of Council, Black River, 18 March 1776, Belize Archives, 1-Mos. Sho., 1–7; List of People retailing Rum, Black River, 1776, Belize Archives, 1-Mos. Sho., 77; Revenue Duties Collected, 1785, Black River, Belize Archives, 1-Mos. Sho., 80.

76   Richard Jones to Gov. Trelawny, Black River, 22 September 1748, PRO, CO 137/48, 176.

77   Joseph Otway to Commissioners of Trade and Plantations, Black River, 25 April 1764, PRO, CO 137/33, 168.

78   Memorial of Rev. Warren, 1773, British Library, Add. Ms. 12413, 3–6; Record of Shipment, Black River, 10 July 1773, Belize Archives, Mos. Sho., bk. 2, 8.

79   Sale of a Sugar Estate, Black River, 1 July 1779, Belize Archives, Mos. Sho. bk. 4, 119–20.

80   "Report on the Mosquito Shore," 428; "Descripción del Rio Tinto y del de Mustees formada en el mes de Mayo del Año 1787," *Cartografía y Relaciones Históricas de Ultramar*, 2: map 34.

81   Joseph Otway to Commissioners of Trade and Plantations, Black River, 12 July 1765, PRO, CO 137/33, 233.

82   Bell, *Tangweera*, 41; Offen, "Sambo and Tawira Miskitu," 348–51.

83   Hodgson, *Account of the Mosquito Territory*, 54; de la Haya, "Letter from

Cartago, 8 Oct. 1722," in *Límites de Costa-Rica y Colombia*, 27; Hodgson Sr. to Lord, Mosquito Shore, 4 April 1744, PRO, CO 323/11, 68. See also "Hodgson to Trelawny, Sandy Bay, 8 April 1740," *States of Central America*, 746.

84 Otway to Commissioners, 12 July 1765, PRO, CO 137/33, 232–35; Lawrie to Rev. Robertson, Black River, 10 November 1774, NLS, Robertson-MacDonald Papers, Ms. 3942, 175; Dawson, "William Pitt's Settlement at Black River," 697.

85 Cairns to Lawrie, Tebuppy, 10 May 1777, PRO, CO 137/73, 202; "List of Indian Slaves belong to Colvill Cairns, Tebuppy, Oct. 1776," Belize Archives, Mos. Sho. bk. 4, 78.

86 Robert Hodgson to Duke of Bedford, Jamaica, 21 April 1751, PRO, CO 137/57, 550; Otway to Commissioners, 12 July 1765, PRO, CO 137/33, 232–35; Act for Recovering and Extending the Trade with the Indian Tribes and preventing for the Future some Evil Practices formerly Committed in that Trade, 22 Aug. 1776, Belize Archives, 1-Mos. Sho., 16–18; Indian Chiefs to Earl of Dartmouth, [England], 10 November 1775, PRO, CO 137/70, 155; "Meeting 24 May 1776," JCTP, 14:31; "Meeting 14 May 1776," JCTP, 14:27; Copy of a letter from John Barry, Black River, 22 August 1776, in "An old letter book of the Mosquito Shore," Belize, 1822, PRO, CO 123/32, 11–13; "Letter of thanks from Mosquito Indians," *Calendar of Home Office Papers of the Reign of George III. 1773–1775. Preserved in the Public Record Office*, ed. Richard Arthur Roberts (London: Her Majesty's Stationary Office, 1899), 460–61; Superintendent of Belize to His Lord Duke of Manchester, Belize, 3 April 1824, PRO, CO 123/35, appendix XXII, 87.

87 Hodgson, *Account of the Mosquito Territory*, 21; Joseph Otway to Commissioners of Trade and Plantations, Black River, 12 July 1765, PRO, CO 137/33; Jones to Gov. Elletson, 1768, PRO, CO 137/35, 25.

88 Superintendent of Belize to His Lord Duke of Manchester, Belize, 3 April 1824, PRO, CO 123/35, appendix. XXII, 88; Hodgson, *Account of the Mosquito Territory*, 15.

89 Will of Colvill Cairns, Black River, 20 April 1778, Belize Archives, Mos. Sho., bk. 4, 63–64.

90 A Copy of the Last Will and Testament of Henry Corrin, Bluefields on the Musquito Shore, 25 August 1767, Manx Library, Isle of Man, Ms. 3208; Sobre haver salido voluntariamente 47 Yndios caribes de ambos sexos de la Montaña del Norte en Matagalpa, 1768, AGCA A1.12 leg. 119, exp. 4826.

91 Inventory of the Estate of George Cummings Corrin, Blewfields Bluff, 5 December 1771, Manx Library, Ms. 3248; Inventory and Appraisal of Blewfields Estate, 30 August 1773, Thomas Marshall and Alex. Patterson, Manx Library, Ms. 3250. I thank Dan Krutka for helping me transcribe this document.

92 On Creole ethnogenesis in eastern Nicaragua, see Gordon, *Disparate Diasporas*, 32–40.

93   Inventory of Bluefields Estate, N. L'estrange, Bluefields, 1 December 1772, Manx Library, Ms. 3225; Abstract of Petition of Cookeraw Indians by Richard Jones, 28 May 1770, PRO, CO 137/65, 196.

94   Corrin Estate, 3 December 1774, Belize Archives, 3-Mos. Sho., 34.

95   Colville Cairns to John Lawrie, Tebuppy, 12 September 1775, Manx Library, Ms. 3236.

96   "Diligencias practicadas por el Governador y comandante general de la Provincia de Nicaragua . . . año 1776," AGCA A1, leg. 117, exp. 2478.

97   Copy of Grant of Land to John Bourke from King George (Río Grande) 1775, Belize, 15 October 1845, PRO, Foreign Office, 53/44, 287–90; Will of John Bourke, Black River, 18 July 1778, Belize Archives, Mos. Sho. bk. 4, 75–76; Equiano, *Interesting Narrative*, 168–78; Potthast, *Die Mosquito-Küste*, 237; Presidente de Goatemala al Governador de Panama, sobre impedir el establecimiento de Yngleses en la Costa de Mosquitos, Guatemala, 28 February 1776, AGI Guatemala 665, 407–9. What little we know about sugar production at Cape Gracias is gleaned from Gonzalo Vallego, "Plano de la Ensenada del Cavo de Gracias á Dios en la Costa de Mosquitos," Map, Archivo del Museo Naval, Madrid, 12-B-7, 1788. Vassa's time in Mosquitia is discussed in Lovejoy, "Autobiography and Memory," 317–47.

98   Offen, "Sambo and Tawira Miskitu," 350–51.

Slave Wages in Omoa

Rina Cáceres Gómez

In 1790 Florencia Palma began lengthy litigation before the military authorities of the Omoa fort for the payment of her back wages. She had worked for six months in the construction of one of the boats destined for the Motagua River trade and in the clearing of brush and woodcutting of the uninhabitable lands surrounding Omoa's San Fernando Fort without the promised payment being made. They had offered her a daily wage of three reales, while Luis Aque, master ship's carpenter, received six reales per day and Luis Gonzáles, a woodcutter, four. The complaint was made on her behalf and that of her family, and on behalf of several free blacks who made up one of the work gangs; the other gang was made up of slaves. It was not uncommon for free blacks and slaves to work together on construction projects in Central American lands; what is surprisingly uncommon is that the complaint indicates that four woodcutters, Manuel Toquero, Pedro Narciso Udole, Juan Mateo Nobondo, and Juan Colorado Musinga, all slaves of the king, had also received daily wages, along with the "English blacks," a group of runaway former slaves from Belize housed in the fort.

It is certainly noteworthy that among the work gangs there were some salaried royal slaves, for the payment of salaries has usually been associated with workers in capitalist enterprises. However, the topic of wage-earning slaves is not new, and at least in other settings they clearly appear in the social terrain.[1] In the case of the caliphate of Sokoto in Africa, for example, we find slaves who paid their owners for the right to work on their own account. By means of this payment they could acquire a certain degree of autonomy and with it the possibility of buying their freedom, marrying, and even owning their own residence, blurring the distinctions between free and slave.[2]

The rental of slave workers occurred in many parts of America and was a source of income for many owners. According to Mieko Nishida, it was a typically urban phenomenon, with part- or full-time rentals, after which they were obliged to turn over to their masters a predetermined daily or weekly portion of their earnings. They worked as peddlers, gangs of porters, and artisans and took care of market stalls.[3] In regions such as Bahía slaves on their own account (*escravos de ganho*) were in charge of practically all transportation, movement, and delivery of goods. João Reiss has shown that to pursue these occupations for their masters' profit slaves needed a certain degree of independence and freedom to move about, maintain their own accounts, and even accumulate enough cash to be able to buy their freedom. This autonomy created not only a work culture but also an organization that made them powerful enough to paralyze the city in 1857, when the authorities sought to restrict their freedom of movement.[4]

These were the wages that Florencia Palma spoke of. Was this the case of an exceptional work gang, or part of a general crown policy in San Fernando de Omoa? And if the latter were the case, did this slave community as social microcosm witness any social differentiation, the product of inequalities in work distribution, whether in social or economic benefits or privileges?[5]

Works by Mario Argueta, Manuel Rubio Sánchez, Juan Manuel Zapatero, and Victor Cruz have called attention to the strategic and architectural, not to mention the military and social, importance of the fort.[6] But thereafter little attention has been paid to the people who lived there, to the soldiers and laborers who built the fort and who created one of the most complex societies of colonial Central America. For years the stone slabs of its enormous walls have seemed to silence the existence of a large and active community tied to the rest of the Central American and Caribbean region, subjected to the strictest patterns of social control and violence.

OMOA SOCIETY

Omoa society was organized around the construction of the fort and by the second half of the eighteenth century had more than 1,300 residents. The majority of the inhabitants were permanent residents; others were just passing through, since in addition to the fort the site was a port that grew in importance over the years.

The social scene of Omoa was made up of six clearly defined social ranks: authorities and commanders, militiamen from different parts of the region, prisoners, enslaved Africans, a group formed in 1790 by "English Blacks" escaped from Belize, and an important group of Indians brought to Omoa from different localities as forced laborers from the second half of the eighteenth century to the beginning of the nineteenth, although fewer in number over time.

In 1777 the commander González Fermidor reported that 1,343 individuals lived in the entire establishment, including the town, where 404 inhabitants lived, among whom we find several slaves with *castizo* or Latinized names who likely worked as domestics. Nearby were the huts of the Africans, containing 611 people, most born in Africa, and the 314 troops, militiamen, and volunteers in the barracks. To these groups must be added the port workers, the shipyard workers, those who repaired the sails, and others, who may have lived in the town or in nearby settlements.

The construction of the fort began in 1745. Ten years later the chapel, the hospital, and houses for the officials were finished. In this first phase of the work the number of workers assigned to construction was limited and made up of Indian laborers from Tenoca and Gracias a Dios, as well as free blacks and mulattos from coastal Honduras, too few for the magnitude of the enterprise.[7]

In the decade beginning in 1750, because of the slow pace of construction there were bitter disputes among the officials. But in view of the need to reinforce the Caribbean frontier in response to the fear of a British invasion and the reinforcement of British establishments on the Mosquito Coast and in Belize, the High Court, or Audiencia, authorities requested new funds to complete the fort. In that context, in 1756 the crown purchased the first one hundred enslaved Africans from Gaspar Hall, resident in Jamaica.[8] The intermediaries on this occasion were the English merchants Guillermo Pitt and Robert Hodson, residents in Río Tinto and Bluefields, respectively, who controlled the commercial triangle with Belize and Jamaica. On the island of Jamaica the slave price depended on the region of origin, with the highest prices for those coming from the Akan region, called the Gold Coast by Europeans. The traders sold them "in groups of one hundred, made up of 50 men, 30 women, 10 boys and

10 girls."[9] According to the report, the Spaniards preferred other groupings at a lower price, but without indicating origin. In 1759 the Royal Treasury officials reported a second group made up of two hundred Africans.[10]

In 1770 and in the context of the conflict between England and Spain for control of the Central American Caribbean, the Captaincy General of Guatemala decided to expel the English from Rio Tinto and Blue Lagoon, for which it requested help from Cuba. However, owing to the lack of funds for the transfer of troops to Central America, Havana preferred to authorize the purchase of another one hundred slaves, but taking care that this not contribute to smuggling, by that time common throughout the Caribbean region. The Cubans indicated that slaves could be gotten "in another foreign colony but transported in Spanish shipping and without other trade goods." Don Alonso de Arcos y Moreno, then captain and governor of Guatemala, acknowledged receiving through Robert Hodgson an offer of slaves for sale, once again from Gaspar Hall.

In 1770 the double-masted sailing ship (*bergantín*) *Honduras*, captained by Juan Monerief and escorted by a war convoy, took one hundred men and one hundred women from Jamaica for delivery to the president of the Audiencia of Guatemala. They were purchased for 184 pesos each, plus two hundred clothing outfits for three hundred pesos and one hundred hats and one hundred shawls or scarves at two reales each. The crown had advanced a total of thirty-seven thousand pesos in a commercial agreement with Gaspar Hall. The captives arrived late owing to a recent downturn in slave supplies. From Kingston on 24 April 1770 Hall explained, "To comply with my obligation I have had to purchase a group of 450 from which to choose that group of 200." The crown had agreed to pay Hall promptly upon the slaves' arrival and authorized him to sell any that may have arrived in ill health. Hall assured the crown that the ships would carry no "prohibited" products to sell, as he had refrained from doing in the past.[11]

At the end of 1770 another 211 slaves arrived in the ships *San Marcos* and *Diamante*. The slave *asiento*, or license, of Aguirre and Arestegui, a Cádiz company based in Puerto Rico, made this last shipment to Central American lands.[12]

There are different versions of the number of slaves sold, as well as of the total cost paid in the decade beginning in 1770. Some speak of 220, 221, or 217 slaves. An order for payment from October 1770 mentions a payment to Don José Piñol, a merchant resident in Guatemala and representative of the Cádiz asiento concession, of 15,760 pesos for the remainder of a total debt of 55,760 pesos, of which 40,000 had already been paid to José Melchor de Ugalde, agent of the same asiento. But there is another authorization for 24,422 pesos, 6 reales in payment for the slaves sent on the *San Marcos* and delivered to José Casimiro Fernández, sergeant of the dragoons, plus the 100 pesos advanced to José del Castillo and 577 pesos in taxes (*por derechos*), for a total of 25,000 for the Omoa expenses. Thus we know of three ships transporting Africans: the *Honduras*, the *San Marcos*, and the single-mast sailboat *Diamante*.[13]

The Africans joined a conglomerate of people of different origins, in which the militiamen played a central role. In 1771 the regular militia was made up of thirty-six infantrymen and eighteen artillerymen, a number that changed little over the entire late colonial period. They attended to the watch and the fort construction, although we also find them out at sea. In the packet boat *San Fernando*, property of the crown, for example, twenty-nine artillerymen, thirty-four sailors, eight sailor apprentices (*grumetes*), one cook, and four officials worked, alternating between that vessel and other launches, sloops, and schooners the Comandancia had charge of.

In the town were many different workers, from the midwife Catarina Padilla to those in charge of manufacturing sails (*triquetes y foques*) for the canoes that shipped goods, as well as those in charge of draining the marshes, clearing brush, cutting wood, and moving earth.

In the fort's hospital a corporal attended, daily caring for the health of slaves, prisoners, sailors, and soldiers, always lacking medicine and tools, who was paid seven and a half reales per month, considerably lower than the officials' salary. In the chapel the sacristan and catechist Felipe Bardales, a mulatto, received the same pay, seven and a half reales, for each of these posts. Among his duties were the care and cleaning of the furnishings, jewelry, and ornaments, tolling the bell, officiating at mass, praying the rosario de Maria Santísima every Saturday and Sunday, and teaching Christian doctrine to the Africans.[14]

In the fort construction work gangs made up of "volunteers" and militiamen also participated. In 1771 we find thirty volunteers who received two reales per day during the nine months they were hired; fifty-two militiamen from Gracias a Dios and thirty-eight from Tenoca also received four reales each "to return home." The carpentry workshop (*mae-stranza*)—the shops where war materiel, artillery pieces, and ships' gear were repaired—brought together a goodly number of skilled workers as carpenters, caulkers,[15] brick masons, stonemasons, and blacksmiths.

CONSTRUCTION WORK

The building of Spanish forts in Central America was part of a broader policy developed in America but dating back to medieval Spain and North Africa. According to Quijano, there were three engineering schools: the Italian in the sixteenth century; the Flamenca, dominant in the seventeenth century; and the French in the eighteenth century. These last two are visible in Central American military architecture, where three forts located in the north of the region stand out: San Felipe de Bacalar in the Campeche peninsula, the Castle of San Felipe del Golfo Dulce in Caribbean Guatemala, and San Fernando de Omoa. Farther south in Nicaragua are the Castle of San Carlos and the Fort of the Immaculate Conception on the San Juan River.[16]

But it would be the siege, the taking of Havana by the British between July 1762 and August 1763 and the loss of the Royal Treasury, estimated at a million silver pesos, that would make for a state of emergency in military construction in the region.

Spain regained the city at the negotiating table in exchange for Florida and permission for the British to log in Belize or British Honduras, at its border with Campeche. Immediately thereafter Spain named a new governor with special powers in Cuba and assigned new resources to defensive reconstruction in the region, decreeing an annual subsidy of 300,000 pesos for Havana's fortification, 100,000 for San Juan in Puerto Rico, and another 100,000 for Honduras, to be taken from the revenues of New Spain. Construction was supervised this time by engineers trained in the French tradition, among whom were Agustín Cramer and Luis Díez de Navarro.

A central problem for the construction was finding labor. For that reason among the powers that the new captain general of Cuba received was the right to buy, in the king's name, hundreds of enslaved workers directly from slave traders. Jennings argues that at the end of the 1760s the Spanish crown in Havana had the largest group of slaves employed in public works and became the largest owner and employer on the island, using slaves in its military, naval, infrastructure, and productive enterprises.[17]

The reconstruction work was carried out in a large number of forts, among them La Cabaña, Atares, El Príncipe, and La Muralla in La Habana; San Severino and Jagua in Matanzas; and Aguadores, Juragua, and Sardineros in Santiago de Cuba, where hundreds of slaves worked, along with prisoners, in the trenching of the fortifications. At these sites they were trained to work as stonemasons, stonecutters, masons, woodcutters, and drainage and construction workers (*canteros, picapedreros, albañiles, aguaderos y peones*).[18] After 1763 most of the assistants were slaves; according to the authorities, this ensured a stable supply of skilled labor. Moreover, when sold they would fetch a much higher price based on the skills they had acquired.

However, the system turned out to be very costly, and despite the recommendations of an engineer named Cramer regarding the preference (*pertinencia*) of using African workers owing to their great capacity for work, they began to be replaced by prisoners. In 1768 the number of enslaved Africans was 1,136, compared to 636 prisoners. One year later the numbers had been inverted, with 1,115 prisoners and 766 enslaved blacks. According to Governor Bucareli, the change was owing to the high cost of buying and maintaining slaves and their high rate of mortality. Hiring free workers was not economically feasible because that required spending three reales per day per man, so the government concluded that the only way to keep costs within the limits of the 300,000 peso budget was by employing prisoners, a policy followed from the beginning in the constructions in San Juan, Puerto Rico.[19]

In Cuba by 1777 the crown owned 350 slaves (and their children as well), of whom 100 were artillerymen and 250 were used in construction, "to whom [King Charles III] give rations, clothing, and medical care"; they were organized into gangs identified by letters of the alphabet.[20] That same year in Omoa the Spanish crown owned 611 individuals organized by order of arrival, the first, second, third, fourth, and fifth groups (*contratas*),[21] located around the fort. Two years later some of these slaves were sold by the Royal Treasury to places distant from Omoa.[22]

The colonial administration fostered family formation by allowing pregnant women to avoid work; thus we find a sustained increase in the number of unions and births. In Cáceres Figure 1 we can see the numbers

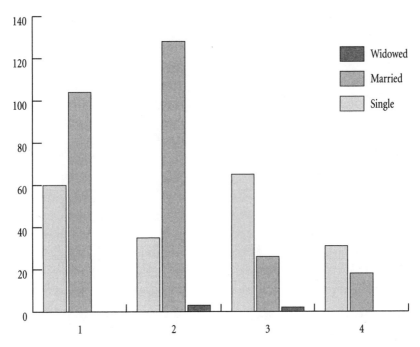

FIGURE 1 Number of single, married, and widowed slaves, by *contrata*, in Omoa, 1777. *Source*: Archivo General de Centro América, Guatemala City, A3.1, leg. 1293, exp. 22187.

of single and married slaves by shipment in 1777, where the last to arrive show the highest number of single persons, a situation that would change over the late colonial period.

A review of the Royal Hacienda's records shows that over the whole period from the mid-eighteenth to the early nineteenth century the population maintained a constant rhythm without abrupt changes despite a high mortality rate, perhaps compensated for by a high birth rate, an average of four children per nuclear family. An in-depth study of the evolution of Omoa's population awaits future work. Here I can only point out the general trend.

The colonial documentation indicates that the majority of the Africans were *mondongos* brought from the Congo-Angola region and *carabalíes* from eastern Nigeria, but only a linguistic study can confirm this or offer new clues as to possible origins. Among the African surnames maintained we find, for example, Hete, Sibuanza, Evo, Ovy, Ocara, Mabanado,

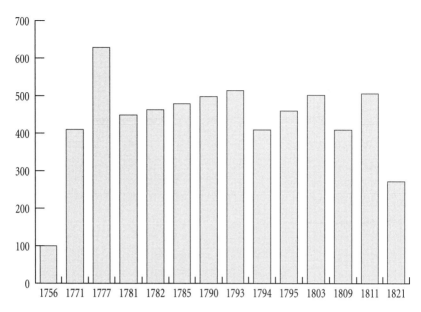

FIGURE 2 Evolution of Omoa's slave population. *Source*: Archivo General de Centro América, Guatemala City, A3.1, legs. 1093, 1287, 1293, 1067, 1307, 692, 588, 1328, 1305.

Cofy, Acuanavo, Ensangua, Pemba, Oququene, Acue, Ocore, Mangandi, Novoro, and Udenda. Such names were indeed uncommon, since in most of Central America slaves were assigned Hispanic given and family names each time they were sold.

THE ORGANIZATION OF LABOR

The organization of the labor force involved two tasks: organizing the labor regime and supplying the subsistence needs of the enslaved workers. Regarding the former, workers were organized in gangs for the clearing of land, building, and military defense. Regarding subsistence, the system foresaw, as the king had indicated, the need for "rations, clothing, and health care," as well as housing. But Omoa was located on an unhealthy site, and disease ensured that construction would be costly not only in economic terms but in human lives. Its distance from the capital and from other population centers made access to basic consumption goods as well as provisioning of the workers difficult, explaining in part the attention paid to politically controlling the enslaved labor force.

In reviewing the royal accounts we discover that the rations the king spoke of consisted of the payment of a daily wage (*gratificación diaria*) for the work slaves were to carry out. This reward or wage of one real, only one-third of what a free worker received, was to cover the subsistence needs of the slaves, minus clothing and medical attention. However, in reality, as we will see later, this was insufficient. The building work required different kinds of workers since some tasks were more complex than others, demanding greater technical skills, and in some cases involved overseeing a work gang, which gave access to a certain share of power. Thus different pay rates were established based on the work carried out and the level of experience required.

The accounting report of 1781 lists several gangs of workers. Among them were carpenters who worked alongside the officers and the blacksmiths in the town's workshop (*mediania*) and were in charge of making and repairing doors, windows, and gun carriages.[23] The daily rates varied between one and a half and four reales. That year the carpenter José Tovi, a slave, earned fourteen pesos, five reales, while for the same period Lopez Crebu, also a slave, earned 121 pesos, a sum comparable to the approximately 150 pesos per year free blacks earned for their labor. In the category of ship's carpentry, where workers were in charge of the repair and maintenance of the ships as well as the construction of wooden storage trunks, we find a master carpenter in charge of a foreman and a caulker, both enslaved. These two slaves manned two canoes, the mail boats charged with aiding vessels arriving from Spain or Havana.

But wages were not always enough to keep someone in Omoa, which was the case with Diego Mabala, who took advantage of an opening to flee his post in April 1781 without claiming the six pesos owed him. The shortage of skilled workers was an ongoing problem for the authorities. Very few skilled individuals were willing to move from Spain to these lands, although we do know of one work gang of eight master masons who left Cádiz for Omoa in 1769.[24] They earned a daily wage ranging from ten to fourteen reales plus the right to carry with them trunks with their personal effects and work tools. In such a context it is no surprise that several enslaved youth were sent to Guatemala and Cuba for specialized training.

The group of masons was made up of Juan Acue, Joseph Ordo, Luis Aca-
nique, Joseph Ocara, and Agustín Uron, supervised by the master mason
Joseph Espinoza, joined for a few days by one referred to as Ayaloya. The
base salary was the same as that for the carpenters, one-half real per day,
except in the cases of Juan Acue, who was paid four reales daily, and Espinoza, the foreman, who earned one peso daily. Both salaries were far
above the daily rates earned by the carpenters. Thus in the annual accounts we see that Juan Acue earned 153 and Joseph Espinoza 64 pesos, the
lower sum for having worked only from May to December, but a significant amount in comparative terms.

Another important occupation was that of Captain Francisco Palma,[25]
Juan Arroyo, Francisco Ocori, Miguel Occu, and Domingo Malli; they
were were in charge of the work routines and responsible for their orderly
execution. Yet contrary to what one might have imagined, they earned
daily wages of no more than one or two reales, not much more than the
rest of the workers. The captains or foremen directed the laborers to cut
palm in the bush, which they then carried back to town and stored in
the foremen's houses. The foremen were also in charge of supervising the
transport of dirt and the removal and discarding of straw from the roofs,
a task performed by the women's work gangs.

The blacksmiths were in charge of repairing axes, machetes, picks, hoes,
saws, and iron goods. The gun cabinet makers Gabriel Cofi and Francisco Encuro, for example, earned a daily wage of one real, amounting to
twenty-nine and thirty-six pesos, respectively, during that year.

Those royal slaves who demonstrated the "greatest dedication to their
work," but especially those who had technical abilities, received a higher
salary, as was the case of the caulker and barrel maker José Chaparro and
the carpenter Manuel Pancho. Living entirely on their royal wages, they
earned one and a half reales per day, in recognition of the shortage of
free workers, which increased their work load and prevented them from
spending more time on growing their own food and providing for themselves like the other slaves.[26] Last but not least, and the subject for another
day, there was a company of fifty-four enslaved artillerymen attached to
the regular troop artillery company of the royal forces.[27]

Access to cash was not limited to skilled workers or those regularly employed full time. On the contrary, from the Cuban experience forward it
was clear that the sums assigned by the crown for the subsistence of the

TABLE 1 Wage (*Grafiticaciones*) Distribution among Slaves in Omoa

	CHILDREN 7 AND UNDER	CHILDREN OVER 7	ADULTS OVER 25
Rough sack cloth*	½ to 2 *varas*, or yards	3 *varas*	4 *varas*
Tobacco			ration
Daily foodstuffs	½ real (half-ration)	1 real (full ration)	1 real (full ration)
Fresh meat	½ pound	1 pound	1 pound

* Hemp, cordage, sackcloth *(bramante, o brabante, hilo de cáñamo).*
Source: Archivo General de Centro América, Guatemala City, A3, leg. 1324, exp. 22332.

slaves and their families were entirely insufficient. In Omoa the crown decided to offer part of the subsistence in kind and part in cash, by which they transferred responsibility to those enslaved for satisfying their basic needs (Cáceres Table 1). A family with two children older than ten received four reales daily for its subsistence.[28] For clothing the authorities delivered every six months thread, sack cloth, and four and a half reales for tailoring, except for the artillerymen, who were assigned uniforms. The crown also provided tobacco to the married and widowed men and women, as well as a ration of meat. The meat, which cost *un cuartillo* (one-fourth of a real; the half-ration for the children equaled one-eighth of a real), was very often deducted from the daily real payment. The crown also deducted for the rice and salt stored in the royal warehouse.

Hospital stays were paid for by the Royal Treasury and cost one real per day, although by the early nineteenth century they began to deduct this from the slave's daily rations. Pregnant women were exempted from work during the last months of gestation and received an extra real during the eight days following the birth.[29]

VIOLENCE AND SOCIAL CONTROL

In building and maintaining the fortress and in the military defense of the port individuals were subjected to daily violence. Just as in other societies structurally based on slavery, physical punishments, whippings, fear, and exemplary punishments were used as means of social control.[30] From the moment of the first African's arrival the radical nature of the slave's circumstances was evident. The first challenge was to survive work in a land where malaria and yellow fever were widespread. Second, slaves had to face the violence of their owners. As throughout the Caribbean, most authorities in the region clearly recognized that the slaves could undermine the system. On 14 September 1764 this fact was violently proven, when the foreman don Eusebio Cabeza de Vaca was murdered. Marcos Agi and Antonio Polopo were charged with the crime, along with three others whose names remain unknown. The act led the authorities to fear an uprising by the entire population.[31]

The information currently available does not clearly indicate the motives for the murder, but the nature of the work could be the cause. The foreman was the visible face of the system, giving orders, controlling the slaves' movements and assigning them to gangs. Every Monday morning the slaves congregated around the front door of his house, where one by one he handed out work assignments. He also supervised the cutting of palm fronds for roofs of the offices, the church, headquarters, the treasury, the small warehouse, the hospital, and the barracks, as well as the carpentry and blacksmithing work.[32] On a daily basis he took a roll call of those present and rigorously controlled the movements of everyone.

In the months preceding the incident the authorities feared the possibility of an uprising, and they informed their superiors in the Audiencia that, even though the slaves came from "different nations among whom it appears there is mutual opposition," it was possible they might unite and organize themselves to rise up. Fearing the "strength of the resistance," the authorities even requested crown support.

Thus following the foreman's death fear invaded all levels of command in the fort. Paradoxically the fear that was the authorities' weapon to subjugate the enslaved population was, at least for a few days, inverted, but it eventually regained its place. The command organized in utmost secrecy the dispatch of militiamen from Comayagua. In lengthy discussions they planned in detail the course to follow; they sought no ordinary punishment but one that would instill fear and serve as a lesson to the slaves. Deciding how to punish those detained took many hours, but the commander finally settled on the gallows, writing to the king, "[They will be shot] by firing squad, in the back, and once dead, I will hang them in the gallows as I have said. After three or four hours their heads and arms will be cut off and placed on hooks in the designated site, issuing license for the burial of their bodies in sacred ground. Their heads and right arms will be placed along the public roads of the city. Or if not, they will be beheaded as Your Mercy chooses." Beheading was not actually possible since there was no executioner.[33]

Short of this brutal death were two other control strategies, public whippings and the threat of sale to distant places, which represented the breakup of the slaves' social and family groups. But despite the physical threats and the use of violence as punishment many slaves fled the fort. Such was the case of thirty-one-year-old Ramón Macabala, who after many years was recaptured. He was thirteen years old when he joined up with Francisco Apalito, who had planned the escape from Omoa to Belize. Ramón was the son of Francisco Macabala and had three brothers; he was born and raised in Omoa and decided to flee owing to mistreatment by the foreman. In Belize he grew up under the control of Commandant Salvador Tablos, who, according to witnesses, also beat him. He married a free black woman, María, with whom he had a son. When he was twenty he planned to flee once again, together with four or five of his fellows, but he was captured by a French pirate vessel on its way to Cuba via Trujillo after passing by Belize. The region had a great deal of commercial activity, so it was common to find English and North American ships as well as pirates of various nationalities carrying anything from wood to flour, crackers, rice, or onions.

Under interrogation Ramón Macabala said that in Belize there remained five royal slaves: Toribio Gangi, José Julián Toquero, Pedro Pascual Gamboa, Antonio Mavengo, and María Niebes. Three others had even more remote destinations. José García had been sold by the English in the city of Mérida (Yucatán), Domingo Novondo was sold in Jamaica, and Francisco Apalito had gone to Spain in a frigate.

In his statement Ramón indicated that he had not returned for fear of the punishment given slaves who ran away. After being given fifty lashes he was removed from prison and turned over once again to the foreman. Francisco Ubi had also been the victim of lashes, in his case numbering two hundred, this time administered in public, in "the plaza to teach a lesson to those of his class," for having fled in a canoe (*cayuco*) to Wallis, Belize, land of refuge for many, where a similar or even more cruel destiny awaited them.[34]

The women's work gangs had basically four tasks: clearing land, moving earth to fill in low spots, and transporting new palm fronds and gathering and disposing of the old palm from the roofs of the buildings. They also worked in agriculture, planting and cultivating in the patios of their huts for family consumption and local trade.

When it was time to clear land to thin the hillside growth the women went in gangs with the men, always under the supervision of foremen. It is not surprising that there was tension between the gangs and the foremen, since they along with the officials in town were the intermediaries of power, often exercised abusively. Unrestrained power was exercised in the fields and women were abused. As María Josefa Loango recounted, it was "very painful" to watch her sixteen-year-old daughter, Juana Bautista, go to work every morning out in the countryside, dragging cane and reeds from the hillsides, for María Josefa knew of the "abuses, violence, and infamies that the very same blacks and deportees carried out against black women in the hills." That was why she had saved her money and asked the authorities to set a price for her daughter in order to manumit her, to "remove her from that work."[35]

Allowing slaves to earn personal income was part of the crown's organizational system, but its use was left to the initiative of the enslaved. Like María Josefa, many families were able to accumulate their own savings "with which to attend to their own and their children's needs," as Josefa Arroyo, Manuel Tamo, and Luisa Nobondo declared. However, there were also collective mutual aid funds, whose resources came from the slaves' wages and even more so from the crops sold in town.[36]

The amount of the food rations varied based on age and occupation, and, as I have said, the cost of rice, meat, and salt were very often deducted from wages. Problems with food supply, as well as the food's poor quality, were a constant complaint in the region. The foodstuffs arrived from the interior, ordered under contract with merchants from different places in the province; the meat came from the cattle ranches of Comayagua and the wheat from Quetzaltenango and Totonicapán in Guatemala.[37] It was no accident, then, that food supplies were a sphere of negotiation and tension between administrators and the enslaved, where women were to play the role of protagonists near the end of the period. On a day in March

1800 the women of Omoa brought the fort to a standstill. That morning, when the men and women lined up to receive orders and the commandant "urged them" to take their meat rations, which would be deducted from their monthly income, José Domingo Ordo took one or two steps forward and said to the others, with his hat on and puffing on a pipe, or *cachimba*,[38] "these formal words": "Sir, nothing, nothing, nothing, no one will take meat." His son-in-law Santiago Macanda continued, "Fellows [*compañeros*], the Caribs eat no other meat than crab, and with water and honey they are fat." Immediately thereafter all the women shouted in a row (*argumentaron en algarabia*) that the meat was more expensive than before. In the streets, in the plazas, and before the scales for weighing they exclaimed, "No one should take meat, leave it to rot," an argument that "they repeated and repeated, in unison, many times." According to Gabriel Aguanato, "The woman is braver than the man, because she doesn't take meat, and if she doesn't, why should we?" María Malacate shouted as she was being taken away to prison, "Even if they slit my throat I don't want to take meat, I'll eat turtle."

That night, according to Bernardo Marenco, first corporal of the San Pedro militia, the twelve to fifteen "black troops . . . spoke in their native (African) language" and were seen at two in the morning. That same night in the home of Juana "la colorada" (Juana Antonia Paria, a slave born and raised in town), the customary site for gambling, Manuel Necore, Pedro José Ocori, Sambruno, Domingo Palma, Manuel Domingo Piquinimi, Carlos Ofíon, José Ignacio Piquinimi, Carlos Guvi, and Juan de Dios Arroyo, all black slaves, and the Englishmen (*inglés*) Juan Pedro and Chico Vizente, both free blacks, had gotten together. They all knew that the black women were going to send a letter with a petition to Guatemala complaining of the excessive charges made for meat. Antonio Nicolás had even offered the money they needed to send the letter. It was in Manuel Domingo Pancho's house that the petition was written, in the presence of Luisa Novondo and Pancho's wife, as well as the prisoner Manuel Monatalla. The resistance to consuming meat was a severe blow to both the slaves' diet and the fort's trade, since there were not enough Spaniards to consume all the meat sent there. (These food provisioning and distribution contracts will be taken up in future work.) But more important, it meant that the enslaved were aware that they were in control of the cash that reached their hands and could determine the fate of their economic resources. This position was reinforced by the Audiencia's resolution ordering the freeing of those detained and exonerating them from the obligation to buy meat.

The meat problem foreshadowed the beginning of the end. By 1808 the protests had increased, this time owing to a reduction in the clothing allowance and the nonpayment of daily wages for subsistence. In the preceding few years the crown had been unable to cover basic needs. By 1808 the authorities had accumulated a debt with the enslaved of the fort of 15,335 pesos for daily wages and for three years of clothing rations.

The amount of cloth assigned to each family had increased in recent years since the amount originally defined had proved inadequate for the climate, as the comandante noted, where "owing to perspiration and sweat [clothing] wore out faster than anywhere else (in the world)." But it was the high cost of provisions and the deterioration of the cloth stored in the fort's warehouse that led the authorities to change the system of cloth rations to cash payments, made in four different categories based on the individual's size and age. Ranging from three and a half to thirty-one and a half reales, these sums were inadequate, according to the authorities, for making pants, shirts, skirts, and blouses.

Since 1806 the lack of cash had prevented the payment of obligations, and unrest had begun to grow in the fort. Multiple demands by both men and women inundated the Comandancia, which found the problem impossible to resolve. To this were added the voices of the townspeople. The economic crisis had moved beyond the fort, since many merchants in town had given credit to the slaves, counting on the Comandancia payments.

The problem's origins were not only in the misadministration and corruption that had always prevailed in the fort, but in Spain. That same year, 1808, popular uprisings had exploded in the streets of Madrid as well. The military defeat at the Battle of Trafalgar in 1805 had revealed that war was consuming most economic resources, worsening the quality of life of the popular sectors. But it would be the French invasion and José Bonaparte's substitution as king of Spain that would propel the system to its moment of crisis.

That same year the military authorities of the fort at San Fernando de Omoa arrived at their final crossroads. Pressure from the children and grandchildren of those *mondongos* and *caravalies* who had been taken to Central American lands, plus the inability to cover financial debts, provoked the decision to grant freedom to the 506 enslaved individuals who had managed to survive. On 19 January 1812 manumission was decreed in Spain and executed at the fort in July. Twelve years later, after the achievement of independence and the creation of the Central American Federation, the abolition of slavery would be declared in all of Central America.

CONCLUSION

The gang of wage-earning slaves reported by Florencia Palma in 1790 was not an isolated case in the San Fernando de Omoa Fort. On the contrary, as we have seen in this analysis, the organizational system implanted there began with the delivery of goods and the payment of wages to provide a minimum subsistence, but paradoxically this precariousness and hyperexploitation opened doors for the slaves to seek their own means of subsistence in agriculture and to permanently renegotiate the use of their subsistence allowances.

The assignment of lands, or the feasibility of personal use of the lands, removed responsibility for slave reproduction from the Comandancia and transferred it to the enslaved, who, as Turner says, behaved as peasants in the face of the owner-supplier's instability and food shortages, generating a subsistence production that served to support the labor demands of construction.[39] Backyard or garden plot production in the slave quarters gave slaves the legal possibility of participating in the commercial economy, which maximized the value of agricultural production as well as that of fishing and payment in kind. All these elements contributed to the slaves' feeling in control of their own destiny and even to their accumulating cash to purchase their freedom. Even if they were not given any freedom of movement outside of the fort, the local market was dynamic enough to create economic resources for mutual aid, held by the women.

In the work arena, the existence of differential payments reflected the talents and responsibilities required by the division of labor, driven in this case by the construction and military defense of the fort, which required captains, carpenters, blacksmiths, and others. But it also introduced an element of social differentiation and indirectly revealed to the slaves the parameters for the improvement of their labor conditions.[40] As Turner has argued, paying slaves a salary for their labor provided them with means to negotiate their conditions, as they became conscious of the value of their labor and the power of controlling their own cash.

The slaves' capability for violence and the possibility of an uprising provoked a permanent state of fear among the authorities. This shared consciousness of their potential to resist enabled slaves to limit the level of exploitation and contributed in the long term to the freeing of the entire community. As is clear in the case of Omoa, slavery was not a static and undifferentiated condition of servitude but involved options for resistance that helped to shape the system.

NOTES

Research was made possible by the support of the School of History and the Institute of Social Research of the University of Costa Rica and the Collaborative Research Program of the National Endowment for the Humanities.

1 Beckles, "Creolization in Action." See also Díaz, *The Virgin, the King.*

2 Lovejoy, "Murgu," 168.

3 Nishida, "Manumission and Ethnicity," 369.

4 Reiss, "The Revolution of the *Ganhadores*," 355–93.

5 Turner, *From Chattel Slaves to Wage Slaves.* See also Beckles, "Creolization in Action."

6 Argueta, *Historia laboral de Honduras*; Cruz et al., *Fuerte de San Fernando de Omoa*; Rubio Sánchez, *Historia de la fortaleza*; Zapatero, *El fuerte de San Fernando.*

7 See Argueta, *Historia laboral de Honduras*; Cáceres "The African Origins of San Fernando de Omoa," 115–37.

8 For the sum of 18,400 pesos.

9 Archivo General de Centro América, Guatemala City (hereafter AGCA), A1.56, leg. 5920, exp. 5920.

10 For whom Hall paid 36,800 pesos. AGCA A1.56, leg. 215, exp. 5065.

11 AGCA A1.56, leg. 215, exp. 5066.

12 AGCA A3.2, leg. 709, exp. 13298.

13 AGCA A3.2, leg. 709, exp. 13273.

14 AGCA A3, leg. 133, exp. 2633.

15 Those in charge of fastening the ship's wooden joints with burlap and tar.

16 See Quijano, "Las fortificaciones en América."

17 See Jennings, "Slaves of the State," 4.

18   Pérez Guzmán, "Modo de vida de esclavos," 241–57.

19   Pike, "Penal Servitude," 24–28.

20   Carlos III to don Diego de Navarro, upon taking office as the new governor of the island of Cuba, in Archivo General de Indias, Seville (hereafter AGI), Santo Domingo, 1.217, cited in Pérez Guzmán, "Modo de vida de esclavos," 243, 246

21   These formed part of the slaves returned to the crown from the estate of Comandante José Antonio de Palma, who had taken them illegally.

22   AGCA A3.1, leg. 686, exp. 12958, fol. 45.

23   Casing where the artillery cannon was mounted.

24   AGI, Contratación 5512, N. 1, R. 1.

25   Francisco Palma acquired his surname from an unauthorized appropriation by the former commandant of Omoa, José Antonio Palma, who had taken over some of the royal slaves as his own. After lengthy litigation they were returned to the crown, but they kept the surname Palma.

26   AGCA A3, leg. 133, exp. 2633.

27   AGCA A3, leg. 1328, exp. 22417. Juan de Ofion, "Black Sergeant of my slave class of Your Majesty," had eight children, all located close to the center of power: one an artilleryman, another a drummer, another a carpenter in town, and one son and four daughters working for the authorities. AGCA A1.4, leg. 57.

28   Children over seven were obliged to work daily.

29   AGCA A3, leg. 1324, exp. 22332.

30   AGCA A2(4), leg. 29, exp. 392.

31   AGCA A2.2, leg. 79, exp. 1724.

32   AGCA A1.14, leg. 55, exp. 624.

33   AGCA A2.2, leg. 79, exp. 1724.

34   AGCA A2(4), leg. 29, exp. 392.

35   AGCA A1.4, leg. 57.

36   AGCA A1.4, leg. 57.

37   Argueta, *Historia laboral de Honduras*, 159.

38   According to the Spanish Royal Academy, the term derives from the Bantú word *cazimba*.

39   See Turner, *From Chattel Slaves to Wage Slaves*, 2–3.

40   Ibid., 4.

Slave Emancipation and Mestizaje in Colonial Guatemala

Catherine Komisaruk

In 1527 the conqueror Pedro de Alvarado received a royal concession to import six hundred African slaves into Guatemala.[1] The slave trade continued there for nearly three centuries until shortly after independence, when the Central American Constitutional Assembly declared a general emancipation in 1824. A picture of Afro-Guatemalan slavery in the early and middle colonial eras has been developed in several studies, including Paul Lokken's essay in this volume.[2] Within this picture an overarching demographic pattern is clear: in the space of several generations, free people of African and partly African descent would come to outnumber enslaved people living in Guatemala. The capital city's free *negro* and *mulato* populations surpassed its slave population around the middle of the seventeenth century. Subsequently the growth of the free population of African heritage continued to outpace the growth of the slave population.[3] In the capital city at least, the free population was increasingly African in ancestry, and the population of African ancestry was increasingly free.[4]

This essay is a qualitative study of the emancipation mechanisms that fueled these demographic trends. The research is based largely on secular court records from late colonial Guatemala (from the 1770s to 1821), including the records of both the Audiencia and the capital city's Ayuntamiento. Although the Audiencia's jurisdiction encompassed the territory of present-day Central America and Chiapas, most individuals who appealed to this high court hailed from areas closer to the capital city. (The capital, the seat of the Audiencia, was at Santiago for most of the colonial era. A ruinous earthquake in 1773 prompted the construction of a new city, Nueva Guatemala, today called Guatemala City, a day's ride away. In its early decades the new capital was populated mainly by migrants from

Santiago.) While the notarial books for both cities confirm that slave sales continued throughout the colonial years, it is the court records that more often reveal details of slaves' lives, often from their own point of view. In the aggregate the court records offer an additional revelation: slavery in Guatemala was disintegrating, even before the emancipation law of 1824.

The period from 1790 to the 1820s saw an increase in slave uprisings in various American colonies. Historians have identified several contributing factors: the Bourbon and Pombaline reforms, the Napoleonic wars, and the resulting tax increases and popular political discontent; the French Revolution; the slave revolt in Saint Domingue (Haiti); the demise of that colony's sugar exports and the subsequent uptick in sugar production and slave importation elsewhere; and the political upheavals of the nineteenth century's first two decades, which ended in independence for Brazil and most of Spanish America in the 1820s.[5]

Guatemala, though, did not experience any large slave rebellion. Slave resistance there appears to have been tied only indirectly, if at all, to external political events. I argue that Afro-Guatemalan slavery was dismantled gradually by the responses of slaves and slaveholders to the particular structures of slavery as it existed locally. These structures were products of centuries-old Iberian understandings of slavery, and of long-term social transformations—ethnic and cultural *mestizaje* in particular—in the colonial American context. Such transformations were beyond the control of legislation, and they were largely complete before independence (which in Central America came without large-scale rebellion or violence).

Across the generations preceding independence, slaves had become increasingly integrated into Guatemala's Hispanic society and economy. Court records from the late colonial years show that numerous slaves were paid wages and charged with providing food and other necessities for themselves and their families. Slaves exercised substantial freedom of movement, while slaveholders' efforts to recover absentee slaves were limited. As Hispanic society grew more racially mixed across the colonial era, slaves were increasingly able to pass unarrested into free society. Like the kin networks that Russell Lohse describes among slaves in the Matina Valley of Costa Rica, in both rural and urban Guatemala social networks linked enslaved people to free relatives and acquaintances. Slaves used these networks to press the limits of their bondage. The civil authorities, for their part, tended to legitimize slaves' ability to move freely and negotiate the conditions of their servitude. In this context the institution of slavery could not be sustained.

HISTORIC, DEMOGRAPHIC, AND LEGAL
CONTEXTS OF EMANCIPATION

The outlines of Afro-Guatemalan slavery reflect origins in Iberia, where slavery in the early modern period assumed two basic forms.[6] The first form, rooted in medieval Europe, had persisted in Iberia as Muslims and Christians enslaved captives during alternating waves of conquest and reconquest. These slaves constituted a relatively small minority of local populations. They typically served in urban, domestic (including artisan) work and as auxiliaries to their employers. (Such roles would be seen too in Spanish America, not only in cities but also in agriculture, where slaves often fulfilled managerial jobs.) In this older Iberian pattern slaves were forced to adopt the dominant culture, and their eventual manumission in the enslavers' society was accepted and even expected.[7] This understanding of slavery would resonate in colonial Guatemala.

A second form of Iberian slavery had developed beginning in the fifteenth century, as Portuguese incursions along the west coast of Africa brought sub-Saharan African slaves into a new European slave trade. Enslaved Africans would provide the labor as European investors established commercial sugar production in Madeira and the Canary Islands. By the mid-fifteenth century large shipments of African slaves were arriving in the Atlantic islands and southern Iberia, where they worked in sugar plantations and were kept without the same expectation of integration into Iberian society. A similarly intensive form of slavery, with sizable slave communities providing field labor on large estates, appeared in Guatemala, specifically in sugar agriculture.[8]

However, in Guatemala (as in Mexico and the Andes) the presence of large native labor forces altered the forms seen in Iberia. On many Spanish American agricultural estates slaves filled a niche between indigenous workers and Spanish employers. Indian draft workers and free laborers of various ethnicities did much of the planting and harvesting. Slaves, on the other hand, were held as year-round employees. They were fewer in number than seasonal laborers at most agricultural enterprises and were often trained as artisans or charged with some authority over seasonal workers.

In the second half of the eighteenth century most of Guatemala's slave population was concentrated in a few locations. These included a number of rural estates, the port of Omoa (in today's Honduras), and the urban centers, particularly Guatemala City. The biggest slaveholder in Guatemala was the Dominican order, with several agricultural estates and a convent in the capital, all of which kept slaves. The Dominicans' Hacienda San Jerónimo, a sugar estate in the Verapaz region north of Guatemala City, was home to the largest single group of slaves in Central America. In the twilight years of the colony over six hundred slaves toiled at San Jerónimo, along with permanent and temporary Indian and mixed-race workers.[9] Other sugar estates, mainly in the lowlands south and east of the capital, also figured prominently as slaveholders.[10] However, the crown ranked next among slaveholders after the Dominicans. A few of the crown's slaves labored in the government's urban administrative functions, but the majority—around five hundred slaves in the 1770s—were held at Omoa. Their work, along with that of Spanish and Indian laborers paid by the government, sustained the port's operations.[11] Rina Cáceres's study in this volume describes the arrival of slaves at Omoa and explores the community's social and economic organization.

Finally, a number of slaves lived in the region's urban centers, particularly the capital, where they labored in monasteries and convents, private homes, and artisan shops. Late colonial records suggest that slaves constituted only a tiny fraction of the population in the capital city (at both locations). But slaves had clearly played an important role in transforming the city's population across three centuries of Spanish rule. As numerous slaves in the capital exploited opportunities for manumission there, and as people emancipated elsewhere migrated to the city in search of economic opportunities, the urban population of African (and partly African) descent grew. This growth spanned the colonial period and continued into the early years of independence. By the middle of the eighteenth century free people of African ancestry represented perhaps the largest ethnic group in the capital city.[12]

Certain aspects of colonial law facilitated slaves' efforts to gain freedom. The Spanish judicial system allowed slaves to file civil and criminal charges against any subjects of the crown, including their masters.[13] The crown provided slaves with attorneys through the office of the Procurator for the Poor, and court records demonstrate that slaves in late colonial Guatemala were indeed availing themselves of their right to litigate. Granted, urban slaves had easier access to the courts. But among the rural slaves who trickled into the capital, some came seeking legal recourse, usually against their masters. Their testimonies indicate that even in the countryside slaves knew of their right to appeal to authorities in the cities.

The judicial system was a product of early modern Spanish social views, which (reflecting medieval patterns) generally legitimized individual slaves' goal of manumission. These views are encapsulated in the Siete Partidas, the massive thirteenth-century codification of legal ideology by Alfonso X el Sabio (the Learned), king of Castile.[14] The Siete Partidas continued to influence judicial thought even in late colonial Spanish America, where judges often cited it in their rulings. In addition to Alfonso's scattered references to slaves, in the Fourth Partida he included two titles (sections) specifically on slavery. Title 21, "Concerning Slaves," contains eight laws defining slavery and its parameters. Title 22, "Concerning Liberty," is significantly longer, with eleven laws describing the ways slaves could be emancipated. Notably the Siete Partidas specifically established slaves' right to litigate, albeit in a limited number of circumstances.[15]

Slaves' suits for liberty in Guatemala competed with the colonial state's ideal of protecting its subjects' property (including slaves). But the magistrates upheld slaves' right to seek liberty through litigation. The outcomes of these suits seem to have been unpredictable; the judges did not always award liberty. Still, the earlier Iberian experience with urban domestic slavery clearly appears in the records of late colonial Guatemala, where Hispanic society took slave manumissions largely in stride.

Market regulations in the late colonial years kept self-manumission within the reach of a number of slaves. Despite labor shortages that frequently vexed Spaniards in Guatemala, slave prices were essentially fixed by royal controls. In earlier times resale of slaves for profit had been common, but in the late colonial era the authorities recognized a slave's value as the price paid at the prior sale, or as the figure named by a government-appointed appraiser. The resulting price ceiling expanded the possibility that a slave might gather sufficient money to purchase emancipation.

Most slaveholders would willingly manumit their slaves for cash payment of the appraised value. A few slaveholders refused, but this appears to have been the exception, as I have found only two cases. In one case the slave appealed to the court and was granted her liberty.[16] In the other case the court ruled in the slaveholder's favor.[17] Because of the price regulations, sellers could not easily charge more than their initial investment in a slave, and they typically appear to have been pleased to recoup that cost. A slaveholder who granted freedom to a slave in exchange for payment was protecting himself against loss of property—a sizable risk, given that a slave denied the option to buy freedom might flee.

Slaves of the crown were not excluded from the possibility of freedom through purchase. In 1798, for example, a free black man ("negro libre") named Manuel Huebo bought the liberty of his entire nuclear family, all slaves at the crown's fort of Omoa, for seven hundred pesos.[18]

RESISTANCE IN THE COUNTRYSIDE: SLAVES OF THE HACIENDA SAN JERÓNIMO

A long-term dispute between the slaves and the *mayordomos* (managers) of the Dominican order's Hacienda San Jerónimo illustrates the flexibility of slavery in late colonial Guatemala. Early in the second decade of the nineteenth century, some fifteen or twenty slaves traveled the mountainous route from San Jerónimo to the capital city. There they appealed to the royal authorities on behalf of themselves and the other slaves at the estate. The *síndico* (syndic) of the Ayuntamiento, who held the ex officio title of Protector of Slaves, wrote up their request. That document, one of the slaves later recalled, "solicited the liberty of the individuals of the [San Jerónimo] plantation, we who live under the bitter yoke of slavery, [because of] the injurious treatment with which we were being managed."[19] Their appeal demanded the reversal of several specific injustices on the estate: they were given insufficient food, they received larger work assignments than the hacienda's non-slave laborers, they were forced to work even on Sundays and holidays, and they were mistreated by a handful of free *negros caribes* employed as overseers or drivers on the estate. (The negros caribes were probably members, or children, of a group of several thousand Black Caribs deported by British forces in 1797 from the Lesser

Antilles to Roatán, in the Gulf of Honduras; descendants of these deportees today constitute the Garífuna communities of Central America.)[20]

The estate's mayordomo, himself a Dominican friar, denied the slaves' allegations, but nevertheless the order's provincial in the capital proposed some concessions, thereby avoiding, or at least postponing, further litigation. Principal among these concessions was that the slaves would be paid a daily wage of one and a half reales, the same as that received by both free and tributary laborers on the estate. Evidently the slaves themselves owned some livestock; the Dominicans agreed to allow each slave to keep three or four animals, but beyond this they would charge for pasturage.[21] The remonstrant slaves returned to the hacienda, where along with the other slaves they were subsequently paid in silver rather than food.

The slaves' litigation amounted to a conscious, collective renegotiation of the terms of their labor.[22] Clearly the slaves had not entered the dispute on equal footing with the Dominicans in terms of social status or political power. Yet the departure of fifteen or more slaves from the hacienda and their ability to appeal to the state gave them some traction. In addition to the concession of wages, the slaves also extracted from the Dominican administration a promise that their workload would be kept equal to that of the estate's free and tributary laborers. And the administration agreed to the slaves' demand that physical punishments would be given to the slaves only by the mayordomo (an office always filled by one of the Dominican friars) or by local civil magistrates, not by the free Black Carib overseers who, the slaves implied, had acted with excessive brutality.[23]

A series of appeals later that same decade reveals that the San Jerónimo slaves repeatedly returned to the courts in ongoing efforts to loosen their bondage. In 1818 four enslaved men sued the hacienda's administration on behalf of all the slaves there. They charged that the negros caribes persisted in mistreating them, pursuing them even with firearms, and they complained that the management regularly delayed paying their Saturday wages in order to force them to report for overtime on Sundays.

In a written response to the suit the plantation's mayordomo, the Dominican friar Andrés Pintelos, sought to refute the slaves' claims. He denied that the overseers had mistreated them, and he tried to justify the Sunday work assignments; the sugar would deteriorate overnight, he contended, if the workers were not required to haul it just three hundred paces from the boiling house to the building where it would be drained.

Pintelos was unable to mask his annoyance with the slaves' attempt to upend what he considered their proper relationship with the hacienda. "It is odd," he wrote, "that they complain of the retention of one *real* for only one night [on Saturdays], when all or most of them always have many [wage] advances."

Informed of the friar's response, the slaves petitioned again. They retracted their complaint about working Sundays and demanded instead that their daily assignment be reduced in proportion to the Sunday jobs. Pintelos ultimately acceded, grudgingly, to this workload reduction. But his words reveal his perception that the hierarchy of masters and slaves had been inverted; even as he submitted to the slaves' demand, his tone rose in frustration. "These slaves must understand that the master is free to give the chores by task, or by day," he wrote. His response amounts to a protest that his power over the slaves had been successively, and successfully, challenged. In particular he decried their repeated, collective judicial appeals: "Some of these slaves are persuaded that just by going to the capital [to court] everything that they want will be conceded to them, and with this they threaten and intimidate the mayordomos when [the mayordomos] require [the slaves] to perform their work properly, and it is cause for some rebellious ones to hoax those who are less aware into going with them and forming a group in their unjust demands and pretensions." Pintelos recognized the pattern: the slaves on his hacienda were using civil institutions to negotiate collectively the terms of their labor, thereby beginning to restructure the social and economic relationships that constituted slavery.

The friar articulated the crux of the dispute in his closing: "These slaves," he said, "should not judge from the excessive benignity and compliance that their masters have had for them, that they cease to be truly slaves." Indeed, through their repeated litigation, the slaves had altered the conditions that in Pintelos's view made them "truly slaves." The friar brandished one of his remaining instruments of power over the slaves— the possibility of selling them away from the estate—as he admonished, "As slaves, they can be sold when and how their masters wish. And this . . . should be motive for them in the future to be more obedient, and compliant in their obligations."

It was not long, though, before the slaves began seeking an injunction against their masters' power to sell them. Less than a year after Pintelos issued his warning, two of the same plaintiffs, José María Loaisa and Miguel González, appealed again to authorities in the capital.[24] They denounced the mayordomo for cruel and unjust treatment and decried an announcement that the hacienda's management was going "to sell entire families." Loaisa and González were especially alarmed about the material and agricultural investments that they would lose in such a sale. "Our possessions will become the property of the convent," they charged. González revealed that he and his wife had a "piece of irrigated land, and a *vega* [piece of lowland] of assorted fruit" she had cultivated, and a field planted with beans.[25] If he and his wife were transferred away from the hacienda, they would lose the crops they had raised to support their family.

Litigation was not the only strategy the plaintiffs had used in their attempt to alter the conditions of their slavery. Loaisa's and González's imbroglios with the hacienda's administrators were of long standing, having already taken shape outside the courts. By the time they made their judicial appeals, both men had been reporting irregularly for work. Loaisa blamed his inconsistency on Friar Pintelos, saying that the priest had "impeded" him from laboring on the estate. And because slaves there were paid in wages, Loaisa insinuated, his exclusion from work had cut off his livelihood. He said that Pintelos had told him to find someone to purchase him. But witnesses indicated that Loaisa had found paid work elsewhere. His wife was still living on the hacienda; for the record she claimed not to know his whereabouts.

González also had come and gone rather freely from the Hacienda San Jerónimo. Friar Pintelos accused him of fleeing from the managers and living as a fugitive, "moving about these environs [by day and] entering his house by night." The slaves told a somewhat different story; they said González had been unable to work because of injuries suffered when he fell off a horse while herding the hacienda's cattle. In any case, the stories concur in depicting González's irregular attendance on the job even while he continued to live with his family on the plantation. He ultimately returned to work at San Jerónimo in April 1819, evidently because he needed wages. But Friar Pintelos balked. When González went to collect his salary after a week's labor, Pintelos refused to pay him, and an altercation erupted. According to witnesses, González spoke insolently to the friar in front of a group of slaves. Pintelos may have beaten González (accounts vary), and the priest ordered some other slaves to tie and shackle the unfortunate man. The prisoner was dispatched to the capital, where, still in shackles, he was put to work in the kitchen of the Dominican monastery. Pintelos argued that if González had been "left without punishment it would be motivation for the rest of the slaves to do the same." Given the history of the slaves' litigation, it is not surprising that the friar feared the spread of resistance.

González was kept shackled for at least three or four months before he could file a complaint with the Ayuntamiento. (It is unclear if he broke away from the monastery with shackles still on his body, or if they had been removed. Or perhaps he had managed to send for the Ayuntamiento's síndico to take his deposition in the monastery.) The Ayuntamiento was slow to respond; nine months later, still slaving in the kitchen, González made another appeal. Evidently he had received news from San Jerónimo; his petition contended that because of his involuntary absence from home, his wife had lost a crop of beans "that was eaten by the [estate's] cattle." Additionally, he charged, Friar Pintelos had taken his wife's irrigated plot and the land with her fruit trees. González argued that his wife had supported him financially during his recovery from the herding accident. He noted that his health had been further compromised by the months laboring in the heat of the kitchen. Finally, he demanded liberty. It was the only way, he insinuated, that the Dominicans could make right on the damages they had caused. Unfortunately the outcome of González's case is not known (the documentation ends abruptly without a judicial ruling).

His appeal, however, typifies a recurring pattern in which slaves contended that their financial sacrifices and suffering caused by their masters warranted the state to grant them liberty. González's wife had borne the costs as well. "I had to suffer seven months," he said of his recovery from the fall, "[and the hacienda did not] provide me with food and medical treatment, but instead my feeble consort suffered and paid for my illness." She had also supported their children—all slaves of the hacienda—while he was unable to collect wages. Indeed, plaintiff slaves in Guatemala frequently asserted that they or their family members, rather than the slaveholder, had paid for food, clothing, and medical care.[26] Also typical are González's charges that much of his and his wife's property (or lands they had been allowed to use) had been usurped by the hacienda and that their bean crop had been eaten by the estate's cattle. Numerous slaves demanded liberty on the grounds that their masters had caused them to incur expenses or had dispossessed them of property and that their losses amounted to payment of their value as chattel.[27] Although these suits were not often successful, they illustrate the loose nature of bondage in late colonial Guatemala. Slaves were using money, providing for themselves and their families, and cultivating and managing property as their own.

These slaves were integrated into Hispanic society in conditions that recall Russell Lohse's depiction of slaves' "remarkably independent lives" on the Costa Rican cacao estates. The San Jerónimo men were able to negotiate their workload and pay, refuse work when they didn't need it, leave the custody of their masters, get paid work elsewhere, and travel to the capital to litigate. Slaves' litigation itself paralleled that of free people, as they used the same courts and attorneys. Like free people, the San Jerónimo slaves owned livestock and cultivated their own food. Such cultivation was typical among slaves in rural areas, and it placed an extra burden on them. But it also gave them a degree of independence, reducing or eliminating their reliance on the master for sustenance. Further, slaves who cultivated food might be able to sell surpluses and accumulate some cash. Recall that Miguel González's wife kept an orchard and bean field. She probably intended to sell some of her produce since she lived in a community of wage earners.

The multiethnic environment of the Hacienda San Jerónimo, where slaves worked alongside free workers and tributary Indians (who worked as draftees), typified conditions in both rural and urban Central America. The *alcalde mayor* of Verapaz said that the San Jerónimo slaves preferred not to marry Indians because they were subject to tribute, and work by Lowell Gudmundson has shown that there were few marriages between Indians and either slaves or freed people at San Jerónimo.[28] But on smaller Guatemalan estates, where slaves might number only a handful within a worker community, interethnic relationships appear to have been more often the norm and more important to those involved.[29] Slaves held in small numbers had less collective negotiating power than the San Jerónimo slaves did, but interethnic social relationships at smaller enterprises helped link slaves to the free world. Notably, free family members were better positioned to help slaves achieve manumission.[30]

A frequent method of redemption was to pay one's own purchase price or to have a relative pay it. Another path originated with the master. Some slaveholders manumitted their slaves, or some of their slaves, in their wills; a few slaveholders did so while living.[31] Slaves used whatever tactics they had at hand. In the 1770s Juan Alexos de Estrada, a slave of one of the Augustinian order's haciendas, repeatedly kidnapped four or five horses from the estate and then made demands in exchange for their return. The Augustinians' lawyer (himself a member of the order) complained that they had been unable to stop the extortion or catch the slave.[32] In 1796 Isabel Arreze gave her master some winning lottery tickets in exchange for a freedom paper. He didn't know the tickets were forgeries, procured by Arreze's lover specifically for this purpose. When the master realized he had been duped, he tried to revoke the manumission, but the Audiencia upheld the validity of the paper he had signed.[33]

Movement and Flight Flight was a common route to extralegal liberation, and by the late colonial era it had sapped slavery's viability. Slave flight vexed slave owners endlessly. On occasion they reported runaways to the authorities, but it made little difference; fugitive slaves were rarely returned, except by their own volition. I have found only two cases documenting the capture of runaways.[34] One case involved fourteen slaves reported missing by the sugar baron don José Jacinto Palomo in 1775. Eleven were men; three were women, perhaps with children in tow. At least some of these slaves were captured, but only in April 1779, more than four years after Palomo's plea. They had been circulating effectively as free people for years. Palomo knew that one of the missing men was working for the customhouse officer in Jocotenango, just outside the capital; another had become the employee of the *comisario* in the Valley of Chibaque, in the Alcaldía Mayor of Chimaltenango. Both locations were several days' journey from Palomo's estate in Jalapa.

Fifteen years later an absentee slave of don José Jacinto Palomo entered the record in a striking case of de facto liberation. The man was Manuel Antonio Hernández (possibly the same Manuel Hernández whom Palomo had reported among the runaways in 1775). In February 1791 Manuel

Antonio Hernández left Palomo's estate, making his way to the capital despite the crippling effects of syphilis. He was welcomed in the city by his half-sister, a free housekeeper named Apolonia Olavarrieta. Palomo sent his son to Olavarrieta's house to retrieve the slave, but to no avail. Olavarrieta refused to turn him over, and she insisted that Palomo owed her money for medicine and clothing she had bought for her brother.

After three years and no reimbursement from Palomo, Olavarrieta sued him. She said she had invested over two hundred pesos in her brother's medical treatment alone. Among other things, she had hired an Indian man from Jocotenango to take care of him and had paid for him to make a pilgrimage to the Black Christ of Esquipulas in the eastern reaches of Guatemala. (This image carved in the sixteenth century continues today to draw people seeking healing.) "God knows the work it cost me to make that money and see him recovered, back on his feet, as he is today," she said in her suit. She presented eighteen witnesses, demonstrating her connections with a wide socioeconomic cross-section of the city's populace. But Palomo countered, arguing that Olavarrieta had usurped his slave's labor. He demanded that she compensate him monetarily and return the slave. The court ultimately dismissed Palomo's suit and ruled in Olavarrieta's favor, ordering the slave owner to pay her expenses. The judges said nothing about returning the fugitive, who by this time was living in a rented room in the customhouse at one of the entrances to the city.[35]

In similar style, most runaway slaves in Guatemala appear essentially to have taken French leave. Recall Manuel González, who came and went for months at a time from the Hacienda San Jerónimo. The brothers Luca and José Arrivillaga, both slaves of doña Tomasa Castilla, were moving about as fugitives from her sugar estate during most of the 1790s. Castilla noted in 1799 that some of her other slaves had also gone missing.[36] Runaway slaves usually found work elsewhere, selling or bartering their labor as free people would. In the 1770s several Spanish *dons* complained that the colony's provincial officers, rather than aiding in the return of runaway slaves, were employing them.[37]

The preponderance of men among fugitives is no coincidence; women's charge of childcare (not to mention pregnancy) made it harder for them to strike out as migrants. But women did flee, sometimes motivated by a precipitating episode of egregious mistreatment. In 1785 a slave named Mauricia fled Nueva Guatemala for Antigua after her master's widow whipped her with fifty lashes.[38] Another slave, María Josefa Godines, fled her master's home in the capital in 1789, also following a cruel punishment; her hair had been cut off and she had been locked in a dark room, brought food only twice a day. After four days she escaped through a hole she had dug in the wall. She appealed to the Audiencia, but the judge rejected her petition. It is not known whether she returned to her lawful owner.[39]

The Guatemalan capital (at both pre- and postearthquake locations) appears to have been a hub of legal and extralegal emancipations. The concentration of wealth and Spanish homes in the capital city enabled fugitives from the countryside and other former slaves to find jobs. Despite the predominance of adult women in the urban population, Spaniards in the city complained of the shortage of domestic servants.[40] Female slaves pursuing litigation against their masters (or simply fleeing) appear to have readily obtained room and board in Spanish homes where they offered to work.[41] As for men, the construction of the new capital starting in the 1770s increased the demand for male workers and drove their wages up.

Slaves Seeking Employers: The papel de venta   An outstanding feature of slavery in late colonial Guatemala was the *papel de venta*, literally "paper of sale," a mechanism by which slaves solicited their own buyers.[42] Drawn up by the slaveholder, the papel de venta announced that a slave was for sale. It gave the slave's name and price and the name of the master or another person for prospective buyers to contact. The paper was given to the slave, who would carry it in search of a new master. The law did not require slaveholders to sell slaves who wanted to be sold, and records suggest that at least two slaveholders punished their slaves for even asking.[43] But some slaves requested and obtained papeles de venta. This happened so frequently that the phrase *pedir papel* ("to ask for a paper") was understood in court documents to refer to a slave's request for a papel de venta.[44] Occasionally the papel de venta may represent a slaveholder's last-ditch effort to get some money rather than simply freeing a recalcitrant slave or risking the slave's departure with no sale.[45] Often, however, the papel de venta was in earnest, a genuine step to sell a valuable worker, as some examples below illustrate. Slaves soliciting their own purchase were in a position of terrible paradoxes: they were agents in the market in which their bodies and ownership of their labor were being sold.

Behind this horrific irony, though, the papel de venta demonstrates that the distinction between slavery and free labor was crumbling. The papel de venta was useful to slave owners specifically because they did not keep slaves constantly in their custody; the papel was circulated to prospective buyers by the slave's unchaperoned movement in Hispanic society. Yet slaves did not necessarily choose to exit the system by simply disappearing with the papel. Papeles de venta worked precisely because slaves expected continued freedom of movement following their sale. This freedom had become the norm. In effect, slaves soliciting buyers were applying for new jobs; they did so because they needed shelter and sustenance or wages. Free laborers often faced similar circumstances; many of them lived in their employers' houses and changed jobs frequently. The usefulness of the papel de venta—the fact that slaves chose to solicit their sale rather than escape—signals that from the viewpoint of many slaves, slavery had become markedly similar to free labor.

Buying Freedom, Negotiating the Price   The possibility of manumission through payment seems to have been well-known among slaves in Guatemala. In the period studied here the words *rescate* and *rescatar(se)* were understood to refer to slaves' self-purchase or the purchase of freedom by kin.[46] Beatriz Palomo de Lewin has documented the frequency of rescate in Guatemala for the period 1723–73, and indeed the phenomenon was occurring beginning in the sixteenth century, as elsewhere in Spanish America.[47]

For slaves who received wages there was at least in theory a possibility of cash accumulation and, at best, self-purchase. Although slaves in the capital do not appear to have bargained collectively for wages, as did those at the Hacienda San Jerónimo, some urban slaves, perhaps especially those with artisanal skills, earned money.[48] Further, slaveholders were legally obligated to allow slaves two hours a day to work for their own profit, though it is hard to know how often this law was followed. Manuel Trinidad, for one, a free man litigating for the emancipation of his wife and children, complained that in nine years of working for the same master his family members had never been allotted these hours.[49]

Liberty was not cheap. Young adult slaves in late colonial Guatemala City were typically sold for prices between 150 and 250 pesos, an amount that could buy a modest house in town. Small children were appraised at lower values (typically fifty to sixty pesos for a child between age five and ten). Nevertheless, enslaved parents generally liberated themselves before their children, probably with the goal of more rapidly increasing the family's earnings. Guatemalan records do not reveal anything quite like the Cuban system of *coartación*, in which slaves gained partial ownership of their time or labor as they made payments toward their purchase price.[50] Occasionally, though, Guatemalan slaves or their kin paid the slaveholder installments, gradually working toward emancipation.[51]

Facing the high cost of manumission, some slaves tried to negotiate a reduction in their prices. They appealed to both their masters and the government, seeking lower reappraisals of their values. The results of these efforts varied.

The enslaved man José Mariano Sínforo met with an unfortunate refusal. He had been sold in childhood for one hundred pesos, and when he was fourteen years old his price was evaluated at two hundred pesos. At age twenty-five he was sold to the Marqués de Aycinena for 250 pesos. (This was in 1783, when construction in the new capital was in full swing and the demand for labor at an apex.) It was some seven years later, in 1790 (as the urban construction boom waned), that Sínforo petitioned the Audiencia. The sale for 250 pesos "has been greatly detrimental to me," he argued, "[as it precludes the possibility] that I might ever liberate myself from this slavery, or solicit a master, if the present one should fail me." He asked that the man who last sold him be required to refund 150 pesos to the marqués, thereby reducing his price to one hundred pesos. The Audiencia flatly rejected his request.[52] While the judges probably thought such a large refund was unreasonable, their decision was also undoubtedly influenced by the marqués's tremendous social status. Nor was the ruling illogical from a legal standpoint. Since Sínforo was only about thirty-two years old he was still very valuable as property, and the Audiencia's decision served to protect the marqués's investment.

A more successful appeal was that of Manuel Trinidad, a free man who had fathered six children by his enslaved wife. Around 1809 the wife and children were sold to don Miguel López in the Verapaz region for a total of 450 pesos, an average of about sixty-four pesos for each person. Upon his death López distributed the children among his heirs; two of the young slaves died soon afterward. (It is not known what happened to Trinidad's wife, who is mentioned only briefly in the record.) In 1818 Trinidad asked the heirs for papeles de venta for the surviving children. The heirs responded by raising the prices, setting three of the children's values at 120, 90, and 80 pesos; one child, probably the smallest, was offered for 50 pesos. Trinidad went to the Audiencia, accusing the heirs of mistreating his children, and demanding that their prices be reduced. He argued that the masters had denied the slaves the legal allocation of hours to work for their own gain. If these hours had been allowed, Trinidad contended, the family would already have saved enough to free the children. Two of López's heirs conceded, reducing the prices they had set at 120 and 90 pesos to 60 and 50 pesos, respectively. Manuel Trinidad immediately purchased the freedom of these two children. Though the record is incomplete, initial responses from the other two heirs suggest that they too were probably prepared to lower their prices.[53]

The possibility that slaves could dispute their valuations, along with the possibility of requesting a papel de venta, lent them some leverage in the market in which they were being sold. An example is Ignacio Escudero, a León (Nicaragua) house slave. Escudero had been purchased around 1780 by don Pedro Soriano for 300 pesos. When the slave requested a papel de venta, Soriano raised his price to 350 pesos. Escudero appealed to the authorities in León, who reprimanded Soriano for the price hike. But Soriano would not budge. Escudero recounted his next move: "I went with the papel [de venta] to the house of don Manuel Taboara imploring him to do me the favor of buying me; in fact he bought me for 350 pesos." Escudero's situation is suggestive about the slave trade outside Guatemala. Not only were slave prices higher in the more distant provinces, but the crown's market controls may have been especially subject to abuses there. In the sale of Ignacio Escudero, don Pedro Soriano had violated the regulation that set a slave's price equal to that of the previous sale. The violation was ultimately corrected, but only because Escudero had occasion to travel to Guatemala and appeal to the Audiencia in 1786. Apparently he had arrived in the company of his new master, don Manuel de Taboara, who testified in the case. The master's testimony corroborated Escudero's story. "This price increase is very injurious [to Escudero]," Taboara said, "since he is looking to liberate himself, and I am willing to give him liberty provided that he pays me the price that I gave for him." Escudero was requesting that Soriano (the seller) be made to refund fifty pesos to Taboara (the buyer). The Audiencia ordered Soriano to give the rebate, in effect lowering the price of Escudero's liberty. Escudero had configured his sale to a new master as a step toward emancipation.[54]

Other slaves made similar plays in the market. Josefa Ordóñez of Zacapa got a papel de venta from her master, then went to the capital and appealed to the court to reduce her price from 200 to 150 pesos.[55] Isidora Morales petitioned not for a price reduction, but for more time to buy her freedom. Her liberty had been set at one hundred pesos and she had already handed over forty-nine pesos when she was "dismissed" from her mistress's house, she said, for a "trifling quarrel." The mistress was demanding that the slave immediately pay the remaining fifty-one pesos. "But it is impossible for me to pay the fifty-one pesos within the brief period that they are giving me," Morales said, "for one thing because my mother is supporting me, and with her small salary of four pesos she cannot help me any further." Morales added that she herself was ill, unable at the moment to find another job. She was asking for more time until she could recover her health and finish paying for her manumission. Presumably she feared being sold and losing the forty-nine pesos she had already invested. The outcome of her case was not recorded, though apparently the mistress did not object.[56]

Crossing Over on Credit   When a price could not be paid or renegotiated, an additional possibility remained: the purchase of freedom on credit. I can confirm only two cases in which slaves used credit to buy liberty, but probably other slaves and their family members also borrowed the money to pay for redemption. (Unfortunately the scattered records that mention manumission by purchase do not always reveal the sources of the money. Some cases are highly suggestive, though. Recall the free black man Manuel Huebo, who bought the liberty of his whole family for a cool seven hundred pesos—probably at least partly a loan.) Lohse's findings on Matina, Costa Rica, seem similarly suggestive. Like the mechanisms of slave emancipation I described earlier, purchase of freedom on credit demonstrates that chattel slavery was eroding with the growing integration of people of African descent into free Hispanicized social networks. It was precisely these networks that provided access to loans.

One example dates to 1777, when the freedman Eugenio de los Angeles gave his former master six hundred pesos in cash to redeem his wife and their five children from slavery. He had borrowed the money. The case entered the courts because the slaveholder, the sugar tycoon don José Jacinto Palomo, refused to liberate one of de los Angeles's daughters. Apparently quibbling over an appraisal made the previous year, Palomo wanted an additional seventy-four pesos and three and a half reales. De los Angeles appealed to the Audiencia. His attorney, the procurator for the poor, pointed out that the plaintiff owned nothing but his labor as a *labrador* (agricultural worker) and that he still needed to repay much of the six-hundred-peso loan. (At the time of the appraisal de los Angeles himself had been a slave; his value had been set at zero because of his age.) Though the Audiencia upheld de los Angeles's obligation to pay Palomo the additional sum, the judges ruled that the daughter should be freed and the father allowed six more months to make the payment. In effect de los Angeles had received even more credit to pay for the liberty of his family. Although the record does not identify the lender of the six hundred pesos, de los Angeles's attorney mentioned that he had help from relatives. His ability to secure such a sum is in any case suggestive of a redoubtable network of contacts.[57]

A second example is that of Luisa Montúfar. A slave of one of Guatemala's most prominent residents, Montúfar petitioned the Audiencia in April 1806.[58] The problem, she explained, was that her master was planning to sell her to a man from Comayagua (in today's Honduras). It would be burdensome for her, the petition said, "to have to go to such a distant place, to leave her relatives, and above all to go to experience different peculiarities, styles, and customs," especially since she expected within six months to have the 117 pesos to purchase her freedom. She was asking the Audiencia to grant a "moratorium for the payment of her liberty."

Her master responded that he had already sold her. The new owner, don Justo de los Campos, was impatiently preparing to leave for Comayagua. He was unwilling, he said, "to wait six months for the price of her liberty," because he didn't believe she would be able to gather the money. He also complained that on the day she filed her appeal she had left his house (in the capital) and had since been moving about freely. He asked that her petition be denied, and he requested that she be arrested and jailed until he was ready to depart. He did, however, leave one door open. He would consent to her remaining behind in Guatemala if she could find another buyer to pay her appraised price within six months. Essentially de los Campos was indicating that he would accept payment from another Spaniard on credit, but that he did not think Montúfar herself was creditworthy. Montúfar enlisted the aid of a *fiador* (a guarantor to provide surety), a man called Pantaleón Montúfar, who owned a house in the capital and other property that he offered as collateral. Still de los Campos refused. In early June Luisa Montúfar made a panicked appeal to the Audiencia, indicating that de los Campos was preparing to leave with her the next morning for his hacienda in Comayagua. "I ask that don Justo de los Campos be ordered to accept the surety," she said, "and not to compel me to go in his company" to Comayagua. Later that day, however, even as the Audiencia's officials were verifying the offer made by Pantaleón Montúfar, Luisa Montúfar returned to the court and alerted them to suspend the proceedings. She had found another fiador, don Víctor Zavala, who was evidently more acceptable to de los Campos. De los Campos had already agreed to Zavala's surety, she explained, and the problem was resolved. Luisa Montúfar got her freedom on credit provided by don Víctor Zavala.

Like Eugenio de los Angeles, Luisa Montúfar had tapped a social network that included free people to get the loan. It is tempting to think that Pantaleón Montúfar was a relative of hers, since they shared a surname and he was her creditor of first recourse. Indeed her attorney had alluded to her relatives in the area. Though Pantaleón Montúfar owned a house in the city, he appears to have been of relatively humble origins; he lacked the honorific *don*, and his credit was dubious in the opinion of don Justo de los Campos. Pantaleón Montúfar was rarely mentioned again in the city's records. Don Víctor Zavala commanded higher status; he used the title *don*, his credit was honored, and his legal and financial affairs generated numerous surviving records. It is not known how Luisa Montúfar secured Zavala's help. Perhaps she agreed to work for him, or perhaps Pantaleón Montúfar on Luisa's behalf offered something for Zavala's backing.

EMANCIPATION AND TRANSFORMATION OF IDENTITIES

By the late eighteenth century slavery in Guatemala was increasingly unsustainable. Slaves were availing themselves of legal institutions and social structures to unravel their enslavement, and as the numbers of people of African descent grew in free society, so too did the possibilities of slave liberations. Kinship and social networks, as well as passing unstopped into free society, continued as primary mechanisms for emancipation, while the state and reigning social ideologies persisted in legitimizing manumissions.

When the general emancipation was declared in Central America in 1824 the civil authorities registered the names of the slaves who came to the offices in the capital to claim their liberty. Only fifty adults and eighteen children were recorded—barely a blip on the screen in a city where thousands of residents were identified as *negra/o* or *mulata/o*.[59] The emancipation law of 1824 essentially ratified a long-term social transformation that was already almost complete.

The enslavement of people of African heritage in Guatemala ended because of a specific kind of social mestizaje: slaves had used physical mobility, access to wages and credit, and the judicial system to mix into free Hispanic society. On the one hand, the ongoing emancipations of slaves contributed to the growing numbers of blacks and mulattos in the free population. On the other hand, this crossing over into free Hispanic society helped occlude consciousness in the nineteenth century of African heritage in Guatemala. Former slaves were absorbed into a free populace whose members increasingly viewed their ethnically mixed society not as Africanized, but Hispanicized, or *ladino*, a term that came to be defined, as Paul Lokken shows, in contrast to the non-Hispanic cultures of the region's Indians.

By the late colonial years most Guatemalans who moved primarily within Hispanicized circles did not seem to know or care much exactly what their racial background was. Though judicial procedures required defendants and witnesses to state their *calidad* (race or rank), neither the public nor the court notaries adhered consistently to the traditional colonial classifications. The records show slippage among racial and ethnic categories, and often people seem to have been guessing based on their own or someone else's appearance or social circle. (Notaries made entries such as "denota ser mestizo" or "por su parecer mulata.") Witnesses and notaries often used multiple terms to describe a single individual. Recall the slave Manuel Antonio Hernández and his free half-sister, Apolonia Olavarrieta; each was labeled *negra/o* in one moment and *mulata/o* in the next. The former slave José Teodoro Arrese was labeled *mulato* and *moreno*.[60] Leandro Carabantes, a free tailor, was alternately described as *mulato* and *pardo*.[61] Another tailor, Hipólito Vela, entered the record repeatedly for criminal deeds in Guatemala City's underworld. Notaries sometimes pegged him as *mestizo* and at other times *mulato*.[62]

Undoubtedly too there were economic and social motives for people to pass further into Spanish society. Domingo Josef Cisneros, known as a mulatto among his neighbors in Zacatecoluca (in today's El Salvador), identified himself as Spanish when he went to court.[63] Rafael Vivas's neighbors in Santiago said he was the son of a mestiza mother and a Spanish father, but on trial he identified himself as Spanish. Rafael was the live-in lover and employee of Rosalía "Bonita" Castro. (They ran her tavern.) Bonita too said she was Spanish, though Rafael said he didn't know her race.[64] Often notaries neglected to include people's calidad in legal records. Sometimes they simply noted that a person did not know his or her calidad.

The colonial nomenclature of ethnic and racial labels, which had recognized African ancestry in terms such as *negra/o*, *mulata/o*, and the occasional *Guinea*, was ushered out of official use at the time of independence. In the national era both state and ecclesiastical institutions adopted the single label *ladina/o* to describe all members of society not identified as Indians. The term *ladina/o* persists today as the predominant popular and official descriptor for non-Indians in Guatemala.

Thus the social structure of slavery itself underlay several historical transformations in Guatemalan society, including slave emancipation, the incorporation of a partly African-descended population into ladino society, and the collapsing of Afro-Guatemalan identities (along with several others) into a single ladino identity. The same processes by which slaves gained emancipation also contributed to the assimilation of free blacks and mulattos within Hispanic society, and, paradoxically, to the erasure of the slave past in Guatemalan historical consciousness. The essay by Justin Wolfe shows that a related process took place in the sphere of Nicaraguan politics in the nineteenth century.

NOTES

Portions of this essay will appear in a book I am bringing to completion on late colonial Guatemala; I am grateful to Stanford University Press for permission to include this material here. I also thank Christopher Lutz, Jim

Lockhart, and the anonymous reviewers at Duke University Press for their suggestions.

1 Palomo de Lewin, "Esclavos negros en Guatemala," 56.

2 Palomo de Lewin, "Esclavos negros"; M. J. MacLeod, *Spanish Central America*; Leiva Vivas, *Tráfico de esclavos negros a Honduras*; Lutz, *Santiago de Guatemala*; Lokken, "From Black to Ladino"; Herrera, *Natives, Europeans, and Africans,* chap. 8.

3 Lutz, *Santiago de Guatemala*, chap. 4, especially 87. Lutz's estimates are based on marriage records.

4 This was the general pattern across Latin America. See Andrews, *Afro-Latin America*, 41, table 1.1.

5 For overviews of these explanations, see Andrews, *Afro-Latin America*, 37–38; Schwartz, "Resistance and Accommodation," especially 70.

6 For an explanation of slavery in Iberia, see Lockhart and Schwartz, *Early Latin America*, 17–19, 26–28.

7 The idealized model of cultural integration has been modified somewhat by recent scholarship. Debra Gene Blumenthal gives an overview of this literature in the introduction to "Implements of Labor."

8 Indigo estates also may have employed large slave communities, especially in the province of San Salvador. See R. S. Smith, "Indigo Production," especially 189.

9 The alcalde mayor of the district in 1819 noted that the estate had more than six hundred slaves. Archivo General de Centro América, Guatemala City (hereafter AGCA) Sig. A1, leg. 2556, exp. 20577. In the seventeenth century Thomas Gage reported that there were more slaves at San Jerónimo than any other estate in the colony. See Sherman, *Forced Native Labor*, 251.

10 Palomo de Lewin, "Esclavos negros," 139.

11 Ibid., 54; AGCA Sig. A3, leg. 1287, exp. 22142; Sig. A3, leg. 1287, exp. 22144; Sig. A3, leg. 1324, exp. 22332; Sig. A3, leg. 1772, exp. 28371; Sig. A3, leg. 1939, exp. 30117.

12 In *Santiago de Guatemala*, Lutz suggests that by the first decade of the eighteenth century there were more mulattos (most of them free) in the city than Indians, mestizos, or Spaniards.

13 Recent studies have analyzed slaves' appeals to the Mexican Inquisition. See Bennett, *Africans in Colonial Mexico*; Owensby, "How Juan and Leonor Won Their Freedom."

14 *Las Siete Partidas del Muy Noble Rey Don Alfonso el Sabio, glosadas por el. Lic. Gregorio López, del Consejo Real de Indias de S.M.*, 3 vols. (Madrid: Compañía General de Impresiones y Libreros del Reino, 1844).

15 3a. Partida, Título II, Leyes VIII and IX and 4a. Partida IV, Título XXI, Ley VI.

16 AGCA Sig. A1, leg. 5359, exp. 45292.

17 AGCA Sig. A1, leg. 2859, exp. 25856.

18 AGCA Sig. A1, leg. 2296, exp. 16824.

19 Testimony of José María Loaisa, 8 June 1819, AGCA Sig. A1, leg. 2556, exp. 20577. Loaisa reckoned it had been about five or six years since the earlier appeal; Friar Andrés Pintelos recalled in 1818 that the slaves had petitioned in 1810. I am uncertain whether the two men were recalling the same appeal or two different appeals. Regardless, the pattern of repeated appeals and concessions is clear. The appeal in 1810 was presumably the one that resulted in a codified agreement that year, which Lowell Gudmundson presents in "Negotiating Rights."

20 On the forced Black Carib (Garífuna) migration, see Gonzalez, *Sojourners of the Caribbean*; Kerns, *Women and the Ancestors*.

21 On livestock and pasturage, see the agreement of 1810 in Gudmundson, "Negotiating Rights."

22 Their negotiations bear parallels with those of some slave communities in Cuba and Brazil. See Díaz, *The Virgin, the King*; Schwartz, "Resistance and Accommodation."

23 These previous accords about punishment, wages, and workload are referenced by the four slave complainants, the administrator of the hacienda, and the Ayuntamiento's síndico in the litigation of 1818–19 (AGCA Sig. A1, leg. 2556, exp. 20577); some of the same points are specified in the agreement of 1810 (in Gudmundson, "Negotiating Rights").

24 José María Loaisa appealed to the Audiencia on 8 June 1819; Miguel González petitioned the Ayuntamiento on 7 July 1819. AGCA Sig. A1, leg. 2556, exp. 20577.

25 Miguel González, petition of April 1820, AGCA Sig. A1, leg. 2556, exp. 20577.

26 A similar pattern has been identified for late colonial Peru. See Hünefeldt, *Paying the Price*, 121–24; Premo, *Children of the Father King*, 235–40.

27 AGCA Sig. A1, leg. 2859, exp. 25856; Sig. A1, leg. 5359, exp. 45303; Sig. A1, leg. 5359, exp. 45300; Sig. A1, leg. 177, exp. 3633; Sig. A1, leg. 2791, exp. 24470; Sig. A1, leg. 2760, exp. 23915; Sig. A1, leg. 2862, exp. 25957.

28 The alcalde mayor testified in José María Loaisa's suit, AGCA Sig. A1, leg. 2556, exp. 20577. For Lowell Gudmundson's findings, see his "Los afroguatemaltecos," 259.

29 For example, AGCA Sig. A1, leg. 2859, exp. 25856.

30 Palomo de Lewin, "Negros Esclavos," 109.

31 For a quantitative analysis of manumissions by grant and sale, see ibid., 107–9.

32 AGCA Sig. A1, leg. 4069, exp. 32109.

33 AGCA Sig. A1, leg. 2864, exp. 26012.

34 AGCA Sig. A1, leg. 379, exp. 7849; Sig. A1, leg. 5359, exp. 45299 (letter of don Francisco Barcena, 27 February 1785).

35 AGCA Sig. A1, leg. 139, exp. 2732; Sig. A1, leg. 4303, exp. 34471.

36 AGCA Sig. A1, leg. 4358, exp. 35390.

37 AGCA Sig. A1, leg. 5359, exp. 45294; Sig. A1, leg. 379, exp. 7849.

38 AGCA Sig. A1, leg. 2296, exp. 16823; Sig. A2, leg. 157, exp. 3047.

39 AGCA Sig. A1, leg. 2861, exp. 25906.

40 For example, AGCA Sig. A1, leg. 5359, exp. 45292 (see the statement of don Juan de Bacara).

41 For example, AGCA Sig. A1, leg. 15, exp. 383.

42 An apparently similar phenomenon, in which slaves requested a papel, is considered from the perspective of legal history by Alejandro de la Fuente in "Slaves and the Creation of Legal Rights in Cuba." Carlos Aguirre notes that a slave who convinced his master to sell him might be sent "to seek a buyer" ("buscar comprador") in *Agentes de su propia libertad*, 87.

43 AGCA Sig. A1, leg. 2859, exp. 25847; Sig. A1, leg. 5358, exp. 45280.

44 AGCA Sig. A1, leg. 2863, exp. 26000; Sig. A1, leg. 4358, exp. 35390; Sig. A1, leg. 2799, exp. 24580; Sig. A1, leg. 2859, exp. 25847; Sig. A1, leg. 2862, exp. 25957.

45 AGCA Sig. A1, leg. 2775, exp. 24209.

46 AGCA Sig. A1, leg. 1675, exp. 10318, fols. 192–93; Sig. A1, leg. 2800, exp. 24593; Sig. A1, leg. 2556, exp. 20577 (petition of Juana Loaisa); Sig. A1, leg. 2895, exp. 25847.

47 Palomo de Lewin, "Negros esclavos," 108; on the sixteenth century, see Herrera, *Natives, Europeans, and Africans*, 126.

48 AGCA Sig A1, leg. 2859, exp. 25854.

49 AGCA Sig. A1, leg. 2800, exp. 24593.

50 Scott, *Slave Emancipation in Cuba*; L. A. Pérez, *Slaves, Sugar, and Colonial Society*.

51 AGCA Sig. A1, leg. 2870, exp. 26226; Sig. A1, leg. 2861, exp. 25907.

52 AGCA Sig. A1, leg. 2861, exp. 25920.

53 AGCA Sig. A1, leg. 2800, exp. 24593.

54 AGCA Sig. A1, leg. 4068, exp. 32079.

55 AGCA Sig. A1, leg. 2792, exp. 24480. The outcome of the case was not documented.

56 AGCA Sig. A1, leg. 2861, exp. 25907.

57 AGCA Sig. A1, leg. 5359, exp. 45295.

58 AGCA Sig. A1, leg. 2772, exp. 24146. The initial slave owner was don Andrés Saavedra, the alcalde mayor of Sacatepequez.

59 AGCA Sig. B1, leg. 1505, exp. 36042, 36043. I have counted people age fourteen and over as adults.

60 AGCA Sig. A2, leg. 157, exp. 3064.

61 AGCA Sig. A2, leg. 157, exp. 3081.

62 AGCA Sig. A2, leg. 151, exp. 2841.

63 AGCA Sig. A2, leg. 153, exp. 2928.

64 AGCA Sig. A2, leg. 154, exp. 2953.

II

NATION BUILDING

& REINSCRIBING RACE

"THE CRUEL WHIP"

Race and Place in Nineteenth-Century Nicaragua

Justin Wolfe

The nineteenth century saw a sea change in the social prominence of Afro-Nicaraguans.[1] Through social advancement
and kinship ties to prominent Spanish families, a generation emerged that
would dominate political struggle in the decades after independence.[2] The
most politically radical of these emerged from the segregated black barrio
of San Felipe in León and came to dominate the Liberal Party. Nurtured
by a shared history of racial discrimination, family networks, and liberal
education, they promoted a republican vision that challenged Nicaragua's
Conservative oligarchy. Although studies of nineteenth-century Nicaragua have tended to ignore or dismiss the importance of race, I argue that
race underlay the political struggles of the 1840s through the 1860s, a period of popular liberalism, civil war, foreign intervention, and emergent
nationalism.

The historiography of nineteenth-century Nicaraguan politics has
been dominated by studies of the classic political divide between Liberals and Conservatives and the apparent coherence between these parties
and the geographic rivalry of León and Granada, but how and when this
arrangement emerged remains little understood. Both cities initially appeared to be led by the privileged aristocracies that had dominated the
local commercial and political scenes since the late eighteenth century.
Yet Liberals of humbler origins came to control León, while Conservative
oligarchs maintained their grip on Granada. José Coronel Urtecho, one of
the most influential writers on this period in Nicaraguan history, admits
that little is known of this period's political relations or ideologies, or even
how the Liberal leaders of the 1830s came to dominate politics.[3] Instead
of investigating this period's politics, however, scholars have tended to

reify post-Independence localism while ascribing it to societal failings: an unwillingness to put country before self, kin, and *pueblo*.[4]

The Afro-Nicaraguan Liberals who rose to prominence after the collapse of the Central American Union (1838) demanded "absolute equality," but their cosmopolitan outlook led them to eschew the language of race rather than challenge it head-on.[5] Exploring how race informed the social and political struggles of this period reveals the limits of such efforts to deracialize Nicaraguan society, especially as scientific racism began to take root in Central America in the 1870s. At the same time this analysis complicates interpretations of Nicaraguan history based on the assumption of mostly white and mestizo protagonists, including the relationship to the Caribbean coast and to the filibuster expedition of the American William Walker. While this essay takes up these issues, my focus on excavating the history of race in nineteenth-century Nicaragua will leave us with many more questions than answers.

RACE AND POLITICS IN POST-INDEPENDENCE NICARAGUA

A census carried out in the late eighteenth century appeared to confirm what many Spaniards already feared: people of African descent dominated the population. They accounted for 51 percent of the province's inhabitants. In the capital city of León that number rose to 56 percent, and it was even higher in the regions of Segovia (61 percent) and Rivas (72 percent).[6] Legal discrimination sought to limit blacks' social mobility and prevent their participation in what the Spanish considered the most honorable affairs of church and government.[7] But blacks pursued a mixture of legal, social, and economic strategies to subvert this discrimination, leading to what German Romero has called "the slow ascent of the marginalized."[8] These strategies tended to fall into two basic, and quite different, categories: whitening or passing and race-based community formation. The latter frightened Spanish authorities, especially after the Haitian Revolution and in the restive early decades of the nineteenth century. The Audiencia of Guatemala, for example, reported to the crown in 1817 on the risk posed in Nicaragua and El Salvador by "those who are descended from Africa." Their exclusion from political citizenship merited immediate amelioration since "this class [was] the majority of the inhabitants of that Province."[9] The king rejected the request, but it is unlikely that any response would have forestalled Central American independence.

Castas were divided in their responses to the Independence-era struggles, but even royalist castas desired to dismantle the Spanish caste system. The newly independent Nicaraguan state, like much of Latin America, abolished the system and colonial racial terms as part of the effort to institute an enlightenment liberalism free of intrinsic inequalities. Thus just as labels of distinction such as the honorific terms *highness* (*alteza*) and *majesty* (*majestad*) were to be abolished and replaced with *citizen* (*ciudadano*), so too were the terms of caste.[10]

Those Afro-Nicaraguans who pursued whitening marriage alliances tended to become associated with Nicaraguan conservatism and its most powerful families, including the Sacasas, Zavalas, Chamorros, and Cuadras.[11] A typical example was Pedro Benito Pineda, who despite his *mulato* birth married well and in 1815 petitioned the Spanish crown for a *gracias al sacar* to allow him and his children to achieve offices and honors otherwise reserved for whites and mestizos. Among the witnesses for his petition were Crisanto Sacasa, who would support Agustín de Iturbide's imperial plans and eventually lead the *serviles* (Conservatives) in Nicaragua's first post-Independence civil war, and Dionisio de la Quadra, whose son Vicente would serve as a Conservative president from 1871 to 1875.[12] It is unknown if Pineda received the gracias al sacar, but in 1815 Dionsio de la Quadra, whose mother was a freed slave, did receive one.[13] In either event, according to Sofonías Salvatierra, Pineda remained a royalist to the end of Spanish rule. This, along with his prominent connections, might explain why among Conservative circles he "ascended notably on the political scale after the proclamation of independence."[14] Perhaps not surprisingly, when Pineda was tapped as *jefe del estado* in 1826, he chose a close ally, Dionisio de la Quadra's brother Miguel, as his general minister.[15]

Pedro Benito Pineda's spectacular political fortunes suggest how successfully he had pursued a strategy of social whitening (*blanqueamiento*). Pineda's son Laureano, described as "light, rosy colored," compared to his father's "dark color," continued this strategy, marrying Crisanto Sacasa's daughter Dolores Sacasa Méndez.[16] He also rose to the same political heights as his father, ruling as supreme director from 1851 to 1853. Despite these efforts Pedro Benito Pineda seemed to believe that appearance belied the standing he had achieved. He became jefe de estado in 1826, during one of Nicaragua's most intensely bloody periods of civil war. Violence soon caught up with Pineda, who was forced to hide out from Liberal forces under the command of Juan Argüello. Pineda was offered a number of ways to escape, but according to Jerónimo Pérez, writing nearly fifty years later, he "refused, because he said that his hair and his color would guarantee his safety, that is to say, he was dark colored and had rough, kinky hair, and he believed that since he wasn't aristocratic and had this connection to the people [*pueblo*], he wasn't hated, but rather loved because of the sympathies for his origin."[17] Pineda was soon captured, along with Miguel Cuadra, taken to León, and then murdered in prison.

Had Pineda survived he may have worked more to secure the kind of "popular caudillo" role that Ponciano Corral came to occupy among the Conservatives. Like Pineda, Corral married well, joining the Conservative circles of the Chamorro family. The nineteenth-century Liberal historian José Dolores Gámez suggested that the Conservatives used Corral's affinity for the "popular masses" to attract votes away from Liberals in the national election of 1853.[18] It was not simply Corral's appearance, what Jerónimo Pérez described as his "dark color and frizzy hair, which revealed that from one blood line he descended from the African race," that made him "the man of the lower classes."[19] Where Fruto Chamorro, Corral's ally and head of the Conservatives, proved himself a dour and aristocratic leader, Corral was quick to laugh and frequently "roamed the barrios and slums."[20] The Conservatives may have needed men like Corral, but they did not seem prepared to let them truly lead. The election of 1853, like those throughout the rest of the century, took place in two stages, with a popular vote for electors, who then voted for the chief executive. According to Gámez, the Conservatives floated Corral's name in the vote for electors, but in the second round the Conservatives were ordered to put forward Chamorro.[21] Just six weeks before the election Bishop Jorge Viteri, who favored Chamorro's candidacy, still viewed Corral as the odds-on favorite, but when the votes of the electors were tallied Corral had received just two out of 980.[22]

In contrast to the more conservative whitening strategy employed by the Pinedas, the discrimination faced by blacks in the late colonial period led many of the poorer casta barrios of León and Granada to support a

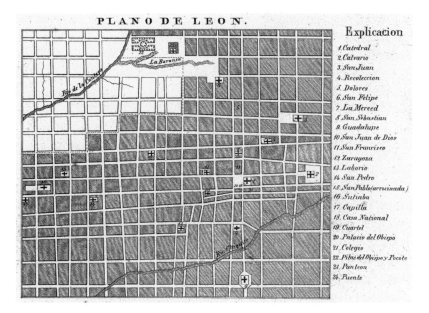

PLANO DE LEON.

Explicacion

1. Catedral
2. Calvario
3. San Juan
4. Recoleccion
5. Dolores
6. San Felipe
7. La Merced
8. San Sebastian
9. Guadalupe
10. San Juan de Dios
11. San Francisco
12. Zaragoza
13. Laborio
14. San Pedro
15. San Pablo (arruinada)
16. Sutiaba
17. Capilla
18. Casa Nacional
19. Cuartel
20. Palacio del Obispo
21. Colegio
22. Pilas del Obispo y Pocote
23. Pan teon
24. Puente

FIGURE 1 "Plano de León." *Source*: Detail from Maximilian von Sonnenstern, *Mapa de la república de Nicaragua* (New York, 1858).

more radical, liberal antioligarchic politics. One of the most important such barrios was San Felipe in León, created as a segregated black barrio in the late seventeenth century.[23] It became the center of León's *pardo* militia in the eighteenth century, and its leaders became active in politics at both the barrio and provincial levels. In the mid-eighteenth century these politics boiled over when a confrontation between the mulatto militia captain Antonio de Padilla and the *gobernador intendente* led to Padilla's execution. The barrio responded with protests and sporadic violence against prominent Spaniards, sealing a contentious and confrontational relationship between San Felipe and León's Spanish population.[24] Despite the barrio's importance in post-Independence politics, its history remains almost unknown. Take, for example, José Coronel Urtecho's reading of the nineteenth-century Nicaraguan historian Tomás Ayón's explanation of Leonese politics in the mid-1820s. Coronel Urtecho cites Ayón reporting, "The military authority of [León] . . . feared the barrio [of San Felipe] because its inhabitants were generally disaffected," only to add, "It is a shame that the venerable historian from León does not say what the military men of León feared about San Felipe, nor for what motives the Felipeños appeared generally disaffected from them."[25]

The community of San Felipe, which numbered about six thousand in the mid-nineteenth century, produced a number of the leading figures who began to assume control of Liberal politics in the 1840s, including the brothers Sebastián and Basilio Salinas, Cleto Mayorga, and Félix Ramírez. A number of other influential Afro-Nicaraguans, such as Francisco Castellón, Rosalío Cortés, and Gregorio Juárez, may also have been from San Felipe.[26] Many of these were connected to one another and to other Liberals by marriage. Despite San Felipe's racialized origin and history, however, there is little to suggest that these men held on to their descent as a political badge. Rather than race, it appears that place—the barrio of San Felipe—served to nurture their political, social, and economic networks. While some of these men pursued whitening marriage alliances, many instead focused on strengthening their links within San Felipe.[27]

These men also found common cause in their education at the Universidad de León. Frances Kinloch noted that the university "constituted a space of sociability where young provincial elites would obtain not just professional titles, but also, not infrequently, promises of marriage."[28] Father Agustín Vijíl, for example, who would become one of William Walker's strongest boosters, was educated at the Universidad de León, where "he made great friends whose influence was hard to avoid, friends like Norberto Ramirez, Trinidad Muñoz, Justo Abaunza, Pablo and Nicolás Buitrago, Hermenegildo Zepeda, Gregorio Juárez and others of no less importance."[29] The university certainly educated the elite, but it also provided opportunity and mobility for the children of much poorer parents. Indeed the list of early post-Independence graduates and later professors is replete with Felipeños and their allies, including Juárez, the Salinas brothers, and Rosalío Cortés.[30] Arturo Cruz has recently suggested that Conservative elites were more socially inclusive than Liberals because Conservatives allowed their illegitimate, frequently mixed-race children to assume family leadership in times of need, whereas Liberals professed equality and leadership based on educational attainment, something Cruz claims was outside the reach of all but León's traditional elite.[31] Cruz's argument is not surprising, given traditional historiography, but it clearly needs reconsideration.

FIGURE 2 Francisco Castellón. *Source*: Jerónimo Pérez, *Obras históricas completas* (1928; Managua: Banco de América, Fundacion de Promoción Cultural, 1977), unnumbered page.

Liberals and Conservatives tended to view race and politics from opposed positions. Conservatives proved capable of incorporating castas into national politics, but only through their adhesion to a conservative social order, one that valued hierarchy and whiteness. Liberals, by contrast, promoted an ideology of social equality where all became equal before the law and the antioligarchic politics of the majority would naturally hold sway. Conservatives like Fruto Chamorro imagined liberalism as the downfall of society and the origin of Nicaragua's bloody civil wars. For them racial difference was natural, and "the desire to establish absolute equality between the races cause[d] great detriment to social well being."[32] Liberals, especially those from barrios like San Felipe, appeared, by contrast, to pursue a strategy of deracialization.

While Liberal Felipeños may have rejected this kind of racialized discourse, they were often reminded of it by political violence and the sting of racial insult. In 1844, for example, Casto Fonseca "made those who were not inclined toward him feel the steel of his fist."[33] This appeared to disproportionately affect Liberals from San Felipe, many of whom fled to Honduras after Basilio Salinas was publicly caned.[34] Memories of this shame reverberated in public discourse more than thirty years later.[35] Given not only the history of violence against blacks from San Felipe, but also the common complaints of physical and sexual abuse among slaves in late colonial Nicaragua, it is hard to imagine that Salinas's flogging was without racial overtones. And though public insults are rarely found in documents from this era, evidence suggests an environment charged with racism. In his memoir of this period Francisco Ortega Arancibia mentioned the "Antillean Thomas Franco," who resided in Granada but who "sympathized with the Democrats, as the antithesis of the aristocracy, which looks down upon those of his race."[36] The private side of such denigration can be found in the letters of the Conservative bishop Jorge Viteri, who referred to Basilio Salinas's brother Sebastián as a "lying Kaffir" and to Castellón and his followers as "Hottentots."[37] That Castellón was described as having "sky blue eyes, a fine white complexion" mattered little then, given his social world and political ideology.[38]

Yet just as hard as whites may have tried to hold Afro-Nicaraguans to their racial origins, Afro-Nicaraguans appeared to deny, or at least sublimate, a racialized sense of self, instead laying claim to their place in the world of liberal civilization. This may help explain the popularity of the term *ladino* in nineteenth-century Nicaragua. The term, which by the end of the eighteenth century was synonymous with *casta*, had by the postcolonial nineteenth century come to mean non-Indian and was used by both ladino and indigenous people.[39] Indians tended to view ladinos as opposed to indigenous community customs and practices and as competitors in the politics of post-Independence Nicaragua. In this context distinguishing between whites, mestizos, mulattos, and *negros* made little difference.[40] Similarly most ladino officials looked upon indigenous communities as an impediment to the establishment of liberal ideals and to their consolidation of political and economic authority. Moreover *ladino* did not carry the pejorative connotations of blackness implicit in the terms *mulato, negro,* and *zambo.* Rather it bespoke a kind of Hispanicized civilization to which so many post-Independence blacks laid claim. Felipeños would likely have been pleased to read that after his travels through Nicaragua E. George Squier defined *ladinos* as "a term signifying gallant men."[41]

Liberal Afro-Nicaraguans like Sebastián Salinas and Francisco Castellón fervently believed in the rights they had achieved as part of an independent, civilized nation. While the racial history of San Felipe might have produced the bonds that united them politically and socially, it seemed to produce no notion of racial solidarity outside this concept of civilization. During their political careers, for example, both Salinas and Castellón tried to resolve Nicaragua's claim over the Mosquito Coast. Neither, however, believed that they should negotiate with the Miskitu inhabitants of the coast, for to do so would undermine the notions of society and civilization to which they pinned their own political claims. In a letter to Frederick Chatfield, the British consul general in Central America, Salinas made plain this view:

> At no time has the Mosquito Kingdom existed, nor does it now. In all truth, Sir, it is reduced to a few savages who wander in the deserts and the woods on the coast of Honduras and Nicaragua, living by the hunt and fishing, without houses, a known language, writing, arts, commerce, laws, or religion, which according to recognized principles would make them appear before the civilized world as composing a regular society, and what is much more, constituting an empire.[42]

While Castellón seemed more willing than Salinas to negotiate British control over San Juan del Norte, he too "adamantly refused to consider the recognition of the Mosquito Indians."[43] To do so, as Salinas argued, "would give to the savage hordes that exist in every continent of the globe the right to form Kingdoms under the protection of other Governments; and put on par with the enlightened states, they would mark the limits of civilization and establish disorder and universal anarchy."[44] Indians and blacks of the Mosquitia were far from brethren to the Felipeños. Their similar origins in slavery and colonial subjugation, if anything, signaled for men like Salinas and Castellón how much they had achieved and distanced themselves from that history. But we need to further historicize and contextualize these relations. There is little in the record to suggest that Liberal Afro-Nicaraguans looked scornfully upon the Afro-Jamaican leadership of San Juan del Norte or the port's numerous African American entrepreneurs as anything but their counterparts in a regional power struggle.[45] As Juliet Hooker's essay in this volume details, however, over the nineteenth century Nicaraguan elites increasingly invoked an exclusionary "spatialization of race" that mapped blackness alongside notions of savage indigeneity in the Atlantic coast. By 1894 and the military annexation of the coast, official discourse was replete with references to "foreign" and "Jamaican" black others.[46]

At the close of the 1840s Nicaraguan Liberals walked a fine line "between fear and hope."[47] They desired a place among the pantheon of nations, one where their equality would be guaranteed by principles of international law, but they had frequently dismaying encounters with Great Britain over the Mosquito Coast. According to José Dolores Gámez, when Francisco Castellón traveled to London as Nicaragua's chargé "every effort he made to settle the current difficulties was in vain, for the English government avoided dealing with Nicaragua, as it seemed very dispiriting to call such a small fraction of Central America a 'nation.' "[48] A contemporary American account of the events described an even harsher encounter: "Signor Castel Leon arrived in London, and was admitted to an interview with Lord Palmerston. He opened the business, but was suddenly checked by her Majesty's minister laughing in his face, and telling him that the question was already closed! Yes, Castel Leon reports that the noble lord did actually laugh in his face. True, it was impolite, but then how could it be helped?"[49] Doubtless it was Castellón who left more dispirited than the British.

The increasingly aggressive stance of the United States was also initially worrying. In 1847 Nicaraguans were shocked at the fate that had befallen Mexico, their far wealthier and powerful neighbor: "We see it subjugated, its national honor insulted, and prisoner to a foreign power, all due to internal divisions."[50] Yet the fault was seen to be as much with Mexico's disunity as with U.S. expansionism. The arrival of E. George Squier as U.S. chargé d'affaires in 1849 seemed to allay Nicaraguan worries as he proclaimed support for Nicaraguan sovereignty and offered a means to counterbalance British influence in the region. In a public speech that cheered Liberals Squier declared, "The American Continent belongs to Americans, and is sacred to Republican Freedom. We should also let it be understood, that if foreign powers encroach upon the territories or invade the rights of any one of the American States, they inflict injury upon all, which it is alike the duty and determination of all to see redressed."[51] Squier's words, which suggested a more reciprocal understanding of the Monroe Doctrine, met wide acclaim, including an impassioned poetic salute to Squier and the American flag by the Liberal Francisco Diaz Zapata. Soon thereafter a newspaper in León reassessed the U.S. invasion of Mexico, now placing blame squarely at the feet of Mexico's own "erroneous conduct."[52]

Squier clearly embraced the Leonese and convinced them of American goodwill. His time in León seemed to attune him to the kind of deracialized image that San Felipe's Liberals envisioned for themselves. He noted, for example, "The fusion between all classes of the population of Nicaragua has been so complete, that notwithstanding the diversity of races, distinctions of caste are hardly recognized."[53] This assessment, however, likely did little to quell Nicaraguan disquiet over foreign representations of the country. During his travels Squier was queried about American Ambassador John L. Stephens's account of his time in Nicaragua: "They had heard of a Mr. Estevens (their nearest approach to Stephens), who had written a book about their 'pobre pais,' their poor country, and were anxious to know what he had said of them, and whether our people really regarded them as 'esclavos y brutos sin verguenza,' slaves and brutes without shame, as the abominable English (los malditos Ingleses) had represented them."[54] Squier's engagement with Nicaragua certainly differed from many of the more common and overtly racist representations of Spanish America in the United States, but more important, it suggests that some Nicaraguans still hoped to be able to embrace U.S. culture without becoming victim to U.S. imperialist impulses.[55]

WILLIAM WALKER, RACE, AND POLITICS IN NICARAGUA

Until 1854 Nicaragua's constitutions tended to promote a weak executive branch, limiting chief executive terms to two years and disallowing consecutive reelection. This, coupled with deep divisions and intense competition, tended to foil political continuity. When no candidate achieved a majority of votes in the election for supreme director in 1853, the decision went to the legislature, which awarded the position to the Conservative Granadino Fruto Chamorro.[56] Chamorro viewed liberal republicanism as a threat to the social order and began to arrest or expel leading Liberals (known then as Democrats). He also ordered a new constitution, one that extended the presidential term to four years. Faced with exile and political exclusion, the Liberals rebelled. Searching for a way to break the back of the Conservatives (known also as Legitimists) and promote American immigration and republican values, the Democrats contracted with William Walker, an American military adventurer, who arrived in June 1855. Seeing in him a kindred political spirit, they hoped he would shift both the military and the ideological balance of power.

It is hardly surprising that the Legitimists had nothing good to say about William Walker. As Walker gained strength in the months after landing in Realejo on 16 June 1855 Legitimists warned against the impending future of filibustering. An article published in the Legitimist newspaper *El Defensor del Orden* on the thirty-fourth anniversary of Nicaraguan Independence seemed prescient:

> Once our country is occupied by North American filibusters, we shall then see an immense immigration of men—declared enemies of our race—who detest our religion, our customs, who regard us and treat us like barbarians, who judge us unworthy of political rights and incapable of fashioning a society worthy of that name. . . . After our territory is flooded by this large immigration, our properties will pass to their hands and they will cast off our institutions and laws.[57]

Within a month Legitimists began to see their prophesies come true, beginning with Walker's execution of Legitimist Minister of Foreign Relations Mateo Mayorga to force the capitulation of Granada.

Given the image of Walker as a pro-slavery demagogue, it is not immediately evident why Liberals, especially Afro-Nicaraguans like Castellón and Salinas, would support him. But they were hardly alone. Felipeño Félix Ramírez, whom Walker described as "swarthy," commanded Democratic troops in Walker's first attempt to capture the southern city Rivas, just two weeks after his arrival in Nicaragua.[58] Ramírez's wife, Bernarda Sarmiento, was also close to José María Valle (alias Chelón), Walker's most important popular military leader.[59] And if Cleto Mayorga mourned his half-cousin, it did not deter his continuing allegiance to Walker. Mateo Mayorga descended from the legitimate Spanish side of the Diaz de Mayorga family; Cleto Mayorga, by contrast, represented the illegitimate black side of the family. While Mateo's family represented the elite of León, Cleto hailed from the barrio of San Felipe.

If Walker and his troops were happily, if judiciously, accepted by Francisco Castellón and other Afro-Nicaraguan Liberals, they were eyed more suspiciously by the more traditional white Leonese elite, such as Nazario Escoto and José María Sarria. Castellón's death on 2 September 1855, just three months after Walker's arrival, left Escoto in charge of the provisional government, and he hoped this command would allow him to redirect his government's efforts. Francisco Ortega Arancibia argues that Escoto and Sarria hoped that a more enduring and stable peace could be established by more moderate figures from both parties, in particular the Liberal José Trinidad Muñoz and the Conservative Ponciano Corral. These were contrasted with Walker and the Conservative Honduran general Santos Guardiola, who were perceived as intensifying the conflict.[60] The deaths of both Muñoz and Castellón in quick succession intensified the fears of these white Liberals and led them to write to the Legitimist leader Fernando Chamorro, seeking an alliance against Walker. Unfortunately their letter of entreaty ended up in the hands of Walker, leading Ortega Arancibia, who recounted his conversation with Chamorro, to "fear that the friends [Escoto, etc.] mentioned in [the letter were] in danger from the vulgar democrats." Who did Ortega Arancibia mean by these "vulgar democrats"? Walker's closest allies, Chelón and Mariano Méndez? Or Afro-Nicaraguan Liberals more broadly writ? While that remains unclear, Chamorro did note that he did not really worry about Escoto and the others "because those friends [were] supported by the barrio of San Felipe."[61] Whatever these talks might have produced became moot once Walker took Granada and forced an uneasy peace upon the Legitimists.

Without more intimate documentation from officials like Sebastián Salinas and Cleto Mayorga it is difficult to assess their belief in the promise of Walker and his filibusters. A reading of the Democratic provisional government's *Boletín Oficial*, however, is suggestive. Until June 1856, when the Democrats broke from their one-year alliance with Walker and joined forces with their former rivals, the Legitimists, the *Boletín* frequently published documents and editorials from newspapers in Nicaragua, Central America, and the United States that were critical of Walker's exploits. They refuted these claims of course, but they still published them in their original form.[62] Such a publishing strategy might have represented Democratic faith in Walker's political ideals, although it may well have been an effort to keep Walker in line by making clear that Democrats were hardly blind to local and international opinion.

Robert May has argued, "Given how entwined slavery and filibustering became, it is not surprising that many Americans habitually came to associate the two, assuming that any expedition must have a proslavery design."[63] May notes that the *New York Herald* claimed that Henry L. Kinney's rival filibustering campaign to colonize land in the Atlantic coast of Nicaragua was either a ruse to introduce slavery or would eventually need to do so to succeed.[64] But evidence suggests that many filibusters and those who encountered them could be otherwise convinced. Soon after Kinney's arrival in San Juan del Norte he was heralded in a sermon by Benjamin Smith, a black Methodist preacher.[65] Smith, who owned the Central American Hotel and ministered to a multiracial flock, praised Kinney as a new Moses who would lead the chosen people into Chontales, a new Canaan.[66]

Reports by Kinney's secretary William S. Thayer to the *New York Evening Post* are equally suggestive of Kinney's racial attitudes, if not that of his fellow colonists. Robert May takes note of Thayer's tale of "respectable" colonists and "an intriguing aside (given American racial mores), that the filibusters danced with women 'of various shades' and that some of their partners were of black and brown complexions."[67] Thayer, who had been a writer for the *Evening Post*, the paper edited by the famed abolitionist William Cullen Bryant, held out Kinney's campaign as a form of legal colonization that should be distinguished from other forms of filibustering.[68] Still, Thayer's claims met disbelief from his antislavery friends. James Gibbons wrote to his son after a family dinner with the Thayers, at which William had announced his plans with Kinney. Gibbons was dismayed:

He [Thayer] is going out to Nicaragua with Filibuster Kinney, to start a "commercial colony," and is entirely persuaded that this is the object and total aim of the expedition. I think, however, that he is mistaken. There is, at least a reservation as to what shall be done when they get there. Powder and ball, no women and children, swords and Saxonism, a rich country with no government, and a weak scattered population—and anyone can guess the rest. Kinney is now detained by government legal process. I suspect the concern to be devilish and piratical, and that they will introduce slavery into their Colony, if they succeed in establishing one.[69]

Kinney's campaign failed, among other reasons because many of his original supporters abandoned him for Walker, yet it is noteworthy how many people within Kinney's circle resisted the conclusion so hastily made by Gibbons.

Whatever good intentions and conciliatory discourse Walker used with the Democrats, the arrival of the filibusters encouraged a withering examination of Nicaragua by foreigners. Foreign travelers had long offered racialized images of the country, making estimates of racial demography and criticizing Nicaraguans' physical appearance and moral qualities. Some of these were despicable, like the German physician Wilhelm Marr's description of the commander of the Castillo Viejo on the Rio San Juan as a "*homo simia*" and "an orangutan." After meeting the "quite white" administrator of the Fort of San Carlos, Marr claimed, "I have discovered a human being."[70] Others were equally blunt, if not so disparaging. Take the description by Félix Belly, the French canal promoter, of his first encounter with Gregorio Juárez and Rosalío Cortés: "[Juárez] was another mulatto, like Mr. Cortez, but much blacker, with almost white curly hair and the face of a very intelligent lion."[71] More common, however, were broadly drawn characterizations of Nicaraguans as "mongrel and degraded races" or "a rabble of ignorant Indians and mulattoes."[72]

Despite these commonplace racist depictions Walker's own words and actions must have conciliated San Felipe's Liberals. Sebastián Salinas, who had been minister of government and foreign relations in Francisco Castellón's provisional government, retained this position even after Patricio Rivas became president.[73] Rivas's son-in-law Cleto Mayorga was charged with helping sort out the finances of Cornelius Vanderbilt's Accessory Transit Company.[74] Gregorio Juárez and Hermenegildo Zepeda were to

FIGURE 3 Rosalío Cortés. *Source*: Francisco Ortega Arancibia, *Cuarenta anos (1838–1878) de historia de Nicaragua: Guerras civiles, vida íntima de grandes personajes políticos, formación de la República* (1912; Managua: Banco de América, Fundación de Promoción Cultural, 1975), unnumbered page.

head up the management of American colonization.[75] This degree of involvement and the dense networks of association between these Liberals challenges the traditional notion that Walker controlled and manipulated his Nicaraguan allies. While some Liberals appeared to fear Walker's designs from his arrival, the more radical ones seemed to imagine they could mold the Americans to their needs. Walker himself claimed that Francisco Castellón hoped to employ the filibusters as a kind of "praetorian guard."[76] In either event it became clear to Felipeños and other Liberals by June 1856 that their faith in Walker's rhetoric and politics was misplaced. In that month Walker came to León and tried to assert himself over the city's Liberals. Informed on 9 June that Walker wanted the presidency of Nicaragua, Sebastián Salinas declared, "We have maintained in good faith that that man [Walker] has not wanted to usurp power or dominate the country." Within a week Salinas and his fellow Liberals had abandoned Walker and the Americans completely, "declaring Walker a traitor."[77] Walker's support did not evaporate completely, but his position became far more tenuous without Liberal support and their resistance to wider Central American intervention against the filibusters.

RACE, PLACE, AND NATION DURING THE
"NATIONAL WAR" AND BEYOND'

William Walker's efforts to claim Nicaragua for himself appeared briefly to unite Nicaraguans under the mantle of Hispano-American civilization, an identity at once gossamer and nebulous. Editorials of support appeared throughout Latin America, often attacking the barbaric and retrograde qualities of the United States while championing those of Latin America. Justo Arosemena's famous essay, "La cuestión americana i su importancia," which pitted the decaying "raza yankee" against the "raza latina," was reprinted in Costa Rica's *Boletín Oficial* just three months after its original publication in the Colombian newspaper *El Neogranadino*.[78] A Chilean editorial decried the North American "enemies of our race," while lauding "our brothers" in the pantheon of "nations of Spanish American origin."[79] Nicaragua's historian-participants in the war also emphasized this discourse, especially its inversion of the racism of North American manifest destiny. Jerónimo Pérez complained, "[It is absurd that Nicaraguans] were called savages because we were defending our lives and property."[80] After all, defending national sovereignty against conquest and colonization had been the core tenet of America's revolutionary experiment. Ortega Arancibia was even more explicit: "In their senseless pride, those foreigners [the filibusters] were a degenerate race and proved . . . that the white race is no more superior than the native one, as their arrogant caudillo [Walker] believed."[81]

If the "raza yankee" or "raza anglosajona" provided a solid target for Latin American attacks, the "raza latina" proved a fraught position from which to take aim. The claim by Justo Arosemena and other, mostly Argentine and Chilean advocates that Hispanic heritage defined the common bond of América certainly enticed some Nicaraguans and served as a compelling counter to U.S. expansionism and Anglo-Saxonism.[82] However, as Aims McGuinness has shown, Arosemena's elitist ire toward "upstart blacks [*negros advenedizos*]" left ambiguous, at best, the position of people of African descent within the "raza latina."[83] Given the disdain of Nicaragua's Afro-Nicaraguan Liberals for the distinction of races, if not the doubtful place of people of African descent within the raza latina, the term appeared to have a short-lived attraction. Indeed the contrast could not be more striking between Arosemena's fear for the "social decomposition" produced by racial heterogeneity—an anxiety that found echo in Fruto Chamorro's conservativism—and the Nicaraguan Liberal Hermenegildo Zepeda's glorying in the creative potential of a people who "are a heterogeneous mixture of indigenous, African and European races."[84]

The same reticence to engage in racial distinctions and the Liberal preference for a cosmopolitan vision of civilization seemed also to guide the Nicaraguan response to Walker's reinstitution of slavery in July 1856. *Slavery* began to creep more regularly into Nicaraguan anti-Walker discourse, but its references were more to colonialism and the loss of national sovereignty than to chattel slavery.[85] The most damning evidence of Walker's intentions to enslave Nicaraguans, in fact, appears to have been faked. In January 1856 the *Boletín Oficial* printed two letters it claimed were from Walker and had been taken off a filibuster trying to escape down the Rio San Juan. Addressed to President Pierce, one letter stated, "I offer on security, under my guarantee, 10,000 Indians from Masaya at 50 pesos each. This capital can be tripled in a moment in New Orleans with just half of them, including the cost of transport: they are very humble and easy to manage."[86] That they were forged is suggested by the fact that Pierce is called "Guillermo" in one letter, rather than Franklin, and the famously reserved Walker penned the other to "My dear Guillermito." Moreover the letters have a half-crazed tone that seems gauged more to incite Nicaraguans against Walker than to attract support for his own designs.[87] Despite these letters, when Tomás Martínez proclaimed "Eternal war before slavery!" he harkened back not to African slavery or Central America's own abolition of slavery in 1824, but to the battle of Covadonga, when Spanish forces first defeated the Moors and began the long centuries of the Reconquista.[88]

Despite the calls for unity against Walker and the Americans, one might imagine that the position of Felipeños like Sebastián Salinas would have been damaged by their close alliance with Walker. After all, it was the established white families of León who first sought to ally with Granada's Conservatives to oust Walker nearly a year earlier. Yet when Máximo Jerez and Tomás Martínez negotiated an agreement to join forces and put aside party differences, the position of minister of government remained in Salinas's hands.[89] Faith in Salinas, moreover, was hardly isolated; San Felipe became a privileged location whose power appeared to grow over the coming years.

On 6 October 1856, just weeks after Liberals and Conservatives joined forces against Walker, Patricio Rivas responded to Felipeño requests for greater political autonomy by establishing a *junta de mejoras* for the barrio. The decree, "responding to the good conduct and industry of the sons of San Felipe," noted that their earlier services to the Spanish crown had been rewarded by a royal grant of lands to the barrio. The new junta de mejoras created an institutional structure that looked and acted much like an independent municipality. San Felipe was not yet liberated from León, but it appeared close. It was to have its own elections, care for its own "governmental, economic, and policing" activities, and manage its own common lands. The decree justified these changes in fundamentally liberal terms: "Responding to the people with the precise amount of power and liberty necessary for their own improvement and well being, with the support of the authority, laws and Government, is to give them what they naturally have the right to ask for and possess."[90] More fundamentally it recognized a juridico-political identity at once tied to its origins in the *pardo* militia and staked to its physical place.[91]

The continued importance of San Felipe may also have been tied to General Tomás Martínez, who had become the de facto head of the Conservative Party through the course of the war. Martínez followed a far more moderate, fundamentally nationalist politics than most Nicaraguan leaders of the time. His most trusted advisors, such as Rosalío Cortés and Gregorio Juárez (often called "El Sabio," the Wise One), were known for their moderation. Both men were also Afro-Nicaraguans from León. Although Martínez had represented the Legitimist army and fought under Fruto Chamorro in the earliest part of the civil war against the Democrats in 1854, he was from León and began his military career under the command of the Afro-Nicaraguan Clemente Rodríguez (alias Cachirulo, "Red Kerchief"), a former Democrat from León. Jerónimo Pérez, who knew Rodríguez, described him as "a son of the people, a man of color, a soldier under Muñoz": "He had risen to Lieutenant Colonel by dint of extraordinary valor; and although he was born in León, and his connections to the Democrats inclined him to their side, he went to serve his political enemies because the Democratic cause was already tainted."[92] Rodríguez's defection to the Legitimists provided them with a fierce military man and, they hoped, a reservoir of popular support like that garnered by Ponciano Corral. Cachirulo's exploits were frequently reported in the Legitimist newspaper *El Defensor del Order*, sometimes in his own voice and often with a mix of admiration and trepidation.[93] Martínez's relationship with Cachirulo and his troops got off to a rocky start, with some of the troops apparently fearing that Martinez "would feel humiliated under the command of a dark colored man."[94] If so he appeared to earn their respect and after Cachirulo's death took command of these same troops.

In the years following Walker's defeat San Felipe continued to receive political favors and cemented its relationship with Tomás Martínez, who would serve as Nicaragua's president for two terms between 1858 and 1867. In 1859 the Martínez government issued a decree that suspended militia duty for any Felipeños who worked on repairs to the Church of San Felipe.[95] Those who worked for free would earn double their time off from militia service. That San Felipe's leaders could wrest such relief for their followers was doubtless a political victory, but it paled in comparison to Martínez's decision to separate San Felipe from León, giving it the status of independent municipality in 1862. This policy is traditionally seen from the perspective of Martínez's pursuit of reelection in 1863 or from his support of Leonese Liberals. In these readings his conciliatory politics toward León is cast as fundamental, and San Felipe is seen as following the political orders of León. In such a scenario San Felipe's independence is instrumental to Leonese politics, rather than part of San Felipe's own politics. Yet Ortega Arancibia's list of León's most ardent supporters of Martínez is topped by the Cortés, Juárez, Salinas, and Mayorga families, all Afro-Nicaraguans and most, if not all, associated with San Felipe.[96] Martínez also promoted a new port near León that would service trade along the west coast and provide competition for San Juan del Sur, and when it opened it was these same leading families who cheered Martínez.[97]

San Felipe's success, however, came at the expense of a more radical democratic politics. The inclusion of Afro-Nicaraguan Liberals (many from San Felipe) into positions of power during Martínez's two presidencies demanded that they share the political stage with former enemies.[98] In 1856, when Martínez opened negotiations with Democrats to join forces against Walker, many of the most hard-line Legitimists looked on disapprovingly. After Martínez and the Liberal leader Máximo Jerez signed the peace accord, the Conservative hardliner Nicasio del Castillo apparently "accused Tomás Martinez of having killed his own party."[99] Imagine the conciliation necessary from both sides for Martínez to put together a cabinet for his first administration that included Castillo and even the moderate Liberals Rosalío Cortés and Hermenegildo Zepeda.

As the more radical Liberal tradition became unanchored from political action, Nicaragua's racial history briefly surfaced, perhaps in search of the solidarities of race that had given form to San Felipe. The same issue of the *Boletín Oficial* that announced the creation of San Felipe's junta de mejoras and recalled the barrio's military services also published an emotional song decrying Yankee racial hatred and championing Nicaraguan racial equality.[100] Its key stanzas declared:

Con desprecio los Yankees nos miran	*The Yankees look upon us with scorn*
Desde sus artes soberbias y vanas,	*From their vain and arrogant arts,*
Nos contemplan cual raza de enanos	*They consider us a race of pygmies*
A quien pueden de un soplo destruir.	*Who can be destroyed with just a blow.*

Ignorantes seremos y pobres,	*We may be poor and ignorant,*
Pero nunca colonos ni esclavos;	*But never subjects nor slaves;*
Somos libres, y altivos, y bravos	*We are free, and proud, and brave.*
Por la patria	*For the homeland*
sabremos morir.	*we shall know how to die.*
Por la patria	*For the homeland*
sabremos morir.	*we shall know how to die.*
Al que negro nació,	*To the one who*
como a un hombre	*was born black, like a man*
De inferior condición	*Of inferior condition,*
lo desprecian:	*they despised you:*
¡Y los Yankees de libres se precian!	*And the Yankees brag of freedom!*
¡Y los Yankees se	*And the Yankees*
llaman cristianos!	*call themselves Christians!*
No tenemos nosotros telégrafo	*We have no telegraph*
Ni vapores ni ferro-carriles;	*Nor steamships nor railroads;*
Mas no nacen aqui	*But here no man*
hombres serviles	*is born servile,*
Negro y blanco se ven	*Black and white live*
como hermanos.	*like brothers.*

After Liberals and Conservatives joined ranks anti-U.S. rhetoric began to appear more widely, but more frequently it recast Nicaraguans as members of the cultured, Hispano- American race and North Americans as barbarian and degenerate. The language of the "Canción" stands out, however, for its direct engagement with Nicaragua's racial history. The claim that "here no man is born servile / Black and white live like brothers" (*servile* was also synonymous with Conservative) is classically liberal, but the Felipeños had long abandoned such a stark black/white divide or any notion of birth to an "inferior condition."

Felipeños seemed uncomfortable with the politics of race even as some turned to it, for it tended to substitute for their radical liberalism without offering its promise. When Tomás Martínez sought reelection in 1862 the Liberal standard-bearer Máximo Jerez turned against him. Most of San Felipe's Liberals, however, stood behind Martínez, and Jerez found himself allying not with his traditional base of Leonese Liberals, but with Granada's Conservatives, notably Fernando Chamorro. Angered by

Jerez's defection, his longtime friend and fellow Liberal Cleto Mayorga (from San Felipe) penned a brief poem that chided Jerez by reaching back into León's racial history. Of the poem, "Amansa Caballos" (The Horse Tamer), Jerónimo Pérez noted, "Among the thousands and thousands of publications in those days, there was one, perhaps the smallest and most vulgar, that so tickled the people, that it was read everywhere, said and repeated with glee."[101] In the poem Jerez is the horse tamer who Mayorga paints as trying to force the masses (the horses) into the Conservative camp. When "the horses speak," however, the masses show that it is only Jerez who has been tamed:

Vino el Amansa Caballos,	*Came the Horse Tamer,*
Y el día que puso un corro,	*And the day that he set up a circle,*
Amansó para Chamorro	*He tamed for Chamorro,*
Negros, retintos y bayos.	*Blacks, dark-browns and bays.*
No tiene miedo a los rayos	*He fears no lightning*
Que fulmina el Occidente:	*That might strike from the West:*
Mansos van para el Oriente	*Broken they head to the East*
A besar la cruel coyunda	*To kiss the cruel whip*
Con que ha de darles la tunda	*With which they'll be beaten*
Su futuro Presidente.	*By their future President.*
HABLAN LOS CABALLOS	*THE HORSES SPEAK*
¡Cuánta habilidad¡, dijeron,	*What ability, they say,*
La de nuestro amansador:	*Has our tamer!*
Pero todavía es mayor,	*But even more so*
La que en él ejercieron,	*Is that exercised over him.*
Pues tan manso lo pusieron	*So tame have they made him*
Como dicen, de *ron plón*,	*As they say, he's humdrum,*
Que lo montan Borbollón,	*That Borbollón, Chamorro,*
Chamorro y hasta las viejas,	*And even the old ladies ride him,*
Y él agacha las orejas	*And he lowers his ears*
Como burra en procesión.	*Like a she-ass on parade.*

The theme of horse taming offered a rich imaginary of race ("blacks, dark browns, and bays") and slavery ("the cruel whip / with which they'll be beaten"). Mayorga's poem, however, is not a call to revolution, but a call for votes. Tomás Martínez won reelection and helped further stabilize

Nicaragua. His two administrations were among the most peaceful periods in Nicaragua's post-Independence history, and San Felipe's Liberals were key to its success. Martínez would be followed in successive elections by the regular and legal turnover of power for twenty-five more years.

CONCLUSION

Almost immediately after Walker was expelled from Nicaragua on 1 May 1857 both popular and scholarly representations of the civil wars leading up to his arrival and the period of Liberal alliance with him were compromised by the Liberal-Conservative coalition and Walker's subsequent representation of the events in *The War in Nicaragua* (1860). Jerónimo Pérez, who participated in the war against Walker, wrote the first significant history of the civil war of 1854 (published in 1865) and what he called the "National Campaign against the Filibuster" (published in 1873). In these and subsequent writings Pérez railed against the failure of Nicaraguan politicians to pursue "real," ideologically based partisan politics: "At the beginning of our revolutions, we adopted names . . . that were expressive of ideas, although at base they were not professed; later . . . each party became recognized by the name of its caudillo, which demonstrates quite well that the factions have not been, nor are they, more than groups or circles that stand in place of their respective leaders."[102] Pérez's contemporaries and subsequent generations have echoed these sentiments.[103] Indeed José Coronel Urtecho's "Introducción a la Epoca de Anarquía en Nicaragua, 1821–1857" all but sealed this era as beyond political comprehension or analysis.[104] Perhaps as important has been the Conservative-Granadino bent of late nineteenth-century and twentieth-century Nicaraguan historiography, against which nineteenth-century Liberal politics and Leonese history hardly tip the scale. Compare, for example, research on Fruto Chamorro and Francisco Castellón, the two leading political figures of the 1850s. Thanks to Pedro Joaquín Chamorro Zelaya and articles published in the *Revista Conservadora del Pensamiento Centroamericano*, we know of Fruto Chamorro's genealogy, career, ideology, and politics.[105] Who can say the same for Castellón? This analytical lacuna has made it difficult to understand Walker's popularity during his first eighteen months in Nicaragua, especially among the mulatto Liberals of San Felipe. Julius Froebel wrote a series of letters to the *New York Times* in 1856 that tried to make sense for North American readers of what he called "The Nicaragua Question."[106] Froebel's analysis stands out for its effort to see Nicaraguan politics at the heart of the ongoing conflict. He chides the typical "observer of recent Hispano-American history" who believes he can explain it "by denouncing the ambition and greediness of political leaders and military chiefs on one side, and the political nothingness of the masses of the people on the other." By contrast, Froebel argues, "The civil dissensions in the Spanish-American countries are by no means void of principle, nor of social and political interest to him who takes the trouble and has the capacity of understanding them,—least of all so in Central America."[107] This rare perspective became equally rare in Nicaragua after Walker's expulsion.

The presidents that followed Martínez had generally Liberal political policies and maintained Martínez's inclusion of Liberal politicians in the cabinet and regional political posts, but the presidents themselves came increasingly from the most exclusive oligarchic families of Granada and Rivas.[108] No longer, however, did Afro-Nicaraguan Conservatives like Laureano Pineda or José León Sandoval figure as Conservative candidates. Instead what Arturo Cruz calls the "grandees of the Conservative circle" increasingly closed ranks around themselves.[109]

León's Afro-Nicaraguan Liberals, the ones who directed the region's politics for most of the 1840s and 1850s, lacked the kind of financial networks available to the leading families of Granada. Their base of power had been built on the claims of mass politics, a politics that derived in many ways from their experiences of cultural and institutional racism and from networks of places like San Felipe. Without that radical project they began to lose their positions of power, and San Felipe was eventually reincorporated into León. The descendants of the Salinas, Cortés, Juárez, and Mayorga (Cleto) families never achieved their parents' political importance in Nicaragua. The same can hardly be said of the Chamorro, Zavala, and Sacasa families, whose sons continued to be vital to Nicaraguan politics well into the twentieth century, if not beyond.[110] In the process Nicaraguan politics reinscribed the colonial hierarchy of race the Felipeños had fought so hard to destroy. A small minority of whites controlled the highest circles of power, while nonwhite ladinos filled the middle-sector roles of local and regional politics. Racialized politics like that suggested in Cleto Mayorga's "Amansa Caballos" fell by the wayside, but racial inequality and discrimination remained.

NOTES

Research for this essay was funded by a Fulbright Scholar Grant and by the Roger Thayer Stone Center for Latin American Studies and the Committee on Research at Tulane University. I am grateful to Robert May, Rosanne Adderley, Michel Gobat, Lowell Gudmundson, and Edith Wolfe for comments on earlier versions of this essay.

1   Discussing the history of race in nineteenth-century Nicaragua is vexed by the often sub rosa quality of racial discourse and a historiography in many ways built on a nationalist ideology of homogeneous *mestizaje*. However, the colonial institutional racism levied against people of African descent and struggles over status distinctions in a postcolonial, postemancipation society marked Nicaragua's social and political history. As such throughout this essay I use the terms *Afro-Nicaraguan* and (at times) *black* to foreground how conceptions of blackness were enmeshed in these conflicts. When specific racial terms were used in the documents I consulted, I have left them in their original Spanish form.

2   The scope of this shift is perhaps most notable at the highest level of executive: José León Sandoval (1845–47), José Laureano Pineda (1851–53), and Francisco Castellón (1854–55) were all of African descent.

3   Coronel Urtecho, *Reflexiones sobre la historia de Nicaragua*, 411.

4   See, e.g., Pérez-Baltodano, *Entre el estado conquistador*, 145; Belli, "Un ensayo de interpretación," 51–53. E. Bradford Burns, by contrast, sees localism as a cynical ploy for power, "a *deus ex machina* to move men and armies" (*Patriarch and Folk*, 21).

5   Sanders similarly notes that "the linchpin of popular liberalism was equality" (*Contentious Republicans*, 43).

6   These figures are from Archivo General de Centro América, Guatemala City (hereafter AGCA) A3.29, leg. 1749, exp. 28130, 1778. The census counted all people of African descent as mulattos. Nicaragua was hardly an anomaly in Central America. See Lutz, *Santiago de Guatemala*. While it might be tempting to dismiss these figures as colonial fantasy, the Nicaraguan census of 1883 reports a nearly identical demographic profile at both the national and regional levels. See Nicaragua, Ministerio de Gobernación, *Informe Ministerio de Gobernación para el Bienio 1883/1884*.

7   On these Spanish strategies, see Twinam, "The Negotiation of Honor"; Martínez-Alier, *Marriage, Class, and Colour*.

8   Romero Vargas, *Las estructuras sociales*, book 3, 285.

9   AGCA B2.7, leg. 36, exp. 817, 1817.

10   Kinloch Tijerino, *Nicaragua*, 41.

11   Stone calls these the "'old' aristocratic families, who can trace their roots to the early colonial period" (*The Heritage of the Conquistadors*, 38). Liberals pursued these strategies too, of course, but their alliances do not appear to have been with León's most important colonial families. More research needs to be done on Liberal marriage patterns, just as it needs to be done on Liberal politics.

12   Salvatierra, *Contribución a la historia de Centroamérica*, 2:424–25. On Crisanto Sacasa, see Coronel Urtecho, *Reflexiones*, 298–315, 342–411; J. Pérez, "Biografía del Coronel Crisanto Sacasa," *Obras históricas completas* (hereafter all works by J. Pérez refer to this collection).

13   See AGCA A1.39, leg. 2651, exp. 22247, 1815. Although the Cuadra family traced its lineage from mulattos on both sides in the nineteenth century, it is more commonly associated with the *mestizo* nationalism championed by Dionisio de la Quadra's grandson (Carlos Cuadra Pasos) and great-grandson (Pablo Antonio Cuadra). On the mulatto history of the Quadra family, see Romero Vargas, *Estructuras sociales*, 357–58; Meléndez Obando, "Presencia africana en familias nicaragüenses," 349–54; Cuadra Pasos, *Obras*, 1:57–58.

14   Salvatierra, *Contribución a la historia de Centroamérica*, 2:424–25.

15   J. Pérez, "Biografía de Don Juan Argüello," 501–2. Nicaragua's constitution of 1826 referred to the chief executive as the "jefe de estado." Only in 1858 would the title become "president of the republic."

16   On physical descriptions of the Pinedas, see J. Pérez, "Biografía de Don Juan Argüello," 502; J. Pérez, "Galería: A Mis Discípulos," 772. The marriage of Crisanto Sacasa's son Salvador to Dionisio de la Quadra's daughter Manuela further strengthened the Sacasa-Quadra-Pineda network.

17   J. Pérez, "Biografía de Don Juan Argüello," 502.

18   Gámez, *Historia moderna de Nicaragua*, 430–31.

19   J. Pérez, "Memorias para la Historia de la Revolución," 37.

20   Ibid.

21   Gámez, *Historia moderna de Nicaragua*, 430–31. It is not clear if the Conservatives actually tried this gambit, or if it had any real effect. In any event, no candidate won outright and the election was through the assembly, which selected Fruto Chamorro.

22   Bishop Jorge Viteri (León) to Agustín Vijil, 20 October 1852, reprinted in Vijil, "El Licenciado don Francisco Castellón," 297. For complete results of the election, see Vega Bolaños, *Gobernantes de Nicaragua*, 186–87.

23   On the barrio's creation, see AGCA A1.10 (5), leg. 21, exp. 142, 1663. See also Buitrago Matus, *León*, 2:121–45.

24   A detailed accounting of these conflicts is beyond this essay. See, however, Ayón, *Historia de Nicaragua*, 2:239–56, 275–90; Buitrago Matus, *León*, 1:271–87. Ayón believed that the barbaric way both Padilla and San Felipe were

treated during the conflict led directly to the continued violence. For violence committed against individuals in response to the execution of Padilla, see, e.g., AGCA A1.15 (5), leg. 101, exp. 780, 1748; A1.15 (5), leg. 103, exp. 786, 1749.

25 Coronel Urtecho, *Reflexiones*, 444.

26 According to Cuadra Cea in "Conferencia," 16, Gregorio Juárez's mother, Concepción Juárez, was a freed slave. Juárez was a notable family name in San Felipe from at least the end of the eighteenth century. See AGCA A1.48.3 (5), leg. 451, exp. 2973, 1801.

27 For marriage within many of these families, see Meléndez Obando, "Presencia"; Cuadra Cea, "Conferencia."

28 Kinloch Tijerino, *Nicaragua*, 76.

29 Vijil, *El Padre Vijil*, 2.

30 Arellano, *Reseña histórica*, 94–114.

31 Cruz, *Nicaragua's Conservative Republic*, 30–31.

32 Chamorro, "Mensaje," 109.

33 Gámez, *Historia moderna de Nicaragua*, 342.

34 Ortega Arancibia, *Cuarenta años*, 50; Gámez, *Historia de Nicaragua*, 342. For Fonseca's defense of his actions, see *Proceso contra el Gran Mariscal Casto Fonseca y ejecución de la sentencia* (León: Imprenta de la Paz, 1849), reprinted in *Revista de la Academia de Geografía e Historia de Nicaragua* 2, no. 3 (1938), 251.

35 See "Notabilidades revolucionarias," *Gaceta de Nicaragua*, 17 July 1869; Dionisio Chamorro, letter to the editor of *El Centro Americano*, 16 October 1880, reprinted in "Cartas históricas," *Revista de la Academia de Geografía e Historia de Nicaragua* 2, no. 3 (1938), 289.

36 Ortega Arancibia, *Cuarenta años*, 213.

37 Bishop Jorge Viteri (León) to Agustín Vijil, 20 October 1852, reprinted in Vijil, *El Padre Vijil*, 103; Bishop Jorge Viteri (León) to Agustín Vijil, 28 March 1853, reprinted in Vijil, "El Licenciado don Francisco Castellón," 297.

38 J. Pérez, "Memorias para la Historia de la Revolución," 56. See also Wells, *Explorations and Adventures*, 96.

39 On the changing meaning of *ladino* in Central America, see Gould, *To Die in This Way*, 136–38; Taracena Arriola, "El vocabulo 'Ladino,'" 89–104. See also Paul Lokken's contribution in this collection.

40 Wolfe, *The Everyday Nation-State*, chap. 5. One exception to the ubiquity of *ladino* appears to be the common use of *mulato* in the indigenous barrio of Monimbó in Masaya. See Gould, *To Die in This Way*, 153, 169; Peña Hernández, *Folklore de Nicaragua*, 79.

41 Squier, *Notes on Central America*, 53.

42 Sebastián Salinas (Managua) to Frederick Chatfield, 14 October 1847, in House of Commons, "Correspondence Respecting the Mosquito Territory," 64. See the much haughtier translation in "British Encroachments

and Aggressions in Central America: The Mosquito Question," *American Whig Review* 11, no. 27 (1850), 243.

43 Rodríguez, *A Palmerstonian Diplomat*, 289.

44 Sebastián Salinas (Managua) to Frederick Chatfield, 14 October 1847, in House of Commons, "Correspondence Respecting the Mosquito Territory," 64–65.

45 On black Jamaicans' and Americans' political and mercantile control of the Caribbean coast, see Letts, *California Illustrated*, 164; Squier, *Travels in Central America*, 73–74; Lapp, *Blacks in Gold Rush California*, 43–47.

46 Gordon, *Disparate Diasporas*, 59.

47 Ramírez, "El Director del Estado," 154.

48 Gámez, *Historia de Nicaragua*, 361.

49 "The Mosquito King and the British Queen," *United States Democratic Review*, November 1849, 416.

50 [Pío J. Bolaños], "A continuacíon el Sr. Presidente expuso," *Registro Oficial*, 11 September 1847, 127.

51 Rodríguez, *Palmerstonian Diplomat*, 301. Squier's speech was reprinted in *Correo del Istmo* (León), 16 July 1849. The full text is also reproduced in Squier, *Travels in Central America*, 251–53.

52 *Correo del Istmo* (León), 7 March 1850, quoted in Kinloch Tijerino, *Nicaragua*, 203.

53 Squier, *Travels in Central America*, 267.

54 "Adventures and Observations in Nicaragua," *International Magazine* 3, no. 4 (1851), 437. See also, Stephens, *Incidents of Travel*.

55 Horsman, *Race and Manifest Destiny*, 116–86.

56 On this election, see Burns, *Patriarch and Folk*, 45–50.

57 *El Defensor del Orden* (Granada), 15 September 1855.

58 J. Pérez, "Memorias para la Historia de la Revolución," 130–31. On Walker's description of Ramírez, see Walker, *The War in Nicaragua*, 39.

59 On Bernarda Sarmiento's relationship with Chelón and other Liberal caudillos, see Ortega Arancibia, *Cuarenta años*, 59. Sarmiento and her husband, Félix Ramírez, adopted her great-nephew Rubén Darío. See Cuadra Cea, "Conferencia," 11.

60 Ortega Arancibia, *Cuarenta años*, 168–80; Walker, *The War in Nicaragua*, 35.

61 Ortega Arancibia, *Cuarenta años*, 202.

62 See, e.g., *Boletín Oficial* (León), 29 May 1856 and 5 June 1856. The Legitimist newspaper *El Defensor del Orden* (Granada), by contrast, often burlesqued Democratic reports and correspondence. In one example, published on 4 July 1854, Francisco Castellón's title is listed as "Chief of the bandits who support me" and ends with the date, "16 days of the month of June of the year of the Devil of 1854."

63 R. E. May, *Manifest Destiny's Underworld*, 267.

64 Ibid.

65   "A Peter the Hermit in Nicaragua," *Littell's Living Age*, 10 November 1855. The article originally appeared in the *New York Evening Post*, for which Kinney's secretary William S. Thayer had worked and wrote on Kinney's efforts. See also "Establishing the Church in Nicaragua," *Frederick Douglass' Paper* (Rochester, N.Y.), 26 October 1855, which mistakenly gives Kinney the credit for Smith's work.

66   Benjamin Smith attended the annual meeting of the African Methodist Episcopal (A.M.E.) Church in Chatham, Canada, in 1856 and discussed his "labors in Greytown" since 1852. He noted in particular that the people of his mixed congregation of whites and blacks "[did] not comprehend the distinction of color." Payne, *History of the African Methodist Episcopal Church*, 384–85.

67   R. E. May, *Manifest Destiny's Underworld*, 189–90.

68   It is notable that when Kinney served in the Constituent Convention of Texas in 1845, against much resistance, he favored the enfranchisement of Tejanos (Mexicans) because they appeared to be good citizens, no matter their "race." M. M. Carroll, *Homesteads Ungovernable*, 44.

69   Quoted in Bacon, *Abby Hopper Gibbons*, 74–75.

70   Marr, *Viaje a Centroamérica*, 145, 155.

71   Belly, *L'isthme Américain*, 107.

72   The former was published in an article in the *New York Herald* and reprinted in "Central American Affairs," *Provincial Freeman* (Chatham, Canada), 14 February 1857; the latter appeared in "The Nicaragua Question," *United States Democratic Review* 41 (February 1858): 115.

73   "Oficial," *Boletín Oficial* (León), 9 April 1856.

74   J. Pérez, "Biografía del Don General Tomás Martínez"; Walker, *The War in Nicaragua*, 153–4. See also United States, Department of State, *Correspondence*, 309–10.

75   "Decreto emitido sobre colonización," *Boletín Oficial* (León), 16 April 1856.

76   Walker, *The War in Nicaragua*, 256.

77   "Efeméridades," *Boletín Oficial* (León), 8 August 1856.

78   "Colombia llama la atención a los republicanos de América," *Boletín Oficial* (San José, Costa Rica), 1 November 1856, reprinted in Costa Rica, Comision de Investigación Histórica de la Campana de 1856–1857, *Crónicas y comentarios*, 350–51. The original was published in *El Neogranadino*, 15 and 29 July 1856, and is reprinted in Tello Burgos, *Escritos de Justo Arosemena*, 247–63.

79   "Chile," *Boletín Oficial* (León), 2 December 1856.

80   J. Pérez, "Memorias para la Historia de la Campaña Nacional," 274.

81   Ortega Arancibia, *Cuarenta años*, 247.

82   Gobat, *Confronting the American Dream*, 44.

83   McGuinness, "Searching for 'Latin America,'" 101–2.

84   Arosemena, "La cuestión americana," 261; Chamorro, "Mensaje," 109; Zepeda, "Discurso [1858]," 6–7.

85　See, e.g., "Los centroamericanos pelean por su libertad," *Boletín Oficial* (León), 24 October 1856; *Boletín Oficial* (León), 5 June 1856.

86　*Boletín Oficial* (León), 16 January 1857.

87　See, however, Ortega Arancibia, *Cuarenta años*, 236; J. Pérez, "Memorias para la Historia de la Campaña Nacional," 231. Both reproduce the implications of these letters (especially the enslavement of Indians) without actually quoting from them.

88　"Proclama del General Martínez a los nicaragüenses," *Boletín Oficial* (León), 29 December 1856.

89　"Convenio," *Boletín Oficial* (León), 20 September 1856.

90　"Junta de mejoras de San Felipe," *Boletín Oficial* (León), 10 October 1856.

91　On the development of identities that linked conceptions of race with locale, see, e.g., Díaz, *The Virgin, the King*, 74–94; Gudmundson, "Firewater," 239–76; Lewis, "Of Ships and Saints," 62–82.

92　J. Pérez, "Memorias para la Historia de la Revolución," 97.

93　See, e.g., *El Defensor del Orden* (Granada), 28 August 1854 and 2 November 1854.

94　Ortega Arancibia, *Cuarenta años*, 149–50. See also J. Pérez, "Galería: A Mis Discípulos," 733.

95　This decree is reprinted in Buitrago Matus, *León*, 2:139–40.

96　Ortega Arancibia, *Cuarenta años*, 327.

97　Ibid., 294.

98　See the fairly complete list of regional political appointments (e.g., prefect, treasurer for public education, customs administration, tax administration) for the years 1844 to 1872 in *Gaceta Nacional* (Managua), 26 January 1874 and 28 February 1874.

99　Díaz Lacayo, *Nicaragua*, 27.

100　Un Chontaleño, "Canción," *Boletín Oficial* (León), 10 October 1856.

101　J. Pérez, "Biografía del Don General Tomás Martínez," 605. The poem is reprinted with Pérez's anecdote. In the poem, "a circle" refers both to the circle in which the horses are tamed but also to Jerez's new political circle. "The West" is León, and "the East" is Granada. "Borbollón" was the nickname of the Conservative leader Fulgencio Vega.

102　J. Pérez, "Biografía de Don Manuel Antonio de la Cerda," 478.

103　Tomás Ayón, José Dolores Gámez, and Enrique Guzmán all helped to create the "historical" narrative for this belief. See, e.g., Ayón, "Apuntes sobre algunos de los acontecimientos políticos de Nicaragua en los años de 1811 á 1824," in *Historia de Nicaragua*, 3:405–32; Gámez, *Historia de Nicaragua*, 248–52; Guzmán, *Editoriales de La Prensa*, 141. Subsequently this conception has found expression in the works of José Coronel Urtecho, Alberto Lanuza, and Humberto Belli, among others.

104　Coronel Urtecho, "Introducción," 39–49. See also Casanova Fuertes, "Hacia una nueva valorización," 231–48; Kinloch Tijerino, *Nicaragua*.

105 Chamorro Zelaya, *Fruto Chamorro.*

106 Julius Froebel, "The Nicaragua Question: Political History of the Central American States: Aims and Prospects of Walker's Expedition," *New York Daily Times*, 16 February 1856, 2; Julius Froebel, "The Nicaragua Question: Natural Advantages of Central America," *New York Daily Times*, 20 February 1856; Julius Froebel, "The Nicaragua Question: Relative Values of Slave and Free Labor—Slavery Unsuited to Nicaragua," *New York Daily Times*, 7 March 1856; Julius Froebel, "The Nicaragua Question: Annexation of Nicaragua Impracticable," *New York Daily Times*, 8 March 1856; Julius Froebel, "The Nicaragua Question: Moral Aspects of the Question—Conclusion," *New York Daily Times*, 12 March 1856.

107 Froebel, "The Nicaragua Question: Political History of the Central American States: Aims and Prospects of Walker's Expedition," *New York Daily Times*, 16 February 1856.

108 Wolfe, *Everyday Nation-State.*

109 Cruz, *Nicaragua's Conservative Republic.*

110 See Stone, *Heritage of the Conquistadors*; Vilas, "Family Affairs."

Blacks in the "White Towns" of
Western Nicaragua in the 1880s

Lowell Gudmundson

As part of the contemporary rush to capitalize on a resurgent tourist trade, a group of a dozen towns in western Nicaragua have been branded as the "White Towns" (*Los Pueblos Blancos*). Day-trip tours to several of these artisan-rich small towns west of Granada and south of Managua come with this color-coded invitation to visitors domestic and foreign. The promoters and government bureaucrats who so unselfconsciously push anything that sells claim that the white reference is based on the whitewashed color of their churches, but no doubt both foreign and domestic visitors occasionally make other, less architectural connections.

With the Los Pueblos Blancos sales pitch, however, Nicaraguans and, to a lesser extent, foreigners are being sold not just a day trip but a complex series of historical simplifications. First, the name recalls the *Los Pueblos* historical label, familiar to Nicaraguans as referring to the arch-Liberal towns of the area critical in the overthrow of Conservative rule after the 1880s and to a whole series of Liberal and revolutionary movements over the next century.[1] Second, it calls upon both Nicaraguans and foreign visitors to conceptually locate themselves with and within the Indian/non-Indian dichotomy basic to all Central American nationalist traditions and sociohistorical interpretations, not to mention their tourism industries and agencies. And finally, it presumes that same audience will be capable of digesting an even more deeply coded message: all that is Indian is folkloric, traditional, backward-looking, and suggestive of a past ever more minoritarian, indeed rare in modern western Nicaragua; all that is non-Indian is (culturally speaking, local) white and the source of good souvenir bargains close at hand. Past generations of Nicaraguans may have taken up arms repeatedly for Left-Liberal causes in Los Pueblos, and national intellectual and political leaders may have taken up their pens just as militantly to argue for a nonwhite (critics would no doubt say pseudo-nonwhite) majority unifying symbol, but in the end all such protest was for naught. All the symbols and terms, from *ladino* to *mestizo* to *Indo-Hispanic* to something so vacuous as *our race*, could be seen as poor euphemisms for *white*, the antithesis of the Indian that Nicaraguans had perhaps once been long ago but certainly not for the past century or more of integrated or progressive national life. Any remaining or recalcitrant Indians would have to get their own day-trip tours and souvenir clients!

Quotidian and pathetic as this example may be, it contains some very powerful elisions in addition to the Indian suppression or avoidance dynamic so very well studied by Jeffrey Gould.[2] Nicaragua is not only one of the best studied cases of Indian identity suppression as nationalism in Central America. It is also one of the most successful cases of black erasure or expulsion to the Atlantic coast of any African American presence or heritage.[3] And the irony of these semantic acrobatics is even greater since Nicaragua and El Salvador are the two Central American nations most closely identified with the Pacific coast and foothills regions as home to their national prototypical non-Indian or Hispanic populations. Everywhere in Central America in colonial and early independent times these were the cattle ranch and sugar-producing populations identified most often by outside observers, whether Spanish colonial or Anglo-expansionist, with what they saw as a predominantly African mixed-race heritage.

Mixed-race nationalism during the nineteenth century and early twentieth was a very powerful force throughout Central America, and no less so in Nicaragua. Moreover white or Spanish American nationalism of the early years of independent life was very often led by the mixed-race sons of leading white patriarchs, nearly always of illegitimate, "outside" birth.[4] However grudgingly such political leaders' whiteness was conceded, or vehemently opposed, by partisan friend or foe, it was not long before inescapably nonwhite, nonelite *mestizos*, *mulatos*, and *zambos* (mixtures of white and Indian, white and black, and black and Indian, respectively) were responding to, when not writing themselves, calls for a far more inclusive social and political system. From the mid- to late nineteenth century Liberals attempted to legislate formal male equality by means of suppressing Indian communal identity and the common lands systems, the latter shared by all ethnic groups in the countryside to one degree or another, as well as the economic, social, and ideological power of the Church. Whatever their intentions, in the countryside the Liberal reforms had the contradictory effect of simultaneously abolishing the official existence and rights of Indians while requiring their continued existence and recruitment as coffee and commercial farm laborers, voters, and militia fighters.

With the triumph of Liberal, insurgent regimes throughout Central America between 1871 and 1893 there was set in motion an ethnic reclassification movement with powerful and cruel ironies for all concerned. Censuses carried out between 1880 and 1920 everywhere in Central America documented, quite miraculously, a dramatic drop in the percentage of the population deemed Indian (something on the order of a 50 to 80 percent decrease), alongside a proportionate increase in the newly minted *ladino* or mestizo population.[5] And yet it was during these same years that a revived and far more effective system of institutionalized labor coercion (and, in Nicaragua at least, political patronage-clientelism) enveloped rural dwellers suspiciously Indian-like, indeed coercible essentially because they were inveterately Indian, contrary to the census taker's welcome erasure of national backwardness by means of reclassification. In Diriomo, Nicaragua, one of the towns discussed in this essay, Elizabeth Dore went so far as to refer to "hunting Indians" as the labor recruitment or policing dynamic of the early twentieth century, complete with pass books, multigenerational debt peonage, and corporal punishments of the vilest sort.[6] Similarly Jeffrey Gould documents many cases of violent Indian community resistance to their institutional suppression, on a whole range of social, political, and cultural and ideological levels.[7]

But liberalism held many meanings beyond "hunting Indians" for coffee labor. Liberalism vastly accelerated the titling of common lands to individuals, and it is now clear from all political angles and case studies that much of the middling peasantry participated in this process in both coffee and non-coffee regions in Nicaragua. Indeed in Diriamba and neighboring areas of Carazo Department, Julie Charlip has presented compelling evidence of remarkably broad distribution of coffee production land in the hands of a peasantry positioned within walking distance of the draconian repression so well documented by Dore for Diriomo.[8] Justin Wolfe and Michel Gobat have provided very detailed evidence of middle and rich peasant resiliency as private landowners from the 1870s through the 1940s in mixed farming and grazing areas, alongside planter encroachments in the Mombacho volcano coffee area close to the city of Granada.[9] Indeed all these authors tend to confirm the original thesis put forward by Gould: anti-Indian nationalism (the myth of *Nicaragua mestiza*) only rarely annihilated Indian communities. More often it forced them to privatize land ownership internally, to decommunalize certain institutions, and to abandon certain cultural practices, including language and distinctive dress. But simple eviction or straightforward proletarianization and *ladinoization* was the exception rather than the rule.[10]

Ideologically as well liberalism had many nuanced meanings. Suppressing Indianness could well be an argument made by the most Jacobin of Left-Liberal leaders in hopes of destroying what they saw as an odious feudal system of oppression of Indians by ladinos or whites whose ethnic heritage was far less important than their landed dominance of local affairs. Many of these firebrands were mixed-race individuals seeking a whole range of radical goals, some more friendly to (ex-)Indians than others. One of the towns I focus on, Diriamba, had the distinction of producing two of the most widely read authors of Left-Liberal, pro-mixed-race Central American nationalism of the time (the 1920s), Juan Mendoza and Salvador Mendieta, both of whom hailed from mestizo families of some wealth but not at the pinnacle of local prestige.[11]

Jacobin liberals such as Mendoza and Mendieta had far greater followings among fellow Central American déclassé intellectuals than within Nicaraguan politics, it is true. But that is precisely what makes their ideas of interest, and their colorful tirades even more so. Their sympathy for the Indian underdog or serf is ever present. So too is their frequent dismissal of Indianness as a noxious mixture of grinding poverty, ignorance, and gullibility at the service of lordly superiors. However often they denounce the crass anti-Indian racism of the local upper classes (all the more disgusting and remarkable in light of their own undeniable if silenced Indian parentage), their implicit dismissal of all things Indian as backward and lamentable places them squarely in the ladino or mestizo camp whose misdeeds they are denouncing. For example, Mendoza's combative left-liberalism denounces ladino snobbery for not fully embracing the "scientific" benefits of generalized race mixture, including the (once) noble Indian, while sparing no praise for the entrepreneurial achievements of

Liberal planters and merchants somehow less condemnable, or perhaps just less hypocritical, in their lesser insistence on mere snobbery.[12] The radical leftism of such a position is readily visible in this end run in the 1920s on social Darwinism to lay claim to the label *scientific*, but the Liberal, ladino, or mestizo upper class bias that sees the suppression of Indianness as a historical good deed or favor to those suffering its consequences is no less so.

Another variant, this time from the Right, of this odd-couple ideology of Indian romanticization cum suppression has been brilliantly studied by both Gould and Gobat.[13] The Conservative Party and the Right in Nicaragua were not the witless bystanders in this process, as many of their critics claimed, not least Mendoza and Mendieta. As part of a complex process of ideological reconfiguration and political maneuvering, the Nicaraguan Conservative Party, and especially its Granadan leadership, generated a solid electoral alliance with certain Indian communities over the first half of the twentieth century. Its intellectual appeal for the "Catholic gentlemen" of Granada had its origins in the visionary leadership of the poet and essayist Pablo Antonio Cuadra, who publicly celebrated for the first time in the 1930s their allegedly mestizo heritage. All of this of course studiously ignored the historical evidence that Cuadra had a wider variety of choices in exalting any mixed-race heritage. His forbearers had proudly endowed the parish church of Nandaime, close by Granada, declaring themselves in a prominent altarpiece the mulatto benefactors of the church's construction at the end of the eighteenth century.[14]

This particular ethnic rebirth and newfound color flexibility was part of a radically rightist, restorationist ideology, one part anti-Yankeeism and one part antimodernism. It shared a contempt and hatred for the various U.S. occupations and interventions in Nicaragua with Left or Jacobin Liberals such as Sandino, in effect their competitors in the quest for a way out of foreign tutelage based on a popular nationalist platform. Just as with Sandino and his followers, red was what best mixed with white, so much so that it fell to another Granadan intellectual leader, Ernesto Cardenal, to join these nostalgic, Conservative elite family values to the Left-Liberal revolutionary tradition, with his extraordinary invocations of Nicaragua's Indian historical heritage as part of the Sandinista Revolution of 1979, in which he served as the Revolution's first minister of culture.[15]

Some of the most engaging recent research has privileged the semiotics of race, the various uses made of racial imageries, and a whole range of written and oral history accounts of the experiencing, making, and performing of race. In the vernacular, what is of interest is not race but its social construction. But then, as Peter Wade perhaps more elegantly than others has put it, there is no other form, and however imaginary in its origins race has been and remains deadly real in social life and in its observable consequences.[16] Wade has also produced one of the most detailed historical, textual participant-observer studies of any black population in Latin America, exploring the extraordinary elasticity and complexity of the concepts of blackness and race mixture in various contemporary settings in Colombia.[17] However, many of the earlier efforts in the social history of Latin America sought to measure, using social scientific methods and traditional documentary sources, the consequences of race in areas as diverse as demography, household and family, the labor market, and educational and professional achievement.[18] To this latter tradition I hope to contribute with the following, while calling for renewed interest in such data-driven or data-rich approaches. After all, the attempt to measure the impact of race, as regards African Americans certainly, was anything but politically naïve or uncritical. Just as with the semiotic approach more recently, the avowed goal was to document and understand the construction and consequences of a wide variety of racist policies in the nineteenth and twentieth centuries.[19]

Unlike the radical differentiation in demographic patterns and life course documented in some studies of race making in modern Latin America, the differences among the races in western Nicaragua, at least those involving people of African descent, were relatively subtle. Where for twentieth-century Cuba, de la Fuente can point to very substantial racial differences in fertility and mortality levels and in marital and fertility timing over the life course, as well as the more familiar differences in educational and occupational achievement, late nineteenth-century Nicaraguans of African descent were far less the bearers of stark demographic distinctiveness. While some might see Afro-Cubans as an archetypical working-class population, both demographically and socioeconomically, mulattos, zambos, and *negros* in western Nicaragua shared many features with *blancos* and mestizos, in contrast to what was usually a surrounding Indian majority. Where Kinsbruner documents Afro–Puerto Rican material advance in the midst of serious disadvantages, their Nicaraguan equivalents would appear to have done at least as well. And while Andrews documents a highly discriminatory urban labor market with visible glass ceilings for Afro-Brazilians in São Paulo in the century following abolition, no such modern, urban labor markets had yet come into existence in this very provincial corner of Nicaragua in the 1880s.

REMEMBERING HOW TO COUNT BY COLORS: THE CENSUS OF 1883

What joins the tourist promoters of today with the firebrand nationalists of yesteryear is their virtual inability to see any black in the white (and red) of their western Nicaraguan towns of the 1880s. In the vast majority of cases the census takers of the period (1880–1920) followed what they understood to be their superiors' intentions in documenting a presumptive process of national integration via a mestizo majority. In this Nicaraguans were simply following a Central American–wide pattern based in the illusion of citizenship and equality for all, Indians included (early liberalism from Independence to the 1850s or 1860s certainly). Second-generation liberalism made its separate peace with the virtual exclusion of Indians from effective citizenship, until and unless they should prove themselves worthy beneficiaries of and participants in the land privatization and community secularization policies forced on them by Liberals after the 1870s. Thus both before and after the 1870s there were powerful reasons not to distinguish based on race, or at the very least not among those defined as non-Indian, whether referred to as ladino, mestizo, or Spanish. Indeed from the earliest days of independent life those whose non-Spanish ancestry had been used against them in colonial times, in particular African Americans, were at the forefront of struggles to prohibit such invidious distinctions in official documentation.

Thus it must have come as a considerable surprise to census takers gearing up for the count in Nicaragua in 1883 to be asked to use their powers of visual discernment and local genealogical knowledge to categorize their informants not in the two familiar categories (Indian or not), but in one of six crisply rectangular boxes on specially prepared worksheets. There was no direct evidence of anyone pursuing novel social Darwinist agendas, but with the two most rapidly growing immigrant communities coming from Germany and the United States such a motivation might logically be suspected.[20] Whatever the reason, this return to a discriminating questionnaire stood out in all of Central America at the time and represents one of the very few resources we have to explore the position and experience of those presumed to be of African descent, nearly always folded into the non-Indian, mestizo majority. It was also confusing enough to leave most census workers mystified and unable or unwilling to comply, although none offered new or different categories not sanctioned by the form itself.

The director in charge of the Office of Statistics, a certain M. Bravo, seemed to recognize that it might not be obvious to all how to proceed. Thus he offered some comments as guides to his subordinates that are worth reproducing here. He first opined that it was quite obvious who was (pure) black, Indian, and white. The mixed-race categories were presumed to correspond to Indian-white (mestizo), black-white (mulatto), and Indian-black (zambo) unions, but here discernment was at a premium. Assigning parents their race was going to be largely an official's duty, and their children would follow the rationalist principles outlined above, although as we will see this was not always the case, and census takers were in the business of educating their superiors as well. Bravo exhorted his subordinates to offer a primitive form of training to the census takers, whose "lack of education [or culture]" could be a serious problem. They should pay particular attention to "facial features, hair, and skin color" as indicators of race, and they should offer their subordinates many examples, such as the following: "An individual of light black skin color, very curly hair, short and stout body is obviously a *zambo*, the hair reveals the pure black and the color and size the Indian."[21] These instructions surely suggest that racial classification was to be done by the census taker, not based on self-identification or questioning. What we are offered here is part social commentary, part group assignment by political officials and their scribes, not voluntary self-definition or expression of self-esteem on the part of western Nicaraguans. Indeed many might well have been surprised, whether gratified or horrified, by the race they enjoyed, however briefly, in the pages of the census of 1883.

Unfortunately records have not survived, or been identified yet, for the city of Granada, where no doubt much or even most of the population was of part-African descent. However, four towns did report something on the order of 10 percent or more of their population as of African descent: Diriomo, Diriá, Diriamba, and Santa Teresa. These were very, very different towns and need to be situated prior to exploring the data. Diriomo and Diriá were small towns thought of as colonial Indian dependencies of Granada, and they remained subject to labor drafts through debt peonage or wage advances by Granada's coffee planters as they developed the Mombacho volcano zone after the 1860s. They were essentially mixed-crop peasant villages that cultivated a wide variety of products, but primarily foodstuffs for sale in the nearby Granadan market. They remained politically dependent on Granada during this entire period; Diriomo's travails with Granadan oppression have been intensively studied by Dore. Each town reported a roughly 10 percent mulatto and zambo population; Diriomo reported essentially all non-Indians as mulattos and Diriá divided them among mestizos, mulattos, and zambos. Neither town had virtually any resident whites, although Diriá registered some non-Indians as mestizos (see TABLE 1). In both cases the non-Indians rigidly dominated the political power structure within the town, and Diriomo's definition of all as mulattos harkens back to colonial usage, when calling someone a mulatto in an Indian town was a way of directly challenging the very legitimacy of his or her presence, non-Spaniards and non-Indians being theoretically forbidden from residence in Indian towns.

Diriamba and Santa Teresa were father from Granada and formed part of the secessionist movement that led to the creation of the new Department of Carazo (1894) as coffee growing expanded after the 1860s. With over 3,200 residents Diriamba was half again as large as Diriomo, nearly three times the size of Diriá, and four times the size of nearby Santa Teresa. However, although both were Carazo settlements, Diriamba was radically unlike Santa Teresa. Just as with Diriomo and Diriá, Diriamba began as an Indian village, and roughly half of its population was considered Indian in 1883. However, it was fast becoming the regional trade center as its coffee and sugar production boomed in the 1870s, no longer

TABLE 1 Percentage Distribution by Age and Ethnicity

| | ETHNICITY | | | | | | |
Village	BLANCO	INDIO	MESTIZO	MULATTO	NEGRO	ZAMBO	*Cases*
Diriá	0	46	40	5	0	8	1,201
Diriamba	10	51	24	9	2	5	3,264
Diriomo	1	75	0	18	0	6	2,382
Santa Teresa	15	6	4	64	5	5	843
Composite	6	53	17	17	1	6	7,690

Age Distribution by Ethnicity

Composite of Four Villages

Age	BLANCO	INDIO	MESTIZO	MULATTO	NEGRO	ZAMBO	*Total*
1–14	38	46	48	48	38	48	46
15–29	28	23	26	24	23	25	24
30–44	18	17	15	17	22	13	16
45–59	10	9	7	6	8	10	8
60+	6	6	4	4	9	4	5
Cases	455	4,042	1,315	1,314	90	461	7,677

Diriamba

Age	BLANCO	INDIO	MESTIZO	MULATTO	NEGRO	ZAMBO	*Total*
1–14	36	43	51	49	42	45	45
15–29	28	23	24	30	23	31	25
30–44	18	17	15	12	14	14	16
45–59	11	9	6	5	8	6	8
69+	8	7	3	4	8	4	6
Cases	307	1,653	786	290	47	172	3,255

Santa Teresa

Age	BLANCO	INDIO	MESTIZO	MULATTO	NEGRO	ZAMBO	*Total*
1–14	45	47	24	46	34	42	44
15–29	30	24	32	27	20	25	27
30–44	15	24	22	17	32	18	18
45–59	8	2	11	6	5	8	6
60+	2	2	11	3	10	8	4
Cases	130	53	37	542	41	40	843

Sources: Archivo Municipal de la Prefectura de Granada, Nicaragua (1883), Caja 184, leg. X5, "Estadística" (Diriá); Caja 191, leg. X7, "Estadística" (Diriomo and Santa Teresa); Caja 192, leg. s/n, "Estadística" (Diriamba).

tied to Granadan commercial networks so much as to the national capital in Managua. It was also strongly identified with Liberal challenges to Granadan Conservative predominance (1858–93). Joining forces with the cities of León and Managua, Diriamba eventually succeeded in installing the Liberal dictatorship of José Santos Zelaya (1893–1909), against which the first American Marine intervention took place. Diriamba was an emerging regional center of great and varied agricultural wealth and large enough to be home to all sorts of ethnic groups, including a growing number of merchants from afar, not all of whom were thought of locally as white. That it gave birth to two of the most famous Central American unionist intellectuals of the 1920s, Juan Mendoza and Salvador Mendieta, is further indication of its sense of itself as a town on the move and at the forefront of progressive ideas both nationally and regionally.

If contemporary politics and common historical origins of much of their non-Indian settlers from among the illegitimate, mixed-race children of Granada's elite joined Diriamba and Santa Teresa, little else made the comparison obvious. Santa Teresa was, to put it kindly, off the beaten path and essentially one continuous field of sugarcane and food crops. Southwest, toward the hot plains of the Pacific, there were scattered peoples amid vastly different landscapes and ecosystems, but at the time they were held in contempt by the political leaders of both Carazo and Granada. In and around the village of Santa Teresa sugarcane and the artisan production of liquors and sweets constituted the local cash economy. Indeed Santa Teresa comes closest to approximating the African American Pacific coastal experience, with sugarcane towns throughout Central America. These were small scale to be sure, but typical of what was always a regional market-oriented and thus spatially limited and diversified agriculture, firmly anchored in cane fields and grinding mills converted from wooden to metal works only at the turn of the century. Its population in 1883 was overwhelmingly mulatto, but with a substantial number of blancos as well.

In what follows I use aggregate figures from all four towns only for the most general questions. I follow up with disaggregated analyses privileging Diriamba and Santa Teresa, very different settlements but in some ways more discriminating in their ethnic categorizations. Most important, they are better reflections of the distinctive processes of commercial agriculture and political enfranchisement that I have chosen to pursue in my pan–Central American project. Thus I use additional documentation from criminal and political archives and sources, sparingly in this initial approximation and hopefully to greater effect in subsequent publications, along with more detailed demographic analyses.

The marriage patterns of western Nicaragua present perhaps the clearest imaginable example of the paradox found throughout much of mainland Spanish America: generalized race mixture alongside a caste-like exclusion of Indian populations in certain circumstances produced extraordinarily high rates of racial or color preference in the selection of spouses by all groups and impressively high rates of marital exogamy for all *except the Indian majority!*[22]

Everywhere mixed unions of all kinds were recognized and involved virtually all color or race and gender combinations (TABLE 2). Census takers restricted themselves to the six categories offered them by the director of the Statistical Office, M. Bravo, but they had to innovate when classifying the resulting children since most mixed unions involved mixed-race couples. Without any guidelines to follow, it is highly significant that children of such unions, as well as those in which one of the parents was *not* of mixed race, could follow the condition of the mother *or* be assigned to the mestizo category. Clearly the mestizo category was the light-complexioned, preferred option, analogous to the *castizo* (one-quarter Indian) or *cuarterón* (one-quarter black) categories of colonial times, and this was no doubt the hope and aspiration of the Nicaragua mestiza officials and statesmen. However, whether they would have welcomed as newly minted mestizos the children of blancos with mulattos, negros, or zambos or those of zambos married to mestizos is not so clear. But that was fairly often what happened, especially when one of the parents had obvious wealth or prestige.

The pervasiveness of race mixture in marriage partner selection was not only characteristic of mixed-race partners. In Diriamba, the one all-inclusive racial setting, blancos, mulattos, negros, and zambos were all more likely to marry outside their group than not. Given the tiny numbers of negros this might not have been avoidable for them, but in all the

TABLE 2 Intermarriage Patterns

COMPOSITE OF FOUR VILLAGES

Husbands	Wives						
	Blanca	India	Mestiza	Mulata	Negra	Zamba	*Total*
Blanco	35	5	11	10	3	2	66
Indio	8	419	32	9	1	8	477
Mestizo	8	25	76	4	1	5	119
Mulatto	11	8	13	94	0	3	129
Negro	5	1	2	1	6	0	15
Zambo	5	11	7	10	0	14	47
Total	72	469	141	128	11	32	853

DIRIAMBA

Husbands	Wives						
	Blanca	India	Mestiza	Mulata	Negra	Zamba	*Total*
Blanco	25	5	10	8	2	2	52
Indio	7	191	20	4	1	4	227
Mestizo	5	16	47	2	0	3	73
Mulatto	7	0	6	10	0	1	24
Negro	2	1	1	0	2	4	10
Zambo	3	2	6	5	2	4	22
Total	49	215	90	29	7	18	408

SANTA TERESA

Husbands	Wives						
	Blanca	India	Mestiza	Mulata	Negra	Zamba	*Total*
Blanco	9	0	1	1	1	0	12
Indio	1	4	0	2	0	0	7
Mestizo	3	0	1	2	1	0	7
Mulatto	4	1	5	56	0	1	67
Negro	3	1	1	1	4	0	10
Zambo	2	0	0	5	0	1	8
Total	22	6	8	67	6	2	111

(*continued on next page*)

TABLE 2 (*continued*)

DIRIOMO

Husbands	Wives						
	Blanca	India	Mestiza	Mulata	Negra	Zamba	Total
Blanco	1	0	0	1	0	0	2
Indio	0	171	2	7	0	3	183
Mestizo	0	2	0	1	0	0	3
Mulatto	0	8	1	27	0	1	37
Negro	0	0	0	0	0	0	0
Zambo	0	3	0	1	0	7	11
Total	1	184	3	37	0	11	236

DIRIÁ

Husbands	Wives						
	Blanca	India	Mestiza	Mulata	Negra	Zamba	Total
Blanco	0	0	0	0	0	0	0
Indio	0	53	10	0	0	1	64
Mestizo	0	9	28	1	0	2	40
Mulatto	0	0	1	2	0	0	3
Negro	0	0	0	0	0	0	0
Zambo	0	1	1	0	0	2	4
Total	0	63	40	3	0	5	111

Sources: Archivo Municipal de la Prefectura de Granada, Nicaragua (1883), Caja 184, leg. X5, "Estadística" (Diriá); Caja 191, leg. X7, "Estadística" (Diriomo and Santa Teresa); Caja 192, leg. s/n, "Estadística" (Diriamba).

other categories this was hardly due to the lack of available partners of the same race. The one group least involved in this process, even though certainly not excluded from it, was the indio majority in Diriá, Diriomo, and even Diriamba, where the diversity of alternatives and a somewhat less rigidly anti-Indian municipal history would perhaps have led to different assumptions. The best way to represent this diverse pattern is to juxtapose the high rates of racial preference (endogamy) alongside simultaneously high rates of race mixture (exogamy) for all groups save one, as can be seen in TABLE 3.

The paradox of powerful same-race preference and the inability or unwillingness to turn that into a prohibition against interracial marriage is

TABLE 3 Measures of Endogamy and Exogamy by Ethnicity

Composite of Four Villages

Males	INDICES OF		Females	INDICES OF	
	ENDOGAMY	EXOGAMY		ENDOGAMY	EXOGAMY
Blanco	7.6	0.5	Blanca	8.2	0.5
Indio	1.6	0.3	India	1.7	0.2
Mestizo	4.0	0.4	Mestiza	3.2	0.6
Mulatto	4.6	0.3	Mulata	4.3	0.3
Negro	30.8	0.6	Negra	38.6	0.5
Zambo	6.4	0.7	Zamba	6.3	0.6

Diriamba

Males	INDICES OF		Females	INDICES OF	
	ENDOGAMY	EXOGAMY		ENDOGAMY	EXOGAMY
Blanco	4.4	1.1	Blanca	4.6	1.0
Indio	1.6	0.2	India	1.8	0.1
Mestizo	3.0	0.6	Mestiza	2.5	0.9
Mulatto	5.2	1.4	Mulata	3.8	1.9
Negro	10.0	4.0	Negra	28.0	2.6
Zambo	4.5	4.6	Zamba	3.1	3.5

Note: Endogamy: measured by dividing the percentage of those married to a spouse of the same race by the percentage of that race in the potential spouse population (males or females fifteen and older). The higher the value, the greater the predilection to select a spouse of the same race compared to a random distribution of spouse selection.

Exogamy: measured by dividing the percentage of those married to a spouse of any of the five other races different from their own by the percentage of the potential spouse population corresponding to those five races. Values lower than 1.0 indicate degrees of endogamy; values above 1.0 indicate those whose marriage patterns are more exogamous than random choice would predict.

Sources: Archivo Municipal de la Prefectura de Granada, Nicaragua (1883), Caja 184, leg. X5, "Estadística" (Diriá); Caja 191, leg. X7, "Estadística" (Diriomo and Santa Teresa); Caja 192, leg. s/n, "Estadística" (Diriamba).

resolved with crystalline clarity by the behavior of all non-Indian groups. Endogamy indices ranging from 4.0 to 30.8 for males and 3.2 to 38.6 for females among the non-Indian population overall, with less extreme but similar values for Diriamba (3.0 to 10.0 for males; 2.5 to 28.0 for females), would never prepare the observer to understand the local marriage market. All non-Indian groups showed a strong preference (likelihood is perhaps a better, less subjective term here) for their own, but this in fact did not lead them into endogamous unions, at least not at anything remotely comparable to the pattern of exclusion and limited choice characteristic of the Indian population. With endogamy indices of 1.6 for males and 1.7 for females overall, and 1.6 for males and 1.8 for females in Diriamba, Indians appeared far, far less committed than their non-Indian neighbors to marrying their own. But that would be the result nonetheless, with dramatically lower percentages marrying outside the group.

Exogamous marriage behavior was prevalent among all non-Indians, with blancos right in the middle of it all. In the specific case of Diriamba, blanco, mulatto, negro, and zambo groups of both sexes were more likely than not to marry outside their group, and mestizas were nearly at that point as well. Indians were radically far removed from this pattern, both overall and in Diriamba. The differences are less spectacular regionwide than in Diriamba, but always in the same direction of relative Indian exclusion. Nevertheless it is important to remember that this exclusion stopped well short of segregation or prohibition, as there were always and everywhere a small number of mixed unions involving Indians, including at times quite prominent and wealthy partners and families. Regionwide only one-third of the Indian males and one-fifth of the Indian females married to non-Indians necessary for a random, race-neutral pattern to obtain actually existed. The figures for Diriamba were even more radically atypical. Only one-fifth of the males and one-tenth of the females needed to reach the roughly comparable equal number of Indian and non-Indian spouses that any random distribution would have led to could be found in the actually existing unions in a general population that was essentially half-Indian and half-non-Indian.

Juan Mendoza, Diriamba's native son intellectual, knew this all too well and reserved some of his most bitter invective for fellow ladinos and their anti-Indian racism. But equally deeply embedded in local society was a long-standing process of race mixture that helps to explain even the partisan political dynamics Mendoza was so dismissive of. Mendoza provides detailed and highly critical portraits of the three dominant political families, the Baltodano, González, and Gutiérrez clans. He does not hesitate to point out which patriarchs were legitimate, which were more or less Indian, and even who "undeservedly" used his biological father's surname when not the product of legitimate marriage. Exploring these issues, first semistatistically, sheds additional light on the underlying realities of racial or ethnic identification.

In TABLE 4 we can see the ethnic distribution of several of Diriamba's most common surnames. Some are obviously nearly all blanco-mestizo (Bendaña, Espinoza, Estrada), others nearly all-indio (Aguirre, Dávila, Hernández, López, Ortíz, Pérez, Ramos, Rodríguez, Romero), and still others all mulatto-negro-zambo (Arias, Bonilla, Rosales, Vargas). Three of those most widely distributed and ethnically diverse are, precisely, the Baltodano, González, and Gutiérrez clans! All have mulatto families carrying the surname, if not necessarily blood brethren, even though the Baltodanos have no negro or zambo families. The same is true of blanco and negro for the Gonzálezes.

Mendoza treats the clan elders of this patrimonial political system at some length. The Baltodano elder, Enrique, was a legitimate white child, true enough, but he remained an illiterate as an adult, and his wife kept the books for the substantial family enterprises. One of his daughters married an Indian named Montiel from Jalteva, a suburb of Granada, who quickly became his righthand man politically, eventually taking control of most of the family's considerable properties.[23] These dominant incumbents were Conservatives nationally from the 1860s to 1893. The early opposition to the Baltodanos by the Gutiérrezes eventually dissipated, and both occupied positions as Conservative officials, more often than not allies by the time Mendoza observed them. At that time they called themselves the *abajeños* against the *arribeños* (Liberals by oppositional definition). These terms might seem to suggest meanings such as "top dog and underdog," "insiders and outsiders," "on top and down below," but in Diriamba the abajeños were in power, and Mendoza explains that the factions corresponded quite simply to "this side" and "that side" of the central town square, the abajeños to the west and the arribeños to the east.[24]

TABLE 4 Common Surnames of Diriamba by Ethnicity

SURNAME	BLANCO	INDIO	MESTIZO	MULATTO	NEGRO	ZAMBO	Total
Aguirre	1	92	10	3	0	4	110
Arias	3	0	26	1	12	0	42
Baltodano	24	3	31	16	0	0	74
Bendaña	19	2	2	0	0	0	23
Bermüdez	1	15	2	21	0	12	51
Bonilla	0	6	9	8	0	15	38
Cárdenas	0	63	3	2	0	0	68
Cruz	3	13	26	14	1	0	57
Dávila	0	89	1	0	0	4	94
Espinoza	10	1	32	0	4	2	49
Díaz	0	48	7	8	1	2	66
Estrada	15	0	11	1	1	1	29
Flores	0	62	34	4	0	1	102
Gago	1	5	32	1	0	5	44
García	11	6	11	0	0	0	28
González	0	97	32	12	0	5	146
Gutiérrez	45	39	57	13	14	6	174
Hernández	1	115	10	0	0	4	130
Jiménez	0	40	0	0	0	0	40
López	0	89	0	5	0	2	96
Medal	10	1	4	0	0	0	10
Medina	0	9	0	0	0	9	18
Mendieta	33	0	42	33	0	0	108
Mendoza	0	1	6	4	0	0	11
Mojica	0	35	18	12	1	6	72
Navarrete	0	12	31	2	1	1	47
Ortíz	0	139	3	0	0	3	145
Parrales	20	7	27	13	0	1	68
Pérez	3	78	40	0	1	0	122
Porras	0	0	0	0	0	3	3
Ramos	0	86	6	0	0	1	93
Rocha	2	1	8	15	0	4	30
Rodríguez	0	104	18	8	0	1	131
Romero	0	112	10	0	0	0	122
Rosales	0	0	0	0	0	10	10
Sánchez	1	6	18	0	3	15	43
Vargas	0	0	1	16	0	11	28
Villavicensio	2	0	3	9	0	0	14

Sources: Archivo Municipal de la Prefectura de Granada, Nicaragua, Caja 192, leg. s/n, "Estadística" (Diriamba, 1883).

The Liberal arribeños were led by the González clan. Their founding figure, Román, is described by Mendoza as someone of humble, illegitimate birth, who as an impoverished youth admirably kept both his Indian mother's surname and her popular attire. His wealthy father, Juan Gualberto Parrales, brokered financial alliances with his own family members, and the son, Román, emerged as the wealthiest individual in the town and thus its natural political leader as well. Román's marriage to Marcela Alemán (listed in the census of 1883 as the four-year-old mestiza daughter of an Indian father and mestiza mother) produced eight children; one of his grandchildren, Crisanto Briceño, was described as the quintessential rich Indian, critiqued by Mendoza in "black" terms.

The elite González clan demonstrates like no other that political power was based on ties to all colors and communities. It also shows that racial classification was neither clear-cut nor a one-way street toward mestizo and away from indio or other inferior categories. Not only was Crisanto's biological heritage from the Parrales line ignored, but his own children by his mestiza wife, Juana Paula Chaverri, were all listed in the census as indios as well. Mendoza repeatedly mocked the tendency of the González third generation of his time to affix the upper-class honorific *don* to their name, just as some of the Baltodanos so foolishly insisted on their "pure Spanish blood." Ironically if this had been literally true in either case, their political dominance would have been something between unlikely and unimaginable.[25]

Perhaps Mendoza's greatest social contempt was reserved for those illegitimate children who assumed the surname of their biological father. He denounced in particular Vicente Rappaccioli and Juan Manuel and José María Siero, all three the illegitimate children of Macedonia Gutiérrez, a market woman who rolled cigars and sold liquor retail to support her children on her own. Rather than remaining Gutiérrezes, two of her five children took the Rappaccioli surname of their Italian father, Juan Rappaccioli, two the Siero surname of their Spanish father, and the only girl the Argüello surname of her Nicaraguan father. Mendoza even reproduced a newspaper story from the local *Eco de Carazo* in which a certain Amelia Aguirre complained from jail of her unjust imprisonment for debt by the coffee plantation owner Vicente Rappaccioli as yet another, biting critique of such parvenu opportunists and usurers unwilling to retain

TABLE 5 Legitimacy by Ethnicity in Percentages, Followed by Number of Cases

Composite of Four Villages

BIRTH

STATUS	BLANCO	INDIO	MESTIZO	MULATTO	NEGRO	ZAMBO	Total
Adulterino	0	0	0	0*	0	0	0
Ilegítimo	0.2	10	14	13	1	21	11
Legítimo	93	84	79	81	70	70	82
Natural	7	6	7	5	29	9	7
Cases	457	4,042	1,321	1,312	91	462	7,685

Diriamba

BIRTH

STATUS	BLANCO	INDIO	MESTIZO	MULATTO	NEGRO	ZAMBO	Total
Ilegítimo	0.3	2	3	2	0	1	2
Legítimo	94	85	85	85	56	79	85
Natural	6	14	11	12	44	20	13
Cases	307	1,652	792	288	48	173	3,260

Santa Teresa

BIRTH

STATUS	BLANCO	INDIO	MESTIZO	MULATTO	NEGRO	ZAMBO	Total
Adulterino	0	0	0	0*	0	0	0
Ilegítimo	0	15	11	7	0	0	8
Legítimo	90	81	86	86	88	78	86
Natural	10	4	3	6	12	15	7
Cases	130	53	37	542	41	40	843

*A single case reported

Sources: Archivo Municipal de la Prefectura de Granada, Nicaragua (1883), Caja 184, leg. X5, "Estadística" (Diriá); Caja 191, leg. X7, "Estadística" (Diriomo and Santa Teresa); Caja 192, leg. s/n, "Estadística" (Diriamba).

their Gutiérrez surname. And yet in the midst of these lengthy diatribes Mendoza points out once again that he himself is the blood relative of these folks, just as certainly as he is of nearly all of the other political and social figures he lampoons.[26]

Mendoza's diatribes on legitimacy were not a reflection of some singular obsession or puritanical bent on his part alone. Legitimacy, just as with access to education, was perhaps the most racially or color-coded of social facts in western Nicaragua. The data presented in TABLE 5 would have us believe that blancos and negros were virtually incapable of being "illegitimate," appearing only as "natural" when not the product of marriage.[27] Unless one wishes to subscribe to this very long-odds race theory, we are left with the fact that western Nicaraguans in the 1880s continued to give voice to centuries-old prejudices and practices in Spanish America, by which mixed races were not only disproportionately the products of sin in the past, but uniquely given to sin in the present. Where one might find it plausible that blancos and mestizos were virtually the only ones with access to education (TABLE 8), these data on legitimacy are as significant as they are implausible, given that, as we are about to see, so very many nonwhites controlled substantial property and exercised political rights that presumed a certain, fairly high level of resources and prestige. Whether or not legitimacy and literacy were "white things" in reality, they very clearly were color-coded as such, strikingly so given the high degree of fluidity and pervasiveness of race mixture within marriage.

STAKING YOUR CLAIM AND GETTING AHEAD:
PROPERTY, POLITICS, AND EDUCATION

To no one was it a secret that most of the earliest non-Indian settlers had come west from Granada seeking land and opportunity not available to them at home. Nor was it any secret that many were the illegitimate, mixed-race children of Granadan patriarchs and their descendants. In fact original land concessions for a few of these towns, Santa Teresa in particular, had come from mulatto and not blanco pioneers. Thus it should come as no surprise that mixed-race men and women held their own and then some when it came to property ownership. What is surprising is that Indians did so as well. Moreover nonwhites of all kinds also stood out as proprietors not only in cattle grazing and food cropping, but also in the most capital-intensive activities and crops: sugar and coffee.

TABLE 6 shows the nominal information comparing those listed in the agricultural census records of 1880 and 1883 with their vital data from the population census of 1883.[28] Diriamba is not only the most important case for further study; it has by far the best, most complete surviving data. The records of 1883 for this village alone actually provide three different lists of agricultural (land or *catastro*, crops or *agrícola*, and output or *estadística*)

TABLE 6 Property Ownership by Ethnicity in Percentages, Followed by (Number of Cases)

Diriamba

	BLANCO	INDIO	MESTIZO	MULATTO	NEGRO	ZAMBO	Total
Population over 19	10	52	23	8	5	1.5	99.5
Agricultura	18 (12)	54 (36)	18 (12)	4.5 (3)	3 (2)	3 (2)	100.5 (67)
Catastro	14 (15)	54 (59)	21 (23)	5 (6)	1 (1)	5 (6)	100 (110)
Estadística	25 (10)	52 (21)	12 (5)	0	0	10 (4)	99 (40)

Santa Teresa

	BLANCO	INDIO	MESTIZO	MULATTO	NEGRO	ZAMBO	Total
Population over 19	15	6	6	62	6	4	99
Agricultura	11 (4)	3 (1)	9 (3)	55 (21)	18 (7)	5 (2)	101 (38)

Diriá

	BLANCO	INDIO	MESTIZO	MULATTO	NEGRO	ZAMBO	Total
Population over 19	0	47	41	5	0	6	99
Agricultura	0	59 (43)	30 (22)	8 (6)	0	3 (2)	100 (73)

Sources: Archivo Municipal de la Prefectura de Granada, Nicaragua (1883), Caja 184, leg. X5, "Estadística" (Diriá); Caja 191, leg. X7, "Estadística" (Diriomo and Santa Teresa); Caja 192, leg. s/n, "Estadística" (Diriamba); Archivo Municipal de la Prefectura de Granada, Nicaragua, Caja 158, leg. 441, "Censo agropecuario," (Santa Teresa, Diriamba, Diriá, and Diriomo, 1880); Caja 182, leg. 490, "Censo agropecuario," (Diriamba, 1882–83).

proprietors and statuses. In all three cases in Diriamba blanco proprietors are, not surprisingly, overrepresented, but the most intriguing finding is that neither the Indian nor the major mixed-race categories are, as far as I can tell, radically underrepresented (with the exception of mulattos and negros in the estadística category). The ability of Indians to retain proportional landownership, in Diriá as well as Diriamba, is indeed striking, as is the mulatto performance in Santa Teresa. And this was not limited to the smallest or poorest of the producers.

The richest sugar producers in Santa Teresa were nearly all mulattos, from the Conrado brothers to the Acevedos, the clan on whose land the village itself was founded.[29] Their political challengers were the Guido and Guadamuz families, also mulattos, and the Vados, who were mestizos. I have already described at some length the largest producer families in Diriamba (Baltodano, Gutiérrez, and González). But among the largest cattlemen and even sugar and coffee producers one finds more than a few indio, mulatto, and zambo owners. Some of the largest coffee growers were Indian men and women, married to Indians and non-Indians alike. Zambo property holders were consistently overrepresented, especially in the most lucrative "output" list. Even more striking, of the ten sugar mills listed (seven wooden, two metal, and one machine powered), seven can be tied to an owner of known ethnicity, three indios and four blancos. The richness of the documentation on this point invites much more detailed analysis in a future version of this research, to which we will be able to add a list of house and lot owners in Diriamba and data on the ownership of firearms as well.

My focus on African Americans in western Nicaragua should not blur an equally important finding: Indians were not uniformly dispossessed as part of the process that sought to officially erase their existence. Gould's research pointed in exactly this direction, while Dore makes much the same point in her study of what may well have been the single most exploitive and oppressive case in the Granada area: Diriomo. Wolfe's more detailed study of the entire region, when read in conjunction with these earlier works, suggests a much more complex model of indio-ladino conflict.[30] Indians were most at risk where they were a large enough minority or majority so that their land and labor were coveted by ladino coffee planters. Where Indians were a large majority (despite the evidence from the Diriomo case) or a tiny minority, their property holding and electoral participation varied little compared to their ladino neighbors. Diriamba, then, is a particularly important case for further study since, unlike much of Charlip's rather rosy description of free land to settlers in Carazo, Indians appear to have participated very broadly in the coffee and sugar revolutions taking place on lands most often previously settled and not subject to homesteading.

Political participation, as measured by the claim in the census of 1883 to have *capacidad política*, was supposedly very widely and equally distributed by ethnicity in all the towns except Diriamba, where only blancos (9 percent) acknowledged more than a 1 percent "yes" to this *capacidad*

TABLE 7 Electoral Rights (Males Only) by Ethnicity in Percentages,
Followed by Number of Cases

Composite of Four Villages

	BLANCO	INDIO	MESTIZO	MULATTO	NEGRO	ZAMBO	TOTAL	*Cases*
Yes	14	8	18	14	13	11	12	438
No	86	92	82	86	87	89	88	3,365
Cases	227	1,952	629	684	45	266	3,803	

Diriamba

	BLANCO	INDIO	MESTIZO	MULATTO	NEGRO	ZAMBO	TOTAL	*Cases*
Yes	9	1	1	1	0	1	2	23
No	91	99	99	99	100	99	98	1,554
Cases	127	788	381	160	21	100	1,577	

Santa Teresa

	BLANCO	INDIO	MESTIZO	MULATTO	NEGRO	ZAMBO	TOTAL	*Cases*
Yes	28	19	30	19	26	16	21	88
No	72	81	70	81	74	84	79	335
Cases	57	26	20	278	23	19	423	

Sources: Archivo Municipal de la Prefectura de Granada, Nicaragua (1883), Caja 184, leg. X5, "Estadística" (Diriá); Caja 191, leg. X7, "Estadística" (Diriomo and Santa Teresa); Caja 192, leg. s/n, "Estadística" (Diriamba).

in any form (TABLE 7). Indians were clearly the least likely to say yes, but mulattos in Santa Teresa were also substantially behind blancos, mestizos, and negros in their claims despite the fact that nearly all leading political leaders were themselves mulattos. Surviving and yet to be processed electoral lists for Diriamba suggest that the census declaration of 1883 was simply unreliable and that the composite and Santa Teresa figures are better guides.[31] As Wolfe found throughout the region, participation rates by ethnicity were not exceptionally skewed in most towns. In any event, whether in Diriomo or Santa Teresa, voting was one thing; counting the votes and ruling were other things entirely.

By the early twentieth century literacy was the sine qua non of political leadership, even if it was not needed to make money in agriculture or

TABLE 8 Education Attainment by Ethnicity in Percentages, Followed by Number of Cases

Composite of Four Villages

	BLANCO		INDIO		MESTIZO		MULATTO		NEGRO		ZAMBO		TOTAL		Cases
	M	F	M	F	M	F	M	F	M	F	M	F	M	F	
None	69	80	97	99	79	91	90	97	96	100	96	99	94	96	7,208
Primaria	28	20	3	1	19	9	9	3	4	2	7	2	8	4	454
Secundaria	3	0	0.2	0	0.3	0	1	0	0	0	0	0	1	0	27
Cases	226	232	1,948	2,095	629	692	684	630	45	46	266	196	3,798	3,891	7,689

Diriamba

	BLANCO		INDIO		MESTIZO		MULATTO		NEGRO		ZAMBO		TOTAL		Cases
	M	F	M	F	M	F	M	F	M	F	M	F	M	F	
None	66	81	99	99	95	95	92	95	100	100	96	99	94	96	3,101
Primaria	30	19	1	1	5	5	7	5	0	0	4	1	6	4	154
Secundaria	3	0	0	0	0	0	1	0	0	0	0	0	0	0	9
Cases	158	150	788	865	381	411	160	130	21	27	100	73	1,608	1,656	3,264

Note: Primaria = primaria, inferior; Secundaria = secundaria, complementaria, intermedia, superior

Sources: Archivo Municipal de la Prefectura de Granada, Nicaragua (1883), Caja 184, leg. X5, "Estadística" (Diriá); Caja 191, leg. X7, "Estadística" (Diriomo and Santa Teresa); Caja 192, leg. s/n, "Estadística" (Diriamba).

trade or to participate, as a follower, in politics. Educational attainment figures thus say a great deal about both public policy and ethnic and color inequality. The extraordinarily low level of public primary education in this boom area of commercial agriculture is depressing enough. But even among the highly favored blanco and mestizo groups mass illiteracy was not an entirely female condition. The virtually total absence of primary education for much of the Indian population is in fact not much worse than the experience of decidedly ladino groups of mulattos, negros, and zambos. Clearly literacy was a very blanco-mestizo young male thing on the eve of sustained political conflict in the 1890s. The somewhat higher composite figures for mulattos in TABLE 8 are perhaps deceptive; the ladino elite in Diriomo is listed here, but if one considers the likely consequences of these figures for Diriamba alone the picture is fairly bleak. Beyond the percentages, among Diriamba's 3,264 residents in 1883 there were, roughly speaking, 75 blancos who had ever made it through the schoolhouse door, fewer than 20 indios, 40 mestizos, fewer than 20 mulattos, no negros, and 5 zambos. One or two mulattos had some high school, along with five or six blancos—not exactly the picture of rapid infrastructural and human capital development made possible by the ongoing boom in commercial agriculture.

BEYOND STRUCTURE: COLOR AND THE LANGUAGE OF CONFLICT

Black was something one did not lightly accuse another of being in Nicaragua or anywhere else in Central America, at least in public. More epithet than descriptor, it ranked right up there with other challenges to honor or masculinity as fightin' words. When María Montiel came to Miss Virgina Mayorga's house in Granada in 1887 looking for a fight, the words Mayorga claimed to have heard were "You horny black whore, you're screwing Carmen Gómez. . . . Come over here if you dare."[32] If indeed her appeal was not granted, Montiel had to pay the small fortune of a fifty-peso fine for her outburst, without having landed a blow beyond some stones she allegedly threw at Mayorga. Despite the uncontrollable anger and hyperbole, this case obviously involved women from quite respectable families of Granada who would otherwise never dream of calling each other black in public.

Wolfe has shown that blackness was both a concept of alterity and a sign of suspiciousness that provided the logic for physical descriptions found in the odious passbook system, seemingly and in reality designed to "hunt Indians" for coffee labor.[33] Descriptions of darkness or "swarthiness" or facial features and hair texture vaguely tied to African descent were being projected onto individuals far more than markers of Indianness were derived from any folkloric or phenotypic inventory originating with Indians. If sexual licentiousness amid slavery's inferiority provided the distant historical template for Montiel's color-coded outburst, then poverty and suitability for conscripted labor as simultaneous uplift and surveillance made for Wolfe's union of darkness and Indianness in the labor records. How close indeed Nicaraguans had come to the original, seemingly absurd Anglophone conjugation of race, class, and oppressed nationality, the black Irish.

But if Indians and the poor of western Nicaragua had become black after a fashion, the terms *negro*, *mulato*, and *zambo* were used in their own right as well. When Juan Mendoza expressed his astonishment and disgust at the racist exclusion by Diriamba's elite ladinos of Indians from their marriage choices, he gave voice to a critique offered by Spanish, English, German, and U.S. immigrants and travelers alike: "Mixture with the Indian was unacceptable for *ladinos*, even though with many of the latter greenish-blue markings revealed black descent." Mendoza was virtually paraphrasing the Spanish-born immigrant and Guatemalan Liberal leader of the Revolution of 1871, Manuel García Granados, who expressed his contempt for the local ladino elite and his astonishment at their arrogance in the following terms: "ignorant, with airs of nobility . . . even though with some the tinge of the African race is visible."[34] Mendoza and García Granados echoed, with their own shadings, the perplexed views of countless foreign observers, arch-racist social Darwinists and antiracists alike.[35] Was this reducible to the mixed-race Hispanic elite's alternately pathetic and arrogant self-delusion, as so many racist foreigners thought? Or was it merely pathetically hypocritical and all that much more odious to those forced to suffer its consequences? Did they, could they really believe it?

Mendoza was anything but a disinterested observer. His own family, and Salvador Mendieta's even more spectacularly, included mestizos, mulattos, and blancos but virtually no indios, zambos, or negros (see table 4). Mendoza was even capable of using the same black Indian dismissive language when describing one of the many "lackeys of the system" he so despised in his hometown, the Indian political boss Crisanto Briceño:

> The ugliest mortal that to this day my eyes have seen. Black, with a huge and stretched out head, covered with thick, loose [or straight] hairs, so rough [or hard] that neither comb nor brush could control them. . . . Measles left him with very visible facial scars . . . marked features all of them, which the artful photographer Christianizes a great deal, softening with careful retouching of the portrait offered here. . . . He is [a] pure-blood Indian who certainly honors his race in the goodness of his sentiments, his tendency to hard work, and the success his efforts have achieved on the road to riches.[36]

While Briceño's alleged physical unattractiveness was inescapably black for Mendoza, he went on at great length to praise his many positive qualities. Moreover this "pure-blood Indian," Mendoza had already told us, was a blood relative of the González clan, the grandson of the patriarch Román. One can only wonder if the blackness associations were meant to extend outward to these political allies, whose leaders were nearly all listed as mestizos in the census records.

Pure-blood Indians became black and miraculously acquired bad (kinky, African American) hair, impervious to the comb or brush even if straight. Non-Indian foreigners could also become black, as the case of the Costa Rican immigrant merchant Miguel Pacheco shows. Mendoza describes Pacheco's rise to commercial and agricultural success in some detail, pointing out that he had married a local woman from a prominent family (Nestora Mendieta). In the same alternately critical or mocking and praiseful tone he took toward so many others, Mendoza portrays Pacheco as a rail-thin drinker and gambler in his impoverished youth, only to become so obese as to be virtually immobile once he abandoned those vices and became wealthy. He began as a goldsmith, graduating to ownership of the best general store in town and eventually to great agricultural wealth in both cattle and coffee. Mendoza provides a tiny portrait of Pacheco, which corresponds fairly poorly with his designation as negro alongside his blanca wife in the census of 1883. Pacheco surely descended

Crisanto Briceño

FIGURE 1 Crisanto Briceño. *Source*: Juan Mendoza, *Historia de Diriamba* (Guatemala City: Staebler, 1920), 388.

Miguel Pacheco

FIGURE 2 Miguel Pacheco. *Source*: Juan Mendoza, *Historia de Diriamba* (Guatemala City: Staebler, 1920), 56.

from Costa Rican mulatto families; indeed his own father, also named Miguel, had even been a slave. One can only wonder whether in Diriamba he may have for too long exuded the airs of racial superiority so common to his countrymen abroad in Central America, leading a local elite rival to vent his anger and envy in the privacy of the census rolls.[37] Whatever the reason, Pacheco's undeniable part-African ancestry became total. Racial inferiority was his official lot, even if in the relatively inconsequential arena of posthumous census identification.

Color surely had consequences, many times for those who were not black at all or had only become black as others abandoned the category. Beyond examples such as these, it should be apparent why we need to focus on the lives led by those of African descent, however inexactly that might be defined. Falling for the sleight of hand by which blackness and blacks disappeared in nineteenth-century Nicaragua and Central America, following those terms into the seductive swamp of semiotic deployment and reinvention, may tell us a great deal about both the language of conflict and the ever-changing set of targets for antiblack racism. However, in doing so we would be doing for our own time what Nicaraguan and Central American census takers and statesmen so often sought to achieve in their own time: institutionalizing the nonexistence of difference in non-Indian society. Once such mythic homogeneity was established it would quickly acquire an air of timelessness, and precious little additional justification would be needed for an all-out attack on Indian difference. Inexplicably, confusedly, perhaps malevolently, late nineteenth-century Nicaraguan officials have offered us a one-time reprieve from this teleological view of nationhood ethnically defined. Whatever their purpose in doing so, their historically out-of-step questioning of presumptive ladino or mestizo homogeneity offers a unique opportunity to deconstruct this unproblematically ethnicized nationalism, not only in western Nicaragua but throughout Central America.

NOTES

Research was funded by the National Endowment for the Humanities Collaborative Research Program (Grant #RZ-20704-01). Exceptionally efficient data entry work was undertaken by Antonio Jara, a graduate student in the Universidad de Costa Rica's history program. Helpful comments by Alan

Tony Briceño, Mauricio Meléndez, Justin Wolfe, and George Reid Andrews on earlier versions of this essay are much appreciated.

1   Cruz, *Nicaragua's Conservative Republic*, 130.

2   Gould, *To Die in This Way*; Gould, "'¡Vana Ilusión!'"

3   For materials on several Central American cases, see "Choosing a Color for the Cosmic Race" on the Mt. Holyoke College website (http://www .mtholyoke.edu/acad/latam/africania.html).

4   Cruz, *Nicaragua's Conservative Republic*, 30, cites the period descriptions of the Conservative leaders Fruto Chamorro as the illegitimate son of Pedro Chamorro and an Indian woman in Guatemala, where the father was a student, and Ponciano Corral as the son of a "Negress, descendant of slaves from the Antilles." Both married well in Granada's aristocratic society and were never specifically challenged in their authority on the basis of their race. Cleto Ordoñez, president of Nicaragua in 1824, was another Granadan of very humble birth. However, as a popular, anti-Conservative leader he was challenged, both racially and politically, during his career by Granadan elite figures.

5   See Gould, *To Die in This Way*, 16–19, for a discussion of the inexplicable declines across censuses.

6   Dore, *Myths of Modernity*, 134–38. See also Dore, "Debt Peonage in Granada," "Land Privatization," and "Patriarchy from Above."

7   Gould, *To Die in This Way*, offers what amounts to a typology of Indian community experiences, from highly successful resistance (Sutiava) to virtual annihilation and forced assimilation (Yucul) in different regions of Nicaragua.

8   Charlip, *Cultivating Coffee*.

9   Wolfe, *The Everyday Nation-State*; Wolfe, "Those That Live by the Work of Their Hands"; Wolfe, "I Must Insist"; Gobat, *Confronting the American Dream*.

10 In direct contradiction to the influential historical and sociological position of the Sandinista rebel leader and minister of agriculture Jaime Wheelock Román, *Imperialismo y dictadura*.

11 Mendoza, *Historia de Diriamba*; Mendieta, *La enfermedad de Centroamérica*. See Gould, *To Die in This Way*, 136–39, for a discussion of their views.

12 Mendoza's blanket support for race mixture included the following extraordinary invocation of social Darwinist language (against itself):

> The *ladinos* were ignorant of what today has been resolved by leading sociologists: race mixture leads to a high level of national improvement and by such an interesting means human degeneration is avoided, as if by introducing a new seed in the molds of life, new energies better disposed for life's struggle might arise.

> Ignoraban los ladinos lo que hoy está resuelto por los sociólogos más avanzados: que el cruzamiento de las razas marca un alto grado de mejora en la faz de las

naciones y que por tan interesante medio se evita la degeneración del hombre, como si al vaciarse un nuevo germen en los moldes de la vida brotaran las energías más bien dispuestas para las luchas de la existencia. (*Historia de Diriamba*, 79–80)

13   Gould, *To Die in This Way*; Gould, "'Vana Ilusión!'"; Gobat, *Confronting the American Dream.*

14   Justin Wolfe, personal communication. See also Germán Romero Vargas's classic work, *Las estructuras sociales de Nicaragua en el siglo XVIII.* The altar image simply states, "By the Lugo and Sandoval familias, mulattos of Nandaime" ("Por las familias Lugo y Sandoval, mulatos de Nandaime").

15   Within Cardenal's vast writings perhaps the most effective in historically reclaiming an Indian heritage for the Sandinista revolutionary project were *El estrecho dudoso* and *Hora cero y otros poemas*, simply because they were among the most widely read. In truth his writings over a half century have never strayed far from an obsessive interest in all things American Indian, within Nicaragua and beyond. See, for example, *Literatura indígena americana, Homenaje a los indios americanos*, and *Golden UFOs.*

16   Wade, *Race and Ethnicity.*

17   Wade, *Blackness and Race Mixture.*

18   The three studies referred to here and in the following paragraph are Andrews, *Blacks and Whites in São Paulo*; de la Fuente, "Race and Inequality in Cuba"; Kinsbruner, *Not of Pure Blood.*

19   As one very pointed example of this, de la Fuente clearly revealed the racist paradox of antiblack prejudice and fear of the blackening of Cuban society peaking in the early twentieth century precisely when, thanks to massive Spanish white immigration, the share of the Cuban population and population growth attributable to Afro-Cubans was at its lowest point in either the nineteenth century or the twentieth. Two brilliant analyses of blackness and its conflictive meanings in Cuban society that, of necessity, have much less to say about blacks in Cuba per se are Chomsky, "Barbados or Canada"; Kutzinski, *Sugar's Secrets.*

20   See Nobles, *Shades of Citizenship* for a brilliant discussion of these agendas. Somewhat ominously, the good Mr. Bravo expressly justified this newfound interest in race by reminding his subordinates that the purpose of the census was to see which races were growing and which declining, echoing the Civil War–era proto-eugenics behind the U.S. census takers' obsession with counting mulattos and not just undifferentiated Negroes:

> The races that populate Nicaragua are of six types more or less well defined and easy to recognize. These types are: pure white, pure Indian, pure black, *mestizo*, *mulato*, and *zambo*. The first three are well defined and offer no difficulty in being determined: regarding the *mestizo*, this is the product of the mixture of Indian and white, as *mulato* is of black and white, and *zambo* of black and Indian, whose

types are recognized in an individual by the mixture of both elements in facial features, hair, and color. . . . As the census needs to be repeated every four years, one needs to know in each period which race(s) are increasing and by what proportion, and which decreasing. Thus, one can never strive too fully to register the (racial) types with the greatest possible exactitude.

Las razas que pueblan a Nicaragua tienen seis clases de tipos más o menos bien manifiestos y que fácilmente pueden ser conocidos. Estos tipos son: blanco puro, indio puro, negro puro, mestizo, mulato y zambo. Los tres primeros son bien definidos y no ofrecen dificultad alguna para ser determinados: y en cuanto al mestizo, este es el resultado de la mezcla de indio y blanco, así como mulato, el de blanco y negro, y zambo el de negro e indio, cuyos tipos se conocen en un indivíduo por la mezcla de ambos elementos que ofrecen sus facciones, pelo y color. . . . Como el censo habrá de repetirse cada cuatro anos, se necesita saber en cada período, que raza y bajo que proporción va en aumento i decadencia. Nunca serán, pues, bastantes sus esfuerzos en el sentido de que se consignen los tipos con la mayor perfección posible. (M. Bravo [Managua] to Jefe Departmental de Estadística, Granada, "Circular No. 4," 18 May 1883, Archivo Municipal de la Prefectura de Granada, Nicaragua [hereafter AMPG], caja 184,1eg. X5, M. Bravo, cited in Wolfe, "I Must Insist," 15–16)

21 "Permítame insistir en esto de la raza. Creo indispensable que Ud. Amplie más estas explicaciones a los ajentes locales, atendiendo a la menor capacidad de comprensión que ellos tienen por su poca cultura. Al efecto, póngales U. ejemplos varios, verbigracia, de esta especie: un indivíduo de color negro claro, pelo mui rizado, cuerpo grueso y bajo, es evidente un zambo, el pelo revela al negro puro y el color y tamaño al indio." M. Bravo (Managua) to Jefe Departmental de Estadística, Granada, "Circular No. 4," 18 May 1883, AMPG, caja 184,1eg. X5, M. Bravo, cited in Wolfe, "I Must Insist," 15–16, n. 42.

22 Marriage partners were never formally defined in these census originals, and thus we might better call them presumptive marriage partners. I have gone through the entire data set of nearly eight thousand individuals and assigned "spouse race" to those whom I believed I could reasonably identify as cohabiting partners, with or without children. This involved simply deducing the relationship from the two individuals being listed one after another, especially when followed by appropriate-age children carrying the presumptive father's surname. Cases where other, more pyramid-like assumptions would have been needed were not assigned "spouse race" and are not included here. A few cases (less than two dozen) of obvious cohabitation by "single" couples with what appear to be their children have also been included here since my goal is to understand the social realities of interethnic cohabitation and its consequences rather than formal marriage or its (obviously already very widespread) acceptability. While more detailed demographic analyses

of ethnicity and gender will not be attempted here, differences were noticeable in the sense that *white* could serve as a surrogate for *upper class* or *status* (younger age at and greater access to marriage for females, for example), closely aligned with *mestizo*, as contrasted with Indian or mulatto majorities in particular village cases. The zambo/a category was also highly distinctive, suggesting both young male predominance and in-migration.

23 Mendoza, *Historia de Diriamba*, 51–56.

24 Ibid., 70. As political leaders in Santa Teresa have explained to me, these were politically polarized neighborhoods and hamlets following each one's strongman leader seeking office and the spoils that came with it. However, these divisions also tended to translate into Conservative and Liberal without much difficulty, and to some extent there may well be a related dynamic of old families and money (with houses) *down here*, near the town center or square, versus the challengers from *up there*, the less prestigious outlying neighborhoods and hamlets.

25 Ibid., 372–75; Parroquia de Santiago de Jinotepe, "Bautizos" 1809–17, fol. 95; Parroquia de San Sebastián de Diriamba, "Sepulturas" 1873–80, p. 35 (1876). The information on the parish record entries was graciously provided by Alan Toney Briceño from his own research in Nicaraguan and Guatemalan archives. His corrections to several of my mistaken identifications and understandings of local family ties, based on a far deeper knowledge of local archival sources and genealogies, are deeply appreciated.

26 Mendoza, *Historia de Diriamba*, 88–89, 289–315. An intriguing if obscure example of this behavior, at the heart of political and social conflict, forms part of local folklore in neighboring Santa Teresa. To this day, without any open hostility toward the family in question, political leaders claim that the Chavarrías simply chose to call themselves the Conrados. Clan leaders and *alcaldes* Ygnacio and Ynocente appear in several documents from the 1880s with these surnames without any change of their race; they are mulatto both before and after. On both sides of intense and even violent conflict between *arribeño* and *abajeño* factions, most politically prominent families in Santa Teresa had been and remained mulatto, not blanco.

27 Entire books would be needed to fully explain these categories to anyone unfamiliar with both Latin American social history and Catholic teaching. Indeed one recent prize-winning study by Twinam, *Public Lives, Private Secrets*, does just that. Legitimate children were those born to Church-sanctioned unions. Next in line in terms of acceptability were *natural* children, or those who were born to an unwed mother who conceived with a lover at a point in time when both *could have* legally married each other (neither was married, neither had taken religious vows, no violation of Church consanguinity rules, etc.). Of course were the couple to subsequently marry, their *natural*, or we might say premarital children would be virtually indistinguishable from their other children. Even if the couple never married

or continued to cohabit, such children were barely distinguishable from legitimates and decidedly superior to illegitimates, all other things being equal, of course, which was rarely the case. Illegitimates were those born to a couple one or both of whom were legally incapable of marrying at the time, presumably owing to the father's already being married, although role reversals were not unheard of here. *Adulterino/a* is an even more specific claim of such (already married) illegitimate parentage, although one suspects here an attempt at even more outspoken condemnation. The ultimate in reprehensible procreative acts involved categories of *incestuoso/a*, that is, too close in consanguinity, or *espúreo/a*, in theory any child of adultery but more often used as an epithet to denounce suspected parentage by clerics or nuns.

28   I considered as a positive identification someone with the same first and last names and of appropriate age (over nineteen), so long as no one else of the same name and age group appeared in the village. Diriamba's agricultural records are much more complete and come from 1883 rather than the material of 1880 for Santa Teresa and Diriá. Diriomo's records for 1880 identify by the name of the property rather than the owner and thus cannot be used here. In the best cases, Diriá and Diriomo, only about half of all the listed proprietors could be identified. In Santa Teresa no more than 10 percent could be found, in all likelihood based on a radical undercounting of the (Pacific coast?) population in the census of 1883.

29   AMPG, leg. 350 (1876), documento no. 3, fols. 1–2.

30   Wolfe, *The Everyday Nation-State*, chaps. 5–6.

31   AMPG, Caja 184, leg. X5 (1883); leg. s/n, "Estadísticas" (1885–86).

32   "Negra puta, arrecha, que te estás echando encima a Carmen Gómez, y si quieres veníte." AMPG, Caja 219, leg. 10, (1887), fols. 69–81.

33   Wolfe, "I Must Insist."

34   Mendoza, *Historia de Diriamba*, 79: "El cruzamiento con indígena era inaceptable por los ladinos, a pesar de que en varios de éstos aparecieron algunos rabadillas verdiazules, que denuncian la descendencia del negro." García Granados, *Memorias*, 7: "Ignorantes, con humos de nobleza, cuyo lenguagje era tan vulgar como la clase más ínfima del pueblo (y en algunos de ellas) la raza africana asomase la punta de la oreja."

35   As antiracist I have in mind the invocation by the jazz greats Jelly Roll Morton and Duke Ellington of the potency for their music of "the Spanish tinge," by which they meant, usually but not exclusively, Afro-Cuban rhythms. The same complex relationship with white supremacist thought has long been noted, including the creation of a separate room assignment category for those of "Latin color" (i.e., mixed-race Latin American whites) in segregation-era U.S. hotels.

36   See Mendoza, *Historia de Diriamba*, 388–92, for the discussion of Crisanto Briceño; 390 for the quoted material.

37 Pacheco's father, while indeed a slave in Costa Rica, had nonetheless been able to marry two different free Spanish women, and thus the free birth of his legitimate children was never at issue. Archivo Histórico Diocesano de León, Nicaragua (hereafter AHDL), Expedientes Matrimoniales, Caja del año 1851, sin número de expediente y sin foliar, solicitud fechada en Diriamba, el 26 de febrero de 1851: "El señor Miguel Pacheco, de 28 años, oriundo de la ciudad de Cartago, criado en San José y residente en Diriamba desde que tenía 15 o 16 años, hijo legítimo del finado Miguel Pacheco y Jacoba Morales, vecinos de Cartago, pide licencia para casar con María Néstor Mendieta." *El Obispado de Nicaragua da autorización el 7 de marzo de 1851.* My thanks to Mauricio Meléndez for the ecclesiastical data and citation. Further details on the Pacheco family can be found in his article, "Los últimos esclavos en Costa Rica," especially 87 and 94. In Diriamba, Pacheco's nephew who accompanied him, Juan José Pacheco, married another Mendieta (María Isidora) in 1872. AHDL, Expedientes Matrimoniales, Caja del año 1872, solicitud del 24 de Julio de 1872, aprobada el 5 de agosto de 1872.

The Mosquito Coast and the Place
of Blackness and Indigeneity in Nicaragua

Juliet Hooker

Anxieties about race played a key role in the construction of the Nicaraguan political community during the nineteenth and twentieth centuries. The racialization of space in particular shaped the contours of citizenship in Nicaragua, where racism operated both in the mapping of racial difference onto region and territory and the spatialization of race.[1] As Floya Anthias and Nira Yuval-Davis observe, "Race is one way by which the boundary is . . . constructed between those who can and those who cannot belong to a particular construction of a collectivity or population."[2] In Nicaragua the racialization of space and the spatialization of race worked to set the boundaries of citizenship and access to political power in different but related ways.[3] The racialization of some regions claimed as part of the national territory as black or indigenous, and therefore as "inferior" and "savage," served to legitimize the political disenfranchisement of their inhabitants by Nicaraguan political elites during much of the nineteenth and twentieth centuries. The mapping of race onto space simultaneously fueled and facilitated the spatialization of race. Thus the designation of some regions of the country as the only ones where racial others resided made it possible to imagine the remaining areas of the country as lacking any kind of racial difference. Specifically it was in contrast to the Mosquito Coast that Nicaraguan political and intellectual elites formulated key elements of Nicaraguan national identity in the late nineteenth century and early twentieth. The sociopolitical dominance on the Mosquito Coast of two mixed-race groups of mostly Afro-Amerindian descent—the Miskitu,[4] who became coded as indigenous, and Creoles (not to be confused with *criollos*, i.e., Spaniards born in the Americas), who came to be seen largely as of African descent—led to the racialization of the region as black, and to a lesser extent as Indian. The marking of the Mosquito Coast as the only place where racial others were present in the nation in turn facilitated the erasure of blackness and indigeneity in western and central Nicaragua, despite the presence of black and indigenous people in those areas of the country as well.[5] The idea of Nicaragua as a "civilized" nation in contrast to the "savage" Mosquito Coast that emerged in the nineteenth century was thus racially coded. It also served to legitimize the notion, which persisted well into the twentieth century, that citizens of western regions of the country were peculiarly entitled to exercise political power in the state as a whole, and over "uncivilized" regions in particular. As Donald S. Moore, Jake Kosek, and Anand Pandian observe, "Racialized discourses mark both living beings and geographical territories with the force of their distinctions."[6] The racialization of space was thus a fundamental feature of nation-state formation in Nicaragua, as was the spatialization of race that it facilitated. Together these processes served to legitimize both internally colonizing state practices toward groups and regions constructed as racial others, and the political exclusion of black and indigenous *costeños* (as the inhabitants of the region are called).

When the newly created state of Nicaragua declared its independence from Spain in 1821 it claimed the Mosquito Coast as part of its territory, but the region's inhabitants did not consider themselves a part of the new nation. As Karl Offen notes in his essay in this volume, they prided themselves on having resisted Spanish attempts at colonization and had little in common with the inhabitants of the new Nicaraguan republic. From the founding moments of the Nicaraguan state, therefore, the Mosquito Coast has occupied an ambiguous position in the national imaginary. On the one hand the region itself was claimed as an indivisible part of the national body, but on the other hand the racial and cultural difference of costeños, combined with their claims to self-government and alliance with foreign colonial powers such as Great Britain, seemed to threaten the very existence of the new nation. This ambivalent, if not contradictory, attitude toward costeños and the territory they inhabited is constitutive of how the Mosquito Coast operated as a racialized space. It became the preeminent place of racial and cultural difference within the nation; its association with blackness and to a lesser extent indigeneity simultaneously facilitated the myths that in the rest of the country there was no African participation in *mestizaje* and that indigenous people had disappeared during the colonial period.[7]

In this essay I analyze key moments in the formation of the Nicaraguan nation-state during the nineteenth century and early twentieth in order to show how the racialization of space and the spatialization of race operated to determine the political inclusion of subaltern racial groups from the Mosquito Coast. First, I show how Nicaraguan national identity was initially constructed in contrast to the "inferior" and "savage" Mosquito Coast during the nineteenth century. I then explain how the racialization of space that marked the region as black and indigenous was used to legitimize the internal colonizing practices of the Nicaraguan state and to justify the political exclusion of costeños until well into the twentieth century. Finally, I analyze the persistent effects of the spatialization of race on the practice of citizenship in Nicaragua today by tracing the links between current attempts to undermine the self-government rights gained by costeños and older discourses about the lesser nationalness and unfitness for citizenship of the black and indigenous inhabitants of the Mosquito Coast.

THE STRUGGLE FOR THE MOSQUITO COAST AND THE CONSTRUCTION OF THE NICARAGUAN NATION

Nationalism as an ideology is by definition both inclusive and exclusive. It sets boundaries between nationals and foreigners, but it may also be used to legitimize the privileged access of certain groups within the state to political power. One of the basic tenets of nationalism is that all members of the nation share a common identity that differentiates them from outsiders, and all nationals possess it equally. The historic association between the growth of nationalist movements and the induction of the masses into politics in Western Europe noted by scholars of nationalism reflects this inclusive aspect of nationalist ideologies.[8] Yet nationalist movements may rely on the support of the lower classes without necessarily wishing to extend them full political rights.

This was certainly the case in Central America at the time of independence, where non-Europeans were a majority of the population and one of the initial spurs of the independence movements was the fear of slave and Indian uprisings by the criollo elite.[9] Independence in Central America was declared by the criollo elite to ward off the specter of another Haitian revolution. The Acta de la independencia of the Central American Federation, enacted in 1821, bluntly explains that criollos declared independence in order to preserve their economic, political, and social dominance: "Independence from the Spanish government being the general will of the people of Guatemala . . . Mr. Political Chief should declare it in order to prevent the consequences which would be fearsome in the event that it were in fact proclaimed by the people themselves."[10] At the same time, however, the Central American Federation's Constitution of 1824 specified that all inhabitants of the republic, white and nonwhite alike, were nationals. Slavery was also abolished that year, and slave traders were barred from citizenship. But as in other republics of this era, only those who had a "useful profession" or owned property could be citizens, and the citizenship of those who worked as "domestic servants close to the body" was suspended.[11] Central American criollo ruling classes may thus have embraced nonwhite populations as their fellow nationals, but they did not necessarily conceive of them as their fellow citizens.

In Nicaragua the existential threat represented by the existence of a large nonwhite majority was exacerbated by the existence of the Mosquito Coast, where political rule was exercised by black and indigenous groups under the protection of the British. While both the Central American Federation and later the state of Nicaragua (after the Federation's dissolution in 1838) claimed sovereignty over the Mosquito Coast, the region was never under Spain's control during the colonial period. In the colonial era Spanish settlers resided mainly on the Pacific coast of what was to become Nicaragua, while the central region was populated mainly by indigenous groups organized in their own communities with few Spaniards or *mestizos*, and the Mosquito Coast was primarily under British influence. British pirates first established relations with the region's indigenous inhabitants in the sixteenth century, and by the seventeenth and eighteenth centuries "an incipient African-Amerindian polity," the Mosquito Kingdom, emerged parallel to the British superintendency for the Mosquito shore, as Offen explains at greater length in his essay on the colonial Mosquitia in this volume.[12] During this period the Spanish crown periodically tried to establish control over the Mosquito Coast, but it was not until 1783 that Britain formally recognized Spanish colonial rights to the Coast. The

British temporarily left the region, but Spain was unable to fill the re- sulting power vacuum, and the Mosquito Coast thus continued to enjoy relative autonomy from Spain's colonial administration. Following Na- poleon's invasion of Spain in 1808 the British returned to the Mosquito Coast and in 1843 officially reestablished their protectorate over the Mos- quito Kingdom. The impetus for doing so was the desire to gain control over a possible interoceanic canal route through Central America, as the Atlantic entrance to a Nicaraguan canal would have been located on the Mosquito Coast.

Great Britain's territorial designs for the Mosquito Coast could not have come at a worse time for the nascent Nicaraguan state, as the period following independence (1821–57) was one in which Nicaragua, like the rest of its Central American neighbors, was engaged in continuous in- trastate and domestic civil wars.[13] The result of the constant warfare and instability was an economy in ruins and a weak and ineffective state that could not impose order, collect taxes, improve the living conditions of its citizens, or assert its rights internationally. Taking advantage of the chaos in Nicaragua, the British sought to secure the port of San Juan del Norte, the Atlantic entrance to the proposed canal, in the name of the Mosquito king. In 1841 British forces tried (and failed) to take over the port.[14] Again in 1848 Britain announced that the limits of the Mosquito Kingdom in- cluded San Juan del Norte, and the British Navy overpowered Nicaraguan forces guarding the port. The Nicaraguan government was forced to let the port remain in Mosquito and British hands until the dispute over the region was finally resolved in 1860.[15] The importance of the dispute over the Mosquito Coast to Nicaragua is reflected in the claim of the country's foreign relations secretary at the time, Sebastián Salinas, that the issue had "absorbed everyone's attention, from that of the first magistrate to that of the last Nicaraguan."[16] While the idea that ordinary citizens were as preoccupied with the dispute as members of the elite strains the imagina- tion, it is at least clear that in the course of Nicaragua's struggle with Great Britain for control of the region Nicaraguan elites first began to articulate certain conceptions of national identity, of who they were as a nation.

Nationalism is an essentially comparative endeavor. One of the funda- mental features of nationalism is the existence of other nations relative to which the standing of the nationalist's homeland can be compared. Charles Taylor, for instance, has argued that nationalism is a response to the very modern predicament of nonrecognition by more "advanced" societies. Nonrecognition is "felt existentially as a challenge" by modernizing elites in less developed countries, he argues, because modern societies are "direct-access" societies in which belonging to the state is conceived as a direct relation between each individual citizen and the nation; it is not mediated by hierarchical relationships such as those between peasant and lord. As a result in modern societies identities are formed in a space of recognition, and nonrecognition is a matter of dignity in which the self-worth of the individual is engaged. It is this feature of modern societies that endows nationalism with its ability to bestow recognition and hence accounts for its "emotive power," according to Taylor.[17] The content of particular nationalist discourses is thus fundamentally shaped by elites' perceptions of and concerns about their nation's standing relative to other nations.

In the case of Nicaragua no event had a more profound effect on the emerging notions of national identity being forged by the country's political and intellectual elites than the dispute with Great Britain for control of the Mosquito Coast.[18] The dispute was extremely troubling for elites because it underscored the fragility of Nicaragua's claim to nationhood and brought to the fore anxieties about the country's racial composition (Was it a white, black, indigenous, or mixed-race nation?), which was crucial to its standing in the international hierarchy of nations. Indeed the nationalist discourses formulated by Nicaraguan elites in the nineteenth century relied explicitly on the racialization of space to shore up the new republic's claim to statehood. In these national narratives the Mosquito Coast was consistently portrayed as savage in contrast to civilized Nicaragua and its black and indigenous inhabitants as incapable of self-government or political agency.

During the nineteenth century the dominant social and political groups on the Mosquito Coast (in addition to the British) were two mixed-race groups of African and Amerindian descent: Creoles and Miskitu. While the racial designation of both of these groups was ambiguous, by the late nineteenth century the former had become identified primarily as people of African descent and the latter as indigenous. The mixing process between Miskitus and Africans who arrived in the region in the seventeenth century had initially resulted in a distinction between "pure," or Tawira, Miskitu on the one hand and Sambos, or Zambos-Mosquitos, on the other. By the nineteenth century, however, these differences had dissolved into a single Miskitu group that was identified as indigenous or Amerindian.[19]

The Creoles were a group of free people of color that emerged in the late eighteenth century in the southern Mosquito Coast. Of mixed African, Amerindian, and European ancestry, they were predominantly mulattos, the descendants of free and enslaved Africans who had arrived on the Mosquito Coast in the seventeenth century. After the departure of the British from the Coast at the end the eighteenth century they founded maroon communities at Bluefields and the sites of other British settler communities and developed a creolized English language and hybrid culture.[20] Creoles became increasingly socially and politically dominant on the Mosquito Coast over the course of the nineteenth century. As a result a rivalry for political power in the region developed between them and the Miskitu. While the Miskitu retained control at the local level, both the Mosquito Kingdom and the Mosquito Reserve created after 1860 were governed by an advisory body to the Mosquito king, the Council of State, which was composed of Europeans and Creoles but no Miskitus.

By the middle of the nineteenth century Creoles were playing a central role in the politics and society of the Mosquito Coast. Contrary to the assertions of Nicaraguan officials in the second half of the nineteenth century, people of African descent involved in the politics of the Mosquito Coast at this time were thus not simply foreign Jamaican blacks.[21] Jamaican and other West Indian immigrant laborers began arriving in the region in the late nineteenth century to work in the developing enclave economies controlled by U.S. companies (a migratory stream that would reach its peak during the early part of the twentieth century). As was the case with the Miskitu, where Tawira and Zambos-Mosquitos fused into one group, these immigrants were gradually integrated into the Creole group.[22]

The dominance on the Mosquito Coast of two Afro-Amerindian groups, one identified with blackness and the other with indigeneity, posed a challenge to Nicaragua's claims to the area. In response Nicaraguan officials deployed a discourse of civilization and savagery that was racially coded to bolster their claim of sovereignty over the Mosquito Coast.[23] Nicaraguan elites were dismayed at not being recognized as a civilized nation by European states and fiercely resisted being equated with the savage Mosquito

Kingdom. When, for example, France explained that it could not intervene on Nicaragua's behalf in the dispute with Great Britain because "European nations cannot, without demeaning themselves, negotiate with those little Mosquitian governments," Nicaraguan elites were powerfully reminded of the fact that in the minds of Europeans there was little difference between them and the inhabitants of the Mosquito Coast, and hence of the precariousness of their claims to civilization.[24] The desire to align Nicaragua with civilized nations as opposed to the savage Mosquito Kingdom is a constant theme in Nicaraguan government correspondence and proclamations of this era. Nicaraguan officials continually chided Britain for violating the international norms that governed interactions between civilized nations. In 1847 Nicaragua's supreme director (the highest office in the executive branch, later renamed the presidency) argued that the British takeover of San Juan del Norte would now serve as a model for "the savage hordes of any country under the protection of a strong Power to consider themselves with the same right to constitute a nation."[25] It would encourage "savage hordes" in all parts of the world to "put themselves on equal footing with civilized States, which would place limits on civilization, and establish disorder and universal anarchy."[26] The dispute over the Mosquito Coast thus played a pivotal role in the evolving self-understanding of Nicaragua's ruling class in the postindependence era. It led political and intellectual elites to construct a vision of their new nation that was premised on the opposition between civilized Nicaragua and the savage Mosquito Kingdom.

NEITHER BLACK NOR INDIAN: CIVILIZED NICARAGUA
VERSUS THE SAVAGE MOSQUITO COAST

Nicaraguan officials' fear of being equated with the savage Mosquito Kingdom was rooted in part in anxieties about race. As a state run by blacks and Indians the Mosquito Kingdom violated prevailing ideas about race, which endorsed racial hierarchies based on the notion that only certain "races" (which were understood to be distinct human groups characterized by permanent inherited physical differences) were capable of being civilized.[27] This kind of racialist thought, which assigned different characteristics to different nonwhite races, was the underpinning of the Nicaraguan claim that the Mosquito Kingdom was savage and inferior.

Nicaraguan officials could not understand how the British government could recognize as a state "a savage horde that lacks all the constitutive principles of a sovereign society," while refusing to do the same for their own, much more civilized nation.[28]

Nicaraguan officials consistently used racist stereotypes of blacks and Indians to portray the inhabitants of the Mosquito Kingdom as incapable of governing themselves. Initially officials tended to associate the region with indigeneity, as reflected in their claims in the 1840s (at the start of the conflict with Britain over the Mosquito Coast) that the Mosquito Kingdom was savage and inferior.[29] The kingdom was thus described largely in terms of savagery, as savage tribes lacking civilization could hardly make credible claims to sovereignty. The mixed Afro-Amerindian heritage of the Miskitu also lent itself to the use of racist stereotypes associated with blackness. The Miskitu were thus said to possess a number of character traits common in racist stereotypes about blacks, including drunkenness, loose morals, and indolence. According to Nicaraguan officials, the Miskitu had been reduced to "a state of moral stupor and brutishness" by the liquor with which the British "encouraged the vice of drunkenness," and possessed loose sexual mores.[30] The older daughter of King Robert Charles Frederick was said to have "manifested a greater preference for foreigners, with whom she used to share her favors to the detriment of her husband."[31] The Miskitu king himself was said to be "famous at the time for his ignorance, by the deep passion with which he adored Jamaican rum, and for the generous largesse with which he gave away and ceded the lands that he was made to believe he owned."[32] Nicaraguan elites delighted in mocking not only the idea of the Miskitu monarchy itself, but also the aesthetic practices adopted by the Miskitu to signify their equal standing as a nation.[33] The Miskitu king's robes were described by Nicaraguan officials as consisting of "tails or a formal coat with a sash but without a shirt or drawers, which he augmented on festive days with a wig on his head like the Spaniards used."[34] Such a "fantastic personage" could not be taken seriously, according to Foreign Relations Secretary Salinas.[35]

The officials' racist representations of the inhabitants of the Mosquito Coast were intended to discredit any claims of the latter to political agency. Nicaraguan officials consistently portrayed the Miskitu as dupes of the British. While British support for the Mosquito Kingdom clearly furthered Britain's goal of controlling an interoceanic canal route through

Nicaragua, the relationship between the inhabitants of the Mosquito Coast and their British allies was far more complex than Nicaraguan officials were willing to acknowledge. In fact the British themselves were aware of the precarious nature of their alliances with the various groups that inhabited the region. In a letter from Mr. Christie, the British consul to the Mosquito Kingdom, to his superiors in London in 1848 he notes that the Miskitu king was at that point "quite submissive": "But I think it right to caution your Lordship that he may not always be so." Christie also mentions trying to please the king's mother because she "was supposed to be averse to the English connexion."[36] Instead of being tricked and exploited by the British or being entirely subservient to them, the inhabitants of the Mosquito Coast chose to ally themselves with the British in order to preserve their independence from Spain and later from Nicaragua.

In fact it appears as if more often than not it was internal rivalries between Creoles and Miskitus within the kingdom and later the Mosquito Reserve that served as the impetus for the shifting alliances that these groups (and indeed different factions within each group) established with the various colonial powers vying for control of the region. In 1847, for example, Princess Agnes Ann Frederick (an aunt of the Miskitu king at the time) signed a treaty with Nicaraguan representatives recognizing Nicaraguan sovereignty over the Mosquito Kingdom and declaring that the Miskitu considered themselves Nicaraguans. In his explanation of the event to his superiors in London, Christie suggested that the motive for the alliance was Miskitu resentment of Creole dominance in the kingdom's political structure: "The native Indians . . . see no right to govern in these needy and ignorant African and Creole Councilors."[37] As these examples reveal, Creoles and Miskitus were not simply puppets of Britain or Nicaragua. Rather, despite being the weakest of the parties involved in the struggle for control of the Mosquito Coast, they attempted to play the various outside powers against each other in order to further their own autonomous (and multiple) political agendas.

Creole political dominance in the Mosquito Kingdom and later the Reserve would become one of the main elements of Nicaraguan officials' attempts to discredit the region's claims to sovereignty, such that by the end of the nineteenth century the region was increasingly identified with blackness. Despite Creoles' long-standing presence in the region (which certainly predated the arrival of the Nicaraguan state), Nicaraguan officials portrayed Creoles as foreign, inferior, and incapable of managing the political affairs of the Mosquito Coast. They referred to Creoles as "Jamaica Negroes," implying that they were foreigners who had improperly taken control of both the Mosquito Kingdom and the Reserve. The basis for this claim was the Treaty of Managua, signed by Great Britain and Nicaragua in 1860, which recognized Nicaragua's claims to the Mosquito Coast. According to the treaty a Mosquito Reserve would replace the Mosquito Kingdom (although encompassing a much smaller geographical area). But while the Reserve would be under Nicaraguan sovereignty, within it the Miskitu enjoyed "the right to self-government and to govern all persons residing in said district, according to their own customs, and in conformity with the rules that may on occasion be adopted by them, as long as they are not incompatible with the sovereign rights of the Nicaraguan Republic."[38] By officially recognizing only Miskitu rights to self-government, despite Creoles' involvement and indeed dominance in the politics of the Mosquito Kingdom, the Treaty of Managua thus provided Nicaraguan officials seeking to bring the Mosquito Coast entirely under Nicaragua's control with a powerful weapon to discredit the autonomous political structures established in the region.

By the late nineteenth century Nicaraguan officials sought to discredit the right to self-government of the inhabitants of the Mosquito Coast by simultaneously claiming that Creoles were foreigners with no authority to govern the Reserve and that the Miskitu had forfeited any claim to political autonomy by allowing Creoles to gain control of the region's political structures. Following the Treaty of Managua, Nicaraguan officials would hereafter claim that the Miskitu could hardly be said to be exercising their right to self-government when the Reserve was in fact controlled by Creoles.[39] Carlos Lacayo, the commissioner to the Mosquito Reserve appointed by the Nicaraguan government, claimed, "The self-government granted to the Mosco Indians was eliminated and supplanted with a tribal regime by a black oligarchy."[40] He argued that the Miskitu could not claim that their self-government rights had been violated by Nicaragua's forcible reincorporation of the region in 1894, given that "they are in the present case the ones to blame, because they have renounced their rights, allowing themselves to be supplanted by an invading colony of Negroes."[41]

The objections of Nicaraguan officials to Creole political power in the Reserve did not stop with their supposed status as foreigners, however; it also had everything to do with their assumed racial inferiority. Government by blacks violated the accepted racial hierarchy of the era, in which Indians were supposed to rank higher than blacks and in which neither group was thought to be capable of self-rule. From the perspective of Nicaraguan officials blacks were not fit to rule themselves or others. Lacayo argued that before reincorporation the Mosquito Coast had been ruled by "a black oligarchy, whose lack of political and administrative ethics, and the vice from which they came, would justify, even if there were no other causes, the destitution which its members have been made to suffer."[42] For Nicaraguan officials the mere fact of Creole political power on the Reserve justified the end of self-government in the region, since blacks had neither the right nor the capacity to govern themselves, much less others.

The inhabitants of the Mosquito Coast did not allow racist representations of the region as savage to stand unchallenged. In a letter to the British written in 1877 the Miskitu chief William Henry Clarence lists the reasons why "the Mosquito Indians [were] not willing to enter into closer connection with Nicaragua." He discredits the claim that Nicaragua was civilized by pointing to the chaos experienced by the country during the period of anarchy following independence from Spain. In contrast, he argues, "The Reserve has maintained during the above-mentioned period a peaceful Government, whilst in Nicaragua there are continued revolutions, wars, and rumours of wars, destruction of property, &c." Clarence also explains why the people of the Mosquito Coast could not be said to enjoy better living conditions under Nicaraguan rule than they had under their own: "There are established on the coast of the Reserve seven Mission stations, with schools, where the people are educated, and instructed to become good members of society, but nothing has been done by the Government of Nicaragua to improve the places or instruct the Mosquito people given over by the Treaty [of Managua]." He also alludes to the fact that the people of the Mosquito Coast had by this time acquired a very different national identity than that of Nicaragua: "The religion, customs, manners, and laws of Nicaragua are in no way compatible [with those of the people of the Reserve]."[43] In another letter he also describes Miskitu claims to the region in nationalist terms: "[The Miskitu] have been a free and independent people from time immemorial—long before Nicaragua became a Republic—and should be left to their own suitable manner of improvement and government."[44] Political elites on the Mosquito Coast thus clearly did not accept racist representations of themselves and their region in terms of civilization and savagery and vigorously defended their right to self-government.

The struggle for control of the Mosquito Coast was equally important to their Nicaraguan counterparts, as comparisons to the savage Coast played a central role in official discourses about Nicaraguan national identity during this era. It is also at this time that representations of the Mosquito Coast as indigenous and black in contrast to the rest of Nicaragua begin to emerge. Ultimately this racialization of space would become a central feature of the practice of citizenship in Nicaragua; it would be used to justify the internally colonizing practices of the state toward regions of the country coded as black or indigenous in the late nineteenth century and early twentieth.

THE RACIALIZATION OF SPACE IN NICARAGUA AND THE POLITICAL EXCLUSION OF COSTEÑOS

The unequal incorporation of black and indigenous costeños and the region in which they lived was a fundamental element of the state-building efforts of Nicaraguan elites following the end of the postindependence period of anarchy. In the late nineteenth century and early twentieth the civilizing and colonizing imperatives of Nicaragua's nation-building elites manifested most clearly in the drive to "reincorporate" and "Nicaragua-nize" the Mosquito Coast on the one hand and dismantle indigenous communities in the Pacific and Central regions of the country on the other hand.[45] As Edmund T. Gordon has noted, in Nicaragua the political exclusion of black and indigenous people was mapped onto region and territory.[46] The racialization of space operated in such a way that certain regions of the country became associated with blackness and indigeneity, thus marking these spaces as (figuratively at least) both inside and outside the nation. Racialized spaces (of which the paradigmatic case is the Mosquito Coast) were seen as part of the nation insofar as the geographical terrain itself was claimed as part of the national territory, but they were also treated as if they existed outside of it insofar as their black and indigenous inhabitants were deemed unfit for citizenship. Black and indigenous costeños were thus treated as second-class citizens by the way the spaces they inhabited were racialized, as the racialization of space served to justify the internally colonizing policies adopted by Nicaragua's Conservative and Liberal elites during this period. In the case of Conservatives in particular this was one element of a wider project to reimagine the internal contours of the Nicaraguan political community in the second half of the nineteenth century in distinctly less egalitarian terms.

Following the postindependence period of anarchy Conservatives, who blamed the chaos of the era on misguided Liberal egalitarian ideas, dedicated themselves to the project of building a strong state with a dominant executive. Their efforts to reform the constitution in order to strengthen the power of the executive branch and restrict access to citizenship by means of new property qualifications for voting and running for public office put them in direct conflict with Liberals, who objected to the aristocratic bent of the reforms. The conflict between the two parties eventually led to William Walker's expedition to Nicaragua (at the Liberals' behest) and the subsequent alliance between Liberals and Conservatives to expel him from the country during the National War of 1855–57, after his alliance with the Liberals had soured. Following the National War both parties began a period of peaceful coexistence (1858–93) under the hegemony of the Conservatives, who dedicated themselves to state-building activities. During this era economic growth fueled by the promotion of agricultural exports led to general prosperity and new state institutions were created.

One of the fundamental elements of the political project pursued by Conservative elites during the second half of the nineteenth century was the unequal inclusion of nonwhites and members of the lower social strata (which tended to overlap). This aim was pursued by means of two principal policies: the attempt to restrict the highest levels of political power to the descendants of the criollo elite and the effort to bring outlying regions of the country inhabited by uncivilized blacks and Indians under direct state control. The Conservative Fruto Chamorro, who served first as supreme director and later as president of Nicaragua, claimed that states should

> be careful not to prostitute and desecrate such a handsome title [of citizen] and such a noble quality by granting it unconditionally, without taking into account merit, virtue and property. Social equality does not consist in making citizens of all, and in granting to all the same rights, standing and immunities.

Giving the same rights to the evil as to the good man, to the lazy and unruly as to the hard working and peaceful, is to destroy that equality; it is to create elements of anarchy.[47]

For Conservatives citizenship and individual rights were the privilege of those who possessed "virtue, merit and property," qualities that they assumed were related. The state should therefore mete out individual rights and protections sparingly.

The inegalitarian political ideology of Conservatives was reflected in the moral and property qualifications for citizenship enshrined in the constitution of 1858. This charter established that Nicaraguan citizens were individuals of all races who were twenty-one years of age or older (or eighteen-year-olds who possessed some education or were a male head of household), who were of good conduct, and who possessed property worth at least one hundred pesos or had a job or profession that produced the equivalent yearly.[48] Property requirements for running for the highest offices of the state were also introduced; citizens could run for the office of president only if they possessed four thousand pesos and for senator only if they had two thousand pesos. Conservatives also introduced moral criteria for citizenship, which was reserved for persons of "good conduct" and could be permanently lost if one was declared a fraudulent debtor, exhibited "notoriously depraved conduct" (offenses that in 1838 had merited only temporary suspension of citizenship), or showed "ingratitude toward one's parents or unjust abandonment of one's wife or legitimate children."[49] Further only married men with children could become president or senator, and only Catholics were eligible for government posts.[50] Religious freedom (which had been protected in the constitution of 1838) was also revoked, and Roman Catholicism was declared the religion of the republic.

In addition to introducing new property and moral qualifications for citizenship, which de facto excluded certain persons from political participation (especially members of lower socioeconomic strata, who were mostly nonwhite), Conservatives also created special regimes to govern savage regions of the country, which automatically disenfranchised the black and indigenous inhabitants of those areas. Conservatives characterized subaltern racial groups as responsible for the anarchy of the postindependence period, conveniently forgetting that although indigenous and other popular sectors participated in the conflicts of the era, they were not the originators of those conflicts.[51] The main causes of the anarchy were conflicts among the ruling class, but Conservatives nevertheless argued that Indians were not yet fit for citizenship. In 1854, for example, Fruto Chamorro argued that racial heterogeneity and political equality were incompatible:

> The absolute equality between one [race] and the other that has tried to be established works to the detriment of the public good. The indigenous race, more underdeveloped in everything than the other, alone possesses habits, preoccupations and customs so antiquated that only time and civilization can gradually modify them; eliminating them suddenly could give rise to disturbances, clashes, and conflicts; and for the same reason, prudence suggests that special institutions be created for the regime of the Indians, adequate to their customs and character.[52]

Similar arguments were made about people of African descent, whose backwardness was said to pose the greatest obstacle to the nation's progress. In an article on indolence published in 1849 the editors of the newspaper *El Correo del Itsmo de Nicaragua* wrote:

> We could develop an idea of the various degrees of laziness, by examining men, from the highest state of society, to those in the most ignorant state in the desert: from the Indian, from the Negro most abandoned to inaction and brutishness among savages, to the most learned and industrious man of the great capitals: What a difference from man to man! . . . men who are similar to God, men who are like beasts.[53]

The republic envisioned by Conservatives was thus a profoundly inegalitarian one in which subaltern racial groups were granted rights according to their level of civilization. Conservatives sought to replace Liberal visions of a republic of equal citizens with a state in which the social, political, and economic dominance of the descendants of the criollo elite was woven into the very fabric of the political community.[54]

When Liberals regained power at the end of the nineteenth century with the ascension of José Santos Zelaya (1893–1909) they removed many of the restrictions on citizenship introduced by Conservatives; they did

not, however, end the political exclusion of black and indigenous costeños. Indeed it was under the Zelaya regime that the Nicaraguan state undertook the military "reincorporation" of the Mosquito Coast by force in
1894. The political disenfranchisement of black and indigenous costeños
that was a result of the internally colonizing policies of the Nicaraguan
state toward the savage regions thus persisted well into the twentieth century. The Treaty of Managua contained a clause requiring the consent
of the Miskitu in order for any incorporation of the Mosquito Reserve
into Nicaragua to take place. As a result costeños retained some self-
government rights on paper even after 1894. The Mosquito Convention of
1894, in which the Miskitu purportedly consented to becoming a part of
Nicaragua, nevertheless reiterated the rights of the Miskitu to elect their
own authorities, be exempt from taxes and military service, and benefit
from the proceeds of all taxes extracted from the region.[55] The Harrison-
Altamirano Treaty of 1905 between Nicaragua and Great Britain, which
superseded the Treaty of Managua, similarly guaranteed Miskitus and
Creoles born before 1894 the right to exemption from taxes and military
service for a period of fifty years, to continued respect for all property
rights gained prior to 1894, and to live according to their own customs as
long as these did not contradict Nicaraguan laws; in addition they were
granted the same rights guaranteed to all Nicaraguan citizens.[56] In practice,
however, the Nicaraguan state never honored either the self-government
or equal rights provisions of the treaties.

Instead the government followed a dual policy of political disenfranchisement and forced cultural assimilation. These policies produced very
different results from their stated aims, however. Nicaraguan officials
maintained that their goal was the "nationalization" of the Mosquito
Coast and its inhabitants, but the policies they pursued had the effect
of further alienating costeños and rendering them second-class citizens.
Early in the twentieth century the governorship and other local government posts on the Coast were filled by officials from outside the region
who were appointed and sent from Managua; the region's representatives
before the national legislature (senators and congressmen) were also appointed directly by the national government. This was possible due to
a clause in the constitutions of 1893 and 1905 that designated as an at-
tribute of the executive branch the "establishment of the special regime
with which uninhabited regions, or those inhabited by uncivilized Indi-

ans, should be temporarily governed."[57] The racialization of space thus served to justify the political exclusion of costeños in Nicaragua during the twentieth century by coding black and indigenous regions as savage and incapable of self-rule.

By the 1920s a variant of official mestizo nationalism had emerged in Nicaragua that portrayed the country as an overwhelmingly mestizo nation and that described *mestizaje* as a mixing process between Spaniards and Indians in which Spanish contributions were determinant and African participation was minimized or erased outright.[58] This nationalist ideology justified the political power of the descendants of the Spanish *conquistadores* by suggesting that only they were destined for political rule; it also served to invalidate costeño demands for self-government. A report on the Atlantic coast commissioned by the president of the republic and compiled by Frutos Ruiz y Ruiz in 1925 argued that it was not possible for the central state to name costeños as mayors or to fill other local government posts in the region because such officials needed to "possess the qualities which adorned those advanced men who during the Spanish colonization were the heralds of Civilization."[59] Naturally none could possess such qualities in as great abundance as the actual descendants of the Spanish conquistadores, the members of the great oligarchic families. The report also argued that black and indigenous costeños were simply not advanced enough to exercise political power in the region.

> On the Coast the native element is of diverse uncivilized Indian races, with aboriginal languages, and furthermore, there is the imported English-speaking component of African descent. These heterogeneous tribes, so lacking in culture and so numerous, far from possessing the capacity and means necessary to govern the Coast instead need the civilized peoples of Nicaragua to come to their lands, mix with them, elevate their race, and impose Nicaraguan civilization and language.[60]

As late as 1925, then, the discourse of civilization and savagery was still being invoked to justify the political exclusion of black and indigenous costeños. We also see here the emergence of the spatialization of race that accompanied the racialization of space, whereby the association of the Atlantic coast with blackness and indigeneity facilitated the depiction of other areas of the country as devoid of black and indigenous people (this in spite of their presence in these regions, as the essays by Wolfe and Gudmundson in this volume demonstrate).

Since 1894 the Nicaraguan state's policy toward the Atlantic coast combined costeño political disenfranchisement with the state's deep desire to "nationalize" the region. The latter aim is especially evident in the educational policies pursued by the central state in the region after 1894, particularly the attempt to replace education in English with mandatory Spanish.[61] In his report Ruiz advocated the creation of schools "in which only Spanish should be taught, while prohibiting speaking other languages in the school" because this was fundamental to national unity.[62] For Nicaraguan nationalists education in Spanish was necessary because it would attract Creoles (who, as we have seen, were viewed as especially foreign) "to the love of the Nicaraguan nation," thus helping to nationalize them. "Unity of language so that there is unity of nation. Castilian language, Nicaraguan language, in Nicaraguan lands to be considered Nicaraguans," Ruiz fervently suggested.[63] Nationalization was a prerequisite for the political inclusion of costeños because only once they were fully national could they be citizens. Spanish schools, Ruiz observed, functioned as "center[s] where citizenship is taught, where the fire of patriotism burns brightly."[64] According to this discursive logic, costeños could not be citizens because they were not sufficiently national. Yet it was precisely because the region in which they lived was considered outside the nation that they were now being denied equal political rights in the Nicaraguan political community of which they had forcibly been made members. This paradox is reflected in the conflicting terms used by Nicaraguan nationalists and costeños to describe the events of 1894. To the former it is known as "reincorporation," while Creoles refer to it as "the overthrow." The contradictory terms themselves illustrate the diametrically opposed outcomes of the event for costeños, who were politically disenfranchised as a result, and Nicaraguan elites, for whom it represented a nationalist triumph.

Costeños were keenly aware of the paradoxical character of the state's policies toward their region. They vigorously contested their political disenfranchisement within the Nicaraguan political community and repeatedly denounced their status as second-class citizens. They noted that the use of the word *reincorporation* to describe the abolition of the Mosquito Reserve suggested that costeños were the conationals and fellow citizens of other Nicaraguans, yet they were treated as anything but. Dr. George Hodgson, a prominent Creole leader in the early twentieth century, shared costeño frustrations with his friend Luis Mena Solórzano, who recorded them in his memoirs:

What is the matter . . . with the government in Managua, which forgets the Coast and when it remembers us it is only to hurt us? The last time, with a simple ministerial order they took away the municipal rents from the Bluff Customs House, violating the Congress' decree. They would not cause that kind of damage to any of the country's other municipalities; furthermore, it is offensive and humiliating. They never name a native governor, nor to any of the lesser posts. . . . We cannot elect our own senators and deputies, because they impose them on us from Managua and, in the majority of cases, they do not even reside in our region. We cannot elect our own mayor. . . . The Department of Zelaya is not a colony of Nicaragua on the Atlantic: it is an integral part of the national territory, and we Coast people have sacred and inalienable rights that we are obliged to demand and protect.[65]

Costeños, as Hodgson notes, were forced to become part of Nicaragua against their will without the political rights that usually accompany such membership. Costeños also contested the arguments used by Nicaraguan elites to justify their political exclusion, such as the discourse of civilization and savagery, which they attempted to recast in their favor by inverting the equation of Nicaraguanness with civilization and the Atlantic coast with savagery. Creoles, for example, claimed that they were in fact *more* civilized than Nicaraguans of Hispanic descent as a result of their British heritage, since Anglo-Saxon nations were more advanced than Iberian nations. In a memorial presented to Congress in 1933 Senator Horacio Hodgson (a Creole) challenged the view that the Atlantic coast was uncivilized by invoking Anglo-Saxon superiority. "When the Government of Nicaragua came to this region, it did not find us enslaved," he wrote, "but as a civilized people; with a good system of education based on the methodology of the Anglo-Saxon race."[66]

Costeños pointed out the inherent contradictions in the nationalist rhetoric surrounding the events of 1894, specifically the paradox of Nicaraguan elites claiming as part of their nation a region whose black and indigenous inhabitants they refused to recognize as full and equal fellow citizens. They noted that nothing was more contradictory than the argument of Nicaraguan nationalists that costeños first needed to be nationalized in order to gain full political inclusion. Or, as one Nicaraguan commentator observed with resignation shortly after 1894, "Nicaragua had to be satisfied [at present] with the physical reincorporation of the Reserve, leaving to circumstances and the passing of time the difficult task, not yet completely accomplished, of the spiritual reincorporation of the Atlantic Coast, or to put it another way the Nicaraguanization of the Mosquitia."[67] The justification for costeño political disenfranchisement was thus that only after that arduous task had been accomplished could they be entrusted with citizenship. In contrast costeños argued that they would feel they belonged to Nicaragua only when they were treated as full and equal citizens.[68] In a letter to the president in 1925 Creole notables argued that the "reconciliation" and "true nationalization of the Atlantic Coast" that nationalists professed to so ardently desire could occur only once the central state ceased to treat the region as "a conquered and disaffected province that needs to be governed with an iron hand and forced to pay tribute." If the goal in 1894 was truly to make the Atlantic coast a part of Nicaragua, they insisted, that objective would be fulfilled only when the central state appointed costeños to fill government offices in the region and complied with the provisions on economic autonomy contained in the treaties governing reincorporation.[69]

The unequal political inclusion of subaltern racial groups that was a fundamental element of the political project of Conservatives during the second half of the nineteenth century thus continued to shape the attitudes and policies of Nicaraguan elites (including those of the Liberals who succeeded them) toward the Atlantic coast well into the twentieth century. The colonizing and civilizing mission that late nineteenth-century and early twentieth-century Nicaraguan elites prescribed for themselves toward regions of the country associated with blackness or indigeneity indelibly "shaped the character and nature of the Nicaraguan national state." As Dora María Téllez observes:

> The construction of the Nicaraguan national state did not denote, from its inception, the homogenous and simultaneous inclusion of all the inhabitants and regions of the territory, but instead has been a double process of inclu-

sion and exclusion of different social classes, specific communities, or ethnic groups. The excluded in each stage have had little or no access to the basic rights derived from belonging to the greater community that is the national state.[70]

More specifically the political exclusion of black and indigenous costeños from the Nicaraguan political community occurred because the region they inhabited was racially coded as both savage and inferior and therefore in need of colonization and civilization. The racialization of space was thus critical to the political exclusion of black and indigenous costeños in Nicaragua.

CONCLUSION: THE SPATIALIZATION OF RACE AND THE POLITICAL INCLUSION OF COSTEÑOS

The racialization of space associating the Atlantic coast with blackness (and to a lesser extent indigeneity) that was a central element of the nationalist discourses formulated by Nicaraguan elites in the nineteenth century and early twentieth in turn facilitated a spatialization of race that has had profound political consequences for costeños. In particular the racialization of the coast made possible the erasure of racial difference from the rest of Nicaragua, a notion that served to justify the view that only the descendants of the Spanish criollo elite who resided in the western regions of the country were suited to exercise political power. The close connections between race and place have thus had profound consequences on the practice of citizenship in Nicaragua. These legacies of spatialized racism have also proven particularly difficult to overcome. Despite the adoption in 1987 of multicultural citizenship policies that recognized a number of collective rights for costeños, including the right to regional autonomy or self-government, costeño attempts to exercise political agency and achieve political equality are still viewed with skepticism by many of their fellow citizens.[71]

We see this clearly in contemporary attempts to dispute the legitimacy of the self-government rights gained by costeños that draw on the Atlantic coast's association with blackness. A case in point is a political caricature of Atlantic coast regional autonomy that appeared in 2002 in *La Prensa*, one of the country's leading newspapers. The objects of the political satire are the different views surrounding regional autonomy held by black and indigenous costeños, who fought to gain collective rights, and more recent mestizo migrants to the region. The drawing is striking not only because of what it suggests about contemporary attitudes toward the rights of costeños to self-government, but also because of the way it harkens back to nineteenth-century representations of costeños. In the drawing the Atlantic coast is personified by a black man wearing dreadlocks who has enormous white lips, a broad nose, and large ears. He is holding a banner on which the word *autonomía* (autonomy) is written and is saying, emphatically, "La Costa para los costeños [The Atlantic coast for costeños]!" Meanwhile, standing nearby under the "no mía [not mine]" portion of the banner, is a mestizo *campesino*. He is uttering only a large question mark, as if wondering "What about me?"[72] The mestizo figure carries a sack, which is presumably meant to evoke industriousness. In contrast to the black costeño figure, whose racial identity is unmistakable as a result of the exaggerated, distorted manner in which the character is drawn, the racial and ethnic identity of the mestizo figure is suggested mostly by the traditional peasant garb he is wearing. In fact the black figure is drawn in a manner characteristic of older racist caricatures of blacks rarely seen today.

Among the many noteworthy elements of this contemporary depiction of the Atlantic coast, one of the most striking is the persistent association of the region with blackness, particularly when issues of political power are at stake. It is remarkable that the coast is still being represented in this way given that Creoles and Garifuna (the other ethnoracial group in the region identified as being of African descent) are certainly not the majority of the coast's inhabitants. In fact indigenous groups, the Miskitu in particular, represent a significantly larger proportion of the region's population today than Creoles. Moreover mestizos (who began to arrive in the region after 1894) are not only major players in the region's politics; they are also now a majority of the population on the Atlantic coast. As the question asked by the political cartoon makes clear, these demographic changes challenge the traditional spatialization of race in Nicaragua whereby mestizos (and only mestizos) live in western and central Nicaragua, while the Atlantic coast is the place of blackness, and to a lesser extent indigeneity. Contemporary mestizo migration to the region thus

FIGURE 1 "El humor de M. Guillén." Courtesy of *La Prensa*, Managua, Nicaragua

raises the prospect that black and indigenous costeños will wield political power over mestizos if they are able to effectively exercise the right to self-government gained during the 1980s, a development that would contradict long-standing ideas about who is entitled to wield political power in Nicaragua that first emerged during the nineteenth century. The fact that it is precisely such anxieties about race and the space of citizenship that are at stake in contemporary debates about costeño regional autonomy has been explicitly acknowledged by politicians from mestizo-majority areas of the coast, who want to carve out a separate department outside the jurisdiction of the two autonomous regions created in 1987. They argue that the creation of a separate department for Atlantic coast mestizos is necessary: "Blacks cannot govern us because they do not think as we do."[73] As was the case with the arguments of nineteenth-century Nicaraguan officials that the Mosquito Coast was undeserving of self-government because it was ruled by a foreign "black oligarchy" of Jamaican origin, mestizo Nicaraguans today find the idea of black costeños exercising political power illegitimate because of the persistence of racist ideas that have marked the development of citizenship in the country. The mapping of racial difference onto region and territory that marked the Atlantic coast as a predominantly black (and to a lesser extent indigenous) space thus continues to justify mestizo political power in Nicaragua because it continues to figuratively and discursively construct costeños as not fully national and makes it difficult to imagine them as political equals.

The racialization of space and the concomitant spatialization of race that served to legitimize the political disenfranchisement of black and indigenous costeños in the nineteenth and twentieth centuries thus continue to shape the contours of citizenship in contemporary Nicaragua. Anxieties about race not only fundamentally influenced state formation in Nicaragua, but they continue to shape the political inclusion of black and indigenous costeños today. The irony of the civilizing and colonizing projects toward regions of the country marked as black and indigenous that were a central element of the political imaginary of nineteenth- and twentieth-century Nicaraguan elites is that they were carried out on behalf of a national political community that, when confronted with the actual bodies of black and indigenous costeños, could not conceive of them as either fully national or political equals. Unfortunately the access of black and indigenous costeños today to full and equal citizenship continues to be delimited by the ambivalent and contradictory attitudes toward the region that emerged during previous eras. The fundamental paradox with regard to race and the space of citizenship in Nicaragua first instantiated by the dispute over the Mosquito Coast has yet to be resolved. Black and indigenous costeños are both of and not of the nation: the region they inhabit is claimed as an indivisible part of the national territory, while they have yet to be seen as either fully national or embraced as political equals.

NOTES

Research for this chapter was carried out at the library of the Instituto de Historia de Nicaragua y Céntroamerica at the Universidad Centroamericana in Managua. Earlier versions were presented at the international conference Revolution, Independence and Emancipation: The Struggle against Slavery in Limón, Costa Rica, 26–28 August 2004. I am grateful to Justin Wolfe, Lowell Gudmundson, and Rina Cáceres for the opportunity to participate in the conference Between Race and Place: Blacks and Blackness in Central

America and the Mainland Caribbean at Tulane University, 13–14 November 2004, and to Jemima Pierre and Ivy Wilson for helpful conversations on questions of race and space, nations and bodies. Unless otherwise noted all translations from texts originally in Spanish are my own.

1 There has been much recent work, both theoretical and empirical, in a variety of disciplines (including anthropology, geography, and history) exploring the relationship between race, place, and space. Some examples are J. N. Brown, "Black Liverpool"; Delaney, "The Space That Race Makes"; Durkheim and Dixon, "The Role of Place and Metaphor"; Gilroy, *The Black Atlantic*; Moore, "Subaltern Struggles."

2 Anthias and Yuval-Davis, *Racialized Boundaries*, 2.

3 In the field of Latin American studies a growing body of literature has begun to emerge that seeks to map how ideas of race construct social and geographical space. See, for example, Appelbaum, *Muddied Waters*; Appelbaum, Macpherson, and Rosemblatt, *Race and Nation*; de la Cadena, "The Racial-Moral Politics of Place"; Orlove, "Putting Race in Its Place"; Wade, *Blackness and Race Mixture.*

4 The contemporary spelling of the group's name is Miskitu, but during the nineteenth century the most common spelling was Mosquito. I use the contemporary spelling when referring to the group, but use the older term when referring to the name of the region as a whole.

5 The innovative work of Justin Wolfe and Lowell Gudmundson on the African presence in western Nicaragua in their essays in this volume represents a welcome corrective in this regard to the traditional historiography and complements similar recent work on the survival of indigenous communities in the western and central regions of the country. One of the most prominent examples of the latter is Gould, *To Die in This Way.*

6 Moore, Kosek, and Pandian, *Race, Nature*, 2.

7 On the development of these myths and their hegemonic role in nationalist discourses, see Gould, *To Die in This Way*; Hooker, "'Beloved Enemies.'"

8 See, for example, Hroch, "From National Movement to the Fully-Formed Nation"; Hobsbawm, "Mass-Producing Traditions"; Nairn, *The Break-up of Britain.*

9 B. Anderson, *Imagined Communities*, 49.

10 "Acta de la independencia [15 de Septiembre de 1821]," *Las constituciones políticas y sus reformas en la historia de Nicaragua*, ed. Antonio Esgueva Gómez (Managua: Editorial El Parlamento, 1994), 144. The Central American Federation replaced the Captaincy General of Guatemala, which included contemporary Guatemala, Honduras, El Salvador, Costa Rica, and Nicaragua.

11 "Constitución de la República Federal de Centro América [22 de Noviembre de 1824]," in Esgueva Gómez, *Las constituciones políticas*, 196–97.

12 On the Miskitu monarchy, see Helms, "Of Kings and Contexts"; Dennis and Olien, "Kingship among the Miskitu."

13 This era is known in Nicaraguan historiography as the "period of anarchy." See Coronel Urtecho, "Introducción a la Época de la Anarquía."

14 On British efforts to take over San Juan del Norte, see Rodríguez, *A Palmerstonian Diplomat.*

15 In 1850 Britain and the United States signed the Clayton-Bulwer Treaty, which established the principle of self-government for the Mosquito Indians and guaranteed that neither the United States nor Britain would try to occupy Central American territory in order to control the canal route. The Nicaraguan Congress rejected this and other treaties that followed it, however. They objected to the fact that it recognized the Mosquito Coast as an entity separate from Nicaragua; they also did not recognize the right of foreign powers to make decisions about a region claimed as part of the country's territory. The dispute was finally resolved in 1860 with the Treaty of Managua between Nicaragua and Great Britain, which recognized Nicaraguan sovereignty over the region but also created a Mosquito Reserve, whose inhabitants enjoyed self-government rights.

16 Salinas, "Memoria a las cámaras legislativas [27 de Febrero de 1849]," 58.

17 Taylor, "Nationalism and Modernity," 45–46.

18 The struggle for the Mosquito Coast was not the only territorial dispute in which Nicaragua was involved during the period of anarchy. But it was the most important of these disputes because it involved the largest expanse of territory (almost 50 percent of the country's land mass), port revenues from San Juan del Norte that were crucial to the state's finances, and ownership of the potential interoceanic canal route.

19 As Offen explains in greater detail in his essay in this volume, the Sambos, or Zambos-Mosquitos, initially lived apart from the "pure," or Tawira, Miskitu and were the first to form an alliance with the British. Both groups joined British raids on different parts of the Captaincy General of Guatemala and captured members of other indigenous groups and sold them to the British as slaves. But both British and Spanish colonial officials distinguished between the Tawira Miskitu, who were perceived as more open to an alliance with Spain, and the Zambos-Mosquitos, who were believed to be more loyal allies of the British. Despite these differences, by the second half of the eighteenth century both groups referred to themselves in proto-national terms as part of a single Mosquito nation, and by the nineteenth century it appears as if the distinction between the two groups had disappeared entirely. Indeed there is little acknowledgment among the Miskitu today of the group's mixed African Amerindian ancestry; they view themselves solely as indigenous. See Romero Vargas, *Las sociedades del Atlántico.*

20 For a more detailed account of Creole ethnogenesis, see Goett, "Diasporic Identities"; Gordon, *Disparate Diasporas,* 35–50.

21 Unfortunately this claim is still uncritically reproduced in much contemporary historiography about the Atlantic coast. Notable exceptions are Goett, "Diasporic Identities"; Gordon, *Disparate Diasporas.*

22 Gordon, *Disparate Diasporas,* 66–67.

23 Justin Wolfe is technically correct when he argues in his essay in this volume referring to mulatto Liberals (such as Sebastián Salinas) from San Felipe who rose to prominence in Nicaragua in the 1840s, "There is little in the record to suggest that Liberal Afro-Nicaraguans looked scornfully upon the Afro-Jamaican leadership of San Juan del Norte or the port's numerous African American entrepreneurs as anything but their counterparts in a regional power struggle." It is also the case, however, that the discourse of civilization and savagery that they and other Nicaraguan officials used to delegitimize Mosquitian claims to sovereignty implicitly and explicitly contested the legitimacy of black and indigenous political power *as such.* Indeed the "deracialized" universalism that Wolfe claims these mulatto Liberals professed was certainly not an option open to the black Creoles and indigenous Miskitu of the Mosquito Coast, precisely because of the racial overtones of the discourse of civilization and progress.

24 Cited in Gámez, *Historia de Nicaragua,* 425.

25 Proclamation of the "Supreme Director of the State of Nicaragua to its Inhabitants, and to the others of Central America [12 November 1847]," enclosed in letter from Frederick Chatfield to Lord Palmerston, 24 December 1847, in United Kingdom, Foreign Office, *Correspondence Respecting the Mosquito Territory,* 2:70.

26 Letter from Sebastián Salinas, secretary of the government of Nicaragua, to Frederick Chatfield, 14 October 1847, in United Kingdom, Foreign Office, *Correspondence Respecting the Mosquito Territory,* 2:66.

27 For further discussion of ideas of race in nineteenth-century Latin America, see Stepan, *The Hour of Eugenics.*

28 Letter from Simón Orosco to Frederick Chatfield [10 November 1842], in Vega Bolaños, *1840–1842,* 317. Underlying British arguments at the time was

> the assumption that the Miskito, though perhaps savages, were a sovereign people, who deserved to be taken seriously as political partners. This view not only accorded with British interests at that time, but could also be justified by the historical traditions concerning relations between the Miskito and British colonial officers, soldiers and traders. In order to undermine these notions it was necessary for the USA and the countries of Central America to demonstrate that the Miskito were not in a position to decide on their own fate and that they could therefore not be considered parties to a treaty. The anti-British side therefore tended to depict a primitive, cruel tribe manipulated by Great Britain for her own purposes, whose chief had been dressed up by the British as a "puppet king." (Wünderich, von Oertzen, and Rossbach, *The Nicaraguan Mosquitia,* 26)

29 The attitudes of Latin American ruling classes toward indigenous people varied considerably in the pre- and postindependence eras. During the Conquest Indians were portrayed as savage cannibals, which served the purpose of justifying the colonizing enterprise, but toward the end of the colonial era criollos rejected European views of Indians as lazy and unproductive because of their natural environment, as such ideas impacted perceptions of criollos as well. In the era preceding independence criollos therefore argued that Indians could be civilized by being brought into contact with European culture and the civilizing process fostered by the use of racial mixing as a form of whitening. After independence, when indigenous groups resisted interference by the new republican states, the pendulum swung back and Latin American elites once again portrayed Indians as savage, anarchic, and in need of forcible civilization.

30 Gámez, *Historia de la costa de Mosquitos*, 78.

31 Ibid., 212.

32 Ibid., 211.

33 Offen, for example, provides a very different reading of the meaning of Miskitu aesthetic practices in his essay in this volume.

34 Gámez, *Historia de la costa de Mosquitos*, 78.

35 Letter from Sebastián Salinas to Chatfield, 14 October 1847, in United Kingdom, Foreign Office, *Correspondence Respecting the Mosquito Territory*, 2:70. Wolfe identifies Salinas as one of the liberal mulattos from San Felipe who rose to prominence during this era.

36 Letter from Mr. Christie to Viscount Palmerston, 5 September 1848, in United Kingdom, Foreign Office, *Correspondence Respecting the Mosquito Territory*, 2:138.

37 "Memoria dirigida por el Ministerio de Estado y el Despacho de Relaciones de Nicaragua a Asamblea Constituyente del mismo Estado, en Diciembre de 1847, sobre los derechos territoriales del propio pais en la costa del norte llamada Mosquitos," enclosure no. 1 in Frederick Chatfield's letter to Lord Palmerston, 19 April 1848, in United Kingdom, Foreign Office, *Correspondence Respecting the Mosquito Territory*, 2:50.

38 "Tratado de Managua," in Pérez Valle, *Expediente de Campos Azules*, 116–20.

39 In 1867, for example, Nicaragua refused to comply with the Treaty of Managua because "the last election of the Mosquito Chief was carried out: first, by foreigners and Creoles without the co-operation of the Indians; and secondly, against the desire of these Indians, who wish to be governed by a bastard son of the last Mosquito Chief." See memorandum and letter from Marshal Martinez, envoy extraordinary and minister plenipotentiary of the Republic of Nicaragua, to Lord Stanley, Britain's foreign minister, 1 October 1867, in United Kingdom, Foreign Office, *Correspondence Respecting the Mosquito Territory*, 3:77.

40 Letter from Carlos Lacayo to F. H. Bingham, the British consul in Bluefields, 16 February 1894, in Cuadra Chamorro, *La reincorporación de la Mosquitia*, 38.

41 Letter from Carlos Lacayo to F. H. Bingham, 3 March 1894, in Cuadra Chamorro, *La reincorporación de la Mosquitia*, 176.

42 Ibid., 191–92.

43 Letter from Chief of Mosquito William Henry Clarence to the Earl of Derby, 6 December 1877, in United Kingdom, Foreign Office, *Correspondence Respecting the Mosquito Territory*, 3:25.

44 "Memorial to the Government of her Britannic Majesty by William Henry Clarence Chief of the Mosquitos," 4 April 1879, enclosed in Letter from Mr. Graham, British consul to Central America, to the Marquis of Salisbury, 8 May 1879, in United Kingdom, Foreign Office, *Correspondence Respecting the Mosquito Territory*, 3:76.

45 I do not discuss the Nicaraguan state's attack on indigenous communal lands in detail in this essay, as my focus is on its policy toward the Mosquito Coast. As was the case with the Mosquito Coast, however, efforts to dismantle indigenous communities and displace indigenous identities in Central and Pacific Nicaragua coincided with the emergence of discourses about the problematic nature of indigenous forms of organization and of Indians' unfitness for citizenship. For more on the Nicaraguan state's efforts to suppress indigenous communities in these regions of the country, see Gould, *To Die in This Way*; Téllez Argüello, *¡Muera la gobierna!*; Wolfe, *The Everyday Nation-State*.

46 Gordon, *Disparate Diasporas*, 122.

47 "Mensaje del Director Supremo, Fruto Chamorro, a la Asamblea Constituyente del estado de Nicaragua, en el día de su instalación [22 de Enero de 1854]," in Esgueva Gómez, *Las constituciones políticas*, 381.

48 "Constitución Política de la República de Nicaragua [19 de Agosto de 1858]," in Esgueva Gómez, *Las constituciones políticas*, 421.

49 Ibid., 421–22, 425.

50 Ibid., 421, 425.

51 Indigenous groups in western and central Nicaragua participated in these struggles as a result of patron-client networks and in order to further their own political agendas, the most important element of which was to resist new taxes and other kinds of state interference in their economic activities, but they did so under the guise of supporting a faction of the ruling class. In the conflict between the Liberals of León and the Conservatives of Granada in 1844–45, for instance, Matagalpa Indians confronted Subtiava Indians on the battlefield, where many of them lost their lives. The former were allies of the Conservatives and the latter of the Liberals, both of whom used the Indians indiscriminately as cannon fodder. Indians had their own reasons for

participating in these struggles, however, one of which may have been obtaining arms to confront local authorities. See Ortega Arancibia, *Cuarenta años*, 61, 73, 81, 108.

52 "Mensaje del Ministerio de estado a Asamblea Constituyente," in United Kingdom, Foreign Office, *Correspondence Respecting the Mosquito Territory*, 2:383.

53 "La pereza," *El Correo del Itsmo de Nicaragua* (Granada), 1 October 1849, cited in Kinloch Tijerino, "Civilización y Barbarie," 266–67.

54 As Wolfe explains in his essay in this volume, this did not mean that Liberal mulattos from San Felipe were excluded from government posts in the first decades of the era of Conservative hegemony, but they never regained the prominence they achieved in the immediate postindependence period. The realignment effected by Conservatives did result in the reinscription of racial hierarchies into the distribution of political power, with a small minority of white families controlling the highest political posts and mestizos, mulattos, and Indians filling lesser government roles.

55 "Decreto de Reincorporación, La Convención Mosquita," in Pérez Valle, *Expediente de Campos Azules*, 227–31.

56 "Tratado entre la Gran Bretaña y la República de Nicaragua, Relativo al Territorio Mosquito," in Pérez Valle, *Expediente de Campos Azules*, 268–69.

57 "Constitución Política de la República de Nicaragua [10 de Diciembre de 1893]" and "Constitución política de la República de Nicaragua [30 de Marzo de 1905]," in Esgueva Gómez, *Las constituciones políticas*, 508, 533.

58 For more on official mestizo nationalisms in Nicaragua in the twentieth century, see Hooker, "Beloved Enemies."

59 Ruiz y Ruiz, *Informe sobre la Costa Atlántica*, 31. Perhaps not coincidentally, Ruiz was a naturalized Nicaraguan citizen of Spanish origin.

60 Ibid., 112–13.

61 The schools run by Moravian missionaries (who had arrived on the Mosquito Coast in 1849), where instruction was in English, were a particular sore spot for Nicaraguan officials. See "Memoria de instrucción pública presentada a la Asamblea Legislativa, 1897," in Pérez Valle, *Expediente de Campos Azules*, 243.

62 Ruiz y Ruiz, *Informe sobre la Costa Atlántica*, 33.

63 Ibid., 77.

64 Ibid., 75.

65 Mena Solorzano, *Apuntes de un soldado*, 235,

66 Cited in Cuadra Chamorro, *La reincorporación*, 164.

67 Ibid., 106.

68 Gordon argues that there was a shift in Creole political attitudes throughout the twentieth century, from an incipient Mosquitian nationalism associated with the Mosquito Kingdom and the Reserve, which initially resulted in a rejection of the Nicaraguan state during the period immediately following

the annexation of the region in 1894, to a more acquiescent position toward Nicaraguan rule from the 1930s onward (*Disparate Diasporas*, 51).

69   "Exposición de los costeños," collected in Ruiz y Ruiz, *Informe*, 133–39.

70   Téllez Argüello, *¡Muera la gobierna!*, 36.

71   The constitution approved in 1986 enshrined the following collective rights for costeños: to "preserve and develop their cultural identity within national unity," to regional autonomy, to "live and develop under forms of organization that correspond to their historical and cultural traditions," to bilingual education, to "the preservation of their cultures, languages, religions and customs," to the communal ownership of land, and to "the enjoyment, use and benefit of the waters and forests of their communal lands." *Constitución Política de Nicaragua* (Managua: Editorial el Amanecer, 1987), 30, 56–57.

72   M. Guillén, *La Prensa*, 21 July 2002, online (accessed 17 May 2007).

73   Cited in Ronald Hill Alvarez, "Un reto al proceso de autonomía del Caribe," *La Prensa*, 5 August 2004: 11A.

The Multigenerational Saga of British
West Indians in Central America, 1870–1940

Lara Putnam

This is the story of the making of a mobile world, a transnational migratory sphere created by hundreds of thousands of men and women who moved between the islands and the rimlands of the Greater Caribbean at the turn of the twentieth century, building multiple and overlapping circuits within which news, remittances, and wayward children circulated. It is the story of the vagaries of race and public authority within one subregion of that mobile world, the coastal lowlands of Central America, where at the start of the twentieth century no bright line separated officials' treatment of dark-skinned immigrants from the lot of other working men and women. And it is the story of the unmaking of that mobile world in the late 1920s and 1930s, as unprecedented antiblack legislation truncated migration across the region, making travel from port to port costly, risky, at times humiliating, at times impossible, fracturing the precarious prosperity the internationalization of household economies had wrought. Scholars studying West Indian migration to individual receiving societies have tended to explain the rise of restrictive legislation in each country on the basis of local issues and national debates. Adopting a regionwide perspective, however, reveals just how sudden and comprehensive the shift was, suggesting that the underlying causes were supranational rather than local in scale. International economic and political developments in the 1920s made nativism an irresistible campaign plank and border control a new hallmark of state sovereignty. This was as true of the agro-export societies of Middle America as it was of the industrialized nations of the North Atlantic. Around the Caribbean it was black men and women who paid the price.

By the end of the nineteenth century British West Indian migrants to Central America had created far-flung social networks that facilitated a continuous flow of people and news between the islands and the isthmus. From the 1870s to the first decade of the twentieth century the main circuits of migration linked Jamaica to Panama and Costa Rica, where canal and railroad construction and expanding banana plantations employed tens of thousands of British West Indians.[1] Some migrants traveled under contract to railroad concessionaires, banana exporters, or Ferdinand de Lesseps's short-lived French canal company, but many more traveled at their own expense. They found work in the expanding service economies of Limón, Colón, Panama City, and other ports or felled trees in the surrounding rain forest to grow bananas and provisions. Others, moving north and south along the coast, created new ties to the English-speaking populations of partial African origin who had carved spaces for themselves in the borderlands between Spanish and English imperial domains in the colonial era, on the Bay Islands and Honduras's northern coast, San Andrés and Providencia, Bluefields, San Juan del Norte (Greytown), Turtle Bogue, Bocas del Toro, and Isla Bastimento.

Meanwhile in the Eastern Caribbean a separate circuit linked the Leeward and Windward Islands, Barbados, and Trinidad to the Guianas, Venezuela, Brazil, and Colombia. Several thousand working men and women did travel from Martinique and Guadeloupe to the isthmus of Panama during the French canal-building effort in the 1880s. But not until the U.S. government began recruiting laborers in Barbados for its own Panama canal project in 1905 did sustained circulation between the Eastern and Western Caribbean begin. Some forty-five thousand Barbadians traveled to Panama during canal construction, roughly half of them formally recruited under contract by the Isthmian Canal Commission.[2] Thousands born elsewhere in the Eastern Caribbean boarded the Panama-bound steamers in Bridgetown; as Bonham Richardson notes, many of these Trinidadians and small islanders had Barbadian roots, for "the extraisland network of families that had been established by Barbadian emigrants late in the nineteenth century" shaped access to the new destination.[3] Eric Walrond, known in the United States as a chronicler of the Harlem

FIGURE 1 "Loading holes with dynamite, Point 2, June 6, 1909." Stereocard image of Panama Canal construction, ca. 1910. Copyright by J. A. Bruce, New York, 1910. *Source*: Prints and Photographs Division, Library of Congress, LC-USZ62–117408.

Renaissance, typified in his own biography the way each wave of migration created resources, networks, and skills that encouraged and inflected the next wave. Walrond was born in 1898 in British Guiana but spent his early years in his mother's native Barbados while his Guyanese father labored in Panama. Walrond's mother and the children followed in 1911. Reared speaking Spanish and English on the streets of Colón, Walrond grew up to be a reporter for the Panama *Star and Herald* before moving on to Harlem in 1918, where he worked as an editor, first for Marcus Garvey's *Negro World* and then for the National Urban League's *Opportunity*. He relocated to England in 1932 and died there in 1966.[4]

The sequential dynamism of construction projects, rain forest logging, and fruit exports at site after site along the Western Caribbean coast meant that, like Walrond, migrants moved on frequently. Some eighty thousand men and women left Jamaica for Panama during canal construction in the first decade of the twentieth century, but only a small portion stayed on the isthmus.[5] The stories of young people involved in court cases in Costa Rica at the turn of the century bear witness to these traveling lives. Constance Porter Brown's baptismal certificate declared that she had been born in "Port Lemon" on 21 August 1883 and baptized the following year by the Protestant chaplain of the Canal Company in Colón, Republic of Colombia.[6] By 1901 Constance and her father, both described as Jamaicans, were back in Port Limón.[7] Eight-year-old Sarah White and her younger sister were orphaned in Bocas del Toro in 1903 and taken in by their "blood aunt and godmother" Wilhemena Parker, who had been born in Penomené, Panama, and now lived in Cahuita, Costa Rica, with a Jamaican husband.[8] Adelaide Brown was born in Colón in 1886; eight years later she was living in Costa Rica's highland capital San José, running errands for the West Indian woman into whose care her mother had placed her.[9]

Opportunities in the expanding economies of Central America had become part of the laboring repertory of the British Caribbean working classes.[10] The Panama Canal's completion in 1914 would redirect those energies rather than end them. The sudden drop in construction jobs in Panama, the virtual halt of banana exports from Jamaica and Costa Rica during the First World War, and the meteoric rise of sugar prices during and immediately after that war combined to reconfigure the Caribbean migratory field. After 1915 Cuba's booming sugar economy became the prime destination for workers from the Western Caribbean, while the Dominican Republic came to occupy a similar position for Eastern Caribbean sojourners. A few Barbadians and St. Lucians made their way to Costa Rica in this era, and a few Jamaicans settled in the Dominican Republic. A yellowing hymnal that lies today in the San Esteban Episcopal Church of San Pedro de Macoris is inscribed in careful script, "Mary Buchanan, Port Limon, Costa Rica, 1922," silent testimony to a young woman's travels (or a multigenerational journey) from the British islands to Central America to a Dominican sugar port.[11] However, in general the Eastern and Western Caribbean remained separate migratory circuits during the interwar years, overlapping only on the isthmus of Panama—"labour clearing-house for the region," as one journalist put it—and in New York City.[12] Large-scale migration to this last destination began as U.S. canal construction commenced and grew rapidly, averaging 4,800 arrivals each year from 1905 to 1919 and 7,300 each year from 1920 to 1924. By 1930 Caribbean immigrants and their children made up nearly a quarter of the population of Harlem.[13]

The circular and repeat migration that had been typical of both Western and Eastern Caribbean circuits before the Great War was replicated in the widening migratory circuits of the interwar years. Some ten thousand Eastern Caribbeans found work on the oilfields of Maracaibo, Venezuela, after 1916; Methodist preachers from Port-of-Spain traveled every Sunday to preach in the camps.[14] A generation later the population of Trinidad would include over three thousand people born in Venezuela.[15] British West Indian migration to Cuba began when travel to Panama was at its height and included significant numbers whose search for opportunity had already taken them far from home. In 1913 Cuban officials reported 1,010 arrivals from Costa Rica, essentially all of whom must have been British West Indians, since only thirty-three people of Central American nationality arrived that same year.[16] Nearly one-fifth of the more than seven thousand Jamaicans who entered Cuba in 1916 reported that their previous place of residence had not been their country of birth; in 1917 more than one-fourth of the nearly eight thousand incoming Jamaicans said the same.[17] By 1940 the cumulative total of Jamaicans who had arrived in Jamaica *from* Cuba exceeded direct departures *for* Cuba from Jamaica by more than six thousand, a statistic that reflects Cuba's role as a subsequent destination for Jamaicans who had originally left for Central America and for the children of such migrants.[18] The United States was another rising destination for those whose traveling days had started long before. In 1918 and 1919 British West Indians from Central America made up roughly one-sixth of West Indian immigrants arriving in the United States.[19]

Travel to Panama, Cuba, and the United States had become integrated into the rhythms of kinship and rites of passage of the British Caribbean

FIGURE 2 "Down by the old sea wall—passengers embarking for an ocean steamer, Panama."
Stereocard image of travelers leaving Panama by boat, ca. 1907. Copyright by H. C. White,
North Bennington, Vermont, 1907. *Source*: Prints and Photographs Division, Library of
Congress, LC-USZ62–120164.

islands. Born in rural Jamaica in 1901, Miss Gatha recalled for an inter-
viewer in 1975 how her father's wife, her stepmother, had been shamed
by the birth of a child whose dark skin seemed evidence of infidelity:
"When de baby born, de baby was dark, and it should be brown because
me moder . . . me foder brown, she brown. Well, dat was the breaking up
of dat. . . . She go away and go to Panama." Her father spent the rest of
his life as the local butcher, Miss Gatha reported, adding only later on, as
an afterthought, "And him go Cuba plenty time."[20] Another interviewee,

born in St. Catherine's parish in 1888, was bemused by a question regarding her schoolmates: "I don't know if they die now, or they alive for everybody travel gone out. Some gone to Cuba, some gone America, some gone to New York and all about."[21] A third respondent explained that his aunt ran a farm in the 1920s: "Her husband went on to Cuba and he from Cuba to Colon and all the rest. Well she never travel but he travels and he comes and go, and then she would run the farm while he is away. . . . You know he would spend a year. Come back, spend a few months and then goes again."[22] Novels written in Jamaica in the first decades of the twentieth century likewise abound with offhand references to a husband "away in Colon," a brother seeking success in "Costa Rica or Panama," a shopkeeper who holds forth nightly on "the Government and the Parochial Board, and the tax on the land, and the women he had met some time before in Nicaragua."[23] Central American destinations had become part of the local landscape.

THE INDETERMINATE COLOR OF THE LAW:
CARIBBEAN CENTRAL AMERICA IN THE
FIRST TWO DECADES OF THE TWENTIETH CENTURY

It was the generalized absence of legal restrictions on migrants' comings and goings that made this kind of circulation possible. At the end of the nineteenth century the policies of circum-Caribbean states regarding race and immigration were internally contradictory and sporadically enforced. In Costa Rica, for instance, a law enacted in 1862 prohibited colonization schemes offering land to immigrants of "African or Chinese race."[24] Yet Costa Rican officials actively encouraged West Indian former railroad workers to claim homesteads in Limón in the 1880s and 1890s.[25] In the same years Afro–North American and Afro-Caribbean men not only labored on the railroads of Guatemala, but opened cantinas, ran licensed gambling dens, and wooed Guatemalan women in towns up and down the line.[26] For black migrants, as indeed for all working people of the Western Caribbean, there was a fundamental distinction between the region's U.S.-controlled zones, such as the Canal Zone in Panama or the "white zones" within United Fruit Company towns, and the Central American ports and towns and the countryside that surrounded them. The former were directly administered by North American authorities, who enforced Jim Crow segregation and offered nonwhite noncitizens few formal rights and no court of appeal.[27] In contrast the spaces outside the zones, although similarly oriented to export production and international commerce, were policed and governed by Central American states. Here there were different authorities and different laws, structures that migrants might, with enough connections, money, persistence, or luck, get to work for them.

Indeed in the early twentieth century, reflecting the historical development of Central America's Caribbean lowlands within the Atlantic system, it was not uncommon for state authority here to have a black face and speak English creole. Along Nicaragua's Atlantic coast in the 1920s, wrote the journalist Carleton Beals, "A large proportion of the officials are Negroes, originally from Jamaica or Belize. In Greytown a Negro customs official directed the Negroes and one Indian inspecting my baggage. In Bluefields a Negro youth filed my cables; another accepted my registered letters."[28] Custom dictated no sharp color line in the public offices of these ports, and expedience demanded bringing newcomers into the structures of governance. In early twentieth-century Limón, Afro-Caribbean immigrants were regularly appointed as *jueces de paz* (justices of the peace) in their communities of residence, charged with registering civil data, levying fines, responding to crises in the public order, and transporting arrestees to authorities in Port Limón.[29] Other black foreigners were hired as salaried police.[30] Two policemen together patrolled Matina's public market in 1902, one whom locals described as "blanco" and who came from Costa Rica's highland capital of San José, and one whom locals described as "negro" and who gave his nationality as French (most likely an immigrant from Guadeloupe or Martinique).[31] When the Costa Rican policeman assigned to 12 Mile got drunk and picked a fight with some West Indian workers in 1912, he was removed from the post and replaced by forty-six-year-old Ernesto Evans, originally of Kingston, Jamaica, who had already served for several years as a *policía de orden y seguridad* in San José, Costa Rica.[32]

Panama's politicolegal system too had room for immigrants willing to work the system, as Walrond captured in his portrait of "the dean of the *tinterillos*, the celebrated Dr. Cecilio Rhodes, a West Indian Negro," presiding over the Colón *alcaldía*. (The same short story underlines the potential frailty of immigrants' clientelist claims, though, for in it the Panamanian *alcalde* ultimately disavows the Anguillan immigrant journalist who has loyally championed the alcalde's Partido Liberal in the *Aspinwall Voice*.)[33] Just who could police where and by what means became an enduring point of contention within and around the Canal Zone. Afro-Panamanian policemen with at least de jure race-blind authority patrolled the terminal cities (Colón and Panama) outside the Canal Zone in the Republic of Panama, a fact some northern travelers found more than a little disturbing. Harry Franck, a U.S. government employee, wrote of the Canal Zone boundary in 1913, "There is no more line of demarkation between Cristobal and Colon than between Ancon and Panama. A khaki-clad Zone policeman patrols one sidewalk, a black one in the sweltering dark blue uniform and heavy wintry helmet of the Republic of Panama lounges on the other side of a certain street. . . . Cross the street and you feel at once a foreigner."[34]

Dismissing the Panamanian police force with characteristic condescension, Franck nevertheless noted the integration of some British West Indian immigrants into the webs of patronage it represented. Describing Panama City he wrote, "Policemen with their clubs swarm everywhere, for no particular reason than that the little republic is forbidden to play at army, and with the presidential election approaching political henchmen must be kept good-humored. Not a few of these officers are West Indians who speak not a word of Spanish—nor any other tongue, strictly speaking."[35] Yankees did not always laugh off so lightly the role of police in Panamanian national claims. After police used force to end rioting by U.S. canal employees and servicemen in Panama City's red-light district in 1915, U.S. authorities demanded the Panamanian force be permanently disarmed, inspiring enormous resentment.[36] In these years and later at least a quarter of the Canal Zone police force was made up of West Indians serving under white American officers. Within the Zone men of color were assigned only to "local-rate," that is, nonwhite, neighborhoods, and even there their authority was circumscribed by race: "They could not arrest a white American even for a traffic violation in a colored neighborhood."[37]

The fact that immigrants could become policemen did not mean that the policing of immigrants was fair. Denunciations of arbitrary arrest and mistreatment appeared periodically in Port Limón's West Indian press.[38] Abuses in Panama seem to have been more frequent and more violent.[39] In Guatemala black migrants found local officials eager for profit and not

FIGURE 3 "A picturesque corner in the market, native women assorting fruit, Panama City." Stereocard image, ca. 1907. Stereo copyrighted by H. C. White Co., North Bennington, Vermont, 1907.
Source: Prints and Photographs Division, Library of Congress, LC-USZ62–75741.

loath to use force to get it.[40] National authorities were still in the process of institutionalizing their rule over Central America's Caribbean lowlands, attempting to build the state presence that indigenous and Afro-descended populations' manipulation of imperial rivalries had denied the Spanish crown up through the end of colonial rule.[41] In the early decades of the twentieth century it was local impulse, improvisation, and greed rather than national policies or fixed racial boundaries that determined the treatment immigrants met in Central America. The same official might side with an "insolent negro" in one instance and jail a black woman without cause in another.[42] Where state formation had proceeded to the point that there were multiple branches of government at work in the lowlands, migrants played officials off each other. In this way even penniless and illiterate immigrants might acquire well-placed allies. In 1907 the wealthy Costa Rican Pánfilo Valverde filed an eviction suit to remove West Indian men he called squatters from lands he claimed just south of Port Limón. The local justice of the peace arrested one West Indian defendant for taking coconuts from the disputed property; the local police officer set him free and gave him back his coconuts. Valverde's lawyer complained, "The *negro*, advised by don Lucas [Alvarado, former alcalde of Limón], not only believes himself the rightful owner of the terrain, but has gone so far as to file criminal charges against the justice of the peace, who fearing for his life has disappeared from town."[43]

Thus British West Indians at the turn of the century found in Central American officialdom both ad hoc access and ad hoc abuse. In this they were not alone: local populations as well as highland working folk passing through were met with a similar mix. It was a moment in which national governments up and down the isthmus sought to expand their authority over and increase profits from the Caribbean lowlands. That the labor force building the railroads, plantations, telegraphs, and docks essential to that expansion was largely black-skinned raised few eyebrows as yet in the highland capitals. For the steamy lowlands to be worked by men of African descent seemed not merely traditional but climatologically inevitable, and thus immigrant workers' blackness was neither alien nor inherently menacing. Over the course of the nineteenth century Central American elites had rewritten their cities' largely mulatto and *pardo* past with a set of racialized myths that claimed only Spanish and indigenous progenitors for the nation. These myths soon became robust enough to admit black and part-black Madonnas, saints, and soldiers as national heroes. Turn-of-the-century Central American social hierarchies did not rest upon claims of black inferiority. Other ideas played that role: ideas about virtue, piety, and obedience to paternal authority in Costa Rica; ideas about Indian moral and intellectual backwardness—and the redemptive potential of state intervention—in Nicaragua, El Salvador, and Guatemala. Claims of cultural characteristics "borne in the blood," of national character and racial progress were batted about, usually with respect to indigenous populations. But before the 1920s we find no polarized notion of black vice as the antithesis of white virtue in Central American public debate.

THE SUDDEN RISE OF ANTIBLACK STATE RACISM
IN THE CIRCUM-CARIBBEAN

In 1915 the Costa Rican congressman Leonidas Briceño—alarmed, he said, by recent murders of Costa Rican women by black husbands or lovers in Port Limón—proposed a law to prohibit Costa Rican women from marrying black or Asian men or any others with biological conditions that might lead to "degeneration of their descendants."[44] Briceño's inclusion of racial criteria within a proposed program of marital prophylaxis was a harbinger of things to come; a decade later eugenicist analyses would be invoked across the region to justify black exclusion laws and premarital certification alike. But in 1915 the proposal did not prosper. Indeed what is striking when we survey the Spanish-speaking receiving societies of the Western Caribbean is that despite the republics' avowed desire to "improve" the "national stock" by promoting "good immigration," usually specified as "European immigration," entry by immigrants of African ancestry was nowhere outlawed, and rarely even restricted, up until the mid-1920s.[45]

Instead it was Asian and Middle Eastern immigrants who bore the brunt of early exclusionary laws. Panama forbade immigration by Chinese, Turks, and Syrians in 1904 (that is, in the first year of its independent existence); in 1917 this was expanded to include "North Africans of the Turkish Race."[46] El Salvador declared all Chinese "pernicious aliens" and prohibited their entry in 1897; later laws excluded Arabs, Malayans, Libyans, Turks, Gypsies, Syrians, and Palestinians as well.[47] The Costa Rican state forbade all future Chinese entry in 1897, and in 1904 added Arabs, Turks, Syrians, Armenians, and "gypsies of any nationality" to the list of "prohibited races." A decree of 1912 extended the prohibition to "individuos de la clase coolie," with the intention of stemming the immigration of South Asian former indentured workers by way of Jamaica and Panama, touching off an extended inquiry into "the ethnography of India" in search of markers to identify the particular "degenerate class," of "aboriginal race," whose exclusion was intended.[48] Small but visible Chinese and Lebanese communities grew up in cities and towns across the region in these years, testimony to the systematic illegalities that characterized the policing of borders and ports.

By banning Asian and North African immigrants Central American states could indulge in fantasies of racial exclusivity without incurring economic costs. The United Fruit Company, the Isthmian Canal Commission, and other powerful employers wanted access to West Indian workers willing to labor cheaply and sought to put them to work in regions whose populations owed much to earlier waves of the African diaspora, lands already linked to blackness in the imagined geography of national elites. Under these circumstances the arrival of black immigrants seemed a small price to pay for the expansion of transportation infrastructure and plantation agriculture seen as essential to the long-term progress of these regions (and equally essential to the short-term profits of the men passing the laws). One can find scattered writings by Central American elites before the 1920s that question this calculus or call attention to perceived problems posed by the thousands of West Indian immigrants making space for themselves on "national soil." Yet the fact is that circum-Caribbean Latin American states did not forbid black immigration before the mid-1920s, nor did they systematically restrict black entry through extralegal means.

In contrast, beginning in the late 1920s governments across the region not only outlawed black immigration on the explicit basis of race, but in fact employed legal sanctions alongside extralegal pressures to limit West Indian entry and in some cases even expel significant numbers of Afro-Caribbeans, some of whom were second- and third-generation residents of the lands they left behind. In Honduras new laws enacted in 1923 and 1926 restricted black immigrants' employment; in 1929 blacks were added to the list of "restricted races" obliged to tender a $2,500 deposit to enter the country; and in 1934 a new law flatly prohibited the entry of "Negroes, coolies, gypsies, and Chinese."[49] A law in Panama in 1926 added "Negroes whose native language is not Spanish" to the list of "undesirable" races and forbade immigration; a law in 1928 limited access to citizenship for those already in the country. In 1941 a new constitution stripped black immigrants' children born after 1928 of their Panamanian nationality.[50] In 1931 Guatemala outlawed immigration by foreigners of the "Negro race" yet retained an exception for those able to pay an entry fee of two hundred dollars; in 1936 even this loophole was removed, replaced with total prohibition "for ethnic reasons" of entry by those of the "Negro" or "yellow or Mongolian" race or "gypsies of any nationality."[51] Similarly in 1936 Nicaragua excluded negros along with Chinese, Arabs, Syrians, Armenians, Gypsies, and "coolies" (these prohibitions could be waived with special permission and a deposit of one thousand dollars).[52] Even nations with no black immigrants embraced the antiblack immigrant fervor. A new law in El Salvador outlawed the entry of "members of the coloured races," including "Negroes" for the first time, in 1925—this in a country with no access to the Caribbean Sea and no West Indian population to speak of.[53]

What had changed? Economic crises shook the region beginning in the 1920s, as world commodity prices contracted and the largely monocropdependent economies of the circum-Caribbean found their export engines stalled. No longer was labor scarcity the problem in Central America. Rather there was rising unemployment, and in each receiving society there was an increasingly vocal labor movement demanding national action to remedy it. The crisis was real. Yet that fact should not be allowed to naturalize the racially defined xenophobia that resulted. After all, the region had experienced export shocks before—North Atlantic financial crises in the 1890s, shipping disruption during the First World War—and receiving societies had not legislated against black immigrants in response. The explanation lies not merely in local conflicts over employment, but in an international shift in the definition, aims, and technologies of state sovereignty.

THE INTERNATIONAL CONTEXT OF MIGRATION RESTRICTION

The U.S. Johnson-Reed Act of 1924 endorsed eugenic criteria and cultural "assimilability" as the guiding principles of U.S. immigration policy. Whereas before only Asian immigration had been barred on the basis of race, now Southern, Central, and Eastern Europeans found their numbers restricted as well. [54] The new limits on visas issued in the British West Indies cut annual black immigration to the United States by 90 percent in a single year. [55] Bowing to pressure from agribusiness interests dependent on Mexican migrant labor and Department of State and Department of Commerce officials reluctant to antagonize neighboring nations and their potential markets, U.S. restrictionists ultimately agreed to class those born in Mexico, Cuba, Haiti, the Dominican Republic, and "the independent countries of Central and South America" as nonquota immigrants, subject to screening for individual eugenic qualities but with no categorical limitation by nationality or race.[56] Thus unlike governments of the British West Indies, Central American governments faced no onslaught of distressed would-be immigrants. (In 1929 the U.S. consul in Jamaica had a total of 140 visas to allocate and a waiting list of three thousand.)[57] Yet governments across the region were well aware of the shift in U.S. policy. Indeed with the move to "remote control" screening via U.S. consulates abroad, Central American officials, like their counterparts elsewhere, became part of the international apparatus of U.S. migratory control.[58] Beginning in 1924 they had to issue passports to their own nationals in accordance with new U.S. entry regulations and provide all those wishing to travel to the United States with the official documents (birth certificate and certificate of good conduct) now demanded by U.S. consuls in order to *visar* the passports.[59]

The increasing prominence of immigration issues in inter-American affairs was reflected in the first Pan-American Conference of Eugenics and Homiculture, held in Havana in December 1927. Sixteen nations, among them Panama, Costa Rica, El Salvador, Guatemala, and Honduras, as well as other key British West Indian receiving societies, including Cuba, the Dominican Republic, Venezuela, Colombia, and the United States, sent delegates.[60] The conference was convened and guided by Dr. Domingo Ramos, a Cuban health authority, working in close consultation with Charles Davenport, head of the Carnegie Institution's Eugenics Record Office, whose advocacy had been crucial in shaping the Johnson-Reed Act.[61] The first item on the agenda: "Immigration in relation to physical, mental and moral conditions of population."[62] As Dr. Rafael Martinez Ortiz, Cuban secretary of state, explained in his opening remarks, "Efforts to improve man at the individual level in our respective countries [would be for naught if] we observe with indifferent neglect the entry into our societies of individuals or of races incapable of amalgamating or fusioning with ours . . . [or with] defective cerebral organization insufficient and inadequate for the development of the high functions of modern people."[63] Likewise Ramos insisted that the first of two steps necessary "to defend and seek out for America the seed capable of evolving in a positive way" was to institute "an immigration policy similar to that adopted by the United States of North America, imitating them in this as they were imitated by other countries of the New World in the emancipatory Revolution and the Abolition of Slavery."[64] (Ramos's grip on historical chronology was weak, to say the least, since with the exceptions of Cuba and Brazil *all* Latin American nations had abolished slavery at least a full generation before the United States managed to do so.) The stakes of population management could not be higher: "Future generations will depend upon our present decisions. Those nations that guided by science strive to create biologically strong populations will in the future dominate those who do not wish to see this truth."[65]

The very notion of a pan-American eugenics presumed that all nations attending the conference were peers and allies in this pursuit of biological strength. In their opening statements Ramos and Martinez Ortiz had made sure to celebrate "the two great and principal stocks to which [the participants] belong[ed]": "[We are] fortunate [that] our Hemisphere is, in great majority, populated by two superior races . . . the Latin . . . and the Saxon."[66] In other words pan-American parity in the eugenicist project depended on the claim that the "Latin" race in Latin America was unitary, eugenic, and prevalent, a claim that Davenport, in this setting, left undisturbed. But in other venues U.S. eugenicists had not minced words. Less than 10 percent of the population of Latin America was white, concluded the Princeton economist Robert Foerster in a report in 1925 solicited by Senator Johnson's Committee on Immigration and Naturalization (to which Davenport and his deputy, Harry Laughlin, were regular advisors). "In no comparable area of the earth's surface has there been so extensive a crossing of diverse or distant races"—with predictably lamentable results.[67] To permit Latin Americans entry to the United States was short-sighted folly. The "economic argument for immigration has always been dangerous. No man is a worker alone. He is also a citizen and must further be viewed as the father of more citizens also."[68] Thus the "political effects" of "race factors" persist and spread. "In its simplest terms, then, the question of Latin American Immigration may be stated thus: Are the race elements involved therein such as this country should to-day welcome into its race stock? To this question the answer is bound to be negative."[69]

Such views could not be uttered in Havana. Davenport carefully eschewed statements about the relative worth of different races, even as he sustained—in lectures on "immigration and race crossing" and "race crossing, with picture plates"—a belief in racial distinction that was reductionist even by the standards of the day.[70] Responding to Davenport's account of U.S. immigration law, the Mexican delegate Dr. Rafael Santamarina came close to puncturing the pretense of pan-American mutuality. Davenport, noted Santamarina, claimed that radical legislation had proved necessary for the United States "to limit the number of [immigrants] who do not have desirable physical, mental, and moral conditions." "And I ask myself," Santamarina went on, "these physical, mental, and moral conditions, considered inferior, is that referring to the inferiority of the country of origin?" As he pointed out, the world had already witnessed the "unscrupulous" misuse of test results by "some American authors, including prestigious psychologists," to claim that Mexican immigrant children were "of inferior mental ability—which is absolutely false."[71] The example encapsulated a broader truth: that in the eugenic project actually undertaken by the United States, Latin American nations were not respected peers and partners but targets of disdainful study.

Some delegates joined the Mexican representative in expressing discomfort with the U.S. approach to restriction. (Given the gravity of the subtext, the discussion was framed as an elliptical debate over whether Davenport's presentation had been a "proposition," a "reference," an "exposition," or a "clarification.") The Panamanian delegate, in contrast, embraced Davenport's position, proudly asserting that his own country, like the United States, had "found it necessary [to] act drastically in this problem," because West Indian workers introduced to build the canal had "scattered in the populations of Panama City and Colon, impeding the establishment of appropriate eugenic regulations."[72] His presentation of his country's solution encapsulated the intellectually incoherent, politically indispensable slippage between biological, cultural, and imperial boundaries typical of policymakers' contortions in this era:

> Instead of a prohibition by nationality in our laws, what exists is a prohibition on races, so that, as was discussed at length in the Congress of my country, when that law was subjected to debate with respect to the term that was used at first, what first was said was that Antilleans of inferior race, of coloured race, could not enter my country, and precisely because there are other countries of Latin origin, located within the Antilles, therefore we made a specific exception for those countries, that is, Puerto Rico, Santo Domingo and Cuba.[73]

In other words, the claim to Latin American racial homogeneity and eugenic worth would be sustained by tracing a bright line between the populations of the British Caribbean and those of the Spanish-speaking Greater Caribbean. The overlapping eddies of African diasporic migration into and around the Caribbean, formerly accepted as a climatologically necessary component of the tropical lowlands, had to be retroactively erased so that territory, nationality, and race could be treated as coterminous.

Until the 1920s the U.S. government position on immigration restriction in Central America, to the extent that one existed, had been identical to the United Fruit Company's: employers should be free to combine workers and worksites at will regardless of territorial boundaries, citizenship, or color. After the passage of the new U.S. immigration acts and regulations of 1924–29 this was no longer the case. Immigrants who pushed the national stock of nonquota states in noneugenic directions constituted a future challenge to the United States itself. Latin American delegates at the Pan-American Conference understood this perfectly well. More than once Ramos reminded those present, "Fortunately, up until now there is no migration problem among the nations of the Americas, [but if their nations do not design immigration policies to] accept the desirable ones and reject the others . . . it will result that the United States, in accordance with their policy on this matter, will fix a quota for the entrance in their country of individuals proceeding from American nations, as they are doing now with individuals proceeding from Europe."[74] Even as delegates weakened or removed from Ramos's drafted Eugenic Code provisions for national eugenic registries, premarital screening, and involuntary sterilization, Ramos's proposed provisions regarding immigration control were preserved largely intact. Item 9 of the final text read, "The nations of America will issue and apply laws of immigration with intention to bar the entry into their territory of individuals from races whose association with the natives may be considered biologically undesirable."[75] Given Davenport's conference presentation on the "disharmonies" of "negro-white hybrids," which spawned mulattos with "conflicting instincts," "dissatisfied and often rebellious," discontent with their own "intellectual inadequacy," and with an "extraordinarily high rate" of tuberculosis and venereal disease, there could be no doubt that black immigrants were among those to be barred.[76] In rewriting immigration laws in the following years Latin American republics positioned themselves as proud collaborators in rather than targets of the U.S.-led project of eugenic exclusion.

Even as U.S. restrictionists worked behind the scenes to curtail Caribbean migration into Latin republics, Latin American anti-imperialists agitated publicly for the same goal in similar terms. Perhaps this should not surprise us. Historians note that "eugenics belonged to the political vocabulary of virtually every significant modernizing force between the two world wars."[77] Certainly this was true of the populists and progressives of the Spanish-speaking circum-Caribbean. Denouncing the racial menace of the "alien" workforce introduced by foreign capitalists became a key rhetorical tool of rising politicians across the region, who thus positioned themselves as defenders of the nation's "blood stock," "native soil," and "national" wealth, all at the same time.[78] The middle-class politicians and labor leaders who began to demand a voice in political debate in the 1920s and 1930s repeatedly cited U.S. companies' "importation" of "servile" foreign labor as evidence of investors' rapacious disregard for the host nation's long-term interests. A typical editorial in 1927 asked, "Is Cuba being Africanized?": "It is the truth, the sad and painful truth, that for many years Cuba has been Africanizing . . . by allowing the entrance of undesirable, cheap, and exploitable immigrants, who dislodge the native and the good immigrant and reaffirm even more the economic power of Yankee capitalism."[79] Costa Rican congressmen debated the terms of a new United Fruit Company contract in remarkably similar terms in 1930, denouncing the imperialists' self-interested "Africanization" of the Atlantic coast.[80] Ironically the simultaneous decisions of governments across the region to stop "allowing the entrance" of those "undesirable, cheap, and exploitable" black immigrants itself bore witness to Yankee power. As local economies contracted in the worsening worldwide economic crisis, U.S.-owned enterprises around the region had ever-increasing numbers of hungry, unemployed workers to choose from. The simultaneous shifts in the U.S. government position and in employers' labor force needs made immigrant workers an irresistible target for Latin American politicians, whether they were pursuing substantive populist reforms or were merely seeking to mask with nationalist rhetoric the continued lack of popular participation in the economic and political systems of their nations.

LOCAL CONSEQUENCES, LOCALIZATION AS CONSEQUENCE

When economic crisis hit in the 1920s, it did so at a moment when international political developments had raised the cachet of certain exclusionary technologies and decreased the weight of certain residents' claim to political voice and individual rights. The new fusion of culture, population, and nation was summed up in Panamanian nationalists' call for state action to remove the Afro-Caribbeans now seen as alien bodies and analogized to microbial infestation: "We have a Latin civilization which is profoundly endangered unless we take the measures necessary to counteract the establishment here of a powerful nucleus of an alien race, with all of its characteristic manifestations."[81] At a very basic level the role of the state in relation to something now reified as "the national population" had changed, in a way that meant that the movement of Afro-Caribbeans in and out of territories they had long settled came to be denounced as a menacing incursion, a threat to working-class welfare and national destiny alike.

The case of Costa Rica is instructive. As late as 1924 Costa Rican congressmen voted to *reduce* the entry fee paid by immigrants—essentially all of whom were Afro-Caribbean—in order to stimulate immigration, increase the labor supply in the Caribbean lowlands, and reduce the wage differential then tempting central highland peasants to seek work in the lowland region, whose "treacherous climate," the congressmen insisted, ruined highlanders' health.[82] Only a decade later the Costa Rican government was attempting to ban all Caribbean immigration, treating racial mixing as a far greater public health threat than climate shifts. In 1934 the Costa Rican foreign minister instructed all Costa Rican consuls abroad "to refrain from issuing passports or visas to persons belonging to the Black race, until further notice," as an interim measure while the government considered reforming immigration laws to restrict the entry of "persons of the Black race."[83] Explaining these shifting politics of race in Costa Rica, British observers claimed that economic crisis and demographic change were bringing black people into white places for the first time. British Consul Sir J. Crosby wrote from Panama to the British Foreign Office:

When reporting on my last visit to San Jose, I made mention of the threat to the racial purity of the Costa Rican highlands arising out of the tendency of coloured labourers of West Indian (negro) extraction to drift up in search of work from the low-lying region on the Atlantic seaboard. These people, the majority of whom are either British subjects or their locally-born offspring, are now many of them without means of subsistence on account of the languishing condition of the banana and cacao industries, which used to provide them with a livelihood. Their employment on the development of the banana plantations in the neighbourhood of Port Limon has always been tolerated, and even encouraged, by the native Costa Rican, who is himself a highlander, and does not take kindly to the tropical heat at lower altitudes, but it is another matter when the negro gives evidence of a desire to invade the more elevated districts.[84]

The eugenic risks denounced by Congressman Briceño two decades earlier to no avail now claimed the attention of a wide range of government officials: "The menace, economic no less than ethnological, thus offered is potentially a serious one, and Sr. Gurdián, the Foreign Minister, is fully alive to it." Such a menace demanded government action, both to regulate national space by closing borders to new arrivals and geographically segregating those British West Indians already settled in Costa Rica, and to regulate intimate space by banning intermarriage. Foreign Minister Gurdián, Crosby wrote, "would like to see the enactment of legislation forbidding the negro to settle above a certain limit, and he would go so far as to prohibit mixed marriages even in the lowlands." The regulation of residential space in turn depended upon policing the borders of civic belonging: civil rights must be redefined as dependent upon citizenship, and citizenship must be reaffirmed as a matter of ancestry rather than birthplace. In his confidential dispatch Crosby added, "The late minister for Foreign Affairs (Sr. Pacheco) once told me that there were constitutional difficulties in the way of a policy of residential restriction for the black elements among the population, but Sr. Gurdián apparently does not regard this obstacle as being insurmountable, since most of the negros born in Costa Rica are of foreign parentage, and are therefore not nationals of the country in contemplation of the local law." The proposed measures met with the British diplomat's frank approval, given the alternative: "Of the unpleasant possibilities of the situation there can be no doubt, and, if Costa Rica is not to imitate the example of Panama, which is already on the way to becoming a black republic, it behooves her statesmen to grapple with the problem while it is yet time."[85]

Calls for racial segregation sounded loudly in Costa Rica's Spanish-language press, with the railway tunnel at Turrialba repeatedly cited as the proper boundary between black lowlands and white highlands. Such pronouncements were met with a mixture of incredulity and derision by the West Indian press in Port Limón, who stood by the long-standing definition of citizenship as determined by birthplace rather than ancestry and clearly expected the national government to do the same. The editors of the Limón *Searchlight* wrote in 1930:

There is much complaint on the part of some thoughtless Costa Ricans of what is considered "Encroachment of coloured people beyond the Tunnel" in a complaint by some "egoist" to the correspondent of The Tribuna, he claims there is a law forbidding the entry of coloured people Beyond the Tunnel; does that gentleman forget that [former president] don Thomas Guardia, contracted those coloured people here to do the work that could not be done by him [during railroad construction in the 1870s], and after those people fulfilled that mission is it fair to tell their progeny "Costa Ricans" by birth that they cannot have free access to any part of the country in which they were born??

Is that gentleman suggesting the Division of the Country from the Tunnel to San Jose white, and Tunnel to Limon governed by blacks?[86]

Predicating their mockery on the assumption that local birth conferred territorial entitlement and political rights, the *Searchlight*'s editors were sadly behind the times.

No policies of race-based geographic restriction were ever formally enacted within Costa Rica, although the persistence of widespread beliefs to the contrary attests to the intensity of extralegal practices that accomplished similar results.[87] "If a *negro* came into the white side of town, we drove him out with stones [*le echábamos a pedradas*]," reminisced one woman from Turrialba. "My parents were forced off the train in Turrialba, they weren't allowed to continue," insisted a Costa Rica–born woman in Jamaica, sixty years after the fact.[88] The informal violence that policed spatial segregation within the Costa Rican territory left scarred memories but no legislative trace. Ultimately constitutional guarantees and the ambiguous boundaries of citizenship did indeed stand in the way of legal restrictions on mobility within the national territory.[89] But the same was not true of Costa Rica's external frontiers. In 1942 "the black race" was for the first time included alongside the Chinese, Arabs, Turks, Syrians, Gypsies, and "coolies" whose immigration to Costa Rica had long been forbidden.[90] With this move the ban on black immigration to the Spanish-speaking republics of Central America was complete. In less than a generation the ports of the isthmus's Caribbean coastline, long open gateways to the sea highway that carried folks from place to place over the course of their laboring lives, had become instead the outermost limits of lawful mobility.

CONCLUSION

The British West Indian communities of the Spanish-speaking Greater Caribbean, home to more than a hundred thousand immigrants and their descendants in 1930, would survive despite the economic pain and political pressures of the interwar years. But from the 1930s onward these communities no longer functioned as parts of a single social whole. The transnational character of the circum-Caribbean migratory sphere had been fractured by radical new limits on migrants' comings and goings, limits put into place by a new class of politicians who claimed to speak for the needs of mestizo nations. It was against those claims, and within those national frames, that Afro-Caribbean communities in Panama, Costa Rica, Nicaragua, Honduras, and Guatemala would be forced to define their collective identities and political destinies over the following half-century.

Where once the porosity, flexibility, and corruption of early twentieth-century Central American states had offered British Caribbean sojourners ad hoc access alongside extralegal abuse, by the middle of the twentieth century Central America's more ambitious and effective nation-states demanded encompassing change in return for permanent citizenship. Yet even when the price of cultural assimilation was paid—when ackee and salt-fish breakfasts gave way to *gallo pinto*, tortillas, or *arepas*—that new citizenship often offered no more than second-class status for black immigrants and their communities.[91] For the children and grandchildren of the islanders who had reached Puerto Barrios, Bluefields, Limón, Bocas del Toro, Colón, and the coastlands in between in the late nineteenth century and early twentieth the shifting international politics of race and nation in the interwar years created previously unimaginable constraints and highly constrained opportunities.

NOTES

I am grateful to Rina Cáceres, Rebecca Scott, Ronny Viales, and the members of the Programa de Estudios de Diáspora of the Centro de Investigaciones Históricas de América Central of the Universidad de Costa Rica for comments on earlier drafts of this material. The research reflected here began under the auspices of the David Rockefeller Center for Latin American Studies at Harvard University and was financed by the Vicerrectoría de Investigación of the Universidad de Costa Rica as part of Proyecto No. 806-A2-047.

1   V. Newton, *The Silver Men*; Thomas-Hope, "The Establishment of a Migration Tradition," 66–81; Petras, *Jamaican Labor Migration*; Richardson, "Caribbean Migrations"; Putnam, *The Company They Kept*, chap. 2.

2   In addition to the sources cited in the previous note, particularly good treatments of migratory circuits in the Eastern Caribbean are offered by Richardson, *Panama Money in Barbados*, 100–111; Marshall, "A History of West Indian Migrations," 15–31. The estimate of forty-five thousand Barbadians is given in Richardson, *Panama Money*, 125.

3   Richardson, *Panama Money*, 131.

4   Parascandola, introduction.

5   For more detailed discussion of movement between Jamaica, Panama, and Costa Rica in these years, see Putnam, *The Company They Kept*, chap. 1; Putnam, "Work, Sex, and Power."

6   Panama was a province of Colombia until 1903.

7   Archivo Nacional de Costa Rica (henceforth ANCR), Serie Jurídica, Limón Alcaldía Única 540 (injurias, 1901). I have used pseudonyms for judicial case participants throughout.

8   ANCR, Limón Juzgado del Crimen 69 (violación, 1904).

9   ANCR, Serie Policia 3088 (sumaria, 1894).

10 For a literary analysis that strongly underlines this observation, see Frederick, *"Colón Man a Come."*

11 I am grateful to April Mayes for sharing this anecdote with me (personal communications, 2000, 2004). See Mayes, "Sugar's Metropolis."

12 Beals, "The Black Belt of the Caribbean," 363.

13 See Winston James, *Holding Aloft the Banner of Ethiopia*, chap. 1, statistics on 356–57.

14 Tinker Salas, "Relaciones de poder y raza," 77–103.

15 Proudfoot, *Population Movements in the Caribbean*, 96.

16 Cuba, Secretaría de Hacienda, Sección de Estadística, *Informe y movimiento de pasajeros . . .* (Havana, 1916), 17, 19. The Cuban government had just imposed a new system of contract labor importation, and the United Fruit Company had just acquired sizable new lands in eastern Cuba. See Chomsky, "'Barbados or Canada,'" 433; F. U. Adams, *Conquest of the Tropics*, 122. United Fruit was authorized by presidential decree to bring one thousand West Indian workers into Cuba in 1913 (de la Fuente, *A Nation for All*, 102). It would seem that they chose to bring them all from their Costa Rican plantations, where a combination of labor strife and declining yields were cutting into profits. See Putnam, *The Company They Kept*, 62–63.

17 Cuba, Secretaría de Hacienda, Sección de Estadística, *Informe y movimiento de pasajeros . . .* (Havana, 1916, 1917). See also V. Newton, *Silver Men*, 162.

18 Proudfoot, *Population Movements*, 77–80, 101.

19 In 1918, 906 foreign black immigrants named Central America their region of previous residence, while 3,993 listed the Caribbean; in 1919 the figures were 799 and 4,027, respectively (Winston James, *Holding Aloft the Banner of Ethiopia*, 356). Some of these immigrants may have been Spanish-speaking Central American citizens perceived as black by U.S. immigration officials (whether or not the immigrants would have categorized themselves in the same way). But analysis of Central American census data suggests that Spanish-speaking citizens' emigration to the United States was negligible to nonexistent in this era. See Castillo G., "La migración en Centroamérica," 27–56.

20 "Life in Jamaica in the Early Twentieth Century; A Presentation of Ninety Oral Accounts" (unpublished transcripts housed at Institute of Social and Economic Research, University of the West Indies, Mona, Kingston, Jamaica), Portland volume, Respondent 31Pfa Caenwood, "A Father's Daughter," interviewed April 1975.

21 "Life in Jamaica in the Early Twentieth Century," St. Catherine volume, Respondent 49StcFb Orangefield, Aunt Dore, interviewed March 1975.

22 "Life in Jamaica in the Early Twentieth Century," St. Catherine volume, Respondent 52StcMb Treadways, "Deacon," interviewed 1973, 1975.

23 de Lisser, *Jane's Career*, 64, 1, 76, 17. See also McKay, *Gingertown*, 172, 200, 222, 233.

24 Ley de Bases y Colonización, Decreto no. 24 del 3 de noviembre de 1862, in Costa Rica, *Colección de leyes y decretos* (San José: Imprenta la Paz, 1872), 159.

25 The minister of development reported in 1884, "In order to attract to the Atlantic coast African immigrants, the only ones who can bear the elevated temperatures of those localities, the government expanded . . . the land concessions made previously with that same goal, removing all restrictions and facilitating the means to acquire property." Costa Rica, Ministerio de Gobernación y Policía, *Memoria* (San José, 1883), 27. See also Chomsky, *West Indian Workers*, 27–28.

26 Opie, "Adios Jim Crow," chap. 5.

27 See Harpelle, this volume; Bourgois, *Ethnicity at Work*; Bryce-Laporte, "Crisis, Contraculture and Religion"; Opie, "Adios Jim Crow," 118.

28 Beals, "Black Belt," 362. For a discussion of the ways northern travelers' presumptions regarding race, climate, and character shaped their perceptions of the Central Americans they encountered, see Putnam, "Contact Zones," 113–25.

29 See ANCR, Limón Juzgado del Crimen 530 (homicidio, 1908); Limón Juzgado del Crimen 681 (homicidio, 1909); Limón Juzgado del Crimen 104 (homicidio, 1906).

30 Some immigrants also came to occupy the higher-ranking position of *agente de policía*. See ANCR, Policia 06196 (communicaciones con el gobernador de

Limón, 1911: telegram 24 September 1911); Limón Juzgado del Crimen 930 (violación, 1907).

31 ANCR, Limón Juzgado del Crimen 217 (homicidio, 1902).

32 ANCR, Policía 06199 (correspondencia con la gobernación de Limón); San José Juzgado Primero del Crimen 3332 (hurto, 1906): one witness referred to him as "Edwards, un policia negro"—note that residents of the neighborhood he patrolled could mistake his name but not his color. See also ANCR, Limón Juzgado del Crimen 531 (homicidio, 1908).

33 Walrond, "The Voodoo's Revenge," 94–103 in Parascandola, *"Winds Can Wake up the Dead,"* 97.

34 Franck, *Zone Policeman 88*, 81–82. See also F. Palmer, *Central America and Its Problems*, 259–61. On an earlier period, see McGuinness, "Searching for 'Latin America.'"

35 Franck, *Zone Policeman 88*, 231.

36 See Greene, *The Canal Builders.*

37 Bryce-Laporte, "Crisis, Contraculture," 103, 107. See Great Britain, Public Record Office, FO 371/5602, "Annual Report of the British Legation in Panama, 1914–1921," 29; Franck, *Zone Policeman 88*, 145.

38 See ANCR, Policía 1310; Policía 890 (3 September 1903); Policía 364 (comunicaciones con la gobernación de Limón, letter 8 May 1903); "Another outrage by police officer," *Searchlight* (Limón), 26 December 1931, 3; Chomsky, *West Indian Workers*; Echeverri-Gent, "Forgotten Workers," 275–308.

39 See, for instance, Great Britain, Public Record Office, FO 288/202, file 461/1919, "Mistreatment of British West Indians by Police," November 1919.

40 See Trefzger, "Making West Indians Unwelcome"; Opie, "Adios Jim Crow," chap. 6.

41 See introduction and essays by Offen, Hooker, Lohse, this volume.

42 See, for instance, the contrasting roles played by Federico Aymerich with individual black immigrants in ANCR, Limón Juzgado del Crimen 821 (abuso de autoridad, 1908) and Policía 1564 comunicaciones 1907, letter 30 September 1907.

43 ANCR, Policia 1565 (Comunicaciones 1907: letters 3 September and 12 September 1907). For further discussion of the patron-client ties that gave West Indian migrants political access in Costa Rica in this period, see Putnam, *The Company They Kept*, chap. 5.

44 "Se va a prohibir que las mujeres costarricenses se casen con negros, asiáticos o también con degenerados. Cada aspirante al matrimonio deberá exhibir un certificado de buena salud." *La Prensa Libre*, 17 June 1915, 2, cited in Buska, "'Marimba Por Tí Me Muero,'" 179. Briceño's perception of the prevalence of deadly conjugal violence in Limón was quite accurate: see Putnam, *The Company They Kept*, chap. 6.

45 S. Palmer, "Hacia la 'auto-inmigración'"; Soto Quirós, "Inmigración e identidad nacional"; Euraque, "The Banana Enclave"; Alvarenga Venutolo, "La inmigración extranjera" (accessed 7 February 2008).

46   Panama, Ley 6ª de 11 de marzo de 1904 and Ley 31 de 1917, in "Indice cronológico de la leyes de a Asamblea Nacional 1904–1956, confeccionado por el personal de la biblioteca y archivos, bajo la dirección de Gavino Sierra Gutiérez, Secretario General de la Asamblea Nacional" (Panama, n.d.).

47   Suter, "'Pernicious Aliens,'" 26–57; Laughlin, "The Codification and Analysis of the Immigration-Control Law," 61.

48   Soto Quirós, "Inmigración e identidad nacional," 217–21, 232–34; Putnam, "Ideología racial," 147–49; ANCR, Serie Gobernación 8101 (telegrams 6–10 September 1924).

49   Euraque, "Banana Enclave," 152; Honduras, Laws, etc., *Ley de inmigración* (Tegucigalpa: Tipografía nacional, 1929), 7–9.

50   Davis, "West Indian Workers on the Panama Canal," 141–42; V. Newton, *Silver Men*, 162–63; Conniff, *Black Labor on a White Canal,* 65–66, 80–84, 98–106, 127–30. The retroactive denationalization was reversed in 1945, but exclusions in employment and access to public education persisted. See Westerman, *Los inmigrantes antillanos en Panama,* 95–101.

51   Guatemala, Decreto Número 1735 de la Asamblea Legislativa de la República de Guatemala del 30 de mayo de 1931, artículo 2; Guatemala, "Ley de Extranjeria," Decreto no. 1781 de marzo 23 de 1936, artículo 9, cited in Zorraquín Becu, *El problema del extranjero,* 55–56.

52   Laughlin, "Codification and Analysis," 57.

53   "Salvador Passes Law Barring All Coloured Immigration," *Panama Star and Herald,* 4 May 1925, 1 (reprinted Associated Press item). See El Salvador, *Ley y reglamento de migración* (San Salvador: Imprenta Nacional, 1933), 18.

54   Ngai, "The Architecture of Race," 67–92. On the political context of these shifts, see King, *Making Americans,* especially chap. 6.

55   See Reid, *The Negro Immigrant,* statistics on 235, discussion on 31–35. The Johnson-Reed Act (1924) did not prohibit black immigration as such; unlike "asiatics," blacks had been and remained eligible for citizenship.

56   See *Annual Report of the Commissioner General of Immigration . . . 1924* (Washington: Government Printing Office, 1924), 24–25. Those from Canada and Newfoundland were likewise categorized as nonquota immigrants.

57   Jamaica National Archive, 1B/5/77/24: Emigration to USA (Individual Enquiries), Minute, 5 November 1929.

58   Zolberg, *A Nation by Design,* especially chap. 8.

59   ANCR, Gobernación 8101 (letters 21 July–8 August 1924).

60   *Actas de la Primera Conferencia Panamericana de Eugenesia y Homicultura de las Repúblicas Americanas, celebrada en la Habana, Cuba, desde el 21 hasta el 23 de diciembre de 1927* (Havana, 1928), 179. Argentina, Bolivia, Chile, Mexico, Peru, and Uruguay also sent delegates.

61   Stepan, *The Hour of Eugenics,* 174–82; García González and Álvarez Peláez, *En busca de la raza perfecta,* 150–229.

62   *Actas,* 185.

63 Ibid., 34–35, 206. Here and elsewhere I have translated from the original Spanish, while also consulting the (frequently awkward) English translation published in the same volume.

64 Ibid., 52, 221.

65 Ibid., 55, 224.

66 Ibid., 34, 36–37, 205–6, 208.

67 Robert F. Foerster, "The Racial Problems Involved in Immigration from Latin America and the West Indies to the United States," *Hearings of the Committee on Immigration and Naturalization, House of Representatives, March 3, 1925* (Washington: Government Printing Office, 1925), 329.

68 Ibid., 334.

69 Ibid., 335. The report, and reaction to it, made news in the Caribbean. See "International Row Threatens over Report," *Daily Gleaner* (Kingston), 27 August 1925, 13.

70 See, for instance, the review of Davenport's *Race Crossing in Jamaica* (coauthored with Morris Steggerda): Castle, "Race Mixture and Physical Disharmonies," 605–6.

71 *Actas*, 68.

72 Ibid., 70, 236.

73 Ibid., 72, 238.

74 Ibid., 70–71, 257.

75 Ibid., 323.

76 Ibid., 284–285, 288.

77 Dikötter, "Race Culture," 467, 468.

78 Chomsky, "West Indian Workers," 11–40; Chomsky, "'Barbados or Canada'"; Tinker-Salas, "Relaciones de poder y raza," 94–95; de la Fuente, *A Nation for All*, 46–50. Across the region communist labor leaders stood out in this era for their consistent rejection of racist argumentation.

79 Roig de Leuchsenring, "¿Se está Cuba africanizando?," 27, cited in Chomsky, "'Barbados or Canada,'" 458–59.

80 Chomsky, *West Indian Workers*, 223; Beals, *America South*, 158. See Harpelle, "Racism and Nationalism," 29–51.

81 Alfaro, *El peligro antillano*, quoted in Westerman, *Inmigrantes antillanos*, 96–97.

82 ANCR, Serie Congreso no. 13460, fol. 4, cited in Alvarenga Venutolo, "La inmigración extranjera."

83 Letter from Frank Cox, British consul in Costa Rica, to British Legation in Panama, 19 April 1934, Great Britain, Public Record Office, CO 318/413/1: Immigration of British West Indians into Central America.

84 Extract of Confidential Dispatch No. 87 from Sir J. Crosby to Sir John Simon, Panama, 9 April 1934, Great Britain, Public Record Office, CO 318/413/1: Immigration of British West Indians into Central America.

85 Ibid.

86 "No Blacks for the Interior," *Searchlight* (Limón), 22 February 1930.

87 On the nonexistence of legal prohibition, see Meléndez Chaverri and Duncan, *El Negro en Costa Rica*, 87–89; Koch, "Ethnicity and Livelihoods." Adding to the confusion on this point, Costa Rica's census publication of 1950 would credit the administration then in power with having "repealed" the "discriminatory law" that since "the past century . . . prohibited people of color from settling west of Turrialba." Costa Rica, Dirección General de Estadística y Censos, *Censo de Población de Costa Rica, 22 de mayo de 1950* (San José, 1953), 81.

88 Testimony from audience members at Seminario "Culturas Populares y Políticas Públicas en México y Centroamérica (siglos XIX y XX)," Museo Histórico Cultural Juan Santamaría, Alajuela, Costa Rica, 20–22 September 2000, and "The Socio-economic and Cultural Impact of West Indian Migration to Costa Rica," Latin American–Caribbean Centre, University of the West Indies, Mona Campus, Jamaica, 4–5 July 2002.

89 The banana contract signed in 1934 by the Costa Rican government with the United Fruit Company did bar the company from employing workers "of color" on their new Pacific plantations but placed no formal restrictions on Afro-Caribbeans' travel to the Pacific region or their employment on private plantations there. Putnam, *The Company They Kept*, 73–75; Harpelle, "Racism and Nationalism."

90 Costa Rica, *Colección de leyes y decretos*, Decreto no. 4 del 26 de abril de 1942. This law would stand until 1960, when all race-based limits on immigration were removed from Costa Rican law. *Colección de Leyes y Decretos.* Ley no. 2694 del 26 de noviembre de 1960.

91 See, for instance, Senior Angulo, "La incorporación social"; M. Anderson, "'Cahuita Gone, Cahuita Gone'"; Westerman, *Los inmigrantes antillanos*; Insanally, Clifford, and Sheriff, *Regional Footprints*.

American Enclave Communities of Central America

Ronald Harpelle

In the early twentieth century the United Fruit Company built a number of corporate enclaves along the Caribbean and Pacific coasts of Central America for their American employees. Along with port facilities, railways, and other trappings of industry, the corporations also constructed exclusive housing compounds for their American employees. Popularly known as "white zones," these compounds were planned communities constructed to house the families of managers, mechanics, engineers, and other skilled workers of European descent. With paved streets, schools, social clubs, and an army of domestic servants, the white zones existed in contrast to the native communities that surrounded them. The barbed-wire fences and armed guards that separated the two worlds of the corporate enclave marked the boundary between the leaders and the led. This essay looks at the white zones of Central America as the domestic front of the corporate conquest of the region. Central to this study is the place of the Euro-American women who accompanied their husbands to the white zones. Little is known about the role of these "company wives," but their presence was part of a corporate strategy developed by multinational corporations in their "conquest of the tropics."[1]

The women of the white zones of Central America were among the many thousands from the United States, Canada, and Europe who ventured to Latin America to live in communities built for the managerial elite who were brought to the region by the United Fruit Company and other corporations.[2] In Latin America they entered a world that was engineered in the boardrooms of Boston and New York, and they became domestic adjuncts to American enterprise. Company wives abroad were elite women assigned a rearguard role in justifying and maintaining the hegemony of U.S. corporations over the people and countries of the region. The position they occupied was a logical extension of the business of bananas in Central America, but this meant that ordinary Euro-American women were put in positions of power for the first time in their lives. Consequently the women of the white zones had agency and the means to impose themselves on the communities they shared with the people who lived outside the walls of the compound.

The wives of administrators, skilled workers, missionaries, and others who grasped at the opportunities afforded by the banana companies were individuals who brought with them their particular class, ethnic, and social backgrounds. In Central America and elsewhere they immediately became conscious of the rank extended to them as the wives of specific individuals and of their apparent superiority over those who lived outside the compound walls. Gender and class interests diverged within the company compounds, but as members of the corporate elite they enjoyed a status that, in their own estimation, was above that of all but the wealthiest people in the countries they found themselves in. Because the identity and power of the Euro-American males were extended to their wives, many women were confronted with the exigency of reorienting class barriers to conform with the identity imposed upon them. Not all of these women were upper class, and many had to learn how to be.

Although women like those connected to the banana plantations of Central America seldom worked outside of the home, they were not merely housewives. Corporations offered superior housing and other privileges to the people who were posted to the frontiers of the American Empire, but along with status came an obligation to maintain and defend the distinctions between the leaders and the led. Their husbands, and by extension the women of the community, were a cadre of trustworthy employees who were selected because they shared the values, cultural attitudes, and racial identity of the corporation's directors. The men who went to Latin America were entrusted with the profitability of operations abroad, and their families played a functional role in ensuring corporate interests. The realm of the company wife was the home, where cultural identity and common values were maintained as a safeguard against the moral degradation of the men who were leading the campaign.[3]

According to A. Grenfell Price in a report on European settlements in the tropics published in 1939, the presence of women was a civilizing influence that "prevented some of the worst evils of tropical white settlement" and "contributed greatly" to the success of enterprises abroad. Significantly Price's *White Settlers in the Tropics* included the Panama Canal Zone, the most important center for U.S. activity in the circum-Caribbean region, as one of the cases in the study. Most Euro-American women associated with the banana industry in Central America were familiar with the Canal Zone because it was nearby and provided respite from long months of isolation on the banana plantations.[4] Company wives in Central America may not have been familiar with Price's work, but the similarities between the Panama Canal Zone, the biggest white zone of them all, and the enclaves established by the banana industry are obvious. Not surprisingly the role of Euro-American women on the banana plantations matches the role their counterparts played in the Canal Zone.

For example, one of Price's main concerns was the biological "threat" posed by the cohabitation of whites and nonwhites in a tropical environment. His research showed that northern Europeans could "survive and breed" in the tropics despite "racial competition and tropical disease," and that they were "making definite and encouraging progress" in warmer climates.[5] However, Price believed that "degenerate members of the more advanced people will always mingle with their belated neighbors" and that this was a serious drawback to having white people live in the tropics.[6] Price's preoccupation with racial purity is not surprising given that at the time debates on race were raging among academics and many people believed in the superiority of the racially pure. Such beliefs inevitably led to discussions of racial hierarchies, and in this respect company wives were infused with the concept of their superiority over their nonwhite neighbors. One of the principal roles of company wives was therefore to maintain the social barriers that reinforced the barbed-wire fences that surrounded their communities.

Unfortunately little is known about the private lives of the people who pushed expansion in Central America, and women, when they do appear, are usually just a footnote in a male-centered story of conquest. When scholars have looked at women in multinational enclaves they have encountered the silence of the official record, and few alternative sources of information exist. If women are mentioned they tend to appear in the society pages of local newspapers or as characters in travelogues or autobiographies, but never as the central focus of government, industry, or general historical records.[7] The only developed literature on white women in the tropics focuses on European colonial experience in the nineteenth and twentieth centuries.[8] The differences between the European imperialism and its modern American equivalent are significant, but the structure of power relations between the leaders and the led, in both cases, were identical social constructions. The literature on European women in imperial settings offers a foundation upon which to build a study of Euro-American women in the American tropics. For example, in South Asia one of the most enduring female figures in colonial history was the memsahib, or "Madame boss," a European woman who joined her husband in the campaign to "civilize" the region.[9] The memsahib was a product of a nineteenth-century colonial culture and society that was defined in terms of gender relations. She was both feminine and imperial in her presence, and the literature makes clear that these women saw themselves as the female expression of European superiority. Men were the explorers, the soldiers, and the commanders of the colonial campaign, while women, if they were present, remained in European compounds where they were engaged in a struggle on a domestic level that was every bit as important as that of their male counterparts. As Rosemary Marangoly George argues, in colonial discourse "management of the Empire" is represented as "'home management' on a larger scale," and "housekeeping in the colonies [was] often represented as a military/imperial campaign."[10] Women played a complementary role by ensuring that the domestic sphere, which was reserved for the family, was free of the debauchery and corruption men were obliged to face in their daily lives. As a result memsahibs carried the weight of the empire on their shoulders and took their responsibilities seriously. Their homes were sanctuaries of evangelical Christian family values and they were entrusted with the defense of their realm against internal threats posed by the presence of servants and other non-Europeans in their midst. Memsahibs were expressions of what was considered to be European superiority and modernity, and their presence defined the female role in European domination while at the same time assisting in the civilizing of the colonized.[11] The homes of the European elite, with servants working in it, became cultural battlegrounds where European and non-European identities clashed.

However, like the memsahib, the company wife was a contradiction. Euro-American women abroad enjoyed power and prestige that most were denied in their home societies.[12] The company wife's was an American home reproduced in a tropical setting and decorated with a combination of local and imported furnishings. Within its confines different standards and rules were applied to domestic tasks. Hispanic and West Indian servants took orders from Euro-American women and children, and the rituals of daily life followed an American design. Within the confines of these compounds the company wife was the guarantor of an idealized home life for her family.

The Euro-American women whose lives intersected with the corporate expansion of the United States in Central America lived in the exclusive world of an enclave elite. In a corporate enclave, as in a European colonial setting, the "white woman's status in society was the norm, the yardstick by which 'native' lack was measured."[13] White women were immediately recognizable as an elite because their presence in Central America was inextricably tied to the investments made by a multinational corporation. As a result of their corporate identity Euro-Americans lived in enclosed compounds where middle-class America, with its social life, household accoutrements, and dietary preferences, were re-created. Town planning, landscape design, housing, home furnishings, social clubs, and anything that related to daily life were drawn from a model developed by the corporation.[14] Corporate managers believed that "an adequate standard of living was almost as vital to the employee in the low tropics as the work of the medical scientist and the sanitarian in safeguarding health."[15] The communities built for Euro-American workers were more than mere housing compounds; they were an instrument engineered with precision to maximize production and profits. When company wives arrived they were given command of the home and became the custodians of the social atmosphere of the company compound.

Upon arrival in the company compound women found that their duties included the management of household finances and the supervision of cooks, laundresses, houseboys, and servants. In addition they were expected to live up to the moral and social expectations the corporation had for its Euro-American employees. The problem was that "whiteness" and "Americanness" afforded company wives positions of power they were not accustomed to. Servants and an enormous amount of leisure time were new to the mainly working-class and lower-middle-class women who became company wives.[16] Consequently they not only learned on the job, but they were made aware that their status was tied to the corporation to which they were indebted for the opportunity to participate as a manager of sorts in the exploitation of Central America's natural and human resources.

One of the best descriptions of a housing compound for the corporate elite by a company wife is Frances Emery-Waterhouse's *Banana Paradise*, which is the story of life in the community of Siguican in western Guatemala. Like other company housing complexes, Siguican was a restricted community built behind a "high wall of woven wire." It was referred to by some of Emery-Waterhouse's contemporaries as the "Graveyard of Guatemala," "Monkey-Man's Burden," and "Malaria Gulch," but to her it was "Paradise."[17] According to Emery-Waterhouse the community was ideal because, in addition to being cosmopolitan, it was "welded into something approaching perfect harmony."[18] Siguican was a state-of-the-art United Fruit Company compound built in the late 1930s after plant disease in the Caribbean region forced the corporation to move much of its operations to the Pacific coast of Central America. If Siguican was paradise, it was because years of corporate architectural refinement went into its planning.[19] Emery-Waterhouse was also exceptional; the account of her stay in Central America reveals a woman who genuinely enjoyed the adventure of life in the tropics.

Banana Paradise offers a frank description of the consciousness of hierarchy that was evident in the community of managers and other Euro-American employees. According to Emery-Waterhouse, social strata were as "sharply observed as machete blade" in Siguican, and everyone was obliged to conform.[20] The highest positions in the community were occupied by the men who worked in the Department of Engineering. Below them on the social scale were employees from the Department of Accountancy, followed by the Department of Construction and finally the Department of Agriculture. Frances Emery-Waterhouse enjoyed the privileges that came with being married to an engineer, and her status was built in. All of the houses in the white zone were single-family dwellings surrounded by private yards, but the quality and size varied because the accommodations were used as an "incentive for acceptable work and promotion."[21] The families of the corporate hierarchy lived in wooden structures that signified the status of the family within the community created by the corporation.[22] In this respect Siguican was a typical white zone, built in the mold of similar communities that once dotted the Central American coastlines.

One of the few remaining United Fruit Company compounds built in the early part of the twentieth century is in Tela, Honduras, where the white zone has been preserved as a hotel complex. The Tela Railroad Company, a subsidiary of the United Fruit Company, established its headquarters there in 1914 and soon began construction of an exclusive community for its managerial class. Within a few years the company had constructed a sprawling company town across the Lancetilla River from the original settlement. Tela Nuevo is a testament to the concepts in town planning made popular in the late nineteenth century and early twentieth by Frederick Law Olmsted, Raymond Unwin, and Lewis Mumford. Along with the company's headquarters, a wharf, the main railway yard, and the central commissary for the region, the Tela Railroad Company built approximately six hundred houses and barracks for its Hispanic and West Indian employees. The houses were color-coded to identify family dwellings and varied in size according to individual needs and seniority. An inventory by the Grounds and Maintenance Department was constantly updated to ensure that employees received only what they deserved. Tela Nuevo included schools, one of Central America's best hospitals, a company cemetery, green spaces, a baseball field called Dodger Stadium, and one of the first golf courses in Central America.[23] A veritable Fordlandia in Central America.[24]

Within Tela Nuevo the fruit company also constructed an exclusive neighborhood known originally as "The White Zone," then later, when the barriers to integration began to drop, as "The American Zone." The White Zone was the segregated world reserved for the families of company officials, managers, foremen, and other specialized workers who were brought in from abroad. Security guards were posted at the entrances to the zone and patrolled the streets to make certain that the corporate families and their possessions were safe.[25] The zone fronted on an exclusive beach and was nestled safely within the corporate enclave. The area immediately surrounding the zone functioned as a security barrier, which was in operation and guarded around the clock. The families of white managers were buffered from the rest of the world by the company headquarters, the bachelors' quarters, a church, and the wharf on one side. On the other side was the company hospital, a dispensary, housing for nonwhite skilled or professional employees and their families, a baseball field, and a cemetery. Behind the community and across the main road was the commissary, which was a large general store and supply warehouse, the machine shop, and the railroad yard. On the other side of the tracks was the golf course and housing for the company's permanent workers. The majority of the housing in Tela Nuevo was for permanent employees. They were designated as being either A, B, or C houses and they were grouped in segregated neighborhoods, with better houses and "better" employees living closest to the white zone.

The chief administrators lived in the largest houses, which were located in a row along the beach. Farther away from the beach the houses were smaller; the smallest and least attractive were located just inside the wall that ran along the main road. There, on the outskirts of the white community, lived the skilled tradesmen and their families. A notable feature of the housing at the rear of the compound is that it did not come with huts for domestic servants, which meant that lower-level personnel in the corporate echelon were restricted to daytime service. Life among the Euro-Americans of the zone was as stratified as it was outside the walls of their exclusive community. Members of the zone's elite, the managers, engineers, physicians, and others, enjoyed special privileges. They were given membership in the company golf club, even though some had never played golf before arriving in Tela, and they were welcomed into the Masonic Lodge and other exclusive organizations formed by and for the elite inhabitants of the white zone. Lower-ranking residents might take up golf and join a club, but some privileges were restricted to an inner circle of those who held the most important positions with the company. Members of the local Hispanic elite might also enjoy the occasional invitation to participate in activities within the white zone, but during the first decades of its existence Hispanics were not allowed to live within its confines.[26]

The geographic, social, and racial isolation of white zones like those in Siguican and Tela is highlighted by the Costa Rican national census of 1927.[27] In Puerto Limón, the provincial capital and the location of the United Fruit Company's headquarters in Costa Rica, a small enclave community of managers and highly skilled workers lived together behind fences and walls, similarly surrounded by a barrier of corporate installations. The Barrio del Hospital de la United Fruit Company contained 129 individuals living in thirty-five households. The community comprised seventy-one females and fifty-eight males, who were described on the original census forms as being of the white race. Eighty-six were adults and forty-one were under eighteen. Similarly thirty of the thirty-five households comprised married couples and their immediate families, but not everyone had children and several households had extended family members or servants living with them.[28] In most respects the white zone in Puerto Limón was typical of those described in reports of similar communities elsewhere.

In 1927 the banana industry in Costa Rica was half a century old, and the bulk of the population of the province of Limón was no longer made up of transient plantation workers. The white zone had been in existence for approximately twenty years, yet most of the foreign residents had arrived within the previous three years. Among the people living in the exclusive white zone, the majority were non-Hispanics who were born in the United States. There was also a scattering of British, Canadian, German, and Swedish nationals within the community. However, the Euro-Americans were not the only white people in the zone; a number of "white" Costa Ricans also shared the compound.[29]

Although approximately 25 percent of the residents were Spanish-speaking Costa Ricans, their presence was measured by their social class and not their skin color. Five households were headed by Spanish-speaking men, most of whom were living with their families. The only Costa Rican men who were permitted to live with their families among the foreigners in the zone were medical professionals working at the United Fruit Company hospital. Three were physicians, one was an x-ray technician, and another was a pharmacist. In addition to the Hispanic husbands and their wives, there were ten Spanish-speaking children, nine domestic servants, and six Spanish-speaking women married to foreigners. All were identified as being of the "white race" in the 1927 census.

The exclusivity and homogeneity of the white zone in Puerto Limón stands out when compared with samples from other neighborhoods in the town. Like all other banana enclaves, housing in Puerto Limón was strictly regulated and communities were segregated by race. Samples from two other neighborhoods, one primarily Hispanic and one mainly West Indian, reveal the distance between the different socioethnic groups. Of particular interest are the adult women in Limón because so little is known about them and because the contrast between females from different ethnic groups is remarkable. Whereas the vast majority of women living in the white zone were married, educated, and living in single-family households, their neighbors lived a different existence.

In the census sample of Hispanic households, which consisted of a total of 160 people (89 males and 71 females), 20 were married, 6 were classified as living in common-law relationships, and 4 were single mothers.[30] Together these 30 women had a total of 56 children under the age of 16; the ages of the mothers ranged from 17 to 70. The sample of West Indian households also revealed differences between women of African descent and other women living in Limón. To begin with, there were twice as many males as females (92 males and 45 females) living in the 35 houses selected for the study. Among the women, only 3 were legally married, 16 were living in a common-law relationship, and 9 were single heads of households.[31] Although approximately the same number of women were in all three samples, the West Indian women had only 28 children among them. In the white zone 30 women had 38 children under the age of 16. West Indian women were, on average, younger than their Hispanic neighbors but older than the women living in the white zone, who ranged between 24 and 46 years of age. One of the most obvious differences between the women in the different groups was their level of education. Whereas almost 90 percent of company wives had a secondary or postsecondary education, 70 percent of the Hispanic and West Indian women had only a primary education. Although these differences are easy to explain, they were used by Euro-Americans to justify the attitudes the enclave elite had toward outsiders.

Upon closer inspection the apparent superiority of company wives was not justified because the white zone was not a random or typical conglomeration of individuals who happened to come together as a community. Most were foreign residents who came specifically to live among the enclave elite. Their families were, by definition, nuclear because housing in the white zone was reserved primarily for married members of the elite, with only a couple of exceptions; two houses contained senior administrators without families, and in one lived three Euro-American women who worked in the hospital, but the residents of these dwellings were "respectable" individuals. There may have been other types of relationships between men and women who were technically eligible for membership in the exclusive community, but they were obliged to live elsewhere.

Company wives were also younger than their Hispanic and West Indian counterparts because their husbands tended to be men who were merely performing a compulsory tour of duty in the tropics. For this reason, and perhaps because they had access to much better health care, company wives appeared to be more fertile. They could provide a more sanitary and secure home life for their children than the women who lived outside their community, with its manicured lawns, gardens, and playgrounds.[32] Young children went to English schools within the company compound, and there was no need for high schools, as those with older children could send them to boarding school in the United States with financial support from the company. With all of the amenities and the homogeneity of the white zone distinctions between themselves and others were easy to make.

These distinctions were not, however, limited to people who lived outside the walls of the compound. For example, on average, white women were better educated than their Hispanic or West Indian counterparts because they came from countries where universal education was the norm, and as children none of them had had to work to help support their families—something that is typical of a poverty-stricken childhood in a poor country. In the white zone most women had a secondary school education, and four of them were described as professionals. There is no clear indication of what their training was, but two of these women were Euro-American and two were Hispanic. The two English-speaking women worked as teachers in the exclusive community school located within the walls of the white zone; the two others were described as housewives. Though limited to observations of a small number of cases, the implication of the data is that there was no work befitting a professional Hispanic woman outside the zone and little possibility for work within the confines of the community. White Hispanics were allowed to live with the Euro-Americans, but there were limits to conviviality within the confines of the fabricated communities of the self-styled elite.

According to don Rafael Elvir, a former employee in the accounting department of the Tela Railroad Company, during the first decades of the twentieth century the United Fruit Company, which was formed in 1899, prohibited its American employees from having relationships with local women; if the managers caught wind of an affair the employee would be "sent back home."[33] However, when Samuel Zemurray of the Cuyamel Fruit Company took control of United Fruit everything changed. Relationships between Euro-Americans and local women became acceptable to the company, so long as the woman came from the right social and ethnic background. The corporation generally made all the decisions with respect to an individual's provision of housing, and for the most part people living in the white zones respected the unwritten rules governing their conduct. Transgressions did occur, but the company was not always in a position to reprimand employees. On some occasions the burden of regulation fell on the community itself, and company wives, as the guarantors of moral standards, were obliged to take action.

The tree-lined streets of the white zone in Tela offer one example of how pressure from within was used to force residents to adhere to what was considered to be acceptable conduct. When David Creighton, a Scottish engineer, lost his wife to illness he decided that his children would be better cared for at boarding schools in the United States. After a time he began a relationship with his cook's daughter. The young woman, who was of African descent, lived behind the house in one of the one-room shacks that housed servants in the zone. This "mingling," as A. Grenfell Price put it, was seen by the company wives as a serious threat to the well-being of their community. When the affair became public knowledge the white women in the community were enraged and took action. Creighton went from being an unfortunate widower to being a pariah within the community, and his life was made uncomfortable. The women in the community refused to "recognize his company any more"; this caused him to move across the river to the town of Tela where he could live openly with the young woman. The move spared him and his lover the indignation and ostracism of the company wives.[34]

Not everyone who crossed the boundary between acceptable and unacceptable conduct was obliged to leave the community. A few years after the Creighton episode, when Mr. Hancock, a company manager, arrived at Tela with a black woman as his mistress, he moved into the community, thereby defying the unwritten rules of life in the zone and sentencing his partner to a life of isolation. Unlike Creighton, Hancock was unwilling to give up the pleasures and security of life in the white zone, and he was too high up on the corporate ladder to be bullied into leaving. As a result Hancock compromised by living a dual life: "He didn't appear with her publicly or socially, it was a private affair."[35] Charivari worked once again as his private affair became his lover's sentence to isolation. The attitude displayed by the Euro-American elite in Tela highlights the issue of *méstissage* in colonial discourse. As Ann Laura Stoler argues, Europeans were wary of the "mixed-blood problem," which they saw as an "embodiment of European degradation and moral decay."[36] The threat of méstissage, as A. Grenfell Price discovered, was especially serious when the "mingling" occurred on the internal frontier, within the community itself.

Shunning was also popular in Siguican, where Frances Emery-Waterhouse reveals the class distinctions that characterized life in the white zone she lived in. *Banana Paradise* demonstrates a heightened awareness of the ranks that existed among members of the corporate forces by exploring the attitudes of the Euro-Americans toward the locals. Emery-Waterhouse was exceptional because she embraced Siguican and took an interest in the people who lived around her. She worked hard to learn enough Spanish to be able to communicate with the young women who waited on her at the commissary and even invited Spanish-speaking women into her home. She also witnessed how the "fine and cultured Latin-American employees and their families were snubbed and slighted by the North Americans and the Britishers." Hispanics were "more often than not treated with ill-disguised contempt . . . left strictly to themselves and very seldom invited to parties or dances." Once she was entertaining a young Spanish woman when a group of her Euro-American neighbors dropped by unexpectedly and refused to shake hands with her guest. After that incident she was obliged to entertain her English- and Spanish-speaking guests at different times and was even threatened with the loss of her "social position" if she continued inviting "Latinos" into her home.[37] In addition to protecting their community from external threats of méstissage company wives also guarded the internal boundaries against incursions by the local elite.

Still, as the wife of one of the top administrators, Emery-Waterhouse did draw the line between herself and others. She shared her husband's status and enjoyed a position within the community that commanded the highest level of comfort and several perks that were denied to other people. Higher-grade employees were allowed "special furnishings" that distinguished their homes from the others in the corporate compounds.[38] For example, after patiently waiting for a shipment to arrive from England, the author and her husband were able to enjoy the privilege of eating from "gold band" china, a service that did not carry the company name and that was restricted to the homes of administrators of the highest rank. The fact that it was important to her to have a table service that could be considered personal, despite its being supplied by the corporation, is echoed in a study of similar expatriate women, who were "conscious of the difference between ladies and something-nothings [low-class white women]."[39] Unlike tablecloths, napkins, blankets, sheets, and many other items that came with the company stamp, gold-band china was "virgin" and therefore desired by the women of Siguican. Reliance on the corporation to supply everything also meant that "when some of those people left [the company], they didn't even have a suitcase to take with them." That was the observation of Rand Garo, who as a boy did odd jobs in Tela's white zone and later worked in the merchandise department that supplied the furnishings for all the company houses. Class distinctions within Siguican were important to the Euro-American elite, but little if anything obtained in the tropics was worth bringing back home.

Another reason for wanting gold-band china was that it was for the exclusive use of the Emery-Waterhouses and their guests. Prior to the arrival of the exclusive dinnerware the family and their guests ate from the same plates used by their servants. Consequently, during what must have seemed an eternal wait for the shipment from England, the author insisted that the servants wash the dishes in hot soapy water before serving white people. Domestic servants were not the "fine and cultured Latin-American employees" the author was willing to share her table service with. The arrival of the china from England meant that the Emery-Waterhouses finally had their whites-only service. Unfortunately gold-trimmed plates were reserved for the homes of the people in the highest positions; company porcelain, like the kind used in the dining halls, was all that some members of the community could get.[40] Moreover in Siguican people ate out at least twice a week, and common practice in enclave communities was to socialize around the dinner table. Homes without gold-band china were homes of lower ranking employees. The line was drawn at the dinner table and on many other domestic fronts.

A chance at obtaining a separate table service was just one of the perks afforded company wives during their stay in a corporate enclave. The corporations subsidized housing and all of a family's basic needs. Duty-free imports were available at the company commissaries, and the corporations made sure that the products on the shelves were familiar to the company wives.[41] Refrigerated banana boats arrived regularly with a store on board whose sole purpose was the provision of goods from the United States to the passengers and the residents of company white zones. Company ships also brought special orders to the plantations, thereby ensuring that company wives had access to anything that was available through a mail-order catalogue.

Although not all company enclaves were as well-serviced as Siguican, one thing women could count on no matter where their husbands were posted was a pool of domestic laborers to assist with every task around the house. Domestic servants were considered an indispensable part of life in a corporate enclave, but they posed a constant challenge to the women who were their bosses. Emery-Waterhouse puts it best when she admits that the "ladies of Siguican were pampered and spoiled by the quiet, lovable and, for the most part, efficient" servants they employed.[42] Inefficiency among the hired help enters into virtually every account of the trials of establishing a home in what were considered to be the frontier regions of the world. Order was essential to the well-being of the community, and finding reliable, efficient, and deferential domestic workers was a central concern for company wives.[43]

In Siguican and elsewhere within the United Fruit Company empire the corporation paid the wages of domestic servants, but the women determined the wage scales in their own homes.[44] The result was that company wives, like their husbands, managed a sector of the local labor supply and had the corporation's resources at their disposal. Domestic servants, like all other company employees, were mindful of the omnipotence of the corporation and were often required to rely on the benevolence of the company. Inez McNabb, a long-time cook and domestic worker, explained that when she left her abusive husband she was able to get the company to supply her with the furnishings for her new home.[45] Unlike other workers, the wage scales for domestic workers were determined according to convention within the white zone and not established by the corporation. This means that working conditions, pay raises, and fringe benefits were also set on an individual basis and that the decision was made by the individual's direct supervisor. Moreover, like memsahibs, company wives brought with them notions of a proper work ethic, cleanliness, and morality and a determination to instruct their charges on the "American way" of doing things.

One of the main obstacles to finding suitable domestic labor was the general shortage of workers. The enclaves were usually located in remote regions where the existing communities were often too small to supply the demand for women workers deemed suitable by company wives. In addition to working in the homes of the elite, women were also hired by the corporations to cook and clean for the single white males who lived in company housing. The labor camps often consisted of company barracks housing hundreds of single males whose meals and basic domestic needs were provided for by their employers. The upper classes of the local Hispanic population also provided employment for women, and a number of other opportunities, such as operating a market stall or a commercial establishment, taking in boarders or doing laundry, also existed. The result was that company wives were forced to compete for labor, so there were limits to what could be expected from domestic servants and to the disciplinary actions that could be taken against them.

Another major stumbling block was the double barrier of language and culture. The reports by women who went to Central America are filled with stories that illustrate the enormous cultural gap existing between the company wife and the hired help. Linked to this were language differences. Because company wives were often unwilling to socialize with Hispanics of any social class and because their communities were islands of Anglo-Saxon solidarity, few women learned Spanish well enough to be able to fully communicate their desires to the Spanish-speaking women who came to work in their homes. Therefore domestic servants who could speak English were in demand; they also tended to be more familiar with the culture of their corporate masters than people who did not speak the language. English-speaking servants could be given instructions and be expected to follow them; expecting Spanish speakers to follow through was always a gamble.

Not surprisingly, finding English-speaking domestic servants was more difficult the farther away the enclave was located from the Caribbean basin. On the banana plantations of the Caribbean coast of Central America and in the region of the Panama Canal English-speaking West Indians were easy to come by. Their familiarity with the language of the elite, their understanding of British culinary tastes, not to mention the racism that kept them out of the homes and businesses of the Hispanic elite and the insecurity of their being foreign workers, meant that West Indians were more attractive as employees than their Spanish-speaking counterparts were. Moreover West Indians were a colonized people who had experience with memsahib-like women in their own society. Even in Siguican, on the Pacific side of Guatemala where there were few West Indians, Emery-Waterhouse was told to get Jamaicans as servants and "save [her]self the trouble of learning Spanish."[46] Unemployed English-speaking women may have been available in western Guatemala, but more likely they were imported from company enclaves in the Caribbean coast region. Although Emery-Waterhouse decided to learn Spanish and employ Mayan women in her home, for many company wives English-speaking domestic labor was essential.

As a result English-speaking women who were considered good workers enjoyed a better bargaining position than their non-English-speaking counterparts did. Good domestic servants would be passed on with the house to the next occupant. This was the case with the Anglican priests of Tela; for more than half a century a series of priests relied on the Wilkinson family to provide them with all their cooking and cleaning needs.[47] Even in her old age, Lola Wilkinson, the last of her family to work for the resident priest, remained defiant in her sense of Britishness and distant from the Hispanic community that surrounded her. Miss Lola never considered working for anyone other than an "English" employer because she would not prepare, or eat, Spanish food.

Another example was Inez McNabb, an English-speaking native of Roatan island, who always had work as a cook and quit several jobs when she had had enough of her employers. Not only was she able to secure employment with little difficulty, but she could also display her contempt for her employer with apparent impunity. On one occasion, while in the employ of a woman she referred to as a "devil," McNabb decided to quit on an evening when guests had been invited for a meal. To exact her revenge, McNabb waited until after she had prepared a roast and put it in the oven to cook; she then slipped out the back door, leaving her employer to discover, in her own time, that the roast was on fire and that there would not be anyone to prepare breakfast in the morning. Inez McNabb lived out H. H. Munro's aphorism "The cook was a good cook, as cooks go; and as good cooks go, she went."

Replacing someone like McNabb was not so easy because not every woman, regardless of her facility with the English language and her skills in the domestic arts, could be welcomed into the home. In addition to maintaining a family residence that resembled an idealized American home, company wives were also responsible for ensuring that their husbands did not stray. Although the potential infidelity of a spouse might be a concern for women everywhere, Euro-American women in Central America were particularly wary of the locals. Therefore an important consideration in the employment of female servants was the individual's marital status. Company wives worried about having single women in their homes because in their eyes the morality of the local population was always suspect. Sidonie Smith argues that in the imperial setting the natives were considered to have an "abnormal sexual appetite," a "'dark' force lurking inside 'civilized man'" and a threat to Western culture.[48] Marital status was important because, by definition, company wives were married women and, since they were the corporate standard by which all others were measured, relationships without legal sanction were evidence of inferiority. A woman's role was to get married, become a good housekeeper, and protect her husband from himself.

One company wife's concerns about the amorality of the domestic labor pool available in Panama is captured in a letter written by Winifred James, a self-described "Woman in the Wilderness," who wrote that there was "one universal calling for old and young alike, and with that profession open to all, irrespective of age or ugliness or any of the arts, you are not going to have much choice of cooks and housemaids." If you did find a woman who was willing to work in your home, according to James, "she would have to be either too young or too old to be able to lift a saucepan." Occasionally, however, a woman would "stray in" and "condescend to combine the two professions."[49] Emery-Waterhouse mentions that servants had to be "watched and sent for venereal disease medicine regularly because 80 percent of [the] labouring class [was] infected."[50] Concerns over sexual promiscuity highlight the opinion many company wives had of the "Other" women who lived in their midst. From all accounts the best domestic servant was one who was chaste and not a threat to the social fabric of the "white zone." This is why the women of Tela were so concerned about the example set by David Creighton, the Scottish engineer who became romantically involved with his cook's daughter and why in the early years the United Fruit Company had a policy of sending men home if they began a relationship with a local woman.

Despite all the problems associated with finding and retaining acceptable domestic servants, they were seen to be a necessary part of life in the tropics. In Siguican, according to Emery-Waterhouse, the "extreme heat" made it impossible for the foreign woman to do "any but the lightest housework." As a consequence some women hired "a cook, a laundress and a house boy," while those whose husbands occupied lower ranks within the corporation would be obliged to settle for the paid services of one all-around domestic laborer.[51] The fact that a family was entitled to only one domestic servant did not mean that the company wife performed the tasks that were left undone. As the lone employee hired to cook for a Euro-American household, Inez McNabb stated that her job was not limited to the kitchen: "I did everything, I did laundry, I cooked, I cleaned, I took care of kids." There was, however, according to Grenfell Price, a risk involved in getting other people to do too much work around the house. With "coloured servants and fair financial resources it [was] probable that American women [were doing] insufficient housework," with the result that their health and communities suffered.[52]

In addition to apparently being better suited to cooking, cleaning, and raising children in the tropics, domestic servants were also necessary because of the active social lives the white community members maintained. To hear Emery-Waterhouse explain it, evenings were spent entertaining and being entertained by one's neighbors. She claimed that everyone entertained or were entertained a couple of times a week; movies were shown regularly, and twice a month "there was a formal dance."[53] Cooks in Siguican were expected to prepare regular meals for the family, cater afternoon teas, and bring their bosses an "early traguito of coffee to [their] bedside." Cooks had to know how to prepare hors d'oeuvres and meals for the large evening get-togethers that were a regular part of social life in Siguican.[54] Although not all social activities involved inviting guests into private homes, when people did show up it was imperative that they be offered refreshments and food tailored to American tastes. Cooks were the labor elite in these homes, and the household pay scale reflected their status.

The problem was that most of the women hired to cook had little or no experience with modern appliances or the kinds of foods they were expected to prepare. To the impoverished women of the enclaves, the modern kitchens in the white zone resembled a scientific laboratory, with its sleek electric appliances, indoor plumbing, and overhead lighting.[55] For company wives the task of managing a household included training domestic labor to work in a modern environment and perform at a level befitting the position and lifestyle of the Euro-American elite. Accounts by women who managed domestic servants often refer to disastrous meals prepared by a cook who had no idea how to use foreign ingredients to produce food they had never heard of before. Emery-Waterhouse recounts her experiences of being served "calves' brains" and her disgust at lifting the cover on a kettle to find turkey feet, "the more unseemly appendages of fowl," protruding from the broth.[56] The only option for a Euro-American woman who did not wish to have her family served unspeakable bits of domestic animals or combinations of ingredients she had never seen before was to train her cook in the finer arts of American cooking.

Training by example, whereby the company wife donned an apron, rolled up her sleeves, and demonstrated the means of creating acceptable results in the kitchen, was the only real option open to most women. However, hands-on training was fraught with difficulties because in addition to being time-consuming and stressing the limits of a white woman's ability to work in the tropics, it involved intimate contact with the hired help. Company wives employed women they considered to be inferior to themselves, and they consciously minimized their social contact with them. "Most prototypical feminine activity," as Susan Leonardi argues, might cross the "social barriers of class, race, and generation." This was not the case for most company wives and their servants.[57] Working with someone in a kitchen and sharing recipes across the table involves divulging personal details. Such innocuous phrases as "My mother always did it this way" or "Where I come from" serve to invite questions prying into family relations and idiosyncrasies that are not normally shared with people who, in addition to being strangers, are considered to be of a lower social order. As Anne E. Goldman argues, in the kitchen women of different races and classes do not "easily fall into sisterhood."[58] In the corporate enclaves the distance between the colonizer and the colonized had to be maintained; familiarity breeds even more contempt when the exploited finds out just how artificial the divide is. The diesel mechanic's wife was not equal to the wife of the superintendent, and domestics knew the difference.

Even if the company wife was someone like Frances Emery-Waterhouse, who spoke some Spanish and was not opposed to fraterniz-ing with the locals, the next great hurdle after teaching the cook to cook was to get her to remember how to cook the same way every time. The logical solution in such a situation was to follow Emery-Waterhouse's example when she encountered problems with "Conchita Maria [who] couldn't cook worth a darn." Conchita claimed she never could remem-ber recipes or read the English in the cookbooks available to her in the home. Consequently Emery-Waterhouse translated and typed up several recipes, only to discover that Conchita could not read in any language.[59] With Conchita and illiterate women like her there was little to do but increase supervision or find someone to replace her who could read.

Finding women who could read was not a serious problem, as evidenced in the data from the Costa Rican census. Most of the women in the sample had at least a minimal education, and cookbooks are not difficult to read because they are repetitive. The real problem was to find a cookbook con-taining recipes designed for the American palate that both the company wife and the cook could understand. With such a tool, orders could be placed with the cook and results could be predicted. Moreover cooks who could read did not require explanations of methods that might lead to prying questions about other personal matters. They could also be kept at a proper distance in order to avoid too much contact with company wives. Familiarity, especially in a "white zone" where differences were imposed, did not lend itself to good labour relations. While West Indian cooks could rely on the company wife's existing collection of cookbooks for inspiration, Hispanic women could not be expected to read English, and books in Spanish did not contain the foods demanded by people living in the artificial confines of a white zone. Moreover cookbooks in Spanish did not permit the English-speaking boss to maintain complete control over the kitchen because they could not read the recipes themselves.

In regions of Latin America where English-speaking cooks were nonexistent, women in enclaves sometimes produced community cookbooks as training manuals that allowed them to share culinary secrets without crossing the social barriers that separated company wives from the women they employed.[60] In Caribbean Central America West Indian women were employed as cooks and Hispanic women were used for other domestic tasks. Consequently West Indian women, like their male counterparts, formed a labor elite within enclave society.[61] Company wives, like their company husbands, preferred West Indian labor because they could more easily communicate with them and because they were in a tenuous position. Throughout Central America West Indians were a group apart who did not enjoy the protection citizenship afforded the Central American workers who went to the enclaves in search of work.

Spanish was a foreign language in the white zones of Central America because life in the tropics was temporary for most Euro-American employees brought in to fill management roles. Senior administrators were often the exception; they moved from one plantation district to another. As a result, company managers and their wives typically spent no more than a few years in the tropics before moving back to the United States. Sojourns in Central America were temporary placements that did not encourage the development of an understanding of the people and customs of the host country. Company wives and their families were the domestic expression of the power of multinational corporations in Central America, and like the companies their husbands worked for, they were quick to move on after they had obtained what they needed in the tropics.

In conclusion, white zones were short-term residences for their inhabitants and were used by multinational corporations as a means of maximizing profits. Corporations needed skilled Euro-American men in the tropics, and it was deemed beneficial to create a wholesome environment for them to live in. But corporations also had to lure Euro-American women to the tropics. To do this they created white zones, model communities protected by high walls, where the English language was spoken, the lawns were manicured, and domestic servants performed all the most mundane tasks. Consequently company wives and "white zones" were as much a part of the banana business as railways and port facilities. Their presence ensured that the managerial elite did not fraternize with the locals and that the enterprise remained American. White zones, managed by "white" women, ensured the comfort of skilled and trustworthy individuals, and they established physical and social barriers between the leaders and the led.

NOTES

1 A classic example of the literature on the development of a multinational corporation is F. U. Adams, *Conquest of the Tropics*.

2 One of the most famous planned communities was built in the Amazon Basin by Henry Ford, a social Darwinist of the first rank. In 1927, seeking to circumvent the British and Dutch rubber monopolies, Ford bought two and a half million acres of Amazonian riverfront property, called his development project Fordlandia, and set in motion a multimillion-dollar scheme in the wilds of Brazil. He built a town complete with miles of roads and railroads, a modern port, a factory, schools, churches, hundreds of brick and stucco bungalows, and a fully equipped hospital that overlooked swimming pools, tennis courts, and a golf course carved from the jungle. Fordlandia was an environmental and economic disaster, and in 1945 Ford abandoned it.

3 For an understanding of a North American expatriate community, see Knapp and Knapp, *Red, White and Blue Paradise*.

4 The Canal Zone was the regional hub for transportation, entertainment, and shopping in the region.

5 Price, *White Settlers in the Tropics*, 177.

6 Ibid., 178.

7 For firsthand accounts by women, see W. L. James, *A Woman in the Wilderness*; Matschat, *Seven Grass Huts*; Shields, *The Changing Wind*. For a somewhat different account, see Cameron, *A Woman's Winter in South America*. Cameron is remarkable because she managed to travel the world at a time when few women ventured abroad on their own. According to Jane Robinson, Cameron "should be the patron saint of cruise liners; although she covered a good 250,000 miles between 1910 and 1925, almost all of them were courtesy of some shipping line, steamer company, or local railway" (*Wayward Women*, 177).

8 See Simon, *Les Exploratrices*, for nineteenth-century insight into the lives of women who traveled the world and wrote of their observations. According to Simon, there are two classes of explorers, "ceux qui découvre et ceux qui observent." The author considered women to be the observers, and he

argues that the reports on their travels shed much needed light on the intricacies of the world.

9   See, for example, Tinkler, "Introduction to Special Issue"; Cooper and Stoler, *Tensions of Empire*; Gouda, "Nyonyas on the Colonial Divide"; Boutiler, "European Women in the Solomon Islands." For a less critical but revealing survey of the lives of the foreign elite, see Hickman, *Daughters of Britannia*.

10 George, "Homes in the Empire," 108–9. See also Anne McClintock's discussion of the exotic and erotic images of empire in *Imperial Leather*.

11 See Stoler, "Carnal Knowledge," 73, for a discussion of the boundaries of elite culture in the colonial context.

12 For an example of the literature on how women projected imperial power abroad while at the same time struggling for political rights at home, see Wildenthal, "'When Men Are Weak'"; Burton, *Burdens of History*; Ware, *Beyond the Pale*; Amos and Parmar, "Challenging Imperial Feminism." Also of interest is the impact of imperialism on women in Europe. In "Imperialism and Motherhood" Davin raises questions about the emphasis placed on motherhood as part of the imperial project.

13 George, "Homes in the Empire," 116.

14 S. May and Plaza, *The United Fruit Company*, 187.

15 Price, *White Settlers in the Tropics*, 134–35.

16 See George, "Homes in the Empire," for a full discussion of race and class in the discourse of empire. See also Stoler, "Rethinking Colonial Categories"; Sharpe, *Allegories of Empire*; Gouda, "Nyonyas on the Colonial Divide."

17 For a visual representation of the multinational enclave and relations between Euro-Americans and other people in a multinational enclave, see Henri-Georges Clouzot's 1953 film, *Le salaire de la peur* (Wages of Fear), staring Yves Montand and Charles Vanel as two stranded French adventurers who are looking for an opportunity to earn enough to purchase a ticket home. The movie portrays the Southern Oil Company, modeled after Standard Oil, as being ruthless, amoral, and money-grubbing. The film offers what might be considered a portrayal of what Georges Arnaud, whose novel by the same name was adapted for the film, and the director Clouzot understood social relations to be in a Central American enclave. Although the book is set in Guatemala, Arnaud cautioned readers not to search for geographic accuracy because, he argued, it is always a delusion: "[Guatemala] does not exist, I know because I lived it." Arnaud was admitting the obvious, that outsiders like himself cannot comprehend the intricacies of a country and a society they have little respect for or interest in.

18 Emery-Waterhouse, *Banana Paradise*, 4.

19 Siguican was not Almirante, Panama, described in 1915 by Winifred James as "no more than a nigger camp with enough white people to break the ground and render it habitable." James's case is interesting because she was British and was "married to the Americanest American." Her husband worked for

United Fruit and they lived on a hill opposite the town. Almirante is the center of a banana plantation complex that is located in one of the remotest regions of Panama. See W. L. James, *A Woman in the Wilderness*, 2.

20 Emery-Waterhouse, *Banana Paradise*, 94.

21 S. May and Plaza, *The United Fruit Company*, 187.

22 Despite the distinctions made by the company, Stacey May and Galo Plaza, who conducted a major study of the United Fruit Company in the 1950s, found that the housing for "clerical, supervisory and executive personnel [was], in most cases, superior to that available to persons of similar income status in the United States" (*The United Fruit Company*, 187).

23 See ibid., 183–99, for a full discussion of the United Fruit Company's social welfare programs. I would like to thank Rand Garo, Inez McNabb, and don Rafael Elvir for sharing their recollections.

24 See Grandin, *Fordlandia*, for a remarkable look at a planned community.

25 The guards had at their disposal a holding cell for intruders.

26 Interview with don Rafael Elvir, Tela, Honduras, January 2000. Elvir's father was one of the richest men in the region until political turmoil in the 1920s and the economic depression of the 1930s bankrupted him. Don Rafael ended up working for the fruit company for forty years and noted with pride that he refused company housing outside of the white zone because he was too "proud" and did not want to be "classified." According to don Rafael, when the company found out that his brother-in-law was the *ministro de fomento*, he was immediately offered a higher salary and first-class housing.

27 Normally original census forms are destroyed and researchers have access only to distilled reports. Fortunately the forms for the Costa Rican census of 1927 were not destroyed after the data were recorded and the material is available to the public. In the province of Limón, the country's center for banana production until the late 1930s, the census revealed that of the 32,000 residents, 58 percent were of African descent. The overwhelming majority of these people were West Indian immigrants or their direct descendants. Except for a small number of indigenous people and a scattering of other people of non-European descent, 40 percent of the people in the census were described as being of the white race. Most were Costa Ricans who, in the country's national discourse of the nineteenth and twentieth centuries, were considered white. Of the white minority, only a small fraction were not Costa Ricans, and they tended to work for the United Fruit Company and live together in corporate housing. In a sample of 6,432 individuals, of the 2,576 people who were described as white, 15 percent were not Costa Ricans; these people accounted for approximately 6 percent of the total. They were a significant but small minority of the provincial population.

28 Of the households that did not contain a married couple, one contained two brothers, a physician and a pharmacist; another two foreign-born men; and the third was home to three women who worked as nurses in the hospital.

Older couples may have had children who had already left home or, as was common, were attending schools in the United States.

29 Forming a buffer just outside the white zone were the bachelors' quarters and a guesthouse, where single Euro-American men of rank were housed. The hospital administrator and his family, who were Jamaicans and described as being "mulatto" in the census, lived outside the fence in a separate house next to the guesthouse.

30 The samples for Hispanic and West Indian households were taken from the original census forms, compiled during a house-to-house survey. Consequently the samples were from small neighborhoods that compared in size with the sample taken in the white zone. Since housing was segregated, all of the houses in a given area could be selected as a representative sample and no houses were left out of the sample because they did not conform to the needs of the study. The term used in the census for a common-law relationship is "sin sanción legal" (without legal sanction).

31 The question of what constituted a marriage among West Indians resident in Catholic Costa Rica needs further study. Unions sanctioned by some religious faiths were not recognized by the Catholic Church, creating a distinction between "legal" and "religious" marriages.

32 Postings in the tropics were also perilous, with numerous tales of white people suffering from disease and lacking adequate health care, and few people tempted fate for any longer than they had to.

33 Interview with don Rafael Elvir.

34 Ibid.

35 Ibid.

36 Stoler, "Sexual Affronts," 514–15.

37 Emery-Waterhouse, *Banana Paradise*, 124.

38 S. May and Plaza, *The United Fruit Company*, 187.

39 See Boutiler, "European Women in the Solomon Islands."

40 Emery-Waterhouse, *Banana Paradise*, 95.

41 Ibid.

42 Ibid., 4.

43 For a revealing account of the difficulties encountered by white women in dealing with domestic labor, see Hickman, *Daughters of Britannia*, 69–89.

44 S. May and Plaza, *The United Fruit Company*, 187; Emery-Waterhouse, *Banana Paradise*, 93.

45 Obtaining items for her home meant getting permission from a company official to dig through the trash on the edge of a hill where old dishes and other discarded furnishings were thrown.

46 Emery-Waterhouse, *Banana Paradise*, 92.

47 Interview with Lola Wilkinson.

48 S. Smith, "The Other Woman," 411.

49 W. L. James, *A Woman in the Wilderness*, 27–28.

50   Emery-Waterhouse, *Banana Paradise*, 92.

51   Ibid.

52   Price, *White Setters in the Tropics*, 160.

53   Emery-Waterhouse, *Banana Paradise*, 94.

54   Ibid., 4.

55   Modern appliances, sometimes referred to in hardware circles as "wife sav-ers," were the exclusive preserve of the households of the enclave elite be-cause the corporations provided all of the furnishings. Some appliances may not even have been found in the homes they left in the Unites States. All of the homes in the white zones were electrified, but in 1930 in the United States 90 percent of rural homes were not connected to the electric power grid.

56   Emery Waterhouse, *Banana Paradise*, 175.

57   Leonardi, "Recipes for Reading," 342.

58   Goldman, "'I Yam What I Yam,'" 172.

59   Emery-Waterhouse, *Banana Paradise*, 239.

60   See *International Cook Book—Recetario Internacional*. For a discussion of community cookbooks, see the articles in Bower, *Recipes for Reading* and Harpelle, "Cooking Class."

61   The literature on the West Indian diaspora in Central America is uneven, but a few significant studies have been produced. See, for example, Conniff, *Black Labour on a White Canal*; Bourgois, *Ethnicity at Work*; Chomsky, *West Indian Workers*; Harpelle, *The West Indians of Costa Rica*.

THE SLOW ASCENT OF THE MARGINALIZED

Afro-Descendants in Costa Rica and Nicaragua

Mauricio Meléndez Obando

Anyone who has taught the history of Central America to the region's youth will recognize the following question: "What happened to the slaves of the colonial period?" The professor thus queried might like to imagine the question as inviting a general description of the lives the slaves led, as in "What happened to them? What transpired in their lives?" But soon enough that wishful thinking is dispelled by a more insistent if inelegant rephrasing of the question as "Where did they go? Why aren't their descendants here among us any longer?"

Rather than attempting a full-scale deconstruction of national origin myths of ethnicity and race, the questioners can often be more deeply engaged by a discussion of who *they* and *them* might actually be, or *we* and *us*, as Rina Cáceres tirelessly reminds us, not where they have gone. This is especially true when even dusty old historical figures can be genealogically connected to portraits or photographs of their more recent and better known descendants. As we have seen in several essays in this volume, particularly those by Wolfe and Gudmundson, numerous Nicaraguan historical figures can be visually represented. What I offer here is a visual and textual rendering of a series of renowned Nicaraguans and Costa Ricans whose African heritage was traditionally obscured, often by their own hand, in favor of a both real and imagined European and Native American heritage more in step with the positions they aspired and ascended to over the past two centuries of independent, national life.

In societies having their distant origins in relatively small groups it is normal that after several centuries many members of today's societies share a large number of original ancestors (*raíces primigenias*). Thus the Arab proverb "All kings descend from beggars and all beggars descend from kings" contains great truth, which should not seem extraordinary in any society. In the case of Hispanic America the Venezuelan Báez Meneses synthesizes this very well:

> Based on unsuspectingly truthful historical documents and with the help of rigorous mathematical logic, given the large number of ancestors that everyone has according to the laws of reproduction, it is easy to conclude that after a certain number of centuries everyone has as ancestors all the people that at that (former) time constituted the nation in question: rulers and ruled, nobles and plebeians, the free and the slave.[1]

What is remarkable about the peoples of Hispanic America is the systematic amnesia regarding their violent and diverse origins, whose basic roots, both genetic and cultural, can be found in three human groups (traditionally characterized racially and culturally): Indians, blacks, and whites.[2] Today Hispanic American official discourses emphasize cultural diversity, past and present, as a positive quality, but in terms of social behavior we still have a long way to go before that quality is seen as such in our societies' hearts of hearts. Of course, structural change cannot be limited to the discursive level of tourism promotion.

Traditionally some of these nations have always emphasized race mixture (but between Spaniards and Amerindians) as a basic element in their societies' foundations. It is undeniable that this biological and cultural reality is the weightiest in some nations; however, the third root, the African, is present everywhere in America since slavery knew no boundaries during the colonial period. Of course, in some nations more than in others this third element is first. Nowhere in Spanish territory in America did these unfree immigrants fail to appear and leave their mark. Even today, when we look at the faces of Chileans, Argentines, Guatemalans, or Costa Ricans and see no element of African ancestry, it is well-known that this heritage reveals itself in their living and material culture as well as in the blood that runs in their veins. Think only of the Argentine tango or Guatemala's colonial architecture.

Invariably in Central America, even in academic circles, when the presence of Afro-descendants is mentioned the popular imagination refers to the Caribbean (in Guatemala, Honduras, Nicaragua, and Costa

Rica, that is; in El Salvador they would say simply that there never were any). Moreover Afro-descendants on the Caribbean coast are perceived as recent immigrants, foreign to the ancient history of the isthmian nations. Thus each country has constructed myths of its people's genesis. For example, the Nicaraguan case emphasizes as fundamental the broad-based race mixture (of course, of the Spanish and Indian) of its people, while the Costa Rican case boasts of its exclusively Spanish origin. Both myths have collapsed in the face of recent genealogical and historical studies that prove the distant, three-part origins of both Nicaraguans and Costa Ricans, peoples moreover so connected by intermarriage since colonial times as to surprise the xenophobes of both nations (perhaps even more the Costa Ricans).[3]

This is the historical reality in all Hispanic America, and it can be proven when genealogical studies abandon their prejudices in order to seriously and systematically consult the documentary sources. Even though the most visible contribution of Africa in America is ourselves, carriers of the seed of African blood mixed with Amerindian and European, the contribution goes beyond genetics. The active participation continentwide began with the arrival of the first slaves, first with their unfree labor in city and countryside, later as free, skilled labor, and finally in areas formerly barred to Afro-descendants, to which they occasionally had access thanks to a gradual, intentional whitening.

In colonial Hispanic America society was socioracially stratified by biological and socioeconomic factors. On the one hand, biological factors such as skin and hair color were expressions of ethnic (or racial, in the traditional sense of the term) differences according to which society was structured in three basic groups: Spaniards (creoles or peninsulars), Indians, and blacks, and their mixtures *mestizos, mulatos,* and *zambos,* among others, better known as "castes." The Spaniards occupied the highest positions as bearers of purity of blood and honor, among other elements, while the rest were beneath them. In the lowest position were black slaves and their descendants, who were barred by law from any possibility of ascent to the pinnacle. However, on the other hand, socioeconomic factors such as honor, dress, speech, work, influence, and wealth were associated with the biological factors in order to reinforce racial separation of the groups.

Nevertheless these socioeconomic factors made stratification much more complex since, with the slow ascent of the castes, especially Afro-descendants, to better positions (access to dress, speech, work, and money that originally only Spaniards had), socioracial divisions became relative. Moreover during the colonial period the opportunities for economic and political ascent by the Afro-descent population depended in large part on the explicit or tacit recognition by their Spanish parents, on the labor experience or skills achieved during or after their enslavement, on the adoption of Spanish customs (dress, speech, etc.), and on the support of influential friends or family members. Already by the last quarter of the eighteenth century (and exceptionally even earlier) in Central America we find lawyers of the Real Audiencia, notaries, and large numbers of clerics who had African ancestors despite the prohibition of Afro-descendants from occupying such positions. Thus the legal limitations against Afro-descendants in place until 1821 began to show cracks through which some of them passed. After the call for independence many more *afromestizos* found the path open to their aspirations, postponed for centuries, for sociopolitical ascent.

Once independence was achieved one of the first steps taken by governments to differentiate themselves from the old regime was the elimination of the socioracial categories and honorific distinctions (these were no longer noted in the civil and ecclesiastical records beginning in 1822), which were replaced by the term *citizen*. Of course, centennial social practices could not be eliminated overnight, and years later (around the mid-nineteenth century) the use of *don* and *doña* reoccurred, limited to economically and politically powerful families (almost always descendants of the old colonial elite, but also new elite members of openly afromestiza extraction). Various cases allow us to see how Afro-descendants, from the last years of the colony to the present, arrived at different social levels.

POLITICS

As I noted, in exceptional cases some afromestizos in colonial times made it into strata barred to them by law; perhaps one of the most outstanding cases in Central America is that of Dionisio de la Cuadra, son of a creole

FIGURE 1 José Vicente Cuadra Lugo. *Source*: Nicaragua, Ministerio de Educación website.

Spaniard and an ex-slave *mulata*, born around 1774 in Granada, Nicaragua, who with crown approval was confirmed in the position of notary in the final days of the colonial period. Dionisio de la Cuadra married Ana Norberta Lugo, also afromestiza, and they were the parents of José Vicente Cuadro Lugo (1812–94), president of Nicaragua (1871–75), and of

FIGURE 2 Anastasio Somoza García (center) with his sons, Anastasio (left) and Luís (right) Somoza Debayle. Courtesy of Instituto de Historia de Nicaragua y Centroamérica, Universidad Centroaméricana.

Manuela Cuadra Lugo, wife of Salvador Sacasa, from whom descend Anastasio Somoza Garcia and his sons, Luís and Anastasio Somoza Debayle, all three presidents of Nicaragua.

In Costa Rica we have the case of Vicente Aguilar Cubero (1808–60), son of a mestizo father and afromestiza mother, born in Cartago, who,

FIGURE 3 Vicente Aguilar Cubero.
Sources: Carlos Meléndez Chaverri, *Dr. José María Montealegre* (San José: Academia de Geografía e Historia de Costa Rica, 1968), 63; La Nacion Digital website.

FIGURE 4 Miguel Ángel Rodríguez Echeverría.
Courtesy of *El Financiero*, San José, Costa Rica.

like his father and maternal grandfather, was a merchant in the trade between Jamaica, Matina, Cartago, and Rivas. By the middle of the nineteenth century he had become the richest man in his country, serving as vice president in 1856. Among his descendants are Miguel Ángel Rodríguez Echeverría, president (1998–2002) and secretary general of the Organization of American States for a single day (before being indicted and jailed on corruption charges); Germán Serrano Pinto, vice president (1994–98); and a large number of ministers. From Francisco Aguilar Cubero, twice first cousin of Vicente, descends another president of the republic, Francisco Aguilar Barquero (1919–20). Vicente Cubero Paniagua, son of an ex-slave, mulatto father and a free mulata mother, was born in Cartago around 1753 and became a merchant, marrying the ex-slave Antonia Francisca Escalante y Paniagua. They were the maternal grandparents of Vicente and Francisco Aguilar Cubero.

HEROES

In the war against the filibusters (1856–57) there are innumerable anonymous heroes, both Nicaraguan and Costa Rican. In Costa Rica every family has its hero, although most do not know it. There are some whose names continue to be venerated today. In Nicaragua one of them is José Dolores Estrada Vado (1792–1869), who in his baptismal entry was registered as mulatto,[4] son of Timoteo Estrada and Gertrudis Vado Lugo. In Costa Rica we have Juan Santamaría (1831–56), son of the afromestiza Manuela Santamaría (1800–1878), who was the daughter of Mateo Santamaría (or Carvajal) and María Narcisa Rodríguez, whose children are registered indistinguishably as mulattos or mestizos.

LITERATURE

In the literary field several persons stand out, the best known being the Nicaraguan poet Rubén Darío (1867–1916) for his universal transcendence as the major creator of modernist poetry. Born Félix Rubén García Sarmiento in San Pedro Metapa, today Ciudad Darío, on 18 January 1867, Darío was baptized in León on 3 March of that year; his godfather and the man who raised him was Félix Ramírez Mayorga (son of Francisco Ramírez and María Gil Mayorga).

FIGURE 5 José Dolores Estrada
Vado on Nicaraguan currency.
Photograph by Mauricio
Meléndez.

FIGURE 6 Statue of Juan
Santamaría. *Source*: La Nación
Digital website.

Darío was the son of José Manuel García and Rosa Sarmiento, who were married in León on 16 April 1866, after obtaining ecclesiastical dispensation based on their close kinship. José Manuel García (1820–88) was the son of Domingo García and Petronila Mayorga, recorded as mulattos in the marital registry in 1819. Rosa Sarmiento was the daughter of Ignacio

FIGURE 7 Rubén Darío, 1898. *Source*: Edelberto Torres, *La vida dramática de Rubén Darío*, 2nd ed. (Mexico City: Biografías Gandesa, 1956), unnumbered page.

FIGURE 8 Rubén Darío, portrait done for the Organization of American States, 1914.
Source: Mount Holyoke College website.

FIGURE 9 Pablo Antonio Cuadra Cardenal. *Source*: La Nación Digital website.

Sarmiento and Concepción Umaña. Petronila Mayorga was the daughter of Rita Mayorga, and Ignacio Sarmiento was the son of Casimiro Sarmiento and Juana Ventura Mayorga. Rita and Juana Ventura were blood sisters, daughters of Darío Mayorga and Catarina Rivas.

The poet Román Mayorga Rivas (1862–1925), a contemporary of Darío, was the son of Cleto Mayorga Buitrago and María Rivas. Cleto was the son of Fulgencio Mayorga, an afromestizo and the blood brother of María Gil and Josefa Simeona Mayorga, both mulatas.

The poet Pablo Antonio Cuadra Cardenal (1912–2002) was the grandson of José Joaquín Cuadra Lugo, son of Dionisio Cuadra and Ana Norberta Lugo, both afromestizos.

From Costa Rica there are no figures with the stature of Darío, but some writers stand out and have transcended national borders. One of them is Carlos Luis Fallas Sibaja (1909–65), the author of *Mamita Yunai* (1940), among other works, and a militant activist in the Communist Party. The son of Abelina Fallas Sibaja, Carlos Luis, better known as Calufa, descends

FIGURE 10 María Isabel Carvajal ("Carmen Lyra").
Sources: Luisa Gonález and Carlos Luis Sáenz,
Carmen Lyra (San José, Costa Rica: Editorial
Universidad Nacional a Distancia, Serie Quien fue y
qué hizo?, 1998), 99; La Nación Digital website.

FIGURE 11 Carlos Luis Fallas Sibaja ("Calufa").
Source: Victor Manuel Arroyo, *Carlos Luis Fallas* (San
José, Costa Rica: Ministerio de Cuļtura, Juventud y
Deportes, Serie Quien fue y qué hizo?, 1973), 111.

from the mulata Ana Cardoso (1649), a *parda* (brown) slave, whose descendants can be found at every social level of the nation.

María Isabel Carvajal (1887–1949), better known as Carmen Lyra, also a communist activist and writer, is best remembered today for her *Cuentos de mi tía Panchita*, a children's delight for several generations of Costa Ricans. She descends from Antonia Carvajal Elizondo (1789), whose family was afromestiza.

Jorge Bravo Brenes, better known as Jorge de Bravo (1938–67), the greatest poet of the mid-twentieth century, descends from the mulatto Captain Tomás del Camino, who was the slave of Captain Cristóbal Martín Cubero.

BISHOPS

Among the ecclesiastical authorities of afromestiza descent in both nations several stand out. Simeón Pereira Castellón (1863–1921), bishop of León (1902–21), was born in that city on 2 July 1863, the son of Pedro Pereira Mayorga and Dolores Castellón Vallecillo. Pedro Pereira Mayorga was the son of Felipe Neri Pereira and Josefa Simeona Mayorga, a mulata descendant of the Spanish creole family Díaz de Mayorga.[5] It may be that Felipe Neri Pereira was also afromestizo, of the Pereira mulattos from the neighborhood of San Felipe in León.

The most outstanding example from Costa Rica is Víctor Manuel Sanabria Martínez (1899–1952), archbishop of San José (1940–52), who was born in Cartago, the old colonial capital, on 17 January 1899, the son of Zenón Sanabria Quirós (1866–1922) and Juana Martínez Brenes. Zenón Sanabria Quirós was the son of Marcial Sanabria Solano and María Francisca Quirós Alarcón. Marcial was descended from Antonio Masís, the black slave of Sergeant Juan Masís and the husband of Josefa Manuela Guerrero, a free mulata whom he married in Cartago in 1716. It is a bit odd that Sanabria, the father of modern genealogical studies in Central America (and perhaps all Hispanic America), chose not to include any mention of the African descent in the genealogical work he did on his own family.

FIGURE 12 Simeón Pereira Castellón. *Source*: Archivo Histórico Arquidiocesano Bernardo Augusto Thiel, San José, Costa Rica.

FIGURE 13 Víctor Manuel Sanabria Martínez. *Source*: Archivo Histórico Arquidiocesano Bernardo Augusto Thiel, San José, Costa Rica.

I could cite many more cases for each nation, but my only intention has been to make visible the presence of the descendants of slaves brought to Central America in colonial times through the Independence era and their genealogical repercussions in our own time. This exercise, carried out for Nicaragua and Costa Rica, could be done for all the other Central American nations, despite the documentary limitations in Honduras and El Salvador.[6] For example, José Joaquín Lindo, president of Honduras, is cited in some documents as afromestizo, and Rafael Carrera, president of Guatemala, clearly has afromestizo roots, which I have been able to document on his mother's side.

As we can see, *they* (in reality *we*) are in all areas of cultural and political life in Central America. The Spanish system that kept afromestizos marginalized from the halls of power for centuries did not in practice prevent some from leaking into the Spanish strata of Hispanic American societies even before 1821. And even though the institution of *gracias al sacar* was not widely used in Central America, it too allowed for such leakage to be legalized in exceptional cases. With Independence and the formal substitution of socioracial categories with the term *citizen*, afromestizos finally witnessed the elimination of legal and social barriers justifying their centuries-long exclusion from the halls of power. Some did not fail to take advantage of the opportunity: they had access to municipal offices, the legislative, executive, and judicial branches of government, and the high clergy throughout Central America.

Now we know the answer to the question frequently posed to those of us who study slavery in Central America. But what happened to the slaves of the colonial period?

NOTES

To prepare genealogies of different individuals I have had to consult dozens of documents in various historical archives, principally in the Archivo Histórico Arquidiocesano Bernardo Augusto Thiel (Costa Rica), the Archivo Nacional de Costa Rica, the Archivo Histórico Diocesano de León (Nicaragua), and the Archivo General de Centroamérica (Guatemala). Some of the documentary sources are cited in the secondary works listed in the bibliography; those that remain unpublished are included in detail on the Mount Holyoke College website.

1   Báez Meneses, "Los estudios genealógicos en Venezuela," 604.

2   There is, of course, only one human "race."

3   However, these myths continue to survive in popular terms.

4   Romero Vargas, *Las estructuras sociales*, 357.

5   The marriage entry was not found in the Sagrario Cathedral in León; rather it was found in the marriage entry of María Gil Mayorga, a mulata (blood sister of Josefa Simeona), and Francisco Ramírez, a mestizo, dated 22 December 1811. Archivo Histórico Diocesano de León, Nicaragua, Matrimonios de El Sagrario de la Catedral de León (1807–24), fol. 84.

6   In reality this could be done anywhere in Iberoamerica. For example, in the Chilean case see what is said of Gabriela Mistral in Retamal Favereau, Celis Atria, and Muñoz Correa, *Familias fundadoras de Chile*, 322: "The person that with certainty can be said not to belong to this family (Godoy), nor to anyone of that surname, is precisely the most famous Chilean celebrity of that name: Lucila Godoy Alcayaga, better known as Gabriela Mistral, Nobel Prize in Literature in 1945. She carried the surname by adoption, as a sixth-generation descendant of Juana Godoy, born in La Serena at the end of the eighteenth century, daughter of the black slaves of the family we have studied."

BIBLIOGRAPHY

Adams, David P. "Malaria, Labor, and Population Distribution in Costa Rica: A Biohistorical Perspective." *Journal of Interdisciplinary History* 27, no. 1 (1996), 75–85.

Adams, Frederick Upham. *Conquest of the Tropics; the Story of the Creative Enterprises Conducted by the United Fruit Company.* New York: Doubleday, 1914.

Adams, Richard N. *Encuesta sobre la cultura de los ladinos en Guatemala.* Translated by Joaquín Noval. Guatemala City: Editorial del Ministerio de Educación Pública, 1956.

Adorno, Rolena. "The Indigenous Ethnographer: The 'Indio Ladino' as Historian and Cultural Mediation." *Implicit Understandings: Observing, Reporting, and Reflecting on the Encounters between Europeans and Other Peoples in the Early Modern Era*, edited by Stuart B. Schwartz, 378–402. Cambridge: Cambridge University Press, 1994.

Aguilar Bulgarelli, Oscar R. "La esclavitud en Costa Rica durante el periodo colonial. (Hipótesis de trabajo)." *Estudios Sociales Centroamericanos* 2, no. 5 (1973), 187–99.

Aguilar Bulgarelli, Oscar R., and Irene Alfaro A. *La esclavitud negra en Costa Rica: Origen de la oligarquía económica y política nacional.* San José, Costa Rica: Progreso Editorial, 1997.

Aguirre, Carlos. *Agentes de su propia libertad: Los esclavos de Lima y la desintegracion de la esclavitud, 1821–1854.* Lima: Fondo Editorial de la Pontificia Universidad Católica del Perú, 1993.

Aguirre Beltrán, Gonzalo. *El negro esclavo en Nueva España: La formación colonial, la medicina popular y otros ensayos.* Mexico City: Fondo de Cultura Económica, 1994.

———. *La población negra de México, 1519–1810: Estudio etno-histórico.* Mexico City: Ediciones Fuente Cultural, 1946.

Alfaro, Olmedo. *El peligro antillano en la América Central (La Defensa de la Raza).* 2nd ed. Panama City: Imprenta Nacional, 1925.

Alvarenga Venutolo, Patricia. "La inmigración extranjera y la nación costarricense." *Istmo: Revista virtual de estudios literarios y culturales centroamericanos*, no. 4 (July–December 2002).

Amos, Valerie, and Pratibha Parmar. "Challenging Imperial Feminism." *Feminist Review* 17 (autumn 1984), 3–19.

Anderson, Benedict. *Imagined Communities: Reflections on the Origin and Spread of Nationalism.* London: Verso, 1991.

Anderson, Moji. "'Cahuita Gone, Cahuita Gone': Struggles over Place on the Caribbean Coast of Costa Rica." Ph.D. dissertation, University of Cambridge, 2002.

Andrews, George Reid. *Afro-Latin America, 1800–2000.* Oxford: Oxford University Press, 2004.

———. *Blacks and Whites in São Paulo, 1888–1988.* Madison: University of Wisconsin Press, 1991.

Anthias, Floya, and Nira Yuval-Davis. *Racialized Boundaries: Race, Nation, Gender, Colour and Class and the Anti-Racist Struggle.* London: Routledge, 1992.

Appadurai, Arjun. *Modernity at Large: Cultural Dimensions of Globalizations.* Minneapolis: University of Minnesota Press, 1996.

Appelbaum, Nancy P. *Muddied Waters: Race, Region, and Local History in Colombia, 1846–1948.* Durham, N.C.: Duke University Press, 2003.

Appelbaum, Nancy P., Anne S. Macpherson, and Karin Alejandra Rosemblatt, eds. *Race and Nation in Modern Latin America.* Chapel Hill: University of North Carolina Press, 2003.

Arellano, Jorge Eduardo. *Reseña histórica de la Universidad de León, Nicaragua.* León, Nicaragua: Editorial Universitaria, 1988.

Argüello, Agenor. *Los precursores de la poesía nueva en Nicaragua.* Managua: Ediciones del Club del Libro Nicaragüense, 1962.

Argueta, Mario. *Historia laboral de Honduras: De la conquista al siglo XIX.* Tegucigalpa: Secretaría de Cultura y Turismo, Dirección General de Cultura, Departamento de Publicaciones, con el patrocinio de la Organización de Estados Americanos, 1985.

Arocha, Jaime. *Ombligados de Ananse: Hilos ancestrales y modernos en el Pacífico colombiano.* Colección CES. Bogotá: Facultad de Ciencias Humanas, United Nations, 1999.

Arosemena, Justo. "La cuestión americana i su importancia." *Escritos de Justo Arosemena: Estudio introductorio y antología,* edited by Argelia Tello Burgos, 247–63. Panama City: Universidad de Panamá, 1985.

Ayón, Tomás. *Historia de Nicaragua desde los tiempos más remotos hasta el año de 1852.* 3 vols. 1882–89; Managua: Fondo de Promoción Cultural-BANIC, 1993.

Bacon, Margaret Hope. *Abby Hopper Gibbons: Prison Reformer and Social Activist.* Albany: State University of New York Press, 2000.

Barberena Pérez, Alejandro. "El fusilamiento del general Corral." *Revista Conservadora,* no. 39 (1963), 31–38.

Barón Castro, Rodolfo. *La población de El Salvador.* Madrid: Consejo Superior de Investigaciones Científicas, Instituto Gonzalo Fernández de Oviedo, 1942.

Barrantes Ferrero, Mario. *Un caso de la esclavitud en Costa Rica*. 2nd ed. San José, Costa Rica: Instituto Geográfico Nacional, 1973.

Báez Meneses, Julio. "Los estudios genealógicos en Venezuela." *Hidalguía* (Madrid) 17, no. 96 (1969), 603–22.

Beals, Carleton. *America South*. Philadelphia: J. B. Lippincott, 1937.

———. "The Black Belt of the Caribbean." *Fortnightly Review*, 1 September 1931, 356–68.

Beckles, Hilary. "Creolization in Action: The Slave Labour Elite and Anti-Slavery in Barbados." *Questioning Creole: Creolisation Discourses in Caribbean Culture: In Honour of Kamau Brathwaite*, edited by Verene A. Shepherd and Glen L. Richards, 181–201. Kingston, Jamaica: Ian Randle Publishers, 2002.

Belaubre, Christophe. "Poder y redes sociales en Centroamérica: El caso de la Orden de los Dominicos (1757–1829)." *Mesoamérica* 41 (June 2001), 31–76.

Bell, Charles Napier. *Tangweera: Life and Adventures among Gentle Savages*. Edited by Philip Dennis. 1899; Austin: University of Texas Press, 1989.

Belli, Humberto. "Un ensayo de interpretación sobre las luchas políticas nicaragüenses: De la independencia hasta la revolución cubana." *Revista del Pensamiento Centroamericano* no. 157 (1977), 50–59.

Belly, Felix. *L'isthme Américain: notes d'un premier voyage, 1858*. Brussels: Weissenbruch, 1889.

Bennett, Herman L. *Africans in Colonial Mexico: Absolutism, Christianity, and Afro-Creole Consciousness, 1570–1640*. Bloomington: Indiana University Press, 2003.

———. "A Research Note: Race, Slavery, and the Ambiguity of Corporate Consciousness." *Colonial Latin American Historical Review* 3, no. 2 (1994), 207–13.

———. "The Subject in the Plot: National Boundaries in the History of the Black Atlantic." *African Studies Review* 43, no. 1 (2000), 101–24.

Berlin, Ira. *Many Thousands Gone: The First Two Centuries of Slavery in North America*. Cambridge, Mass.: Belknap Press of Harvard University Press, 1998.

Binayán Carmona, Narciso. *Historia genealógica argentina*. Buenos Aires: Emecé, 1999.

Blumenthal, Debra Gene. "Implements of Labor, Instruments of Honor: Muslim, Eastern and Black African Slaves in Fifteenth-Century Valencia." Ph.D. dissertation, University of Toronto, 2000.

Bolland, O. Nigel. *The Formation of a Colonial Society: Belize, from Conquest to Crown Colony*. Baltimore: Johns Hopkins University Press, 1977.

Bourgois, Philippe I. *Ethnicity at Work: Divided Labor on a Central American Banana Plantation*. Baltimore: Johns Hopkins University Press, 1989.

Boutiler, James A. "European Women in the Solomon Islands, 1900–1942: Accommodation and Change on the Pacific Frontier." *Rethinking Women's Roles: Perspectives on the Pacific*, edited by Denise O'Brien and Sharon W. Tiffany, 173–99. Los Angeles: University of California Press, 1984.

Bower, Anne L., ed. *Recipes for Reading: History, Stories, Community Cookbooks.*
Amherst: University of Massachusetts Press, 1997.

Bowser, Frederick P. "Africans in Spanish American Colonial Society." *Cambridge History of Latin America*, vol. 2, edited by Leslie Bethell, 357–79. Cambridge: Cambridge University Press, 1984.

Bozzoli de Wille, María Eugenia. "Continuidad del simbolismo del cacao, del siglo XVI al siglo XX." *V.º Centenario de Gonzalo Fernández de Oviedo: Memoria del congreso sobre el mundo centroamericano de su tiempo (24–25–26 y 27 de agosto, 1978)*, 229–40. Nicoya, Costa Rica: Comisión Nacional Organizadora, 1980.

Brown, Jacqueline Nassy. "Black Liverpool, Black America, and the Gendering of Diasporic Space." *Cultural Anthropology* 13, no. 3 (1998), 291–315.

Brown, Wallace. "Mosquito Shore and the Bay of Honduras During the Era of the American Revolution." *Belizean Studies* 18 (1990), 43–64.

Bryce-Laporte, Roy Simon. "Crisis, Contraculture and Religion among West Indians in the Panama Canal Zone." *Blackness in Latin America and the Caribbean*, vol. 1, edited by Norman E. Whitten Jr. and Arlene Torres, 100–118. Bloomington: Indiana University Press, 1998.

Buitrago Matus, Nicolás. *León: La sombra de Pedrarias.* 2 vols. León, Nicaragua: Fundación Ortíz Gurdián, 1998.

Burney, James. *History of the Buccaneers of America.* 1816; New York: Norton, 1950.

Burns, E. Bradford. *Patriarch and Folk: The Emergence of Nicaragua, 1798–1858.* Cambridge, Mass.: Harvard University Press, 1991.

Burton, Antoinette. *Burdens of History: British Feminists, Indian Women, and Imperial Culture, 1865–1915.* Chapel Hill: University of North Carolina Press, 1994.

Buska, Soili Iiris. "'Marimba Por Tí Me Muero': Region and Nation in Costa Rica, 1824–1939." Ph.D. dissertation, Indiana University, 2005.

Cáceres, Rina. "The African Origins of San Fernando de Omoa." *Trans-Atlantic Dimensions of Ethnicity in the African Diaspora*, edited by Paul E. Lovejoy and David Vincent Trotman, 115–37. London: Continuum, 2003.

———. "Migraciones forzadas y mercancías en el Caribe de la segunda mitad del siglo XVIII: El asiento de Aguirre y Arístegui." Unpublished manuscript, 2008.

———. *Negros, mulatos, esclavos y libertos en la Costa Rica del siglo XVII.* Mexico City: Instituto Panamericano de Geografía e Historia, 2000.

———, ed. *Rutas de la esclavitud en Africa y América Latina.* San José: Editorial de la Universidad de Costa Rica y Asociación Pro-historia Centroamericana, 2001.

Camacho, Juana, and Eduardo Restrepo, eds. *De montes, ríos y ciudades: Territorios e identidades de la gente negra en Colombia.* Bogotá: Fundación Natura, Instituto Colombiano de Antropología, 1999.

Cameron, Charlotte. *A Woman's Winter in South America*. London: Stanley Paul, 1911.

Cardenal, Ernesto. *El estrecho dudoso*. Madrid: Ediciones Cultura Hispánica, 1966.

———. *Golden UFOs: The Indian poems/Los Ovnis de oro: Poemas indios*. Bloomington: Indiana University Press, 1992.

———. *Homenaje a los indios americanos*. León: Universidad Nacional Autónoma de Nicaragua, 1969.

———. *La hora cero y otros poemas*. Barcelona: Ediciones Saturno, 1971.

———. *Literatura indígena americana: Antología*. Medellín, Colombia: Editorial Universidad de Antioquía, 1964.

Carney, Judith. *Black Rice: The African Origins of Rice Cultivation in the Americas*. Cambridge, Mass.: Harvard University Press, 2001.

———. "Landscapes of Technology Transfer: Rice Cultivation and African Continuities." *Technology and Culture* 37, no. 1 (1996), 5–35.

Carrera, Magali M. *Imagining Identity in New Spain: Race, Lineage, and the Colonial Body in Portraiture and Casta Paintings*. Austin: University of Texas Press, 2003.

Carroll, Mark M. *Homesteads Ungovernable: Families, Sex, Race, and the Law in Frontier Texas, 1823–1860*. Austin: University of Texas Press, 2001.

Carroll, Patrick J. *Blacks in Colonial Veracruz: Race, Ethnicity, and Regional Development*. Austin: University of Texas Press, 1991.

Casanova Fuertes, Rafael. "Hacia una nueva valorización de las luchas políticas del período de la Anarquía: El caso de los conflictos de 1845–1849." *Encuentros con la Historia*, edited by Margarita Vannini, 231–48. Managua: IHN-UCA and CEMCA, 1995.

Casaús Arzú, Marta. *Guatemala, linaje y racismo*. San José, Costa Rica: FLACSO, 1992.

———. *La metamorfosis del racismo en Guatemala*. Guatemala City: Editorial Cholsamaj, 1998.

Castillo G., Manuel Angel. "La migración en Centroamérica y su evolución reciente." *Revista de Historia* (Costa Rica) 40 (1999), 27–56.

Castle, W. E. "Racial Mixture and Physical Disharmonies." *Science*, new series 71, no. 1850 (1930), 605–6.

Castro y Tosi, Norberto de. "La población de la ciudad de Cartago en los siglos XVII y XVIII." *Revista de los Archivos Nacionales* (Costa Rica) 28 (1964), 3–28.

Chacón de Umaña, Luz Alba. *Don Diego de la Haya Fernández*. San José: Editorial Costa Rica, 1967.

Chamberlain, Robert S. *The Conquest and Colonization of Honduras, 1502–1550*. New York: Octagon Books, 1966.

Chamorro, Fruto. "Mensaje de S. E. el general director supremo don Fruto Chamorro a la Asamblea Constituyente del Estado de Nicaragua, instalada el

24 de enero del año de 1854." *Las constituciones de Nicaragua,* edited by Emilio Alvarez Lejarza, 106–12. Madrid: Ediciones Cultural Hispánica, 1958.

Chamorro Zelaya, Pedro Joaquín. *Fruto Chamorro.* Managua: Editorial La Unión, 1960.

Chaplin, Joyce E. "Race." *The British Atlantic World, 1500–1800,* edited by David Armitage and Michael J. Braddick, 154–72. New York: Palgrave Macmillan, 2002.

Charlip, Julie A. *Cultivating Coffee: The Farmers of Carazo, Nicaragua, 1880–1930.* Athens: Ohio University Press, 2003.

Chaventré, A., and G. Bellis. "Role et importance des généalogies dans les sciences biologiques." *Archivum: Les Archives et les Sciences Généalogiques* 37 (1992), 93–109.

Chávez Alfaro, Lizandro. "El mestizaje y sus símbolos." *Nicaragua en busca de su identidad,* edited by Frances Kinloch Tijerino, 99–115. Managua: Instituto de Historia de Nicaragua, Universidad Centroamericana, 1995.

Chávez Carbajal, María Guadalupe, ed. *El rostro colectivo de la nación Mexicana.* Morelia, Mexico: Univeridad Michoacana, Instituto de Investigaciones Históricas, 1997.

Chomsky, Aviva. "'Barbados or Canada': Race, Immigration, and Nation in Early-Twentieth Century Cuba." *Hispanic American Historical Review* 80, no. 3 (2000), 415–62.

———. *West Indian Workers and the United Fruit Company in Costa Rica, 1870–1940.* Baton Rouge: Louisiana State University Press, 1996.

———. "West Indian Workers in Costa Rican Radical and Nationalist Ideology: 1900–1950." *The Americas* 51, no. 1 (1994), 11–40.

Ciudad Suárez, Milagros. *Los dominicos, un grupo de poder en Chiapas y Guatemala, siglos XVI y XVII.* Seville: Escuela de Estudios Hispano-Americanos, 1996.

Cobos Batres, Manuel. *Carrera.* Guatemala City: Librería Renacimiento, 1935.

Colección de documentos references a la historia colonial de Nicaragua. Managua: Tipografía y Encuadernación Nacionales, 1921.

Colombres, Adolfo, ed. *A los 500 años de dos mundos: Balance y prospectiva.* Buenos Aires: Ediciones del Sol-Cehass, 1991.

Conniff, Michael L. *Black Labor on a White Canal: Panama, 1904–1981.* Pittsburgh: University of Pittsburgh Press, 1985.

Contreras Gallardo, Pedro de. *Manual de administrar los sanctos sacramentos a los Españoles, y naturales desta Nueua España conforme à la reforma de Paulo V. Pont. Max.* Mexico City: Ioan Ruyz, 1638.

Conzemius, Eduard. *Ethnographical Survey of the Miskito and Sumu Indians of Honduras and Nicaragua.* Washington: U.S. Government Printing Office, 1932.

Cooper, Frederick, and Ann Laura Stoler, eds. *Tensions of Empire: Colonial Cultures in a Bourgeois World.* Berkeley: University of California Press, 1997.

Cope, R. Douglas. *The Limits of Racial Domination: Plebeian Society in Colonial Mexico City, 1660–1720.* Madison: University of Wisconsin Press, 1994.

Coria, Juan Carlos. *Pasado y presente del los negros en Buenos Aires.* Buenos Aires: Editorial J. A. Roca, 1997.

Coronel Urtecho, José. "Introducción a la Epoca de Anarquía en Nicaragua, 1821–1857." *Revista Conservadora de Pensamiento Centroamericano,* no. 134 (1971), 39–49.

———. *Reflexiones sobre la historia de Nicaragua: De la Colonia a la Independencia.* Managua: Fundación Vida, 2001.

Costa Rica, Comisión de Investigación Histórica de la Campana de 1856–1857. *Crónicas y comentarios: Año centenario, 1856–1956.* San José, Costa Rica: n.p., 1956.

Costa Rica, Dirección General de Estadística y Censos. *Censo de Población de Costa Rica. 22 de Mayo de 1950.* San José, Costa Rica: n.p., 1953.

Cruz, Arturo J. *Nicaragua's Conservative Republic, 1858–93.* New York: Palgrave, 2002.

Cruz R., Victor C., Sergio Palacios A., Mercedes Oyuela S., Sucelinda Zelaya C., and Olga B. Maldonado S. *Fuerte de San Fernando de Omoa: Época colonial.* Estudios antropológicos e históricos 5. Tegucigalpa, Honduras: Instituto Hondureño de Antropología e Historia, 1985.

Cuadra Cea, Luis. "Conferencia del honorable profesor Don Luis Cuadra Cea, en el teatro municipal de León, Nicaragua, la noche del 6 de febrero de 1936 al conmemorarse el XX aniversario de la muerte de Rubén Darío." *Revista de la Academia de Geografía e Historia de Nicaragua* 32 (1967), 6–22.

Cuadra Chamorro, Pedro J. *La reincorporación de la Mosquitia: Estudio de interpretación histórica.* Granada, Nicaragua: Tipografía El Centro-Americano, 1944.

Cuadra Pasos, Carlos. *Obras.* 2 vols. Managua: Fondo de Promoción Cultural, Banco de América, 1976–77.

Cushner, Nicholas P. *Lords of the Land: Sugar, Wine, and Jesuit Estates of Coastal Peru, 1600–1767.* Albany: State University of New York Press, 1980.

Dampier, William. *A New Voyage round the World.* Edited by Albert Gray. London: Argonaut Press, 1927.

Davidson, William V. *Atlas de mapas históricas de Honduras: Honduras, an Atlas of Historical Maps.* Translated by Jaime Incer Barquero. Managua: Fundación Uno, 2006.

———. "Etnografía histórica y la arqueología de Honduras: Un avance preliminar de la investigación." *Yaxkin* 8 (1985), 215–24.

Davidson, William V., and Fernando Cruz S. "Delimitación de la región habitada por los sumos taguacas de Honduras 1600–1990." *Yaxkin* 11 (1988), 123–36.

Davin, Anna. "Imperialism and Motherhood." *History Workshop Journal* 5, no. 1 (1978), 9–66.

Davis, Raymond Allan. "West Indian Workers on the Panama Canal: A Split Labor Market Interpretation." Ph.D. dissertation, Stanford University, 1981.

Dawson, Frank Griffith. "The Evacuation of the Mosquito Shore and the English Who Stayed Behind." *The Americas* 55 (1998), 63–89.

———. "William Pitt's Settlement at Black River on the Mosquito Shore: A Challenge to Spain in Central America, 1732–87." *Hispanic American Historical Review* 63 (1983), 677–706.

de Friedemann, Nina S., and Jaime Arocha. *De sol a sol: Genesis, transformacion y presencia de los negros en Colombia.* Bogotá: Planeta, 1986.

de la Cadena, Marisol. "The Racial-Moral Politics of Place: Mestizas and Indigenistas in Cuzco." *Gender's Place: Feminist Anthropologies of Latin America*, edited by Rosario Montoya, Lessie Jo Frazier, and Janise Hurtig, 155–75. New York: Palgrave Macmillan, 2002.

de la Fuente, Alejandro. *A Nation for All: Race, Inequality, and Politics in Twentieth-Century Cuba.* Chapel Hill: University of North Carolina Press, 2001.

———. "Race and Inequality of Cuba, 1899–1981." *Journal of Contemporary History* 30 (1995), 131–68.

———. "Slaves and the Creation of Legal Rights in Cuba: *Coartación* and *Papel.*" *Hispanic American Historical Review* 87, no. 4 (2007), 659–92.

———. "Sugar and Slavery in Early Colonial Cuba." *Tropical Babylons: Sugar and the Making of the Atlantic World, 1450–1680*, edited by Stuart B. Schwartz, 115–57. Chapel Hill: University of North Carolina Press, 2004.

de la Serna, Juan, ed. *Pautas de convivencia étnica en la América Latina colonial (indios, negros, mulatos, pardos y esclavos).* Mexico City: Universidad Nacional Autónoma de México, 2001.

de Lisser, Herbert G. *Jane's Career.* 1914; New York: Africana Publishing, 1971.

de Lussan, Raveneau. *Raveneau de Lussan, Buccaneer of the Spanish Main and Early French Filibuster of the Pacific.* Translated by Marguerite Eyer Wilbur. Cleveland: Arthur C. Clark, 1930.

DeKalb, Courtney. "Nicaragua: Studies of the Mosquito Shore in 1892." *Bulletin of the American Geographical Society* 25 (1893), 236–88.

Delaney, David. "The Space That Race Makes." *Professional Geographer* 54, no. 1 (2002), 6–14.

Dennis, Philip A., and Michael D. Olien. "Kingship among the Miskito." *American Ethnologist* 11, no. 4 (1984), 718–37.

Díaz, María Elena. *The Virgin, the King, and the Royal Slaves of El Cobre: Negotiating Freedom in Colonial Cuba, 1670–1780.* Stanford: Stanford University Press, 2000.

Díaz del Castillo, Bernal. *Historia verdadera de la conquista de la Nueva España.* 2nd ed. Mexico City: Editores Mexicanos Unidos, 1992.

Díaz Lacayo, Aldo. *Nicaragua, acuerdos políticos: 1. Acuerdos Jerez/Martínez (1856–1857).* Managua: Aldilá Editor, 1999.

Diez Navarro, Luis. "Costa, y poblaciones que ay en rio tinto." *Cartografía y relaciones históricas de Ultramar. Tomo IV. América Central.* 2 vols. 2nd ed. Edited by Servicio Histórico Militar. Madrid: Ministerio de Defensa, 1990.

Dikötter, Frank. "Race Culture: Recent Perspectives on the History of Eugenics." *American Historical Review* 103, no. 2 (1998), 467–78.

Dore, Elizabeth. "Debt Peonage in Granada, Nicaragua, 1870–1930: Labor in a Noncapitalist Transition." *Hispanic American Historical Review* 83, no. 3 (2003), 521–59.

———. "Land Privatization and the Differentiation of the Peasantry: Nicaragua's Coffee Revolution, 1850- 1920." *Journal of Historical Sociology* 8, no. 3 (1995), 303–26.

———. *Myths of Modernity: Peonage and Patriarchy in Nicaragua.* Durham, N.C.: Duke University Press, 2006.

———. "Patriarchy from Above, Patriarchy from Below: Debt Peonage on Nicaraguan Coffee Estates, 1870–1930." *The Global Coffee Economy in Africa, Asia and Latin America, 1500–1989,* edited by William Gervace Clarence-Smith and Steven Topik, 209–35. Cambridge, England: Cambridge University Press, 2003.

Duncan, T. Bentley. *The Atlantic Islands: Madeira, the Azores, and Cabo Verde in the Seventeenth Century.* Chicago: University of Chicago Press, 1972.

Dunn, Richard S. *Sugar and Slaves: The Rise of the Planter Class in the English West Indies, 1624–1713.* New York: Norton, 1972.

Durkheim, Kevin, and John Dixon. "The Role of Place and Metaphor in Racial Exclusion: South Africa's Beaches as Sites of Shifting Racialization." *Ethnic and Racial Studies* 24, no. 3 (2001), 433–50.

Echeverri-Gent, Elisavinda. "Forgotten Workers: British West Indians and the Early Days of the Banana Industry in Costa Rica and Honduras." *Journal of Latin American Studies* 24 (1992), 275–308.

El Salvador. *Ley y reglamento de migración.* San Salvador: Imprenta Nacional, 1933.

Elliott, J. H. *The Count-Duke of Olivares: The Statesman in an Age of Decline.* New Haven: Yale University Press, 1986.

Eltis, David. "The Volume and Structure of the Transatlantic Slave Trade: A Reassessment." *William and Mary Quarterly,* 3rd series, 58, no. 1 (2001), 17–46.

Eltis, David, and Stanley L. Engerman. "Was the Slave Trade Dominated by Men?" *Journal of Interdisciplinary History* 23, no. 2 (1992), 237–57.

Eltis, David, Philip Morgan, and David Richardson. "Agency and Diaspora in Atlantic History: Reassessing the African Contribution to Rice Cultivation in the Americas." *American Historical Review* 112, no. 5 (2007), 1329–58.

Emery-Waterhouse, Frances. *Banana Paradise.* New York: Stephen-Paul, 1947.

Equiano, Olaudah. *Interesting Narrative of the Life of Olaudah Equiano. Written by Himself.* Edited by Robert J. Allison. 1791; New York: Bedford Books, 1995.

Esgueva Gómez, Antonio, editor and compiler. *Las constituciones políticas y sus reformas en la historia de Nicaragua.* Vol. 1. 2 vols. Managua: Editorial El Parlamento, 1994.

Esquemelin, John. *The Buccaneers of America.* 1678; London: George Routledge and Sons, 1951.

Euraque, Darío A. "The Banana Enclave, Nationalism and Mestizaje in Honduras, 1910s–1930s." *At the Margins of the Nation-State: Identity and Struggle in the Making of the Laboring Peoples of Central America and the Hispanic Caribbean, 1860–1960,* edited by Aviva Chomsky and Aldo Lauria-Santiago, 151–68. Durham, N.C.: Duke University Press, 1998.

————. *Conversaciones históricas con el mestizaje y su identidad nacional en Honduras.* San Pedro Sula, Honduras: Centro Editorial, 2004.

Falla, Juan José. *Extractos de escrituras públicas, Archivo General de Centro América.* 3 vols. Guatemala City: Editorial Amigos del País, Fundación para la Cultura y el Desarrollo, 1994–2001.

Fernández, León, ed. *Colección de documentos para la historia de Costa Rica.* 10 vols. San José, Costa Rica: Imprenta Nacional (vols. 1–3); Paris: Imprenta Pablo Dupont (vols. 4–5); Barcelona: Imprenta Viuda de Luis Tasso (vols. 6–10), 1881–1907.

Fernández Guardia, Ricardo, ed. *Cartas de relación de Juan Vázquez de Coronado, conquistador de Costa Rica.* San José: Academia de Geografía e Historia de Costa Rica, 1964.

————. *Crónicas coloniales de Costa Rica.* 1937; San José: Editorial Costa Rica, 1991.

————. *Reseña histórica de Talamanca.* San José, Costa Rica: Imprenta Alsina, 1917.

Ferry, Robert J. "Encomienda, African Slavery, and Agriculture in Seventeenth-Century Caracas." *Hispanic American Historical Review* 61, no. 4 (1981), 609–35.

Few, Martha. *Women Who Lead Evil Lives: Gender, Religion, and the Politics of Power in Colonial Guatemala.* Austin: University of Texas Press, 2002.

Fiehrer, Thomas. "Hacia una definición de la esclavitud en Guatemala colonial." *Revista del Pensamiento Centroamericano* 31, no. 153 (1976), 41–55.

————. "Slaves and Freedmen in Colonial Central America: Rediscovering a Forgotten Black Past." *Journal of Negro History* 64 (1979), 39–57.

Figueroa Navarro, Alfredo. *Testamento y sociedad en el istmo de Panamá (siglos XVIII y XIX).* Panama City: Impresora ROYSA, 1991.

Floyd, Troy S. *The Anglo-Spanish Struggle for Mosquitia.* Albuquerque: University of New Mexico Press, 1967.

Fonseca, Elizabeth. *Costa Rica colonial: La tierra y el hombre.* 3rd ed. San José, Costa Rica: Editorial Universitaria Centroamericana, 1986.

Fournier García, Eduardo. "Desarrollo de la ciencia genealógica en Costa Rica." *Revista del Archivo Nacional* (Costa Rica) 56 (1992), 51–64.

Fowler, William R., Jr. *The Cultural Evolution of Ancient Nahua Civilizations: The Pipil-Nicarao of Central America.* Norman: University of Oklahoma Press, 1989.

Franck, Harry A. *Zone Policeman 88: A Close Range Study of the Panama Canal and Its Workers.* New York: Century, 1913.

Frederick, Rhonda. *"Colón Man a Come": Mythographies of Panama Canal Migration.* Lanham, Md.: Rowman and Littlefield, 2005.

Fuentes Baudrit, Hernán. "La importancia de la investigación en las ciencias genealógicas." *Revista de la Academia Costarricense de Ciencias Genealógicas,* no. 23 (1976), 305–15.

Fuentes y Guzmán, Francisco Antonio de. *Recordación florida: Discurso historial y demostración natural, material, militar, y política del reyno de Guatemala.* 3 vols. Biblioteca "Goathemala," vols. 6–8. Guatemala City: Sociedad de Geografía e Historia, 1932–33.

Gage, Thomas. *The English-American His Travail by Sea and Land: Or a New Survey of the West-India's.* London: R. Cotes, 1648.

Gámez, José Dolores. *Historia de la Costa de los Mosquitos hasta 1894.* Managua: Talleres Nacionales, 1939.

———. *Historia de Nicaragua desde los tiempos prehistóricos hasta 1860, en sus relaciones con España, México y Centro América.* 2nd ed. Madrid: Gobierno de Nicaragua, 1955.

———. *Historia moderna de Nicaragua: Complemento a mi Historia de Nicaragua.* 2nd ed. Managua: Fondo de Promoción Cultural-BANIC, 1993.

García González, Armando, and Raquel Alvarez Peláez. *En busca de la raza perfecta: Eugenesia e higiene en Cuba (1898–1958).* Madrid: CSIC, 1999.

García Granados, Miguel. *Memorias del general Miguel Garcia Granados.* Guatemala City: Editorial del Ejército, 1978.

George, Rosemary Marangoly. "Homes in the Empire, Empires in the Home." *Cultural Critique* 26 (winter 1994), 95–127.

Ghidinelli, Azzo. "Reconstrucción histórica de las relaciones interétnicas en el área pocomam oriental durante el período colonial." *Guatemala Indígena* 11, nos. 1–2 (1976), 22–35.

Gilroy, Paul. *The Black Atlantic: Modernity and Double Consciousness.* Cambridge, Mass.: Harvard University Press, 1993.

Gobat, Michel. *Confronting the American Dream: Nicaragua under U.S. Imperial Rule.* Durham, N.C.: Duke University Press, 2005.

Goett, Jennifer. "Diasporic Identities, Autochthonous Rights: Race, Gender, and the Cultural Politics of Creole Land Rights in Nicaragua." Ph.D. dissertation, University of Texas, Austin, 2007.

Goldman, Anna E. "'I Yam What I Yam': Cooking, Culture, and Colonialism." *De/Colonizing the Subject: The Politics of Gender in Women's Autobiography,* edited by Sidonie Smith and Julia Watson, 169–95. Minneapolis: University of Minnesota Press, 1992.

Gómez, Ana. "*Al servicio de las armas*: The Bourbon Army of Late Colonial Guatemala, 1762–1821." Ph.D. dissertation, University of Minnesota, 2003.

Gomez, Michael A. *Exchanging Our Country Marks: The Transformation of African Identities in the Colonial and Antebellum South.* Chapel Hill: University of North Carolina Press, 1998.

Gonzalez, Nancie L. Solien. *Sojourners of the Caribbean: Ethnogenesis and Ethnohistory of the Garifuna.* Urbana: University of Illinois Press, 1988.

González Víquez, Cleto. *Apuntes estadísticos sobre la ciudad de San José.* San José, Costa Rica: Imprenta de Avelino Alsina, 1905.

Gordon, Edmund T. *Disparate Diasporas: Identity and Politics in an African Nicaraguan Community.* Austin: University of Texas Press, 1998.

Gouda, Francis. "Nyonyas on the Colonial Divide: White Women in the Dutch East Indies, 1900–1942." *Gender and History* 5, no. 3 (1993), 318–42.

Gould, Jeffrey L. *To Die in This Way: Nicaraguan Indians and the Myth of Mestizaje, 1880–1965.* Durham, N.C.: Duke University Press, 1998.

———. "'¡Vana Ilusión!' The Highlands Indians and the Myth of Nicaragua Mestiza, 1880–1925." *Hispanic American Historical Review* 73, no. 3 (1993), 393–429.

Gould, Jeffrey L., Charles Hale, and Carol Smith, eds. *Memorias del Mestizaje: Cultura política en Centroamérica de 1920 al presente.* Antigua, Guatemala: CIRMA, 2004.

Gould, Jeffrey L. and Carlos Henríquez Consalvi, producers. *1932, Scars of Memory / Cicatriz de la memoria.* Brooklyn, N.Y.: Icarus Films, 2002.

Grandin, Greg. *Fordlandia: The Rise and Fall of Henry Ford's Forgotten Jungle City.* New York: Metropolitan Books, 2009.

Greene, Julie. *The Canal Builders: Making America's Empire at the Panama Canal.* New York: Penguin Press, 2009.

Guardino, Peter F. *Peasants, Politics and the Formation of Mexico's National State: Guerrero, 1800–1857.* Stanford: Stanford University Press, 1996.

Gudmundson, Lowell. "Los afro-guatemaltecos a fines de la Colonia: Las haciendas dominicas de San Gerónimo y Amatitlán." *Rutas de la esclavitud en Africa y América Latina*, edited by Rina Cáceres, 251–68. San José: Editorial de la Universidad de Costa Rica, 2001.

———. "De 'negro' a 'blanco' en la Hispanoamérica del siglo XIX: La asimilación afroamericana en Argentina y Costa Rica." *Mesoamérica*, no. 12 (December 1986), 309–29.

———. *Estratificación socio-racial y económica de Costa Rica, 1700–1850.* San José, Costa Rica: EUNED, 1978.

———. "Firewater, Desire, and the Militiamen's Christmas Eve in San Gerónimo, Baja Verapaz, 1892." *Hispanic American Historical Review* 84, no. 2 (2004), 239–76.

———. "Negotiating Rights under Slavery: The Slaves of San Gerónimo (Baja

Verapaz, Guatemala) Confront Their Dominican Masters in 1810." *The Americas* 60, no. 1 (2003), 109–14.

Gutiérrez Brockington, Lolita. *The Leverage of Labor: Managing the Cortés Haciendas in Tehuantepec, 1588–1688*. Durham, N.C.: Duke University Press, 1989.

Guzmán, Enrique. *Editoriales de La Prensa, 1878*. Edited by Franco Cerutti. Managua: Fondo de Promoción Cultural, Banco de América, 1977.

Harlow, Vincent T., ed. "The Voyages of Captain William Jackson (1642–1645)." *Camden Miscellany* 13 (1923), v–xxvi, 1–39.

Harpelle, Ronald N. "Cooking Class: Order and the Other in the Corporate Kitchens of Latin America." *Negotiating Identities in Modern Latin America*, edited by Hendrik Kraay, 115–137. Calgary: University of Calgary Press, 2007.

———. "Racism and Nationalism in the Creation of Costa Rica's Pacific Coast Banana Enclave." *The Americas* 56, no. 3 (2000), 29–51.

———. *The West Indians of Costa Rica: Race, Class, and the Integration of an Ethnic Minority*. Montreal: McGill-Queen's University Press, 2001.

Harris, Marvin. *Patterns of Race in the Americas*. New York: Walker, 1964.

Hawthorne, Walter. "Nourishing a Stateless Society During the Slave Trade: The Rise of Balanta Paddy-Rice Production in Guinea-Bissau." *Journal of African History* 42, no. 1 (2001), 1–24.

Helg, Aline. *Liberty and Equality in Caribbean Colombia, 1770–1835*. Chapel Hill: University of North Carolina Press, 2003.

Helms, Mary W. *Asang: Adaptions to Culture Contact in a Miskito Community*. Gainesville: University of Florida Press, 1971.

———. "Miskito Slaving and Culture Contact, Ethnicity and Opportunity in an Expanding Population." *Journal of Anthropological Research*, no. 39 (1983), 506–23.

———. "Of Kings and Contexts: Ethnohistorical Interpretations of Miskito Political Structure and Function." *American Ethnologist* 13, no. 3 (1986), 506–23.

Hernández, Omar, Eugenia Ibarra R., and Juan Rafael Quesada Camacho. *Discriminación y racismo en la historia costarricense*. San José: Editorial de la Universidad de Costa Rica, 1993.

Hernández Aparicio, Pilar. "Problemas socioeconómicos en el valle de Guatemala (1670–1680)." *Revista de Indias* 37, nos. 149–50 (1977), 585–637.

Herrera, Robinson A. *Natives, Europeans and Africans in Sixteenth-Century Santiago de Guatemala*. Austin: University of Texas Press, 2004.

Herrera Casasús, Luisa. *Piezas de indias: La esclavitud negra en México*. Veracruz, Mexico: Instituto Veracruzano de Cultura, 1991.

Hickman, Katie. *Daughters of Britannia: The Lives and Times of Diplomatic Wives*. London: Harper Collins, 2001.

Hobsbawm, Eric. "Mass-Producing Traditions: Europe, 1870–1914." *The Invention of Tradition*, edited by Eric Hobsbawm and Terence Ranger, 263–307. Cambridge: Cambridge University Press, 1983.

Houdaille, J. "Negros franceses en América Central a fines del siglo XVIII." *Revista de Antropología e Historia de Guatemala* 6, no. 1 (1954), 65–67.

Hooker, Juliet. "'Beloved Enemies': Race and Official Mestizo Nationalism in Nicaragua." *Latin American Research Review* 40, no. 3 (2005), 14–39.

Horsman, Reginald. *Race and Manifest Destiny: Origins of American Racial Anglo-Saxonism.* Cambridge, Mass.: Harvard University Press, 1986.

House of Commons. "Correspondence Respecting the Mosquito Territory," *Sessional Papers, 1847–48, Accounts and Papers,* 3 July 1848.

Hroch, Miroslav. "From National Movement to the Fully-Formed Nation: The Nation-Building Process in Europe." *Becoming National,* edited by Geoff Eley and Ronald Grigor Suny, 60–78. New York: Oxford University Press, 1996.

Hünefeldt, Christine. *Paying the Price of Freedom: Family and Labor among Lima's Slaves, 1800–1854.* Translated by Alexandra Stern. Berkeley: University of California Press, 1994.

Ibarra Rojas, Eugenia. *Las manchas del jaguar: Huellas indígenas en la historia de Costa Rica (Valle Central siglos XVI–XIX).* San José: Editorial de la Universidad de Costa Rica, 1999.

———. *Las sociedades cacicales de Costa Rica.* San José: Editorial de la Universidad de Costa Rica, 1990.

Insanally, Annette, Mark Clifford, and Sean Sheriff, eds. *Regional Footprints: The Travels and Travails of Early Caribbean Migrants.* Kingston, Jamaica: Latin American–Caribbean Centre, University of the West Indies, 2006.

International Cook Book—Recetario Internacional. Lima: Imprenta del Ministerio de Guerra, 1941.

James, Winifred Lewellin. *A Woman in the Wilderness.* London: Chapman and Hall, 1915.

James, Winston. *Holding Aloft the Banner of Ethiopia: Caribbean Radicalism in Early Twentieth-Century America.* New York: Verso, 1998.

Jefferson, Ann F. "La Gente Parda and the Guatemalan Rebellion of 1837." *Transforming Anthropology* 12, nos. 1–2 (2004), 30–39.

———. "The Rebellion of the Mita: Eastern Guatemala in 1837." Ph.D. dissertation, University of Massachusetts, Amherst, 2000.

Jennings, Evelyn Powell. "Slaves of State: Urban Slavery, Imperial Defense, and Public Works in Colonial Havana, 1763–1840." Ph.D. dissertation, University of Rochester, 2001.

Joyner, Charles W. *Down by the Riverside: A South Carolina Slave Community.* Urbana: University of Illinois Press, 1984.

Juarros, Domingo. *Compendio de la historia del Reino de Guatemala, 1500–1800.* Guatemala City: Editorial Piedra Santa, 1981.

Katzew, Ilona. *Casta Painting: Images of Race in Eighteenth-Century Mexico.* New Haven: Yale University Press, 2004.

Kerns, Virginia. *Women and the Ancestors: Black Carib Kinship and Ritual.* 2nd ed. Urbana: University of Illinois Press, 1997.

King, Desmond. *Making Americans: Immigration, Race, and the Origins of the Diverse Democracy.* Cambridge, Mass.: Harvard University Press, 2000.

Kinloch Tijerino, Frances. "Civilización y Barbarie: Mitos y símbolos en la formación de la idea nacional." *Nicaragua en busca de su identidad,* edited by Frances Kinloch Tijerino, 257–76. Managua: IHN-UCA, 1995.

———. *Nicaragua: Identidad y cultural política (1821–1858).* Managua: Banco Central de Nicaragua, 1999.

Kinsbruner, Jay. *Not of Pure Blood: The Free People of Color and Racial Prejudice in Nineteenth-Century Puerto Rico.* Durham, N.C.: Duke University Press, 1996.

Kiple, Kenneth F. *The Caribbean Slave: A Biological History.* Cambridge, England: Cambridge University Press, 1984.

Klingberg, Frank J. "The Efforts of the S.P.G. to Christianize the Mosquito Indians, 1742–1785." *Historical Magazine of the Protestant Episcopal Church* 9, no. 4 (1940), 305–21.

Knapp, Herbert, and Mary Knapp. *Red, White, and Blue Paradise: The American Canal Zone in Panama.* San Diego: Harcourt Brace Jovanovich, 1984.

Koch, Charles. "Ethnicity and Livelihoods: A Social Geography of Costa Rica's Atlantic Coast." Ph.D. dissertation, University of Kansas, 1975.

Konrad, Herman W. *A Jesuit Hacienda in Colonial Mexico: Santa Lucía, 1576–1767.* Stanford: Stanford University Press, 1980.

Kupperman, Karen Ordahl. *Providence Island, 1630–1641: The Other Puritan Colony.* Cambridge: Cambridge University Press, 1993.

Kutzinski, Vera M. *Sugar's Secrets: Race and the Erotics of Cuban Nationalism.* New World Studies. Charlottesville: University Press of Virginia, 1993.

Landers, Jane. *Black Society in Spanish Florida.* Foreword by Peter H. Wood. Blacks in the New World. Urbana: University of Illinois Press, 1999.

Lane, Kris. *Quito 1599: City and Colony in Transition.* Albuquerque: University of New Mexico Press, 2002.

Lapp, Richard M. *Blacks in Gold Rush California.* New Haven: Yale University Press, 1995.

Láscaris, Constantino. *Historia de las ideas en Centro América.* 2nd ed. San José, Costa Rica: Editorial Universitaria Centroamericana, 1982.

Lasso, Marixa. *Myths of Harmony: Race and Republicanism During the Age of Revolution: Colombia 1795–1831.* Pittsburgh: University of Pittsburgh Press, 2007.

Laughlin, Harry. "The Codification and Analysis of the Immigration-Control Law of Each of the Several Countries of Pan America, as Expressed by Their National Constitutions, Statute Laws, International Treaties, and Administrative Regulations, as of January 1, 1936." Mimeograph. Eugenics Record Office, Carnegie Institution of Washington, 1936.

Leiva Vivas, Rafael. *Tráfico de esclavos negros en Honduras.* Tegucigalpa, Honduras: Editorial Guaymuras, 1982.

Leonardi, Susan J. "Recipes for Reading: Summer Pasta, Lobster à la Riseholme, and Key Lime Pie." PMLA 104, no. 3 (1989), 340–47.

León-Portilla, Miguel, editor and compiler. *Visión de los vencidos: Relaciones indígenas de la conquista*. Mexico City: Universidad Nacional Autónoma de México, 1984.

Letts, John M. *California Illustrated; Including a Description of the Panama and Nicaragua Routes. By a Returned Californian*. New York: William Holdredge, 1852.

Lewis, Laura A. *Hall of Mirrors: Power, Witchcraft, and Caste in Colonial Mexico*. Durham, N.C.: Duke University Press, 2003.

———. "Of Ships and Saints: History, Memory, and Place in the Making of Moreno Mexican Identity." *Cultural Anthropology* 16, no. 1 (2001), 62–82.

Littlefield, Daniel C. *Rice and Slaves: Ethnicity and the Slave Trade in Colonial South Carolina*. Blacks in the New World. Baton Rouge: Louisiana State University Press, 1981.

Little-Siebold, Todd. "'Where Have All the Spaniards Gone': Independent Identities, Ethnicities, Class and the Emergent National State." *Journal of Latin American Anthropology* 6, no. 2 (2001), 106–33.

Lobo Wiehoff, Tatiana. *Entre Dios y el diablo: Mujeres de la Colonia: Crónicas*. San José: Editorial de la Universidad de Costa Rica, 1993.

———. "Los hijos de mi hija." *Revista Asogehi*, no. 2 (1996), 164–65.

Lobo Wiehoff, Tatiana, and Mauricio Meléndez Obando. *Negros y blancos: Todo mezclado*. San José: Editorial de la Universidad de Costa Rica, 1997.

Lockhart, James, and Stuart B. Schwartz. *Early Latin America: A History of Colonial Spanish America and Brazil*. New York: Cambridge University Press, 1983.

Lohse, Kent Russell. "Africans and Their Descendants in Colonial Costa Rica, 1600–1750." Ph.D. dissertation, University of Texas at Austin, 2005.

Lokken, Paul. "From Black to Ladino: People of African Descent, Mestizaje, and Racial Hierarchy in Rural Colonial Guatemala, 1600–1730." Ph.D. dissertation, University of Florida, 2000.

———. "A Maroon Moment: Rebel Slaves in Early Seventeenth-Century Guatemala." *Slavery and Abolition* 25, no. 3 (2004), 44–58.

———. "Marriage as Slave Emancipation in Seventeenth-Century Rural Guatemala." *The Americas* 58, no. 2 (2001), 175–200.

———. "Undoing Racial Hierarchy: *Mulatos* and Militia Service in Colonial Guatemala." SECOLAS *Annals* 31 (1999), 25–36.

———. "Useful Enemies: Seventeenth-Century Piracy and the Rise of Pardo Militias in Spanish Central America." *Journal of Colonialism and Colonial History* 5, no. 2 (2004).

Long, Edward. "Mosquito Shore." *The History of Jamaica: Or, General Survey of the Ancient and Modern State of That Island*. 3 vols. 1774; London: Frank Cass, 1970.

Love, Edgar F. "Marriage Patterns of Persons of African Descent in a Colonial Mexico City Parish." *Hispanic American Historical Review* 51, no. 1 (1971), 79–91.

Lovejoy, Paul E. "Autobiography and Memory: Gustavus Vassa, Alias Olaudah Equiano, the African." *Slavery and Abolition* 27 (2006), 317–47.

Lovejoy, Paul E. "Murgu: The Wages of Slavery in the Sokoto Caliphate." *The Wages of Slavery: From Chattel Slavery to Wage Labour in Africa, the Caribbean, and England*, edited by Michael Twaddle, 168–85. London: Frank Cass, 1993.

Lovejoy, Paul E., and David V. Trotman, eds. *Trans-Atlantic Dimensions of Ethnicity in the African Diaspora*. London: Continuum, 2003.

Luján Muñoz, Jorge. *Agricultura, mercado, y sociedad en el corregimiento del valle de Guatemala*. Guatemala City: Universidad de San Carlos, 1988.

Lutz, Christopher H. *Historia sociodemográfica de Santiago de Guatemala, 1551–1773*. Guatemala City: CIRMA, 1982.

———. *Santiago de Guatemala, 1541–1773: City, Caste, and the Colonial Experience*. Norman: University of Oklahoma Press, 1994.

Lutz, Christopher H., and Matthew Restall. "Wolves and Sheep? Black-Maya Relations in Colonial Times." *Beyond Black and Red: African-Native Relations in Colonial Latin America*, edited by Matthew Restall, 185–222. Albuquerque: University of New Mexico Press, 2005.

MacLeod, Murdo J. *Spanish Central America: A Socioeconomic History, 1520–1720*. Berkeley: University of California Press, 1973.

MacLeod, Philip S. "Auge y estancamiento de la producción de cacao en Costa Rica, 1660–1695." *Anuario de Estudios Centroamericanos* 22, no. 1 (1996), 83–107.

———. "On the Edge of Empire: Costa Rica in the Colonial Era (1561–1800)." Ph.D. dissertation, Tulane University, 1999.

Mallon, Florencia E. *Peasant and Nation: The Making of Postcolonial Mexico and Peru*. Berkeley: University of California Press, 1994.

Manning, Patrick. "Africa and the African Diaspora: New Directions of Study." *Journal of African History* 44, no. 3 (2003), 487–506.

Marr, Wilhelm. *Viaje a Centroamérica*. Translated by Juan Carlos Solórzano. San José: Editorial Universidad de Costa Rica, 2004.

Marshall, Dawn. "A History of West Indian Migrations: Overseas Opportunities and 'Safety-Valve' Policies." *The Caribbean Exodus*, edited by Barry B. Levine, 15–31. New York: Praeger, 1987.

Martínez-Alier, Verena. *Marriage, Class, and Colour in Nineteenth-Century Cuba: A Study of Racial Attitudes and Sexual Values in a Slave Society*. 2nd ed. Ann Arbor: University of Michigan Press, 1989.

Martínez Durán, Carlos, and Daniel Contreras. "La abolición de la esclavitud en Centroamérica." *Journal of Inter-American Studies* 4, no. 2 (1962), 223–32.

Martínez Montiel, Luz María. *Presencia Africana en México*. Mexico City: Dirección General de Culturas Populares, 1994.

Martínez Montiel, Luz María, and Juan Carlos Reyes G., eds. *Encuentro nacional de Afromexicanistas, III*. Colima, Mexico: Instituto Colimense de Cultura, 1992.

Martínez Peláez, Severo. *La patria del criollo: Ensayo de interpretación de la realidad colonial guatemalteca*. Editorial Universitaria, no. 65. Guatemala City: Universidad de San Carlos, 1970.

Matschat, Cecile Hulse. *Seven Grass Huts: An Engineer's Wife in Central-and-South America*. New York: Literary Guild of America, 1939.

Matthew, Laura. "Mexicanos and the Meanings of Ladino in Colonial Guatemala." *Journal of Colonialism and Colonial History* 7, no. 1 (2006).

May, Robert E. *Manifest Destiny's Underworld: Filibustering in Antebellum America*. Chapel Hill: University of North Carolina Press, 2004.

May, Stacy, and Galo Plaza. *The United Fruit Company in Latin America*. United States Business Performance Abroad. Washington: National Planning Association, 1958.

Mayes, April Janice. "Sugar's Metropolis: The Politics and Culture of Progress in San Pedro de Macoris, Dominican Republic, 1870–1930." Ph.D. dissertation, University of Michigan, 2003.

Mazariegos Anleu, José Fernando. *Indice general de informaciones matrimoniales en Guatemala, 1614–1900*. Guatemala City: AHA, 1999.

McClintock, Anne. *Imperial Leather: Race, Gender, and Sexuality in the Colonial Contest*. New York: Routledge, 1995.

McGuinness, Aims. "Searching for 'Latin America': Race and Sovereignty in the Americas in the 1850s." *Race and Nation in Modern Latin America*, edited by Nancy P. Appelbaum, Anne S. Macpherson, and Karen Alejandra Rosemblatt, 87–107. Chapel Hill: University of North Carolina Press, 2003.

McKay, Claude. *Gingertown*. 1932. Reprint ed. Salem, New Hampshire: Ayer Co., Publishers, 1991.

Meléndez Chaverri, Carlos. *Conquistadores y pobladores: Orígenes histórico-sociales de los costarricenses*. San José, Costa Rica: EUNED, 1982.

———. *Hernández de Córdoba: Capitán de conquista en Nicaragua*. 2nd ed. Managua: Hispamer, 1993.

———. "Las migraciones y los procesos de mestizaje: El caso de la Costa Rica colonial." *Revista del Archivo Nacional* (Costa Rica) 56 (1992), 39–50.

Meléndez Chaverri, Carlos, and Quince Duncan. *El negro en Costa Rica: Antologia*. San José: Editorial Costa Rica, 1972.

Meléndez Obando, Mauricio. "Descendientes mulatos del conquistador Juan Vázquez de Coronado." Incorporation address to the Academia Costarricense de Ciencias Genealógicas, San José, Costa Rica, 1996.

———. "Dominga Fallas o Un siglo de engaños, 1684–1786." *Entre Dios y el diablo: mujeres de la Colonia: Crónicas,* by Tatiana Lobo Wiehoff, 114–30. San José: Editorial de la Universidad de Costa Rica, 1993.

———. *La dinastía de los conquistados.* Work in preparation.

———. "La familia de la mulata Josefa Flores. I parte." *Revista de la Asociación Genealogía e Historia de Costa Rica* 2 (1996), 64–117.

———. "La familia de la mulata Josefa Flores: Su descendencia II parte." *Revista de la Asociación Genealogía e Historia de Costa Rica* 3–4 (1997), 349–54.

———. "La investigación genealógica en Centroamérica." Hispanic Family History Conference, Latino Legacy, Provo, Utah, 1997.

———. "Luis Méndez de Sotomayor y su descendencia." *Revista del Archivo Nacional* (Costa Rica) 56 (1997), 33–67.

———. "Presencia africana en familias nicaragüenses." *Rutas de la esclavitud en Africa y América Latina,* edited by Rina Cáceres, 341–60. San José: Editorial de la Universidad de Costa Rica, 2001.

———. "Las raíces mulatas de una ciudad 'española': Los arquitectos afromestizos de Guatemala." Unpublished manuscript, 2003.

———. "Los últimos esclavos en Costa Rica." *Revista de Historia* (Costa Rica) 39 (1999), 51–138.

Mena Solórzano, Luis. *Apuntes de un soldado: Los arquitectos de la victoria liberal.* Seville: ECESA, 1970.

Mendieta, Salvador. *La enfermedad de Centroamérica.* Barcelona: Tipografía Maucci, 1919.

Mendoza, Juan. *Historia de Diriamba.* Guatemala City: Staebler, 1920.

Miller, Joseph C. *Kings and Kinsmen: Early Mbundu States in Angola.* Oxford Studies in African Affairs. Oxford: Clarendon Press, 1976.

Mintz, Sidney, and Richard Price. *The Birth of African American Culture: An Anthropological Perspective.* Boston: Beacon Press, 1966.

Montalván, José H. *Valores nicaragüenses para la historia del derecho.* Managua: Universidad Nacional de Nicaragua, 1955.

Montoya, Salvador. "Milicias negras y mulatas en el reino de Guatemala (siglo XVIII)." *C.M.H.L.B. Caravelle,* no. 49 (1987), 93–103.

Moore, Donald S. "Subaltern Struggles and the Politics of Place: Remapping Resistance in Zimbabwe's Eastern Highlands." *Cultural Anthropology* 13, no. 3 (1998), 344–81.

Moore, Donald S., Jake Kosek, and Pandian, eds. *Race, Nature, and the Politics of Difference.* Durham, N.C.: Duke University Press, 2003.

Morera Brenes, Bernal, and Ramiro Barrantes. "Genes e historia: El mestizaje en Costa Rica." *Revista de Historia* (Costa Rica) 32 (1995), 43–64.

Morera Brenes, Bernal, and Mauricio Meléndez Obando. "El tesoro del genoma humano." *El Financiero* (Costa Rica), 9 November 2000, 42.

Morera Brenes, Bernal, Ramón Villegas Palma, Francesca Calafell, David Comas, Mauricio Meléndez Obando, and Jaume Bertranpetit. "Combined Genealogical and mtDNA Analysis for the Characterization of Early Colonial Historic Female Lineages in Costa Rica." Unpublished manuscript, 2000.

Mosquera, Claudia, Mauricio Pardo, and Odile Hoffmann, eds. *Afrodescendientes en las Americas: Trayectorias sociales e identitarias: 150 anos de la abolición de la esclavitud en Colombia.* Bogotá: Universidad Nacional de Colombia, 2002.

Mörner, Magnus. *La corona española y los foráneos en los pueblos de indios de América.* Stockholm: Almqvist and Wiksell, 1970.

———. "La política de segregación y el mestizaje en la Audiencia de Guatemala." *Revista de Indias* 24, nos. 95–96 (1964), 137–52.

———. *Race Mixture in the History of Latin America.* Boston: Little, Brown, 1967.

Nairn, Tom. *The Break-up of Britain: Crisis and Neo-Nationalism.* London: New Left Books, 1977.

Naveda Chávez-Hita, Adriana. *Esclavos negros en las haciendas azucareras de Córdoba, Veracruz, 1690–1830.* Colección Históricas Veracruzanas, vol. 4. Xalapa, Mexico: Universidad Veracruzana, 1987.

———, ed. *Pardos, mulatos y libertos: Sexto Encuentro de Afromexicanistas.* Xalapa, Mexico: Universidad Veracruzana, 2001.

Naylor, Robert A. *Penny Ante Imperialism: The Mosquito Shore and the Bay of Honduras, 1600–1914.* Rutherford, N.J.: Fairleigh Dickinson University Press, 1989.

Newson, Linda A. *El costo de la conquista.* Tegucigalpa, Honduras: Editorial Guaymuras, 1992.

———. *Indian Survival in Colonial Nicaragua.* Norman: University of Oklahoma Press, 1987.

Newton, Arthur Percival. *The Colonising Activities of the English Puritans: The Last Phase of Elizabethan Struggle with Spain.* New Haven: Yale University Press, 1914.

Newton, Velma. *The Silver Men: West Indian Labour Migration to Panama, 1850–1914.* Mona, Jamaica: Institute for Social and Economic Research, 1984.

Ngai, Mae. "The Architecture of Race in American Immigration Law: A Reexamination of the Immigration Act of 1924." *Journal of American History* 86, no. 1 (1999), 67–92.

Nicaragua, Ministerio de Gobernación. *Informe ministerio de gobernación para el bienio 1883/1884.* Managua: Tipografía Nacional, 1885.

Nishida, Mieko. "Manumission and Ethnicity in Urban Slavery: Salvador, Brazil, 1808–1888." *Hispanic American Historical Review* 73, no. 3 (1993), 361–91.

Nobles, Melissa. *Shades of Citizenship: Race and the Census in Modern Politics.* Stanford: Stanford University Press, 2000.

Offen, Karl H. "British Logwood Extraction from the Mosquitia: The Origin of a Myth." *Hispanic American Historical Review* 80, no. 1 (2000), 113–35.

———. "Creating Mosquitia, Mapping Amerindian Spatial Practices in Eastern Central America, 1629–1779." *Journal of Historical Geography* 33 (2007), 254–82.

————. "Ecología cultural mískita en los años 1650–1850." *Wani,* no. 30 (July–September 2002), 42–59.

————. "The Geographical Imagination, Resource Economics, and Nicaraguan Incorporation of the Mosquitia, 1838–1909." *Territories, Commodities and Knowledges: Latin American Environmental History in the Nineteenth and Twentieth Centuries,* edited by Christian Brannstrom, 50–89. London: Institute of Latin American Studies, 2004.

————. "The Miskitu Kingdom: Landscape and the Emergence of a Miskitu Ethnic Identity, Northeastern Nicaragua and Honduras, 1600–1800." Ph.D. dissertation, University of Texas, Austin, 1999.

————. "The Sambo and Tawira Miskitu: The Colonial Origins and Geography of Intra-Miskitu Differentiation in Eastern Nicaragua and Honduras." *Ethnohistory* 49, no. 2 (2002), 319–72.

Olien, Michael D. "Black and Part-Black Population in Colonial Costa Rica: Ethnohistorical Resources and Problems." *Ethnohistory* 27, no. 1 (1980), 13–29.

————. "General, Governor, and Admiral: Three Miskito Lines of Succession." *Ethnohistory* 45, no. 2 (1998), 277–318.

————. "The Miskito Kings and the Line of Succession." *Journal of Anthropological Research* 39, no. 2 (1983), 198–241.

Opie, Frederick Douglass. "Adios Jim Crow: Afro–North American Workers and the Guatemalan Railroad Workers' League, 1884–1921." Ph.D. dissertation, Syracuse University, 1999.

Orlove, Ben. "Putting Race in Its Place: Order in Colonial and Postcolonial Peruvian Geography." *Social Research* 60, no. 2 (1993), 301–36.

Ortega Arancibia, Francisco. *Cuarenta años (1838–1878) de historia de Nicaragua.* 4th ed. Managua: Fondo de Promoción Cultural-BANIC, 1993.

Ortiz, Fernando. *Cuban Counterpoint: Tobacco and Sugar.* Translated by Harriet de Onis. Introduction by Bronislaw Malinowski. Prologue by Herminio Portell Vila. New introduction by Fernando Coronil. Durham, N.C.: Duke University Press, 1995.

Owensby, Brian P. "How Juan and Leonor Won Their Freedom: Litigation and Liberty in Seventeenth-Century Mexico." *Hispanic American Historical Review* 85, no. 1 (2005), 39–79.

Palmer, Colin. *Slaves of the White God: Blacks in Mexico, 1570–1650.* Cambridge, Mass.: Harvard University Press, 1976.

Palmer, Frederick. *Central America and Its Problems.* New York: Moffat, Yard, 1913.

Palmer, Paula. *"What Happen": A Folk-History of Costa Rica's Talamanca Coast.* 2nd ed. San José, Costa Rica: Publications in English, 1993.

Palmer, Steven. "Hacia la 'auto-inmigración': El nacionalismo oficial en Costa Rica, 1870–1930." *Identidades nacionales y estado moderno en Centroamérica,* edited by Arturo Taracena and Jean Piel, 75–85. San José: Editorial de la Universidad de Costa Rica, 1995.

Palomo de Lewin, Beatriz. "Esclavos negros en Guatemala (1723–1773)." Licenciatura Thesis, Universidad del Valle de Guatemala, Facultad de Ciencias Sociales, 1992.

———. "Perfil de la población africana en el reino de Guatemala, 1723–1773." *Rutas de la esclavitud en Africa y América Latina*, edited by Rina Cáceres, 195–209. San José: Editorial de la Universidad de Costa Rica y Asociación Prohistoria Centroamericana, 2001.

Parascandola, Louis J. Introduction to *"Winds Can Wake up the Dead": An Eric Walrond Reader*, edited by Louis J. Parascandola, 11–42. Detroit: Wayne State University Press, 1998.

Pargellis, Stanley, and Ruth Lapham, eds. "Daniell Ellffryth's Guide to the Caribbean, 1631." *William and Mary Quarterly* 3rd series, 1, no. 3 (1944), 273–316.

Parker, Franklin Dallas. *Travels in Central America, 1821–1840*. Gainesville: University of Florida Press, 1970.

Patterson, Orlando. *Slavery and Social Death: A Comparative Study*. Cambridge, Mass.: Harvard University Press, 1982.

Patterson, Tiffany Ruby, and Robin D. G. Kelley. "Unfinished Migrations: Reflections on the African Diaspora and the Making of the Modern World." *African Studies Review* 43, no. 1 (2000), 11–45.

Payne, Daniel Alexander. *History of the African Methodist Episcopal Church*. Edited by C. S. Smith. Nashville: A.M.E. Sunday School Union, 1891.

Peña Hernández, Enrique. *Folklore de Nicaragua*. Masaya, Nicaragua: Editorial Unión, 1968.

Peralta, Manuel M. de, ed. *Costa-Rica y Colombia de 1573 a 1881; su jurisdicción y sus límites territoriales, según los documentos inéditos del Archivo de Indias de Sevilla y otras autoridades*. Madrid: M. Murillo, 1886.

———. *Costa Rica y costa de Mosquitos; documentos para la historia de la jurisdiccion territorial de Costa Rica y Colombia*. Paris: n.p., 1898.

———. *Límites de Costa-Rica y Colombia; nuevos documentos para la historia de su jurisdicción territorial, con notas, comentarios y un examen de la cartografía de Costa-Rica y Veragua*. Madrid: M. G. Hernandez, 1890.

Pérez, Jerónimo. *Obras históricas completas*. 2nd ed. Edited by Pedro Joaquín Chamorro Zelaya. Managua: Fondo de Promoción Cultural-BANIC, 1993.

Pérez, Louis A., Jr., ed. *Slaves, Sugar, and Colonial Society: Travel Accounts of Cuba, 1801–1899*. Wilmington, Del.: Scholarly Resources, 1992.

Pérez-Baltodano, Andrés. *Entre el estado conquistador y el estado nación: Providencialismo, pensamiento político y estructuras de poder en el desarrollo histórico de Nicaragua*. Managua: Instituto de Historia de Nicaragua y Centroamérica, Fundación Friedrich Ebert, 2003.

Pérez de Antón, Francisco. *Los hijos del incienso y de la pólvora*. Guatemala City: Editorial Santillana, Alfaguara, 2005.

Pérez Guzmán, Francisco. "Modo de vida de esclavos y forzados en las fortificaciones de Cuba: Siglo XVIII." *Anuario de estudios americanos* 47 (1990), 241–57.

Pérez Palma, José S. *Datos históricos de Nicaragua. Tomo I.* Managua: n.p., 1977.

Pérez Valle, Eduardo, ed. *Expediente de Campos Azules: Historia de Bluefields en sus documentos en el 75 aniversario de su erección en ciudad.* Managua: n.p., 1978.

———, ed. *Nicaragua en los cronistas de Indias: Oviedo.* Managua: Fondo de Promoción Cultura, Banco de América, 1976.

Petras, Elizabeth McLean. *Jamaican Labor Migration: White Capital and Black Labor, 1850–1930.* Westview Special Studies on Latin America and the Caribbean. Boulder, Colo.: Westview Press, 1988.

Pike, Ruth. "Penal Servitude in the Spanish Empire: Presidio Labor in the Eighteenth Century." *Hispanic American Historical Review* 58, no. 1 (1978), 21–40.

Piñero, Eugenio. "Accounting Practices in a Colonial Economy: A Case Study of Cacao Haciendas in Venezuela, 1700–1770." *Colonial Latin American Historical Review* 1, no. 1 (1992), 36–66.

Pinto Soria, J. C. *El valle central de Guatemala (1524–1821): Un análisis acerca del origen histórico-económico del regionalismo en Centroamérica.* Colección Estudios Universitarios 31. Guatemala City: Editorial Universitaria, 1988.

Porta Costas, Antonio. "Relación del reconocimiento geométrico y político de la Costa de Mosquitos desde el establecimiento de Cabo Gracias a Dios hasta El Blewfields, 1790." *Wani*, no. 7 (January 1990), 51–64.

Potthast, Barbara. *Die Mosquito-Küste im Spannungfeld Britischer und Spanischer Politik, 1502–1821.* Köln: n.p., 1988.

Potthast-Jutkeit, Barbara. "Indians, Blacks and Zambos on the Mosquito Coast, 17th and 18th Century." *América Negra*, no. 6 (1993), 53–65.

Premo, Bianca. *Children of the Father King: Youth, Authority, and Legal Minority in Colonial Lima.* Chapel Hill: University of North Carolina Press, 2005.

Price, A. Grenfell. *White Settlers in the Tropics.* New York: American Geographical Society Special Publication, 1939.

Proudfoot, Malcolm J. *Population Movements in the Caribbean.* Port-of-Spain, Trinidad: Caribbean Central Secretariat, 1950.

Putnam, Lara. *The Company They Kept: Migrants and the Politics of Gender in Caribbean Costa Rica, 1870–1960.* Chapel Hill: University of North Carolina Press, 2002.

———. "Contact Zones: Heterogeneity and Boundaries in Caribbean Central America at the Start of the Twentieth Century." *Iberoamericana* 6, no. 23 (2006), 113–25.

———. "Ideología racial, práctica social y estado liberal en Costa Rica." *Revista de Historia* (Costa Rica), no. 39 (January–June 1999), 139–86.

———. "Work, Sex, and Power in a Central American Export Economy at the Turn of the Twentieth Century." *Gender, Sexuality, and Power in Latin*

America, edited by Katherine Bliss and William French, 133–62. Lanham, Md.: Rowman and Littlefield, 2006.

Quijano, José Antonio. "Las fortificaciones en América durante la Edad Moderna." *Buenavista de Indias* (Seville) 1, no. 2 (1992), 12–72.

Ramírez, Norberto. "El Director del Estado, a sus Habitantes (León, abril 24 de 1849)." *Gobernantes de Nicaragua: Notas y documentos*, edited by Andrés Vega Bolaños, 154–54. Managua: n.p., 1944.

Reid, Ira De Augustine. *The Negro Immigrant: His Background, Characteristics, and Social Adjustment, 1899–1937*, 1939; New York: Arno Press, 1969.

Reis, João José. "'The Revolution of the *Ganhadores*': Urban Labour, Ethnicity and the African Strike of 1857 in Bahia, Brazil." *Journal of Latin American Studies* 29, no. 2 (1997), 355–93.

Remesal, Antonio de. *Historia general de las Indias: Occidentales y particular de la gobernación de Chiapa y Guatemala.* 2nd ed. 2 vols. Mexico City: Editorial Porrúa, 1988.

Restall, Matthew, ed. *Beyond Black and Red: African-Native Relations in Colonial Latin America.* Albuquerque: University of New Mexico Press, 2005.

———. *Seven Myths of the Spanish Conquest.* Oxford: Oxford University Press, 2003.

Retamal Favereau, Julio, Carlos Celis Atria, and Juan Guillermo Muñoz·Correa. *Familias fundadoras de Chile, 1540–1600.* 3rd ed. Santiago de Chile: n.p., 1993.

Richardson, Bonham C. "Caribbean Migrations, 1838–1985." *The Modern Caribbean*, edited by Franklin W. Knight and Colin A. Palmer, 203–28. Chapel Hill: University of North Carolina Press, 1989.

———. *Panama Money in Barbados, 1900–1920.* Knoxville: University of Tennessee Press, 1985.

Riismandel, John N., and James H. Levitt. "Un estudio cuantitativo de algunos aspectos de la esclavitud en Costa Rica en tiempos de la colonia." *Revista del Pensamiento Centroamericano*, no. 152 (1972), 101–16.

Roberts, W. Adolphe. *Jamaica.* New York: Coward-McCann, 1955.

Robinson, Carey. *The Fighting Maroons of Jamaica.* Kingston, Jamaica: William Collins, 1969.

Robinson, Jane. *Wayward Women: A Guide to Women Travellers.* Oxford: Oxford University Press, 1990.

Robinson, St. John. "Southern Loyalists in the Caribbean and Central America." *South Carolina Historical Magazine* 93 (1995), 205–20.

Rodas Núñez, Isabel. *De españoles a ladinos: Cambio social y relaciones de parentesco en el altiplano central colonial guatemalteco.* Guatemala City: Instituto Centroamericano de Prospectiva e Investigación, 2004.

Rodríguez, Mario. *The Cádiz Experiment in Central America, 1808–1826.* Berkeley: University of California Press, 1978.

———. *A Palmerstonian Diplomat in Central America: Frederick Chatfield, Esq.* Tucson: University of Arizona Press, 1964.

Rodríguez Morel, Genaro. "The Sugar Economy of Española in the Sixteenth Century." *Tropical Bablyons: Sugar and the Making of the Atlantic World, 1450–1680*, edited by Stuart B. Schwartz, 85–114. Chapel Hill: University of North Carolina Press, 2004.

Roig de Leuchsenring, Emilio. "¿Se está Cuba africanizando?" *Carteles* 10, no. 48 (1927), 18, 27.

Rojas Mix, Miguel. *Los cien nombres de América: Eso que descubrió Colón.* San José: Editorial de la Universidad de Costa Rica, 1997.

Romero Vargas, Germán. *Las estructuras sociales de Nicaragua en el siglo XVIII.* Managua: Vanguardia, 1988.

———. *Las sociedades del Atlántico en Nicaragua en los siglos XVII y XVIII.* Managua: Fondo de Promoción Cultural-BANIC, 1995.

Romero Vargas, Germán, and Flor de Oro Solorzano. "Declaración de Carlos Casarola, negro esclavo bozal, 1737." *Wani* 10 (May 1991), 84–90.

Rosés Alvarado, Carlos. "El ciclo del cacao en la economía colonial de Costa Rica, 1650–1794." *Mesoamérica* 4 (December 1982), 247–78.

Rubio Sánchez, Manuel. *Historia de la fortaleza y pueblo de San Fernando de Omoa.* Guatemala City: Negociado de Historia, Departamento de Información y Divulgación del Ejército, 1988.

———. *Monografía de la ciudad de Antigua Guatemala.* Guatemala City: Tipografía Nacional, 1989.

Ruiz y Ruiz, Frutos. *Informe del Doctor Don Frutos Ruiz y Ruiz comisionado del Poder Ejecutivo en la Costa Atlántica de Nicaragua.* Managua: C. Heuberger, 1927.

Ruz, Mario Humberto, coordinator. *Memoria eclesial guatemalteca: Visitas pastorales.* Mexico City: Universidad Autónoma de México, 2002.

———. "Sebastiana de la Cruz, alias 'La Polilla,' mulata de Petapa y madre del hijo de Dios." *Mesoamérica* 23 (June 1992), 55–66.

Salinas, Sebastián. "Memoria a las cámaras legislativas [27 de Febrero de 1849]." In "La voz sostenida: Antología del pensamiento nicaragüense," edited by Orlando Cuadra Downing, *Revista Conservadora*, no. 4 (1960), 56–64.

Salvatierra, Sofonías. *Contribución a la historia de Centroamérica: Monografías documentales.* 2 vols. Managua: Tip. Progreso, 1939.

Sanabria Martínez, Victor Manuel. *Genealogías de Cartago hasta 1850.* 6 vols. San José, Costa Rica: n.p., 1957.

Sanders, James E. *Contentious Republicans: Popular Politics, Race, and Class in Nineteenth-Century Colombia.* Durham, N.C.: Duke University Press, 2004.

Sánchez Saus, Rafael. "La genealogía, fuente, y técnica historiográfica." *Archivum: Les Archives et les Sciences Généalogiques* 37 (1992), 78–92.

Sandoval, Alonso de. *De Instauranda Aethiopum Salute: El mundo de la esclavitud negra en América.* Introduction by Angel Valtierra. Bogotá: Empresa Nacional de Publicaciones, 1956.

Schubert, H. "Some Experiences of a Missionary among the Miskito Indians of the Miskito Coast of Nicaragua." *Proceedings of the Society for Propagating the Gospel* (1926), 93–96.

Schwartz, Stuart B. "Resistance and Accommodation in Eighteenth-Century Brazil: The Slaves' View of Slavery." *Hispanic American Historical Review* 57, no. 1 (1977), 69–81.

———. *Slaves, Peasants, and Rebels: Reconsidering Brazilian Slavery*. Blacks in the New World. Urbana: University of Illinois Press, 1992.

Scott, Rebecca J. *Slave Emancipation in Cuba: The Transition to Free Labor, 1860–1899*. Princeton: Princeton University Press, 1985.

Seigel, Micol. "Beyond Compare: Comparative Method after the Transnational Turn." *Radical History Review*, no. 91 (winter 2005), 62–90.

Senior Angulo, Diana. "La incorporación social en Costa Rica de la población afrocostarricense durante el siglo XX, 1927–1963." Master's thesis. Universidad de Costa Rica, 2007.

Settipani, Christian. "La transition entre mythe et réalité." *Archivum: Les Archives et les Sciences Généalogiques* 37 (1992), 27–67.

Sharpe, Jenny. *Allegories of Empire: The Figure of Woman in the Colonial Text*. Minneapolis: University of Minnesota Press, 1993.

Sherman, William L. *Forced Native Labor in Sixteenth-Century Central America*. Lincoln: University of Nebraska Press, 1979.

Shields, Karena. *The Changing Wind*. London: John Murray, 1960.

Simon, Charles. *Les Exploratrices au XIXe Siecle*. Paris: Lecène, Oudin, 1892.

Smith, Carol A. "Introduction: Social Relations in Guatemala over Time and Space." *Guatemalan Indians and the State, 1540 to 1988*, edited by Carol A. Smith, 1–30. Austin: University of Texas Press, 1990.

———. "Race-Class-Gender Ideology in Guatemala: Modern and Anti-Modern Forms." *Comparative Studies in Society and History* 37, no. 4 (1995), 723–49.

Smith, Robert S. "Indigo Production and Trade in Colonial Guatemala." *Hispanic American Historical Review* 39, no. 2 (1959), 181–211.

Smith, Sidonie. "The Other Woman and Racial Politics of Gender: Isak Dinesen and Beryl Markham in Kenya." *De/Colonizing the Subject: The Politics of Gender in Women's Autobiography*, edited by Sidonie Smith and Julia Watson, 410–35. Minneapolis: University of Minnesota Press, 1992.

Socolow, Susan Migden. *The Women of Colonial Latin America*. New Approaches to the Americas. Cambridge, England: Cambridge University Press, 2000.

Sorsby, William S. "The British Superintendency of the Mosquito Shore, 1749–1787." Ph.D. dissertation, University of London, 1969.

Soto Quirós, Ronald. "Inmigración e identidad nacional: Los 'otros' reafirman el 'nosotros.'" Ph.D. dissertation, Escuela de Historia, Universidad de Costa Rica, 1998.

Soulodre-La France, Renée. "Socially Not So Dead! Slave Identities in Bourbon Nueva Granada." *Colonial Latin American Review* 10, no. 1 (2001), 87–103.

Squier, E. G. *Notes on Central America, Particularly the States of Honduras and San Salvador.* New York: Harper and Brothers, 1855.

———. *Travels in Central America, Particularly in Nicaragua.* New York: D. Appleton, 1853.

Stepan, Nancy Leys. *The Hour of Eugenics: Race, Gender, and Nation in Latin America.* Ithaca, N.Y.: Cornell University Press, 1991.

Stephens, John L. *Incidents of Travel in Central America, Chiapas and Yucatan.* 2 vols. New Brunswick, N.J.: Rutgers University Press, 1949.

Stoler, Ann Laura. "Carnal Knowledge and Imperial Power: Gender, Race, and Morality in Colonial Asia." *Gender at the Crossroads of Knowledge: Feminist Anthropology in the Postmodern Era,* edited by Micaela de Leonardo, 51–101. Berkeley: University of California Press, 1991.

———. "Rethinking Colonial Categories: European Communities and the Boundaries of Rule." *Comparative Studies in Society and History* 31, no. 1 (1989), 134–61.

———. "Sexual Affronts and Racial Frontiers: European Identities and the Cultural Politics of Exclusion in Colonial Southeast Asia." *Comparative Studies in Society and History* 34, no. 3 (1992), 514–51.

Stone, Samuel Z. *La dinastía de los conquistadores: La crisis del poder en la Costa Rica contemporánea.* San José: EDUCA y Editorial de la Universidad de Costa Rica, 1975.

———. *The Heritage of the Conquistadors: Ruling Classes in Central America from the Conquest to the Sandinistas.* Lincoln: University of Nebraska Press, 1990.

Suter, Jan. "'Pernicious Aliens' and the Mestizo Nation: Ethnicity and the Shaping of Collective Identities in El Salvador before the Second World War." *Immigrants and Minorities* 20, no. 2 (2001), 26–57.

Sweet, James H. *Recreating Africa: Culture, Kinship, and Religion in the African-Portuguese World, 1441–1770.* Chapel Hill: University of North Carolina Press, 2003.

Tannenbaum, Frank. *Slave and Citizen: The Negro in the Americas.* New York: Vintage Books, 1946.

Taracena Arriola, Arturo. "El vocabulo 'Ladino' en Guatemala (S. XVI–XIX)." *Historia y antropología de Guatemala: Ensayos en honor de J. Daniel Contreras R.,* edited by Jorge Luján Muñoz, 89–104. Guatemala City: Universidad de San Carlos, 1982.

Tardieu, Jean-Pierre. "Origins of the Slaves in the Lima Region in Peru (Sixteenth and Seventeenth Centuries)." *From Chains to Bonds: The Slave Trade Revisited,* edited by Doudou Diène, 43–54. New York: Berghahn Books, 2001.

Taylor, Charles. "Nationalism and Modernity." *The Morality of Nationalism,* edited by Robert McKim and Jeff McMahan, 31–55. New York: Oxford University Press, 1997.

Tello Burgos, Argelia, ed. *Escritos de Justo Arosemena: Estudio introductorio y antología.* Panama City: Universidad de Panamá, 1985.

Téllez Argüello, Dora María. *¡Muera la gobierna! Colonización en Matagalpa y Jinotega (1820–1890)*. Managua: Universidad de las Regiones Autónomas de la Costa Caribe Nicaragüense, 1999.

Thiel, Bernardo Augusto. *Datos cronológicos para la historia eclesiástica de Costa Rica*. 1897–1902; San José, Costa Rica: Comisión Nacional de Conmemoraciones Históricas, 1983.

Thomas-Hope, Elizabeth M. "The Establishment of a Migration Tradition: British West Indian Movements to the Hispanic Caribbean in the Century After Emancipation." *International Migration* 24 (1986), 66–81.

Thornton, John. *Africa and Africans in the Making of the Atlantic World*. Cambridge, England: Cambridge University Press, 1992.

———. "The African Experience of the '20 and Odd Negroes' Arriving in Virginia in 1619." *William and Mary Quarterly* 3rd series, 55, no. 3 (1998), 421–34.

———. "Cannibals, Witches, and Slave Traders in the Atlantic World." *William and Mary Quarterly* 3rd series, 60, no. 2 (2003), 273–94.

———. "Central Africa in the Era of the Slave Trade." *Slaves, Subjects, and Subversives: Blacks in Colonial Latin America*, edited by Jane G. Landers and Barry M. Robinson, 83–111. Albuquerque: University of New Mexico Press, 2006.

Tinker Salas, Miguel. "Relaciones de poder y raza en los campos petroleros venezolanos, 1920–1940." *Asuntos* (Venezuela) 5, no. 10 (2001), 77–103.

Tinkler, Penny. "Introduction to Special Issue: Women, Imperialism and Identity." *Women's Studies International Forum* 21, no. 3 (1998), 217–22.

Tobar Cruz, Pedro. "La esclavitud del negro en Guatemala." *Antropología e Historia de Guatemala* 17, no. 1 (1965), 3–14.

Tompson, Douglas A. "Frontiers of Identity: The Atlantic Coast and the Formation of Honduras and Nicaragua, 1786–1894." Ph.D. dissertation, University of Florida, 2001.

Trefzger, Douglas W. "Making West Indians Unwelcome: Race, Gender, and the National Question in Guatemala's Banana Belt, 1914–1920." Paper presented at the 23rd annual meeting of the Latin American Studies Association, Washington, DC, 2001.

Turner, Mary, ed. *From Chattel Slaves to Wage Slaves: The Dynamics of Labour Bargaining in the Americas*. Bloomington: Indiana University Press, 1995.

Twinam, Ann. "The Negotiation of Honor: Elites, Sexuality, and Illegitimacy in Eighteenth-Century Spanish America." *The Faces of Honor: Sex, Shame, and Violence in Colonial Latin America*, edited by Lyman L. Johnson and Sonya Lipsett-Rivera, 68–102. Albuquerque: University of New Mexico Press, 1998.

———. *Public Lives, Private Secrets: Gender, Honor, Sexuality, and Illegitimacy in Colonial Spanish America*. Stanford: Stanford University Press, 2001.

United Kingdom. Foreign Office. *Correspondence Respecting the Mosquito Territory*. Vols. 2 and 3. 3 vols. 30 January 1847–29 April 1848; 16 June 1860–29 June 1879.

United States, Department of State. *Correspondence in Relation to an Interoceanic Canal between the Atlantic and Pacific Oceans, the Clayton-Bulwer Treaty and the Monroe Doctrine, and the Treaty between the United States and New Granada of December 12, 1846.* Washington: Government Printing Office, 1900.

Uring, Nathaniel L. *The Voyages and Travels of Nathaniel Uring.* 1726; London: Cassell, 1928.

Valverde Runnenbaum, Enrique. "Breve historia de la genealogía en Costa Rica." *Revista de la Academia Costarricense de Ciencias Genealógicas* 24 (1977), 117–37.

Van Oss, Adriaan C. *Catholic Colonialism: A Parish History of Guatemala, 1524–1821.* Cambridge: Cambridge University Press, 1986.

Vásquez de Espinosa, Antonio. *Compendio y descripción de las Indias Occidentales.* Edited by Charles Upson Clark. Smithsonian Miscellaneous Collections, vol. 108. Washington: Smithsonian Institution, 1948.

Vaughn, Bobby, and Ben Vinson III. *Afroméxico.* Mexico City: Fondo de Cultura Económica, 2005.

Vázquez, Francisco. *Crónica de la Provincia del Santísimo Nombre de Jesús de Guatemala de la Orden De Nuestro Seráfico Padre San Francisco en el Reino de la Nueva España.* 4 vols. 2nd ed. Guatemala City: Tipografía nacional, 1937–1944.

Vega Bolaños, Andrés, compiler and editor. *Gobernantes de Nicaragua: Notas y documentos.* Managua: n.p., 1944.

———. *1840–1842: Los atentados del Superintendente de Belice.* Managua: Editorial Unión, 1971.

Velásquez, María Elisa, and Ethel Correa Duró, eds. *Poblaciones y culturas de origen africano en México.* Mexico City: Instituto de Antropología e Historia, 2005.

Velásquez, Melida. "El comercio de esclavos en la Alcaldía Mayor de Tegucigalpa, siglos XVI al XVIII." *Mesoamérica* 42 (December 2001), 199–222.

Velásquez Gutiérrez, María Elisa. *Juan Correa: Mulato libre, maestro de pintor.* Mexico City: Círculo de Arte, 1998.

Vieira da Cunha, Rui. "Los archivos y la genealogía en las sociedades multirraciales tradicionales, el caso de Brasil." *Archivum: Les Archives et les Sciences Généalogiques* 37 (1992), 173–76.

Vijil, Francisco. "El Licenciado don Francisco Castellón visto por el Señor Obispo Viteri." *Revista de la Academia de Geografía e Historia de Nicaragua* 3, no. 3 (1940), 289–99.

———. *El Padre Vijil: Su Vida.* Granada, Nicaragua: El Centro-Americano, 1930.

Vila Vilar, Enriqueta. *Hispanoamérica y el comercio de esclavos: Los asientos portugueses.* Seville: Escuela de Estudios Hispano-Americanos, 1977.

Vilas, Carlos M. "Family Affairs: Class, Lineage and Politics in Contemporary Nicaragua." *Journal of Latin American Studies* 24, no. 2 (1992), 309–41.

Vincent, Theodore G. *The Legacy of Vicente Guerrero, Mexico's First Black Indian President.* Gainesville: University Press of Florida, 2001.

Vinson, Ben, III. *Bearing Arms for His Majesty: The Free-Colored Militia in Colonial Mexico.* Stanford: Stanford University Press, 2001.

———. "Introduction: African (Black) Diaspora History, Latin American History." *The Americas* 63, no. 1 (2006), 1–18.

von Bülow, Tulio. "Apuntes para la historia de la medicina en Costa Rica durante la colonia." *Revista de los Archivos Nacionales* (Costa Rica) 9–10 (September–October 1945), 458–75.

von Houwald, Götz. *Mayangna apuntes sobre la historia de los indígenas Sumu en Centroamérica contribuciones a la etnología centroamericana.* Managua: Fundación Vida, 2003.

Wade, Peter. *Blackness and Race Mixture: The Dynamics of Racial Identity in Colombia.* Baltimore: Johns Hopkins University Press, 1993.

———. *Music, Race, and Nation:* Música tropical *in Colombia.* Chicago: University of Chicago Press, 2000.

———. *Race and Ethnicity in Latin America.* London: Pluto Press, 1997.

———. "Rethinking *Mestizaje:* Ideology and Lived Experience." *Journal of Latin American Studies* 37 (2005), 239–57.

Walker, William. *The War in Nicaragua.* 1860; Tucson: University of Arizona Press, 1985.

Ware, Vron. *Beyond the Pale: White Women, Racism, and History.* New York: Verso, 1992.

Webre, Stephen. "Las compañías de milicia y la defensa del istmo centroamericano en el siglo XVII: El alistamiento general de 1673." *Mesoamérica* 14 (December 1987), 511–29.

Wells, William V. *Explorations and Adventures in Honduras.* New York: Harper and Brothers, 1857.

Westerman, George W. *Los inmigrantes antillanos en Panamá.* Panama City: n.p., 1980.

Wheelock Román, Jaime. *Imperialismo y dictadura: Crisis de una formación social.* Mexico City: Siglo XXI, 1979.

Wildenthal, Lora. " 'When Men Are Weak': The Imperial Feminism of Frieda von Bülow." *Gender and History* 10, no. 1 (1998), 53–77.

Wolfe, Justin. *The Everyday Nation-State: Community and Ethnicity in Nineteenth-Century Nicaragua.* Lincoln: University of Nebraska Press, 2007.

———. " 'I Must Insist on This Issue of Race': Constructing Race and Difference in Postcolonial Nicaragua." Unpublished manuscript, 2006.

———. "Those That Live by the Work of Their Hands: Labour, Ethnicity and Nation-State Formation in Nicaragua, 1850–1900." *Journal of Latin American Studies* 36, no. 1 (2004), 57–83.

Wood, Peter H. *Black Majority: Negroes in Colonial South Carolina from 1670 through the Stono Rebellion.* New York: Norton, 1974.

Wünderich, Volker, Elenor von Oertzen, and Lioba Rossbach. *The Nicaraguan Mosquitia in Historical Documents, 1844–1927.* Berlin: Dietrich Reimer Verlag, 1990.

Ximénez, Francisco. *Historia de la Provincia de San Vicente de Chiapa y Guatemala de la Orden de Predicadores.* 3rd ed. 5 vols. Tuxla Gutiérrez, Mexico: Consejo Estatal para la Cultura y las Artes de Chiapas, 1999.

Zapatero, Juan Manuel. *El fuerte San Fernando y las fortificaciones de Omoa.* Tegucigalpa: Instituto Hondureño de Antropología e Historia, 1997.

Zepeda, Hermenegildo. "Discurso [1858]." *Revista Conservadora del Pensamiento Centroamericano,* no. 72 (September 1966), 6–7.

Zolberg, Aristide R. *A Nation by Design: Immigration Policy in the Fashioning of America.* Cambridge, Mass.: Harvard University Press, 2006.

Zorraquín Becu, Horacio. *El problema del extranjero en la legislación latinoamericana reciente.* Buenos Aires: Editorial Guillermo Kraft, 1943.

CONTRIBUTORS

RINA CÁCERES GÓMEZ is a professor of history at the Universidad de Costa Rica. She is the author of *Negros, mulatos, esclavos y libertos en la Costa Rica del siglo XVII* (2000), the editor of *Rutas de la esclavitud en Africa y América Latina* (2001), and editor with Paul Lovejoy of *Haití: Revolución, independencia y emancipación* (2008). She coordinates the UNESCO/Universidad de Costa Rica project on Afro-Central American history and memory, Del Olvido a la Memoria.

LOWELL GUDMUNDSON is a professor of Latin American studies and history at Mount Holyoke College. His return to Afro–Central American research after a lengthy absence was thanks to the inspiration of Rina Cáceres and Mauricio Meléndez, as well as the support of the National Endowment for the Humanities Collaborative Research Program (2001–3). His collaborative project at the Universidad Nacional, where he began his academic career in 1975, completes a long-term project on coffee and the lessons of Costa Rican development, with the support of a National Endowment for the Humanities Fellowship (2008–9).

RONALD HARPELLE teaches history at Lakehead University. He is the author of *The West Indians of Costa Rica: Race, Class and the Integration of an Ethnic Minority* (2001). He continues to conduct research on the history of British West Indian immigration and settlement on the Caribbean coast of the Central American isthmus, but he has also been commissioned, with Dr. Bruce Muirhead of the University of Waterloo, to write an intellectual history of Canada's International Development Research Centre. In addition he is conducting research and participating in the production of a six-part series on Canada's role in international development.

JULIET HOOKER is an associate professor of government at the University of Texas, Austin. She is the author of *Race and the Politics of Solidarity* (2009) and articles on multicultural citizenship, race and nationalism, and Afro-descendant politics in Latin America that have appeared in the *Journal of Latin American Studies*, the *Latin American Research Review*, and *Souls: A Critical Journal of Black Politics, Culture and Society*.

CATHERINE KOMISARUK is an assistant professor of history at the University of Iowa. She is completing a book on gender, ethnicity, and labor in late colonial Guatemala, under contract with Stanford University Press.

RUSSELL LOHSE is an assistant professor of Latin American history at Pennsylvania State University. He has published articles in journals and edited collections on African ethnicity and the slave trade, the Yoruba in colonial Costa Rica, and the abolition of slavery in Colombia.

PAUL LOKKEN is an associate professor of Latin American history at Bryant University. His articles on various aspects of the African experience in colonial Central America have appeared in *The Americas, Slavery and Abolition*, and several other journals.

MAURICIO MELÉNDEZ OBANDO completed the master of linguistics program at the Universidad de Costa Rica and since 1989 has worked in different media, in particular his "Roots" (Raíces) column for the digital version of the Costa Rican daily *La Nación*. Since 1984 he has carried out genealogical and historical research in the major historical archives of Central America. His various publications include *Negros y blancos, todo mezclado* (with Tatiana Lobo Wiehoff, 1997) and "Los últimos esclavos en Costa Rica" in *Revista de Historia* (1999), which won the Costa Rican National History Prize in 2000.

KARL H. OFFEN is an associate professor of geography at the University of Oklahoma. He is the coeditor (with Jordana Dym) of *Mapping Latin America: Space and Society, 1492–2000* (forthcoming). His research examines ethnogenesis, environmental history, and the geographic imagination in Central America. He is currently investigating the role of English settlers of Providence Island in bringing West-Central Africans to eastern Central America in the early seventeenth century.

LARA PUTNAM is an associate professor of history at the University of Pittsburgh specializing in the study of gender, kinship, and migration in the Greater Caribbean. She is the author of *The Company They Kept: Migrants and the Politics of Gender in Caribbean Costa Rica, 1870–1960* (2002) and is currently at work on two book-length manuscripts, the first a history of the role of migrants' experiences in shaping political and cultural movements in the twentieth-century Caribbean (tentatively titled *Born a' Foreign: Intraregional Migration and the Routes of Radical Blackness*) and the second on social policy, decolonization, and the Afro-Caribbean family as object of academic inquiry (tentatively titled *The Politics of Parenting at the End of Empire: Family Practice and Collective Destiny in the British Caribbean, 1890–1960*).

JUSTIN WOLFE is the William Arceneaux Associate Professor of Latin American History at Tulane University. He is the author of *The Everyday Nation-State: Community and Ethnicity in Nineteenth-Century Nicaragua* (2007) and is currently working on a history of blacks and blackness in Nicaragua from empire to nation.

INDEX

Page numbers followed by *m* indicate maps.

Gurdián, Raúl, 298
Gutiérrez, Luis, 68
Gutiérrez, Macedonia, 227
Gutiérrez, Manuela, 81

Hacienda San Jerónimo (Guatemala), 19, 31, 152, 155–60
Hall, Gaspar, 132–33
Hancock, Mr., 318–19
Hannibal, John, 98, 102
Harlem, 282
Harrison-Altamirano Treaty (1905), 262
Havana, Cuba, 135
hawskbill turtling, 116
Haya Fernández, Diego de la, 76–77
Hernández, Manuel Antonio, 161–62
hero genealogies, afromestizo, 341
Herrera Campuzano, Diego de, 69
hispanization and Hispano-American identity: *ladino* designation and, 47; Nicaragua and, 193–94; Spanish view of, 55 n. 83. See also *ladina/o* designation
Hodgson, George, 265
Hodgson, Horacio, 265
Hodgson, Robert (the elder), 99–100, 107, 132–33
Hodgson, Robert (the younger), 98–100
Honduras: exclusion laws and, 290; Tela Nuevo white zone and, 313–14, 317–18, 323. *See also* Mosquitos (Miskitu), costeños, and Mosquitia (Mosquito Coast)
Honduras (slave ship), 133–34
Huebo, Manuel, 167

Ibarra y Calvo, Juan de, 74
Iberian slavery, 152

immigrant slaves, African, to Amatitlán, Guatemala, 29–35, 42
immigration from British West Indies. *See* West Indian migration and legal restrictions
incestuosa/o designation, 244 n. 27
Indian labor: on Costa Rican cacao haciendas, 62–65; "hunting Indians" in Nicaragua, 211; slaves in Mosquitia, 35, 116–20
Indianness: African slaves placed higher than Indians, 43; blackness and, in Nicaragua, 235–36; citizenship and, in Nicaragua, 261; dismissal of, in Nicaragua, 212; elite attitude variation by era and, 274 n. 29; Nicaraguan civilization-savagery discourse and, 254
Indian/non-Indian dichotomy in Nicaragua, 209–10, 216–19. See also *ladina/o* designation
Indian uprising in Talamanca, 59
indio ladino designation, 55 n. 79
indios laboríos, 38, 46–47
indios tributarios, 28, 38
Inés (free black woman), 33
ingenio, defined, 49 n. 10
Irving, Charles, 120

Jamaica: migration to and from Cuba and, 282; Mosquito King Jeremy in, 102; slave trade in, 132–33. *See also* West Indian migration and legal restrictions
James, Winifred, 324, 330 n. 19
Jeremy (Mosquito King), 102
Jerez, Máximo, 195, 197–99

Spain, slavery in, 152

Spaniards (*espagnol*), passing as, 171

Spanish Central America (MacLeod), 8

Spanish language, mandatory, 264

spatialization of race in Nicaragua, 246

Squier, E. George, 186–87

state-building in Nicaragua. *See* Nicaraguan state-building and citizenship

Stephens, John L., 187

Stone, Samuel, 6–7, 21 nn. 6–7

sugar cultivation and plantations: ingenios vs. trapiches, 49 n. 10; in Mosquitia, 115–16, 120. *See also* Amatitlán region, colonial Guatemala

surnames, ethnic distribution of (western Nicaragua), 225–27, 243 n. 26

Taboara, Manuel de, 166

Talamanca, 59, 60, 62–65

Tawira Mosquito, 93, 99–101, 120, 251–52, 272 n. 19. *See also* Mosquitos (Miskitu), costeños, and Mosquitia (Mosquito Coast)

taxes, 61

Taylor, Charles, 250–51

Tela Nuevo, Honduras, 313–14, 317–18, 323

Thayer, William S., 190–91, 206 n. 65

trade, contraband, 76–77, 114–15

trapiche, defined, 49 n. 10

Treaty of Managua (1860), 256, 262, 272 n. 15, 274 n. 39

Trelawny, William, 107

Trinidad, Manuel, 164–66

Ubi, Francisco, 143

Umaña, Concepcíon, 345

unemployment and exclusion laws, 291

United Fruit Company, 289, 294–96, 301 n. 16, 306 n. 89, 317–18. *See also* white zones and "company wives"

United States: Clayton-Bulwer Treaty and (1850), 272 n. 15; eugenics and immigration policy and, 291–96; immigration and race statistics and (1918), 302 n. 19; Jim Crow policies of, in Panama, 284–85; Johnson-Reed Act and (1924), 291–92; Mexico invasion by, 186; migration to, 282; Nicaraguan anti-U.S. rhetoric, 193–94, 197–98; relations with Nicaragua of, 186–87

Urinama Indians, 62–65

Uring, Nathanie, 97

Vado Lugo, Gertrudis, 341

Valle, José María (pseud. Chelón), 189

Valverde, Pánfilo, 287

Vargas, Antonio, 120

Vásquez de Coronado, Juan, 59

Vassa, Igbo Gustavas (Olaudah Equiano), 120

Vega Cabral, Antonio de la, 69

Vega Cabral, María Josefa de la, 71

Vela, Hipólito, 171

Vijíl, Agustín, 182

violence: Nicaraguan politics and, 184; Omoa construction work and, 141–43; spatial segregation and, in Costa Rica, 299

Viteri, Jorge, 180, 184

Vivas, Rafael, 171

Wade, Peter, 5, 214

wages: on cacao haciendas, 67–68; litigation for, in Guatemala, 156;

wages (*cont.*)

for slaves at Omoa, 130–31, 139–41, 146–48

Walker, William, 188–95, 200, 259

Walrond, Eric, 279–81

war heroes, afromestizo, 341

Warren, Thomas, 100–101

West Indian migration and legal restrictions: contradictory policies and enforcement of, 284–85; mid-20th-century effects on citizenship of, 300; migratory circuits and (1870–1920), 279–84; nationalism, localization, and Costa Rican segregation and, 296–99; overview, 278; policing and race and, 285–88; rise of exclusion laws in, 288–91; U.S. immigration policy and pan-American eugenics and, 291–96

West Indians: on Mosquito Coast, 252; as servants in white enclaves, 323, 328

Wheelock Román, Jaime, 240 n. 10

whippings, 143, 184

White, Sarah, 281

white designation and class, in Nicaragua, 243 n. 22

whitening strategy (*blanqueamiento*), 179–80

White Towns. *See* Nicaraguan western "White Towns"

white zones and "company wives": children in, 317; class distinctions in, 319–21; corporate conquest and, 307–9; demographic isolation in, 314–17; domestic servants and cooks in, 321–28; elite status and expectations in, 310–12; European colonial experience compared to, 310; housing in, 312–314, 331 n. 22; language and culture issues of, 322–24; local women and white men in, 317–19, 324–25; racial hierarchies and, 309; temporary placements in, 328

wild animals, danger from, 66–67

Wilkinson, Lola, 323

women, Euro-American. *See* white zones and "company wives"

workload of slaves, litigation over, 156–57

Yapiro, Estaban, 65–66

zambo designation: absence of term in colonial Guatemala, 51 n. 37; class and, in Nicaragua, 243 n. 22; in Nicaragua, 216, 231; Sambo Mosquito and, 93, 97–101, 113, 251–52, 272 n. 19

Zavala, Víctor, 169

Zavaleta, Esteban de, 31, 36

Zelaya, José Santos, 219, 261–62

Zemurray, Samuel, 318

Zepeda, Hermenegildo, 191, 194, 197

LOWELL GUDMUNDSON is a professor of Latin American studies and history at Mount Holyoke College.

JUSTIN WOLFE is the William Arceneaux Associate Professor of Latin American History at Tulane University.

LIBRARY OF CONGRESS CATALOGING-IN-PUBLICATION DATA

*Blacks and blackness in Central America : between race
and place / edited by Lowell Gudmundson and Justin Wolfe.
p. cm.   Includes bibliographical references and index.
ISBN 978-0-8223-4787-3 (cloth : alk. paper)
ISBN 978-0-8223-4803-0 (pbk. : alk. paper)
1. Blacks—Central America—History. 2. Slavery—Central
America—History. 3. Central America—Race relations—History.
I. Gudmundson, Lowell. II. Wolfe, Justin, 1968– F1440.B55B53 2010
972.800496—dc22   2010016649*